TEENPLOTS

Chicago Public Library

TEENPLOTS

*A Booktalk Guide to Use
with Readers Ages 12–18*

JOHN T. GILLESPIE
and CORINNE J. NADEN

A Member of the Greenwood Publishing Group

Westport, Connecticut • London

Library of Congress Cataloging-in-Publication Data

Gillespie, John Thomas, 1928–
    Teenplots : a booktalk guide to use with readers ages 12–18 / John T.
Gillespie and Corinne J. Naden.
        p. cm.
    Includes bibliographical references and indexes.
    ISBN 1–56308–921–1 (alk. paper)
    1. Young adult literature—Stories, plots, etc. 2. Book talks. 3. Teenagers—
Books and reading—United States. I. Naden, Corinne J. II. Title.
Z1037.A1G526 2003
001.62'5—dc21   2003047725

British Library Cataloging in Publication Data is available.

Library of Congress Catalog Card Number: 2003047725
ISBN: 1–56308–921–1

First published in 2003

Libraries Unlimited, 88 Post Road West, Westport, CT 06881
A Member of the Greenwood Publishing Group, Inc.
www.lu.com

Printed in the United States of America

The paper used in this book complies with the
Permanent Paper Standard issued by the National
Information Standards Organization (Z39.48–1984).

10   9   8   7   6   5   4   3   2   1

Contents

Preface

Helping young people select books for their reading pleasure is one of the most enjoyable and rewarding responsibilities of teachers and librarians. There are many methods that can be used, such as the preparation of reading lists and use of displays, but perhaps the most potent is actually talking to either an individual or to groups about the books one wishes to recommend. This technique is known as booktalking. A brief guide to the preparation and delivery of booktalks follows this preface.

The primary purpose of this volume is to help librarians and teachers supply reading guidance by way of the booktalk. A secondary purpose is to serve as a collection-building tool. In this volume, 100 highly recommended titles are highlighted with detailed background information on each. This material can be used singly or in combination to provide the basis for booktalks on various topics and at different reading levels. In choosing these 100 books, a serious attempt was made to cover a wide range of subjects and interests at the various reading levels and abilities represented by students in junior and senior high school. In addition to adult and juvenile contemporary fiction, other genres are represented, including the classics, biographies, general nonfiction, and some old favorites. Emphasis has been placed on current titles published from 1998 to 2002. Although considerations involving subject matter, interests, and levels of difficulty were important in choosing these titles, the overriding criterion was the quality of the book. Each had to be highly recommended for purchase in several standard bibliographies and reviewing sources. Many have been winners of major literary awards in the fields of children's and young adult literature.

The 100 books in *Teenplots* have been organized into nine different sections according to subject matter or genres. They are

(1) Teenage Life and Concerns (14 titles)
(2) Social and Family Problems (14 titles)
(3) Mystery and Adventure (12 titles)

(4) Science Fiction and Fantasy (17 titles)
(5) Historical Fiction and Other Lands (13 titles)
(6) Sports in Fact and Fiction (9 titles)
(7) Biography and General Nonfiction (9 titles)
(8) Guidance and Health (4 titles)
(9) Challenging Adult Novels (8 titles)

After bibliographic information and a statement of general grade level suitability, the detailed material on each of the books is divided into nine sections:

1. Introduction. The author is generally introduced with brief biographical information and mention of his or her other works of importance.
2. Principal Characters. The important characters in the book are listed with brief material to identify each of them.
3. Plot Summary. The entire plot is retold, including important incidents and characters. In each case, an attempt was made to retain the mood and point of view of the author.
4. Suitability and Critical Comment. Levels of difficulty and suitability are discussed with an identification of potential readers.
5. Themes and Subjects. A list of both primary and secondary themes and subjects present is given to facilitate the use of the book in various situations.
6. Passages for Booktalking. Incidents suitable for retelling or reading aloud are indicated and the pagination for each is given.
7. Additional Selections. Four books that explore similar or related themes at the same reading level as the main title are listed with bibliographic material and brief annotations.
8. About the Book. To locate further information about the book, there is a listing of reviews from standard current book reviewing sources and when they appeared.
9. About the Author. Sources of biographical information about the author in standard printed biographical dictionaries are listed with their locations. Due to their diversity and variability, Web sites are not included.

Following the body of the work, there are three indexes: the first two are author and title indexes to all the books mentioned in the text, and the third is a subject index to key topics covered in each of the main titles.

The detailed treatment of the main titles is not intended as a substitute for reading the books. Instead, it is to be used by teachers and librarians to refresh their memory about books already read and to suggest new uses for these titles.

This volume is also not meant to be a work of literary criticism or a listing of the best books for young adults. It is a representative selection of books that have value in a variety of situations.

The authors have had many helpers in preparing this book, including several public and school librarians who have given assistance and advice. Special thanks go to our editor at Libraries Unlimited, Barbara Ittner, for her invaluable assistance and patience. It is our hope that this volume will be of help in spreading the word about the joys of reading.

John T. Gillespie
Corinne J. Naden

A Brief Guide to Booktalking

By John T. Gillespie

There is basically just one purpose behind booktalking—to stimulate reading and a love of literature through delivering tantalizing, seductive introductions to books. There are, however, often many different secondary purposes: for example, to introduce specific authors, titles, or themes of books; to develop a specific aspect of literary appreciation; to further a particular school assignment; to present yourself to students; or to encourage visits to and use of the library.

Booktalks generally fall into two main categories: informal and formal. The informal booktalk consists of the spontaneous introduction to books that goes on every day in the library with single or small groups of students, often in reply to such questions as "Could you suggest some good books for me to read?" The formal booktalk is explored here in this brief introduction.

Before preparing a specific booktalk, three "knows" are helpful. First, is to know your audience as well as possible. By this is meant such factors as age and grade levels, the range of abilities and interests, and levels of maturation and sophistication. Take a few moments to inquire about a reader's likes and dislikes. Second, is a knowledge of books. This comes in time through reading about books, in book reviewing journals and other secondary sources, but more importantly from reading the books themselves. It is wise to begin a card file with brief notes on each book read. Although these need not be as detailed as the coverage of each title in *Teenplots*, certain topics should be covered. Basically these are: a brief plot summary; a list of a few key passages, particularly at the beginning of the book, that would be suitable for retelling or rereading to an audience; a note on the major subjects or themes covered; and related book titles that come to mind. As this file grows, it can be used to refresh one's memory of books and thus save rereading time and also serve as a source to create new booktalks by "mixing and matching" titles to create a variety of interesting new combinations of titles and themes.

Third, is a knowledge of and familiarity with the many aids, such as *Teenplots,* available to help in preparing and delivering a booktalk. Some of the most valuable aids are described at the end of this introduction.

Before choosing the books to be presented, a preliminary framework should be established. First, the physical conditions should be studied (place, time, purpose, number of attendees). Second, the length of the talk should be determined. Most booktalk sessions have a time length of fifteen to twenty-five minutes, depending on such factors as the number of books to be introduced and the attention span of the audience. An average length is about twenty minutes. In a classroom period of forty to forty-five minutes, this allows time for housekeeping chores (for example, announcements, attendance taking, the booktalk itself, browsing through the books presented and additional titles, checking out books, and so on).

Deciding on the number of titles to be presented is next. Some booktalkers like to give short one- or two-minute "quickies," whereas others feel more comfortable spending longer periods, perhaps five minutes, on each title, supplying more details of plot or character and perhaps retelling or reading a key self-contained incident. Still others mix both techniques. The conditions of the booktalk and the preference of the booktalker in the end determine the style used. Also, if a large number of books are to be introduced, a bibliography can be prepared and distributed to students to prevent confusion and give them reading guidance for future visits to the library. This bibliography should contain names of authors, titles, and a brief "catchy" annotation for each.

In preparing the talk, a connecting link or theme should be decided on. This could be as general as "Books I think you would enjoy reading" or "Some titles old and new that are favorites of students your age" to something more specific, such as American Civil War novels or family crises as portrayed in fiction. The more specific topics are often suggested by a classroom teacher and are assignment oriented. Regardless of the nature of the theme or subject, it supplies a structure and connecting link to produce a oneness and unity to the booktalk. It is used to introduce the talk, to act occasionally as a bridge from one book to the next, and to serve as a conclusion to round out the presentation.

Next, choose the books themselves. Although this seems an obvious point, each book should have been read completely. The ultimate outcome or denouement in a book will often determine the material to be presented in introducing the book. Lacking this knowledge, the booktalker might misrepresent the contents or give an inaccurate or incorrect interpretation. One should believe in the value of each title to be presented—feel that the book is worthy of being introduced and that it will supply enjoyment and value to the intended audience. The booktalker does not necessarily have to dote on each title, but should choose good books that will enlighten and entertain the audience regardless of the personal preference of the presenter. Be sure the selection represents the interests and reading levels of the group—some difficult, some average, some easy; some old titles, some new; some fiction, some nonfiction; and so on.

Having chosen the theme and the books to be introduced, the method and content of each book introduction should be determined. There are several ways of introducing books. The most frequently used is a brief description of the plot to a certain climactic moment. Words of caution: Do not give away too much of the plot, stick to essential details (for example, avoid introducing subplots or subsidiary characters), and try not to overwork this technique or else students will find the cliff-hanger endings ultimately frustrating. The second method is by retelling or reading a specific self-contained incident, or incidents, that give the flavor of the book. This is sometimes the most satisfying for the audience because a "complete" story has been told and yet, one hopes, a desire for more has also been implanted. One must be very cautious about reading from the book and use that technique sparingly, only when the author's style cannot be produced otherwise. Some booktalkers eschew entirely reading from the book and instead memorize the passages because reading from the book interrupts the immediate eye contact with the audience and can lessen or destroy the rapport one has with the group. Therefore, passages to be read must be chosen very carefully and should be short and fulfill a specific purpose when simple retelling will not suffice. A third method is to introduce a specific interesting character fully and placed within the context of the book. This is a suitable technique for booktalking such works as *Goodbye, Mr. Chips* or *Breakfast at Tiffany's*. Using the setting or atmosphere of the novel is a fourth method. Science fiction or fantasies with their often exotic, fascinating locales lend themselves frequently to such introductions.

Make sure you are honest in interpreting the book. To present, for example, *The Red Badge of Courage* as an exciting action-filled war story is both a disservice to the book and a misrepresentation to the audience.

Some people write down their booktalks and memorize them; others simply prepare them mentally. A rehearsal, however, is necessary to test pacing, presentation, timing, and sequencing. Perhaps friends, family, or colleagues can be an initial test audience. Tape recorders or, better yet, video recorders are also helpful in preparation. Although rehearsals are necessary, always try for sincerity, naturalness, and a relaxed atmosphere in the delivery. Because initial nervousness can be expected, be particularly careful to know thoroughly the beginning of the talk. Once one becomes used to the audience and the surroundings, nervousness usually disappears. Introduce the theme or subject of the booktalk quickly, in a way that bridges the gap between the experience and interests of the audience and the contents of the books you wish to introduce. Be sure to mention both the author and the title of the book (often twice—once at the beginning and once at the end of the presentation), show off the book (dust jacket and covers help sell a book and supply a visual reminder of the book), and then display the book (usually by standing it up on the desk). Try to adhere to principles of good public speaking: include the entire audience in your eye contact; don't fidget, rock, play with elastic bands, or create other distractions; speak slowly, with good intonation, and use pauses effectively; and move quickly from one book to the next. After introducing the last book, conclude by returning to the main theme to round out the booktalk.

Happy booktalking!

Teenage Life and Concerns

Anderson, Laurie. *Speak*. Penguin, 1999. $10.28 (0-3743-7152-0);
pb. $7.99 (0-1413-1088X) (Grades 9–12).

Introduction

Laurie Halse Anderson (1961–) was born in Potsdam, New York, and claims that as a child she read practically every book in her school library. Although she wrote three earlier picture books for children, her first novel for young adults is *Speak*. It was greeted enthusiastically by reviewers. One said that she is a "gifted new writer whose novel shows that she understands (and remembers) the raw emotion and tumult that marks the lives of teenagers." Some parts of the story were drawn from experience. Anderson remembers that when she was a new student in her high school, she was outside the reigning clique, a situation duplicated in the novel when Melinda Sordino is cruelly ostracized by her peers. The author also stated that the beginnings of the novel stem from a nightmare she experienced during which she heard a sobbing girl. Her second novel for teens is the historical *Fever, 1793* (Simon & Schuster, 2000) set in post-Revolutionary times and dealing with a yellow fever outbreak.

Principal Characters

Melinda Sordino, who enters high school ostracized by her schoolmates
    and carrying a dark secret
Rachel Bruin, Melinda's ex–best friend
Andy Evans, an upperclassman who rapes Melinda
Melinda's parents, a dysfunctional couple who have little time for their
    daughter
Heather, a disoriented newcomer to school and the only one who speaks
    to Melinda
Mr. Freeman, a sympathetic art teacher

Plot Summary

This should be the happiest time of her life. However, Melinda Sordino enters Merryweather High as a social outcast. None of her classmates will talk to her, including even her former best friend, Rachel. The cause of the trouble happened during the summer. At a summer party of the gang, Melinda called in the police. A number of her friends got into trouble because of the call and, since that time, they will have nothing to do with her.

Melinda cannot and will not tell them, even Rachel, the reason she made the call. It is her terrible and agonizing secret. The reason is that she was raped at the party by upperclassman jock Andy Evans. Melinda has never told anyone of that dreadful night. She has no one to talk to, certainly not her dysfunctional parents. Even if she could talk to them, they are almost never at home anyway, and even when the three of them are together, her parents have little time for her.

The story is told in diarylike entries, often with dark humor, beginning on Melinda's first day at Merryweather. The long and lonely year continues with almost no respite. Melinda's grades begin to drop. She does acquire a friend of sorts, a newcomer from Ohio. Heather is a perky but flighty girl who does not understand or even appear to realize that Melinda is ostracized. Melinda is not even sure she likes Heather. The days go on, and Melinda makes frequent entries that record her dreary existence.

More and more, the young girl retreats into herself. She views the high-school scene about her with a sometimes sarcastic, sometimes indifferent attitude. Her only outlet in her cloistered world is Mr. Freeman, who gives her a chance to express her emotions and loneliness through creativity.

By the end of the interminable school year, Melinda is now nearly totally isolated at school and at home. Then, unbelievably, she once again finds herself in a situation where she is about to be trapped by Andy Evans. But Melinda has not suffered this year for nothing. This time, when Evans tries to attack her, she finds her voice. She screams over and over again. At first, Evans does not believe her resistance, and he persists. But when he continues his assault, she attacks him with a piece of glass. When he is silenced with fright, she tells him with conviction, "I said no."

This incident is overheard by her schoolmates. It restores Melinda into the land of the talking. Everyone now knows the story. She is suddenly popular. She will not forget what has happened to her or what lessons she has learned, but she is sure that next year promises to be better.

Suitability and Critical Comment

Although well written and compelling, this book may not be for all readers. Even in a situation as compelling as Melinda's, the picture of high-school life that it presents is almost unrelentingly depressing. Added to this are two nearly unbelievably uncaring parents. This is a very strong dose of gritty realism suitable for grades nine through twelve.

Themes and Subjects

Acceptance, cliques, conformity, dysfunctional families, friendship, high-school life, honor, loneliness, peer pressure, rape

Passages for Booktalking

Melinda's ex–best friend ostracizes her (pp. 4, 5); Melinda meets Heather (pp. 22–24); Thanksgiving at home (pp. 57–61); Melinda's parents meet the principal about her falling grades (pp. 113–16); Melinda and Mr. Freeman talk about her work (pp. 152–53); the second assault (pp. 193–95).

Additional Selections

Nice guy Kenyon Baker abandons his girlfriend, Razzle, and becomes infatuated with sexpot Harley in Ellen Witlinger's *Razzle* (Simon & Schuster, 2001), set on Cape Cod.

In *Shayla's Double Brown Baby Blues* (Simon & Schuster, 2001) by Lori Aurelia Williams, thirteen-year-old Shayla gets involved with Lemm Turley, a boy with a severe drinking problem, and with her best friend, Kambia, who has an abusive past.

Set in the slums of Brooklyn, *Every Time a Rainbow Dies* (HarperCollins, 2001) by Rita Williams-Garcia tells of the love sixteen-year-old Jamaica-born Thulani feels for the girl he has seen being raped.

Everyone wonders why fifteen-year-old Skylar Deacon's family is so overly protective and why Skylar is so eager to please his mysterious older sister in *Calling the Swan* (Viking, 2000) by Jean Thesman.

About the Book

Booklist, Sept. 15, 1999, p. 247.
Bulletin of the Center for Children's Books, Oct., 1999, p. 45.
Horn Book, Sept.–Oct., 1999, p. 605.
Kirkus Reviews, Sept. 15, 1999, p. 1496.
School Library Journal, Oct., 1999, p. 144.

About the Author

Authors and Artists for Young Adults, vol. 39, Gale, 2001.
Drew, Bernard A. *100 More Popular Young Adult Authors,* Libraries Unlimited, 2002.
"The Printz Award Revisited—Laurie Halse Anderson," *Booklist,* Jan. 1 and 15, 2001, pp. 933–34.
Something about the Author, vol. 95, Gale, 1998.

Block, Francesca Lia. *Baby Be-Bop.* HarperCollins, 1995. $12.95
(006-02-48793) (Grades 9–12).

Introduction

With the publication in 1989 of *Weezie Bat,* a hip, psychedelic story that is
part magical fairy tale and part funky realism, critics took sides. Some welcomed this imaginative depiction of the teenage punk subculture of
Shangri-L.A., better known as Los Angeles, while others had serious reservations. Regardless of the reaction, the author has, in this and subsequent
novels in this series, taken the young adult novel in a new direction that
explores sensual experiences, the teenage psyche, and the meaning of love
and family in a unique, life-affirming fashion. In the first novel, Weezie Bat,
an unconventional, larger-than-life teenager with a great need to give and
receive love, creates her own family unit, which includes two young gay
lovers, Dirk McDonald and Duck Drake. *Baby Be-Bop* is Dirk's story before
he met Drake.

Principal Characters

Dirk McDonald, a good-looking fifteen-year-old gay boy who has difficulty accepting his homosexuality; called Baby Be-Bop when he was a
baby

Grandma Fifi, Dirk's supportive grandmother who possesses a great love
of life and is an accomplished dancer

Martin and Merlin, two gay lovers who were part of a show-business team
with Fifi years ago

Pup Lambert, an attractive straight schoolmate of Dirk's with whom Dirk
falls in love

Gazelle Sunday, Fifi's mother who survived cruelty from a sadistic aunt

Derwood McDonald, an entomologist who becomes Dirk's grandfather

Dirby McDonald, Dirk's father, a talented poet who was known as Be-Bop
Bo-Peep

Just Silver McDonald, Dirk's mother

Duck Drake, a surfing fanatic who becomes Dirk's lover

Bam-Bam, a gay friend of Duck's who helps him accept being gay

Plot Summary

After the death of his parents, Dirby and Just Silver McDonald, in an
automobile accident, young Dirk McDonald goes to live with his high-
spirited, freedom-loving grandmother, Fifi, who has as best friends two old
showbiz cronies, Martin and Merlin, gay lovers who have remained closeted

through the years. Dirk harbors a guilty secret. He knows he is gay but is afraid to reveal his secret to anyone, even his understanding grandmother. When he is almost sixteen, he meets and falls in love with Pup Lambert, a daring, fun-loving boy who delights in using other people's swimming pools and basketball hoops without permission and engaging in petty thievery to satisfy his immediate needs. Their close friendship ends when Pup becomes infatuated with an attractive girl in their school. Dirk tries to tell Pup about his feelings but is rebuffed. He tries to change his lifestyle; he sports a Mohawk haircut and begins hanging out in leather dives, but one night, he is beaten up by a gang of skinheads who call him "faggot." He manages to get home but there falls into a coma during which he has a series of visitations that represent the past and future. In the first, Gazelle Sunday comes to him and tells her sad life story. She was raised by a cruel aunt who trained her as a dressmaker and kept her locked in their apartment. One day when the aunt is absent, a stranger visits her, orders a dress, and holds her tight. Soon she realizes that she is pregnant and, after the death of her aunt, raises the child she has, named Fifi. Dirk realizes that he is hearing the story of his family. Fifi has great dancing ability and joins the show-business act of Martin and Merlin. Later she meets an introspective, otherworldly young entomologist who marries her. He dies shortly after the birth of Dirby, their only child. Dirby, a talented poet who is known as Be-Bop Bo-Peep in the venues where he reads his poetry, next tells his story about how he fell in love and married Dirk's mother, Just Silver. When Dirk confesses his homosexuality to his father, Dirby replies, "I know you are buddy . . . I love you. I want you not to be afraid." The same stranger, who ordered the dress from Dirk's great-grandmother now appears and gives Dirk a glimpse into the future. He shows him the Drake household in which one of the sons is Duck Drake, a young man who, like Dirk, is gay, unhappy, and unfulfilled. Moving to Los Angeles, Duck learns about the gay lifestyle from a gay friend, Bam Bam, during their platonic relationship. In the last part of the vision, Duck is seen alone waiting to meet his future love, Dirk. When he awakens in a hospital, Dirk is recovering from his wounds and Grandma Fifi is by his bedside. Through his experiences, he has gained an inner peace, a sense of acceptance and self-worth, and the strength to move on.

Suitability and Critical Comment

This novel contains richly lyrical prose that conjures up colorful images with sensual appeal. As well, its plot combines elements of magic realism that often require suspension of belief. Like many novels that are innovative and break new ground, this work challenges new readers but ultimately provides a satisfying reading experience. These elements plus its subject matter and the graphic nature of the language used make it best suited to readers in grades nine through twelve.

Themes and Subjects

Acceptance, California, continuity of life, families, fear, first love, friendship, hippies, homosexuality, life, Los Angeles, punk lifestyles, school stories, social pressures

Passages for Booktalking

Dirk meets Pup (pp. 9–12); their activities together (pp. 20–23); their friendship ends (pp. 29–31); he is beaten up by skinheads (pp. 43–45); Gazelle begins her story (pp. 52–58).

Additional Selections

Two teenage girls attending a summer institute for gifted high-school students experience their first same-sex relationship in *Empress of the World* (Viking, 2001) by Sara Ryan.

In *You Don't Know Me* (Farrar, 2001) by David Kass, John creates an intricate structure of black humor to compensate for such humiliations as the date with his dream girl and abuse from his mother's drunken boyfriend.

Jacqueline Woodson's *If You Come Softly* (Putnam, 1989) tells the story of Jeremiah, who is white, and Ellie, an African American girl; how they fall in love and the prejudices they encounter.

The present and past mingle in Aidan Chambers's award-winning *Postcards for No Man's Land* (Dutton, 2002), a novel of World War II and present-day Holland that explores such themes as sexual identity, love, courage, and family.

About the Book

Booklist, Oct. 1, 1995, p. 308.
Bulletin of the Center for Children's Books, Oct., 1995, p. 46.
Horn Book, March–April, 1996, p. 202.
Kirkus Reviews, July 15, 1995, p. 256.
VOYA, Dec., 1995, p. 297.

About the Author

Authors and Artists for Young Adults, vol. 13, Gale, 1994; vol. 34, Gale, 2000.
Campbell, Patricia. "People Are Talking about Francesca Lia Block," *Horn Book,* Jan.–Feb., 1993, pp. 57–66.
Children's Literature Review, vol. 33, Gale, 1994.
Continuum Encyclopedia of Children's Literature, Continuum, 2001.

Drew, Bernard A. *The 100 Most Popular Young Adult Authors,* Libraries Unlimited, 1997.
Hipple, Ted. *Writers for Young Adults,* vol. 1, Scribners, 1997, pp. 111–20.
St. James Guide to Young Adult Writers (2nd ed.), St. James, 1999.
Seventh Book of Junior Authors and Illustrators, Wilson, 1996.
Something about the Author, vol. 80, Gale, 1995; vol. 116, Gale, 2000.
Something about the Author Autobiography Series, vol. 21, Gale, 1996.
Twentieth Century Young Adult Writers, St. James, 1994.

Brooks, Bruce. *All That Remains.* Atheneum, 2001. $16.00 (0-689-833511-2) (Grades 7–12).

Introduction

Bruce Brooks (1950–) was born in Richmond, Virginia. His parents divorced when he was six, and he spent much of his childhood shuttling between two households. Because his mother was an alcoholic and unstable emotionally, he found living with her so difficult that he once ran away to stay with his grandmother. He has said that many of his books with teenage protagonists were attempts by him to understand his own childhood. His first young adult novel, *The Moves Make the Man* (Harper, 1984), was a Newbery Honor Book and the winner of the Boston Globe–Horn Book Award. In it, Jayfox, a cheeky, incoherent black student, tells about his friend Bix, who is troubled after his mother's mental breakdown. *All That Remains* consists of three novellas for young adults that explore, often with macabre humor, the effects of death on different young people. About it, the author said, "This stuff is definitely new for me. . . . In writing these stories I let myself use a more dicey aspect of my humor, a less classical narrative sense, and generally more peculiar subjects and shadows. . . . but I do hope these stories yield to readers a slightly different sense of order and design."

Principal Characters
All That Remains

Jonny, the thirteen-year-old narrator and prep-school student
Marie, his cousin who attends the same school
Sue Jo, a Japanese-American potter
Judith Roberts, aunt of Jonny and Marie
Captain Hardy and Mr. Geers, employees of a funeral home

Playing the Creeps

Hank, an all-around teenager particularly interested in sports and rock
Bobby, Hank's bookish cousin

Teeing Up

Flipper, Jackson, and Irons, three teenaged friends who are out for a game of golf

Isabel, a young girl who joins them

Plot Summaries
All That Remains

Jonny and Marie take time off from the prep school they attend to visit the deathbed of their aunt, Judith Roberts, who is dying of AIDS. Judith has been living and studying with her gay lover, Sue Jo, a renowned potter, in their rural home in redneck country. Unfortunately, on one of Sue's absences, Judith had a heterosexual fling with a local from Duke's tavern and became infected. Jonny runs afoul of some of these locals when he tries to buy food at Duke's, with the result that he comes back to the house with several stitches in his arm. Before her death, Judith requested that she be cremated. However, local law stipulates that AIDS victims must be buried in a special isolated area. Sue, Jonny, and Marie concoct a wild plan to obey Judith's last wish. They kill a deer, place some of its remains in a specially built clay sarcophagus, fire it in Sue's large kiln, and give the result to the officials from the funeral home, claiming that Judith's body is inside. In the meantime, after firing the sarcophagus, Judith will be cremated in the kiln. The plot works: Captain Hardy and Mr. Geers come from the funeral parlor and take the casket. During their visit, Judith's body is being cremated, and there are some anxious moments when the kiln emits loud popping sounds, but neither of the employees suspects the truth. While driving the two cousins back to school, Sue gets her final revenge by dumping the rest of the deer's remains on the bar at Duke's tavern.

Playing the Creeps

Hank, a young teenager, is a little nervous when he is summoned to his Uncle Frank's hospital room because he knows his uncle is dying. Frank has one last request to make: that Hank encourage and help his son Bobby if he ever expresses an interest in any of Hank's activities, like playing hockey, skateboarding, or even, because he plays a little guitar, joining a rock band, like Hank's group The Weasels. Bobby is very different. He is bookish, quiet, and sensitive; Hank refers to him as a dweep. After his father's death, Bobby purchases a fancy skateboard and asks Hank's help, but he shows no aptitude and soon gives up. Later, Hank notices that Bobby hangs out at parties with kids who could be called effeminate, and on those occasions he guiltily avoids him. Weeks later, Bobby invites Hank to go skating with him and, to Hank's amazement, he proves to be an expert figure skater. Despite the taunts and jeers of Hank's teammates, Bobby buys hockey gear and, to everyone's amazement, he makes the team. However, while trying to save the puck during a game, he suffers a serious concussion and is forbidden by his doctors to engage in any physical sports. At his mother's insistence, Hank invites Bobby to join his band at a gig. Here, at last, Bobby and Hank find a common ground, and they jam together frequently. One day, at Bobby's insistence, they go to the cemetery to play at Frank's grave. The music isn't very good, but their friendship is strengthened.

Teeing Up

At dawn's first light, three friends sneak onto a golf course to avoid paying the greens fee. They are Flipper, a boy with a withered right arm but a remarkably positive attitude; Irons, an African American who has just lost his parents in a plane crash; and Jackson, a witty, smooth-talking, likable young man. They are joined by a stranger—a girl named Isabel—who, in spite of their hostility, invites herself to join them, making it a foursome. Isabel tells them that everything she knows about golf she learned from her father. The three notice that, even while playing, she never takes off her backpack. At Flipper's questioning, she admits that the backpack contains an urn of her father's ashes. He died a month before from an accidental overdose of his medication. As they pass from hole to hole, they become more friendly, easy in their conversation, and willing to exchange confidences. As they approach the eighteenth hole, the boys try to persuade Isabel to accept her father's death and empty the urn. They tell her that there is more to her life than carrying around the past. On the last hole, she agrees and empties a little of the ashes into each of the four sand traps. Together, she and her three new friends take rakes and mix the ashes with the sand of the golf course.

Suitability and Critical Comment

In these stories, the author explores the effect of death on different young people in different locales and shows how people cope with the "remains" of recently deceased loved ones. In each case, self-knowledge and an acceptance of death are gained. Though bordering on the morbid, these stories will hold mature readers, particularly because of the subject matter, realistic characterization, and witty dialogue. They are suitable for readers in junior and senior high school.

Themes and Subjects

AIDS, cremation, death, friendship, golf, hockey, homosexuality, loyalty, music, pottery, skateboarding, sports competitions, sports stories

Passages for Booktalking

All That Remains: Jonny seeks food at the tavern (pp. 14–18); Sue makes a suggestion about Judith's body (pp. 26–29).

Playing the Creeps: Uncle Frank makes his dying request of Hank (pp. 67–70); Hank and Bobby go skateboarding (pp. 77–81).

Teeing Up: Isabel joins the three friends (pp. 117–21); she tells Flipper what's in her backpack (pp. 133–35).

Additional Selections

Death and the Catholic Church's mysticism are the subjects of the eighteen stories in David Almond's *Counting Stars* (Delacorte, 2002), which is based on incidents in his rural English childhood.

The realities of AIDS and death are confronted by twelve-year-old Slim when she goes to live with her sick father and his lover in *Earthshine* (Orchard, 1994) by Theresa Nelson.

Harley, abandoned by his mother in the Arizona desert, meets a collection of fellow rejects who try to build a new family in Ouida Sebestyen's *Out of Nowhere* (Orchard, 1994).

An insecure adolescent remembers vacations during the 1960s with his eccentric "born again" family in *Portofino* (Macmillan, 1992) by Frank Schaeffer.

About the Book

Booklist, May 1, 2001, p. 1682.
Bulletin of the Center for Children's Books, June, 2001, p. 367.
Horn Book, July-Aug., 2001, p. 447.
Kirkus Reviews, April 1, 2001, p. 495.
New York Times Book Review, July 15, 2001, p. 24.
School Library Journal, May, 2001, p. 148.
VOYA, June, 2001, p. 19.

About the Author

Authors and Artists for Young Adults, vol. 8, Gale, 1996; vol. 36, Gale, 2001.
Campbell, Patricia. "Asylum for Nightface (in Sand in the Oyster column)," *Horn Book,* July-Aug., 1996, pp. 462–96.
Children's Literature Review, vol. 25, Gale, 1991.
Continuum Encyclopedia of Children's Literature, Continuum, 2001.
Drew, Bernard A. *The 100 Most Popular Young Adult Authors,* Libraries Unlimited, 1997.
Hipple, Ted. *Writers for Young Adults,* vol. 1, Scribners, 1997, pp. 173–82.
Lives and Works: Young Adult Authors, vol. 1, Grolier, 1999, pp. 93–95.
Major Authors and Illustrators for Children and Young Adults, vol. 2, Gale, 1993.
Marens, Leonard S. *Author Talk,* Simon & Schuster, 2000.
———. "Song of Myself: Bruce Brooks," *School Library Journal,* Sept., 2000, pp. 50–51.

St. James Guide to Young Adult Writers (2nd ed.), St. James, 1999.
Silvey, Anita. *Children's Books and Their Creators,* Houghton Mifflin, 1995.
Sixth Book of Junior Authors and Illustrators, Wilson, 1989.
Something about the Author, vol. 60, Gale, 1990; vol. 72, Gale, 1993; vol. 112, Gale, 2002.
Twentieth Century Young Adult Writers, St. James, 1994.

Cabot, Meg. *The Princess Diaries.* HarperCollins, 2000. $15.95 (0-06-029210-5); pb. $5.95 (0-380-81402-1) (Grades 6–9).

Introduction

Meg Cabot has written several books under various pseudonyms; for example, she wrote juvenile mysteries using the name Jenny Carroll and several romances as Patricia Cabot. According to her dust jackets, she currently lives in New York City with her husband and a one-eyed cat named Henrietta. In *The Princess Diaries,* Cabot has captured the way adolescents think, feel, and speak. As we read Mia's diary entries and follow the new-found princess through darkest adolescence, we are in the presence of a bubbly, cheery young girl who always faces her problems in a positive, commonsensical fashion. The humor, often verging on slapstick, never stops as we move from one hilarious situation to another. In the first sequel, *Princess in the Spotlight* (HarperCollins, 2001), Mia is visited by her maternal grandparents and Hank, a handsome young cousin. As well, Mia has an e-mail admirer, and her mother finally marries Mr. Gianini. In the third volume, *Princess in Love* (HarperCollins, 2002), Mia at last gets a boyfriend of her own.

Principal Characters

Mia Thermopolis, a typical adolescent who discovers she's a princess
Helen Thermopolis, Mia's mother and an avant-garde painter
Phillipe Renaldo, Mia's father and prince of Genovia
Lilly Moscovitz, a precocious teenager who is Mia's best friend
Michael Moscovitz, Lilly's older brother
Grandmere, Mia's demanding maternal grandmother
Lars, Phillipe's driver and later Mia's bodyguard
Tina Hakim Baba, Mia's new friend at school and fellow outcast

Plot Summary

Mia Thermopolis, a fourteen-year-old, good-natured, bright freshman at the posh Albert Einstein High School on Manhattan's fashionable East

Side, is fumbling through adolescence with unruly hair, a flat chest, and a height of five feet nine inches. Her self-esteem sags at times, but living with her liberal single mother, a freelance artist, in a loft in the East Village is a big plus. Another is her long-standing friendship with fellow classmate Lilly Moscovitz, who lives on lower Fifth Avenue with her psychiatrist parents and older brother, Michael, a brainy computer whiz who is a senior at Albert Einstein. Mia and Lilly have many mutual interests, including working together on Lilly's cable TV show and sharing a wild crush on Josh Richter, the most popular, handsome jock in the senior class. Unfortunately, Josh has a girlfriend, the snobby, dislikable Lana Weinberger. Mia spends her summers in Europe with her father, Phillipe Renaldo (Mia is the result of a youthful fling, and her parents never married), and her domineering, aristocratic Grandmere in a castle in the tiny duchy of Genovia. In spite of teenage longings and anxieties, Mia's life is relatively serene until two momentous events occur. First, her mother begins dating Mr. Gianini, Mia's algebra teacher (algebra is the one subject Mia is flunking), and second, shortly after her father arrives on a special trip from Genovia, he announces, in a Plaza Hotel meeting with Mia, that he is actually the ruler of the little country and that Mia is Amelila Mignonette Grimaldi Thermopolis Renaldo, Princess of Genovia. As well, because Phillipe can't have any more children, as a result of testicular cancer, she will become the next ruler! With this news, her life suddenly becomes topsy-turvy, particularly after her autocratic Grandmere arrives at the Plaza to give Mia "princess lessons" every day after school. She begins by giving Mia a beauty salon makeover, including a smashing new hairdo by Paolo. Mia tries to hide her status from her classmates, but Grandmere, anxious for Mia to assume her rightful place in society, blabs to the press and soon the street outside of Albert Einstein becomes a media circus with reporters anxious to interview the new princess. Under the strain, Mia quarrels with Lilly and forms a friendship with Tina Hakim Baba, the daughter of a wealthy Arab sheikh. Tina is an outsider principally because she is always accompanied by a bodyguard named Wahim. At her father's insistence, Mia now also has a bodyguard, whose name is Lars, and the four, isolated from the rest of the crowd, have lunch together. Lilly's intellectual brother, Michael, remains her friend and even coaches her in algebra. Dreamboat Josh breaks up with Lana and surprisingly invites Mia to be his date for the school's Cultural Diversity Dance. Unsuspecting Mia is thrilled, but both her parents doubt the boy's intentions. Grandmere, however, supports Mia and takes her shopping to Chanel for a knockout party dress plus a waxing (which is painful) and new shoes. Before the dance, Josh and Mia have dinner at Tavern on the Green, and Mia realizes that, in spite of his big reputation, Josh is shallow and basically uninteresting. Furthermore, she feels betrayed when she finds a media mob scene again outside the school. Josh has tipped them off about her attending the dance in order to share the limelight with her. Even worse, while the cameras are rolling, he plants a juicy, unwanted kiss on her lips. Mortified, she retreats to the ladies' room, where she is rescued by Tina and Lilly, with whom she has a joyful reunion. Mia spends the rest of the dance with Lilly and her friends and finds that, unlike Josh, Michael Moscovitz and she have a lot in common and enjoy each other's company. Furthermore, Mr. Gianini tells her that her algebra grade has changed from an F to a D. As Mia looks around at her friends and loyal supporters, she has to admit that she is really HAPPY.

Suitability and Critical Comment

Mia's diary entries (she writes everywhere, including in algebra class and the ladies' room at the Plaza Hotel) ring true to teenage speech, interests, and wild humor. Her bubbly, emotional attitudes and opinions, her vulnerability, and her candid, honest view of situations and people add to the refreshing charm of the book. The diary format also adds to its appeal. It is popular with readers in grades six through nine.

Themes and Subjects

Family stories, friendship, humorous stories, New York City, princesses, royalty, school stories, single-parent families, teachers

Passages for Booktalking

Mia reacts to her mother's dating Mr. Gianini (pp. 1–5); Lilly Moscovitz's list of hottest guys (pp. 12–13); Mia confronts Mr. Gianini (pp. 14–16); Mia's father tells her that he is a prince (pp. 35–41); and that she is a princess (pp. 42–47).

Additional Selections

Four teenage girls who are close friends separate for the summer but keep in touch by means of a pair of magical secondhand jeans in Ann Brashares's *The Sisterhood of the Traveling Pants* (Delacorte, 2001).

In Patrice Kindl's lighthearted fairy-tale romp *Goose Chase* (Houghton Mifflin, 2001), magical geese help Goose Girl get rid of two unwanted suitors.

In Anne Fine's very funny *The Book of the Banshee* (Little, Brown, 1992), Will Flowers tells what happens when his sister is transformed into a teenage banshee.

Florida high-school junior Jonah Black continues to be unlucky in love in Jonah Black's *Run, Jonah, Run* (Avon, 2002), the third volume in the series Black Book (Diary of a Teenage Stud).

About the Book
Booklist, Sept. 15, 2000, p. 233.
Book Report, March, 2001, p. 57.
Bulletin of the Center for Children's Books, Dec., 2000, p. 137.
School Library Journal, Oct., 2000, p. 155.
VOYA, April, 2001, p. 35.

About the Author
Contemporary Authors, vol. 197, Gale, 2002.
Something about the Author, vol. 127, Gale, 2002.

Cormier, Robert. *Tenderness.* Delacorte, 1977. $12.85
(0-6143-1156-7) (Grades 10–12).

Introduction
During his career as a writer of novels for young adults, Robert Cormier (1925–2000) wrote about fifteen groundbreaking books, beginning with *The Chocolate War* in 1974 and ending with the posthumously published *The Rag and Bone Man* in 2001. Each is a gripping, unsettling exploration of such themes as corruption, abuse of power, and evil. Like many of his other novels, *Tenderness* deals with the dark side of humanity and tells of the delicate balance between the forces of light and of darkness in our world. It is told in alternating passages from two points of view. A first-person narrative that reflects the thoughts and actions of Lori, a fifteen-year-old runaway, is followed by a passage in the third person that delves into the mind and twisted motivations of Eric Poole, a teenage serial killer. The action takes place in and around a town featured in many of Cormier's novels, Wickburg, a fictitious place in central Massachusetts.

Principal Characters
Lorelei (Lori) Cranston, a fifteen-year-old, very attractive, but discontented girl who is obsessively searching for love and tenderness
Eric Poole, a handsome, intelligent eighteen-year-old who has become a serial killer because of a deep psychological derangement in which he associates tenderness with killing
Lieutenant Jake Proctor, a veteran police officer whose previous experience with a serial killer has led him to suspect Eric

Jimmy Pickett, a young detective who is helping Proctor in his investigation of Eric Poole

Aunt Phoebe, Eric's aunt in Wickburg, who is unaware of her nephew's evil machinations and offers him a home when he is released from detention

Marie Valdez, a striking dark-haired beauty whom Eric first sees while they are both in prison

Plot Summary

After the latest of her mother's live-in boyfriends makes sexual advances to fifteen-year-old Lori and she feels a mutual attraction, the girl decides that it is best to cool it and pretend to visit some fictitious friends for a few days in Wickburg, a nearby Massachusetts town. Her current crush, the rock star Throb, is also appearing there, and perhaps she will get a chance to meet him. Though technically still a virgin, Lori has had some sexual experience and longs for the love and tenderness she finds absent from her life at home. After hitching a ride from a guileless, fortyish driver named Walter Clayton, and extorting thirty dollars from him for a kiss and a quick feel, she arrives in Wickburg, richer also by the wallet she has stolen from the man. She tracks down Throb, fulfills her longings by giving him a big, wet kiss, and is now ready for a new fixation. While watching a TV news program, she sees her new romantic obsession. He is Eric Poole, an attractive eighteen-year-old who was convicted three years before of murdering his parents and is now about to be released from a juvenile detention center. The announcer also states that Eric plans to go to Wickburg and live with his aunt. Lori recognizes Eric as the kind young man who rescued her several years before from a motorcycle gang she encountered while out walking. Lori plans to track him down.

On the exterior, Eric is clean-cut, handsome, and charming, but inwardly he is a cunning, psychopathic killer who finds a perverted feeling of tenderness in holding soft, helpless beings in his arms and killing them. As a child he killed kittens, and while a young teenager murdered three randomly chosen girls without being caught. Later, he carried out a scheme to kill his mother and stepfather and cleverly convinced the judge that the act was justified by the physical and emotional abuse he supposedly suffered. The only people he has not convinced are Lieutenant Jake Proctor, a near-retirement police officer, and his assistant, a young detective named Jimmy Pickett. Both want to link Eric with the death of the teenage girls and, after his release, they follow him, fearful that he might strike again.

Realizing that Proctor and Pickett are out to get him, Eric lays low at his Aunt Phoebe's house for the first days after his release. Soon he becomes increasingly restless and anxious to look up an attractive girl named Marie Valdez, whom he met in prison. He hopes to give her some of his own lethal brand of tenderness.

Eric notices that a young, attractive girl is keeping vigil outside his aunt's house, and he recognizes her as the lonely youngster he helped years ago. Late one night he steals away in a newly purchased van, only to find that the girl, who introduces herself as Lori, is a stowaway. There begins an uneasy friendship. Lori, at last, has a boy she adores, and Eric has a girl he knows he could murder. After a botched attempt, he realizes that Lori's death will not produce the feeling of tenderness he craves. Eric arranges a rendezvous with Marie at an amusement park. He entices the girl into the woods, but Lori, who is sitting atop a Ferris wheel, sees that the couple are being followed by Proctor and the police. Lori gets off the ride and warns Eric. Unknowingly, she has saved not only Eric, but also the life of her female rival.

On the road again, Eric and Lori stop by a lake for some canoeing. Lori, who can't swim, accidentally tips the canoe after banging her head on an oar and drowns in spite of Eric's rescue attempts. After finding Eric and discovering Lori's body, the police charge him with murder. Although Proctor inwardly knows that Eric is not lying when he claims Lori's death was an accident, he also knows that a conviction is possible and that, in a perverse way, justice will be done.

Suitability and Critical Comment

This is a jolting, deeply disturbing portrait of two emotionally dysfunctional teenagers, each on an obsessive search for a feeling called tenderness, an elusive emotion that involves radically different conditions for fulfillment with each. It is also a suspenseful thriller that is a gripping reading experience. Although there are no graphic sex scenes or explicit language in the novel, the darkness of its subject matter, which involves senseless murder, psychopathology, and a perversion of justice, makes it most suitable for mature readers in grades ten through twelve.

Themes and Subjects

Detectives, Massachusetts, murder, mysteries, obsession, prisons, psychopaths, serial killers

Passages for Booktalking

Lori hitchhikes with Walter Clayton (pp. 12–19); she finds Throb and kisses him (pp. 23–25); and sees Eric on TV (pp. 26–28); Eric and Lieutenant Proctor talk before Eric's release (pp. 35–38); Eric kills a mouse in his cell (pp. 69–71); and Lori recalls her first meeting with Eric (pp. 88–94).

Additional Selections

America (Atheneum, 2002) by E. R. Frank is a deeply disturbing novel about the past, present, and future of a fifteen-year-old boy who unsuccessfully attempts suicide.

Ellen Wittlinger's *The Long Night of Leo and Bree* (Simon & Schuster, 2002) tells in alternating chapters of a night spent together by two teenagers, during which Leo intends to murder Bree.

Spanning a period of seven years from the late 1930s to the beginning of World War II, *Her Father's Daughter* (Delacorte, 2000) by Mollie Poupeney is a story of poverty, family problems, and abuse as seen through the experiences of young Maggie.

When Simon Glass, one of a clique run by charismatic Rob Hayes, turns against his classmates, they beat him to death in *Shattering Glass* (Millbrook, 2002) by Gail Giles.

About the Book

Booklist, Feb. 1, 1997, p. 935.
Bulletin of the Center for Children's Books, April, 1997, p. 278.
Horn Book, March-April, 1997, p. 197.
Kirkus Reviews, Jan. 1, 1997, p. 57.
School Library Journal, March, 1997, p. 184.
VOYA, April, 1997, p. 27.

About the Author

Authors and Artists for Young Adults, vol. 3, Gale, 1990; vol. 19, Gale, 1996.
Campbell, Patricia, "A Loving Farewell to Robert Cormier," *Horn Book*, March-April, 2001, pp. 245–48.
———. *Presenting Robert Cormier*, Twayne, 1985.
Children's Literature Review, Vol. 12, Gale, 1987; vol. 55, Gale, 1999.
Continuum Encyclopedia of Children's Literature, Continuum, 2001.
Drew, Bernard A. *The 100 Most Popular Young Adult Authors*, Libraries Unlimited, 1997.
Fifth Book of Junior Authors and Illustrators, Wilson, 1983.
Hipple, Ted. *Writers for Young Adults*, vol.1, Scribners, 1997, pp. 291–302.
Lives and Works: Young Adult Authors, vol. 2, Grolier, 1999, pp. 72–74.
Major Authors and Illustrators for Children and Young Adults, vol. 2, Gale, 1993.
St. James Guide to Young Adult Writers (2nd ed.), St. James, 1999.
Silvey, Anita. *Children's Books and Their Creators*, Houghton Mifflin, 1995.
Something about the Author, vol. 10, Gale, 1976; vol. 45, Gale, 1986; vol. 83, Gale, 1996.
Twentieth Century Young Adult Writers, St. James. 1994.

Dessen, Sarah. *Dreamland.* Viking, 2000. $15.99
(0-670-89122-3) (Grades 9–12).

Introduction

Sarah Dessen (1970–) grew up and still lives in Chapel Hill, North Carolina. She was a shy girl and began writing stories while still in elementary school. The daughter of an English professor, she later studied writing at the University of North Carolina and, after graduation, worked for years as a waitress, an occupation that gave her both the opportunity to study people and the free time to do her own writing. Her first book, *That Summer* (Orchard, 1996), is the story of Haven, an awkward fifteen-year-old girl who is almost six feet tall. She faces such problems as accepting her older sister's marriage to a man Haven doesn't like, adjusting to her mother's new lifestyle after her divorce, and trying to like her father's new bride. In *Dreamland,* the author explores her most challenging subject, physical abuse, in the story of Caitlin and her search for self-worth, a quest that leads her to seek love from a charismatic young man who begins abusing her when he is in one of his violent moods.

Principal Characters

Caitlin O'Koren, a sixteen-year-old who has lived her life in the shadow of her older sister
Cassandra, Caitlin's sister, who runs away as she is about to leave for Yale
Mr. and Mrs. O'Koren, who are shattered when their daughter leaves home
Boo and Stewart, the O'Korens' unconventional next-door neighbors
Rina, Caitlin's best friend
Rogerson Brisco, Caitlin's troubled boyfriend

Plot Summary

On Caitlin's sixteenth birthday, she discovers that her older sister, Cass, has run away from home to be with her boyfriend. Her parents are devastated. Cass has always been the perfect one, great looking, homecoming queen, star right wing on the soccer team, president of the student body, all Ms. Everything. And now, just as she is ready to start at Yale, she runs away. Caitlin can't believe it. She was jealous of her sister now and then, but she'd always counted on Cass to lead the way. Now Caitlin is on her own.

Cass did leave her a birthday present before she ran away, however. It was a blank book, a Dream Journal. When the girls were little, the last thing their mother always said when she tucked them in was, "See you in dreamland." Now Cass expects her to write things in the journal, but Caitlin doesn't have anything to say.

Before long, Cass calls to let her parents know she is okay but that she won't be coming home. Nothing they say can persuade her. Caitlin doesn't talk to her. She has nothing to say.

Surprisingly, life goes on at school and home much as before, except that her mother takes Cass's running away the hardest of all. Boo and Stewart, their unconventional next-door neighbors, are there to offer comfort to all of them. But Caitlin just can't talk about how she feels to anyone. She fits into the school routine and even lets her best friend, Rina, talk her into trying out for the cheerleading squad. Caitlin is amazed when she is accepted, but not so sure she wants to be there.

Then, around Halloween, she meets Rogerson Briscoe. He's different, fascinating looking, maybe even a bit dangerous. But that's all it takes. Caitlin is in love. After she witnesses the brutal way in which his father treats him, Caitlin and Rogerson become inseparable. She is not sure what the attraction is, but she knows it's there. She knows he is into drugs, and she experiments herself. For the first time, she sleeps with him.

No one is too pleased with her association with Rogerson, but Caitlin simply withdraws more and more and lives only for her world with Rogerson. Then one day, in a fit of anger, he slaps her, really hard. She can't believe it at first. After that, Caitlin almost gets used to the treatment. If she's late to meet him, he might punch her. If she annoys him, she gets a bruise on her arm. But nothing matters. She won't talk to anyone about it, and she just keeps going back.

Then comes the day when she is late to meet Rogerson, and he sees her getting out of the car of another boy, who has given her a ride home. That results in a beating so brutal that Caitlin's mother hears what is going on and comes to her rescue.

Caitlin is sent to the Evergreen Care Center where over a long period she learns that she has been trying to replace her sister in her parents' eyes. She learns that she has been trying to pretend to be someone she is not and that pretense led her straight to Rogerson and his treatment of her.

Slowly Caitlin begins to understand who she is and her place in the family. She begins to look at her mother as a person, not just the mother of perfect Cass. And when finally she is able to go home, she walks into a house filled with those who love her, and she sees that Cass is there, too.

Suitability and Critical Comment

This is a frank, somewhat frightening look at the world of physical violence involving teenagers. It presents an understanding picture of a young girl caught in emotions she does not fully comprehend. Well done and gripping, it is nonetheless best recommended for young readers who can handle realism, that is, in grades nine through twelve.

Themes and Subjects

Adolescent sex, drugs, mental breakdown, mother-daughter relationships, peer pressure, runaways, sibling rivalry, violence

Passages for Booktalking

Caitlin reacts to Cass's disappearance (pp. 13–16); Caitlin gets talked into trying out for cheerleading (pp. 27–31); she meets Rogerson (pp. 50–53); Caitlin witnesses the behavior of Rogerson's father (pp. 84–86).

Additional Selections

An extra-tall Alaskan teenager near death by drowning reflects on her life with her drunken father in *Lucy the Giant* (Delacorte, 2002) by Sherri L. Smith.

In Han Nolan's *Born Blue* (Harcourt, 2001), Janie, a product of abuse and foster homes, sinks into alcohol, drugs, and sex until she confronts her problems after seeing her mother dying of AIDS.

In the coming-of-age story *Looking for Alibrandi* (Orchard, 1999) by Melina Marchetta, seventeen-year-old Josie Alibrandi learns to see herself and her family in new ways.

To escape her stepfather and abusive mother, teenaged Chloe goes on the run accompanied by a pregnant Hispanic servant in Matthew Olshan's *Finn* (Bancroft, 2001).

About the Book

Booklist, Nov. 1, 2000, p. 534.
Bulletin of the Center for Children's Books, Oct., 2000, p. 58.
Horn Book, Sept., 2000, p. 566.
Kirkus Reviews, July 15, 2000, p.1036.
School Library Journal, Sept., 2000, p. 228.

About the Author

Authors and Artists for Young Adults, vol. 39, Gale, 2001.
Contemporary Authors, Vol. 196, Gale, 2002.
Drew, Bernard A. *100 More Popular Young Adult Authors,* Libraries Unlimited, 2002.

Flinn, Alex. *Breathing Underwater.* HarperCollins, 2001. $15.95 (0-06-029199-0) (Grades 9–12).

Introduction

While attending law school in Florida, Alex (Alexandra) Flinn tried several domestic violence cases as an intern in the state's attorney's office. She also served as a volunteer in a facility for battered women. These experiences led her to write this, her first novel. The story is told in two alternating narratives. The first is a handwritten journal (which appears in the book in script format) that has been kept by the central character, Nick Andreas, to fulfill a court-ordered punishment, and the second is the account of Nick's experiences in the nine months following his court appearance. In contrast to many other young adult novels about domestic violence, this harrowing story explores its causes, effects, and treatment from the standpoint of the perpetrator, an affluent, likable teenager who, in a moment of self-revelation, describes his desperate condition in this statement: "Ever feel that you're breathing underwater and have to stop because you are gulping in too much fluid?"

Principal Characters

Nicholas (Nick) Andreas, a rich, popular high-school sophomore
Mr. Andreas, Nick's wealthy, abusive father
Caitlin (Cat) McCourt, Alex's attractive but insecure girlfriend
Tom Carter, Nick's best friend and classmate
Mario Ortega, the counselor in Nick's Family Violence Class
Leo Sotolonga, a member of the class with whom Nick feels friendly
Kelly, Tyrone (Tiny) Johnston, and A.J., other members of the class
Patrick "Saint" O'Connor, the star quarterback in Nick's school

Plot Summary

Sixteen-year-old sophomore Nick Andreas seems to have everything: he's rich, popular, handsome, and a strong achiever in both sports and academics at his high school in wealthy Key Biscayne, Florida. Yet he finds himself in a Miami-Dade County courtroom facing Judge Deborah Lehman, accused of beating up his lovely girlfriend, Caitlin McCourt. Although he feebly denies the charges, he is obviously guilty and, in addition to a restraining order, Nick is required to write a journal recounting the events leading up to the beating and also to attend classes on family violence and anger control.

Nick takes the writing of the journal seriously. In it, he reveals his darkest secret. His father, a hugely successful investment banker, possesses a volcanic temper that erupts in physical violence directed at his son, often for minor offenses. These tantrums drove Nick's mother away when he was only five, leaving him with recurring feelings of desertion and insecurity. Nick is able to hide these feelings by becoming one of the school's most popular and liked students, but he never tells anyone, including his best friend of many years, Tom Carter, about his domestic situation, which often involves missing school because of bruises and other injuries. When Nick meets attractive, charming Caitlin McCourt, it is mutual love at first sight. As their love deepens to the point of physical intimacy, Nick becomes increasingly controlling and threatened by her beauty, popularity, and talent. Caitlin, who is herself inwardly insecure and saddled with a domineering mother, forgives Nick's bad behavior and often needlessly blames herself. Nick's fear of losing her, particularly to the hunky quarterback, Saint O'Connor, leads to increasingly irrational, dominating, and belittling behavior that culminates in his attacking her physically because she takes part in a talent show of which he disapproves.

After his court appearance, Nick finds his life completely changed. He is treated like a pariah by all his classmates, including Tom. Messages like "Go Nick! Beat your girlfriend" appear mysteriously on classroom blackboards. Nick, lonely and confused, manages to withstand many of these rebuffs but is pained when his attempts to communicate with Tom and (illegally) with Caitlin are rejected. At his domestic violence class, led by no-nonsense Mario Ortega, himself a recovered perpetrator, Nick meets an odd assortment of people, including the smart-aleck Kelly; an overweight loser named Tiny Johnston; a pathetically withdrawn man named A. J.; and the confident, outgoing Leo Sotolongo, who believes he has been wrongly sentenced to attend these classes. Through this group therapy, Nick gains insights into his own condition, and through these bouts of self-discovery, begins to develop greater control and a sense of responsibility. By persuading his girlfriend to drop the charges against him, Leo is able to leave the class but, shortly afterward, Nick learns that he has murdered this girl and committed suicide. Nick knows he has a long way to go, and at the end of his six-month class he decides to return for further sessions with Mario.

By the beginning of Nick's junior year, there have been several new developments. Caitlin has moved to spend the school year with her father; Nick is able to reestablish his friendship with Tom; and, most importantly, he has successfully confronted his father about his violent behavior, and stopped it by threatening to leave if his father touches him again. Perhaps the cycle of domestic violence in Nick's family has been broken.

Suitability and Critical Comment

This novel portrays realistically and candidly the ugliness and brutality of domestic violence in a case history that proves the truth in the adage "like father, like son." It also explores the causes and treatment of this increasingly prevalent form of violence, through the eyes of a tortured, intelligent young man with whom the reader easily identifies. This novel is read by students in grades nine through twelve, as well as some mature younger readers.

Themes and Subjects

Domestic violence, family problems, father-son relationship, Florida, friendship, group therapy, high schools, jealousy, rage, romance, wealth

Passages for Booktalking

In the courtroom: Caitlin testifies (pp. 2–6); the judge's decision (pp. 6–10); Caitlin and Nick attend their first party (pp. 50–55); Nick begins his controlling behavior toward Caitlin (pp. 60–67); the first group session with Mario (pp. 14–24); and Nick suffers insults from his classmates (pp. 41–45).

Additional Selections

Told in alternate chapters by twelve-year-old Jeremy and his fourteen-year-old sister, Jenna, this is the story of youngsters piecing together the facts after their father, a psychologist, has shot their mother in Julius Lester's *When Dad Killed Mom* (Harcourt, 2001).

In Chris Crutcher's psychological sports novel, *Ironman* (Greenwillow, 1995), Bo is sent to an anger-management program where he learns his real problem is his cruel father.

Taylor Drysdale, a bipolar teen, is devastated when her mother commits her to an outpatient program for problem teens in Dawn Wilson's *St. Jude* (Tudor, 2001).

Using alternate male and female voices, Marilyn Reynolds in *Beyond Dreams* (Morning Glory, 1995) presents stories of teens in crisis.

About the Book

Booklist, Aug., 2001, p. 2106.
Book Report, Nov., 2001, p. 61.
Bulletin of the Center for Children's Books, July, 2001, p. 407.
VOYA, June, 2001, p. 120.

About the Author

No information available.

Kerr, M. E. *What Became of Her.* HarperCollins, 2000. $13.95
(0-06-028435-8); pb. $5.95 (0-06-447210-8) (Grades 7–10).

Introduction

M. E. Kerr (1927–) burst on the world of juvenile literature with an
unconventional novel carrying the attention-getting title, *Dinky Hocker Shoots
Smack!* (Harper, 1972). Before young readers realized the innocence of the
title, they were hooked on M. E. Kerr. Since then, she has written almost two
dozen young adult novels dealing with the problems and bittersweet out-
comes of adolescence. Some, like *I Stay Near You* (Harper, 1985), explore the
relationship between the actions of one generation and the lives of the next.
This is also true of *What Became of Her* in which a wealthy, unscrupulous
woman (the "her" of the title) returns to her hometown to seek revenge on
the people who mistreated her as a youngster. Two of the favorite locales of
Kerr's novels are Seaville on Long Island (modeled after her current home
in East Hampton) and towns in upstate New York similar to Auburn, New
York, where she grew up. *What Became of Her* takes place in another eastern
town situated in affluent Bucks County, Pennsylvania, north of Philadelphia.

Principal Characters

Edgar Cayce Tobbit, known as E. C., the sixteen-year-old narrator of the
novel, who is growing up in the town of Serenity and is named after
the celebrated psychic

Ann Tobbit, E. C.'s mother

Darwin C. Duke, E. C.'s former shrink and currently Ann Tobbit's
boyfriend

Rosalind Slaymaster, formerly Rose Fitch, a tough multi-millionaire
whom E. C. calls "the Boss of Everything" and who owns most of the
property in the town of Serenity

Peale, a two-foot leather mannequin on whom Mrs. Slaymaster dotes as if
he were alive

Julie, a quiet fifteen-year-old girl who has been adopted by Mrs.
Slaymaster

Neal Kraft, the friend of E. C. who is known for his outlandish dress and
behavior

Plot Summary

Sixteen-year-old Edgar Tobbit (known as E. C.), growing up in the town
of Serenity in Bucks County, Pennsylvania, has his share of problems. He is
trying to adjust to his father's recent death, to being jilted by his steady girl-

friend, and to his mother's dating of E. C.'s shrink, Dr. Darwin C. Duke, a social-climbing nerd whom E. C. contemptuously calls "the Duck" or "the Quack." To avoid conflicts, E. C. leaves therapy but retains the friendship of a strange boy he met in group sessions named Neal Kraft, whose father, Perry Kraft, a local druggist, has recently committed suicide. Neal, two grades ahead of E. C. in high school, helps his mother in her dance studio but is celebrated in town for his outlandish dress, bizarre habits, and passion for Stephen King. After seeing Neal steal from a local bookstore, E. C. also knows that he is a kleptomaniac. E. C. tries to help a newcomer in his school, fifteen-year-old Julie, an orphan who has been adopted by Mrs. Rosalind Slaymaster, a formidable, fabulously wealthy widow, who grew up in poverty in Serenity, married extremely well, and has now returned, taking residence in the one palatial mansion in town, nicknamed *Peligro* (Spanish for danger) because of the signs workmen used during its reconstruction. As well as Julie, the icy Mrs. Slaymaster has brought with her a two-foot-high leather doll, Peale, name after Norman Vincent Peale, who officiated at her wedding. Peale, who is treated like a human by Mrs. Slaymaster, has his own wardrobe, bedroom, and television and is Mrs. Slaymaster's constant companion. E. C. and his mother meet Mrs. Slaymaster and Peale one evening when they are invited to Peligro, where Mrs. Tobbit, an amateur psychic, is asked to draw up Peale's horoscope. The intimidating Mrs. S. invites the two to a Christmas party, and E. C. brings along Neal, who arrives too late to meet the hostess but in time to pocket a cigarette case and lighter and impress young Julie. While Mrs. S. is away at New Year's visiting her huge ranch in Texas, Julie entertains E. C. and Neal, who go skinny-dipping in the indoor pool, take pictures, and stay overnight in separate bedrooms. E. C. finds diaries kept by Mrs. Slaymaster dated from when she was known as Rose Fitch and growing up in Serenity as a lonely teenager, scorned and continually humiliated by all her classmates because of her poverty and the fact that she worked after school with her simpleminded father, Sonny, in the funeral parlor run by Mr. and Mrs. Dare. The only boy who paid attention to her was Perry Craft, but this was only out of pity. After being fed alcohol by some tormenting teenagers, Sonny drowns in a pool in an amusement park, and Rose continues her solitary existence until she meets at the funeral parlor Mr. Slaymaster, who has come to town to bury his twin. The diary explains why Mrs. Slaymaster is behaving so ruthlessly to the people of Serenity, including Neal's father, Perry, whose suicide was caused partially by the exorbitant rental demands she made on his drugstore. In Texas, Mrs. Slaymaster receives from a housekeeper copies of the pictures of the skinny-dipping episode and also surveillance camera film that identifies Neal as a thief. She returns to Peligro, intent on bringing Julie back to Texas. To prevent their leaving, E. C. kidnaps Peale, but before he can bury him, his dog rips the mannequin to shreds. In spite of his efforts, Julie and Mrs. Slaymaster leave town. In an epilogue, seven years later, Julie returns to Serenity, now married to one of Mrs. Slaymaster's servants. Her adoptive mother is dead, and Julie is now the mistress of the Slaymaster millions. Neal is in charge of his mother's thriving dance studio, and E. C. is busy writing a novel about the rise and fall of Mrs. Slaymaster and her beloved Peale.

Suitability and Critical Comment

M. E. Kerr combines humor, suspense, mystery, and an interest in the plight of the underdog in this tale told from a teenager's point of view. Her protagonists are facing problems involving loneliness, establishing identities, and relating to adult values and authority figures. Her references to popular teenage concerns and interests, like pop music, add realism to this story. This book is popular with students in grades seven through ten.

Themes and Subjects

Adoption, coming-of-age, death, dolls, friendship, high schools, mystery, popularity, psychotherapy, revenge, single-parent families, stealing, wealth

Passages for Booktalking

E. C. and his mother visit Peligro (pp. 5–11); Neal and E. C. at the bookstore (pp. 17–21); E. C. and Julie talk about themselves (pp. 24–25); E. C.'s mother tells him about Mrs. Slaymaster's past (pp. 30–33); and the in-crowd at school (the Sluts) play a mean trick on Julie (pp. 39–44).

Additional Selections

High school senior Theo, who takes care of all his family, none of whom can hear, seeks escape through a friendship with Ivy in *Of Sound Mind* (Farrar, 2001) by Jean Farris.

In *When I Was Older* (Houghton Mifflin, 2000) by Garrett Freymann-Weyr, Sophie, who is adjusting to her brother's death from leukemia and her parents' divorce, meets Francis, who is also grieving the death of a loved one.

Fifteen-year-old Harley uncovers the truth about her parentage and experiences first love in Cat Bauer's *Harley, Like a Person* (Winslow, 2000).

In *Tender* (Farrar, 2001) by Valerie Hobbs, fifteen-year-old Liv is reunited with a father she scarcely knows and finds that their lifestyles clash.

About the Book

Booklist, June 1, 2000, p. 1875.
Bulletin of the Center for Children's Books, April, 2000, p. 285.

Horn Book, May-June, 2000, p. 316.
School Library Journal, July, 2000, p. 106.
VOYA, Aug., 2000, p. 189.

About the Author

Authors and Artists for Young Adults, vol. 2, Gale, 1989; vol. 23, Gale, 1998.
Children's Literature Review, vol. 29, Gale, 1993.
Continuum Encyclopedia of Children's Literature, Continuum, 2001.
Drew, Bernard A. *The 100 Most Popular Young Adult Authors,* Libraries Unlimited, 1997.
Fourth Book of Junior Authors and Illustrators, Wilson, 1978.
Gallo, Donald. *Speaking for Ourselves,* National Council of Teachers of English, 1990.
Hipple, Ted. *Writers for Young Adults,* vol. 2, Scribners, 1997, pp. 177–80.
Kerr, M. E. *Blood on the Forehead: What I Know about Writing,* HarperCollins, 1998.
Kerr, M. E. *Me, Me, Me, Me, Me,* Harper, 1983.
Lives and Works: Young Adult Writers, vol. 5, Grolier, 1999, pp. 2–4.
Major Authors and Illustrators for Children and Young Adults, vol. 4, Gale, 1993.
Neilson, Alleen Pace. *Presenting M. E. Kerr,* Twayne, 1986.
Roginski, Jim. *Behind the Covers,* Volume II, Libraries Unlimited, 1986.
St. James Guide to Young Adult Writers (2nd ed.), St. James, 1999.
Silvey, Anita. *Children's Books and Their Creators,* Houghton Mifflin, 1995.
Something about the Author, vol. 10, Gale, 1980; vol. 61, Gale, 1990; vol. 91, Gale, 1997; vol. 111, Gale, 2000.
Something about the Author Autobiography Series, vol. 1, Gale, 1986.
Sutton, Roger. "A Conversation with M. E. Kerr," *School Library Journal,* June, 1993, pp. 53–54.
Twentieth Century Young Adult Writers, St. James, 1994.

Koertge, Ron. *The Brimstone Journals.* Candlewick, 2001. $15.99 (0-7636-1302-9) (Grades 7–10).

Introduction

Ron Koertge (1950–) became interested in writing and the power of words at an early age. After receiving degrees in English, he took a teaching position at Pasadena City College in California where he has taught for many years. His first young adult novel was *Where the Kissing Never Stops* (Little, Brown, 1986) in which Walker, a teenager beset by sexual fantasies and yearnings, finally has his first love affair while he is still adjusting to the fact that his mother has become a stripper in a local roadhouse. Perhaps his most famous work is his second novel, *The Arizona Kid* (Little, Brown, 1988), the story of Billy Kennedy, age sixteen, who spends an eventful summer with his gay uncle Wes in Arizona, and learns a lot about growing up, respect for others, horses and horse racing, and the joys of first love. The author uses authentic dialogue, explicit language, good humor, and believable characters to tell interesting, fast-moving stories that probe human relationships.

Principal Characters

Students at Branston High School: Allison, Boyd, Carter, Damon, David, Kelli, Kitty, Jennifer, Joseph, Lester, Meredith, Neesha, Rob, Sheila, Tran

Plot Summary

In a series of letters or journal entries, the students of the Class of '01, Branston High School, jot down their innermost feelings and, in so doing, present a portrait of the life and times of teenagers in the early twenty-first century. It is a startling, poignant, and terrifying picture. Lester knows his father would freak out if he knew his son liked to fondle the gun he keeps hidden, even though the bullets are in another place. Tran worries about being American when his father is still hanging on to his Vietnamese roots. Sheila feels so strongly about her girlfriend Monica that she wonders if she is becoming a lesbian. Damon is a school jock and feels he is king of everything, including all the girls. After all, he says, Kelli will do anything to keep him. As for Kelli, she is starting to wonder if sex is all there should be in a relationship. After she thinks about it awhile, she gives Damon back his beeper phone.

Boyd is an angry young man—angry with his drunken father, angry at the world. He agrees with his gas jockey friend Mike about the whites being superior in this world. He figures school rules are there just to break them. Allison worries herself sick about the social collapse of the world. Kitty is obsessed with her body because she knows she is fat. Jennifer is into religion, which her father stresses, but she is also experimenting with sex, and she finds it all confusing. Meredith sleeps around a lot. She doesn't know why; she just likes to be popular with the guys.

One day Boyd and his friend Mike go off and load up on some weapons. Boyd starts making a list; everyone he doesn't like is on it, everyone who offends him in some way. It's a long list. Rumor gets around school that Boyd has a gun and wants to use it. Finally, Boyd and Mike decide on a date to take it out on the list. Boyd circles the seventeenth on his calendar.

One night Lester goes over to Boyd's house, and he talks about guns and weapons. Lester recounts the conversation to Meredith. He tells her that he is afraid Boyd is planning something. Meredith says that Boyd really wants Lester to stop him, but Lester isn't so sure what the right thing to do is. He doesn't want to rat on Boyd and get him into trouble. What if he tells the police, and it turns out to be nothing? Will his friends talk to him?

Finally, Lester makes a decision. He calls 911. The police come and take Boyd away before anyone is hurt. Because Boyd is eighteen, he is really in trouble. But Lester is a hero for about ten minutes, and that feels good. Kitty is glad she didn't get shot because then she'd have to go to the hospital and she'd have to eat. Damon figures Boyd is a punk anyway and wonders why Kelli isn't so interested in him anymore. Sheila tells her mother about her feelings for Monica. Surprisingly, her mother understands; she says she once had a crush on a girlfriend, too. Meredith is going to the prom with Lester, and Lester figures he'd better lose ten pounds so he doesn't have to wear a fat tuxedo.

Suitability and Critical Comment

This is a sad, funny, poignant, frightening look into the intimate lives and thoughts of teenaged America. Each page is a journal-like entry and easily read. The author portrays an intimate picture of often confused young people in any suburban high school, who are trying to mature in what often seems to be a bewildering society. The entries often read like newspaper headlines. For readers in grades seven through ten.

Themes and Subjects

Bullies, guns, school, teen problems, violence

Passages for Booktalking

Lester's worries about his feelings for guns (p. 3); Kelli wonders about her relationship with Damon (pp. 7–8); Boyd and the purity of the white race (p. 15); Boyd gets the weapons (p. 82); Lester calls 911 (pp. 98–99).

Additional Selections

Three teenagers mount social protests to challenge the dependence on alcohol of many of the inhabitants of their Vermont hometown in *God of Beer* (HarperCollins, 2002) by Garret Reizer.

Thicker Than Water: Coming of Age Stories by Irish and Irish American Writers (Delacorte, 2001), edited by Gordon Snell, is a powerful collection of stories about adolescents that uses the thread of a common Irish heritage to unify this outstanding anthology.

Ten high-school students in Scrub Harbor each narrate a chapter describing concerns and crises of identity in the intriguingly complex *What's in a Name* (Simon & Schuster, 2000) by Ellen Wittlinger.

The aftermath of the unexpected shooting death of a high-school teacher is presented through the eyes of several people in Mel Glenn's *Who Killed Mr. Chippendale? A Mystery in Poems* (Lodestar, 1996).

About the Book
Booklist, April 15, 2001, p. 1548.
Bulletin of the Center for Children's Books, April, 2001, p. 307.
Kirkus Reviews, Jan. 15, 2001, p. 111.
New York Times Book Review, May 20, 2001, p. 21.
School Library Journal, Mar., 2001, p. 270.
VOYA, Aug., 2001, p. 203.

About the Author
Authors and Artists for Young Adults, vol. 12, Gale, 1994.
Contemporary Authors New Revision Series, vol. 25, Gale, 1989.
Drew, Bernard A. *The 100 Most Popular Young Adult Authors,* Libraries Unlimited, 1997.
Gallo, Donald. *Speaking for Ourselves, Too,* National Council of Teachers of English, 1993.
Lives and Works: Young Adult Authors, Grolier, 1999, vol. 5, pp. 5–7.
St. James Guide to Young Adult Writers (2nd ed.), St. James, 1999.
Seventh Book of Junior Authors and Illustrators, Wilson, 1996.
Something about the Author, vol. 52, Gale, 1988; vol. 92, Gale, 1997.
Twentieth Century Young Adult Writers, St. James, 1994.

Lynch, Chris. *Freewill.* HarperCollins, 2001. $15.89 (0-06-028177-4) (Grades 10–12).

Introduction
Chris Lynch (1962–) grew up in a Boston area once entirely Irish but, during his childhood, becoming Hispanic. He remembers that the neighborhood was filled with racism, sexuality, and violence—themes that he has explored in many of his books. While at Boston University, he explored the possibilities of a writing career and, after trying several jobs, took a master's degree at Emerson College, also in Boston, and began writing seriously. Many of his young adult novels deal with disaffected youth whose search for identity often leads to conflict, frustration, and violence. Many of his novels also reflect his love of various sports. His first novel, for example, was *Shadow Boxer* (HarperCollins, 1993), in which two brothers live with the memory of their father, who was killed in the ring. As a result, the older brother and his mother have grown to hate boxing, but the younger one regards his father as a hero and wants to pursue a boxing career. *Freewill* is a disquieting story of guilt and responsibility as told in the second person by the central character, a disturbed boy.

Principal Characters
Will, a seventeen-year-old junior in a vocational high school
Angela, a fellow classmate whose passion is track

Mr. Jacks, Will's shop teacher
Gran and Pops, Will's grandparents
An unnamed fellow male student in Will's class

Plot Summary

Everyone is in awe of Will's unusual skills as a woodworker, including his shop teacher, Mr. Jacks; the boy at his neighboring workbench, who is content to make simple video racks from knotty pine; and an attractive classmate, a loner named Angela, who is more interested in track than shop. Only seventeen-year-old Will is unimpressed. He had wanted to pursue an academic program at school that would lead to his becoming a pilot, but instead he messed up his aptitude tests and has been sent to a school with special vocational programs, nicknamed "Hopeless High." Hopeless also describes Will's state of mind. He lives with Gran and Pops, his grandparents, a well-meaning Italian American couple, but Will is without direction, despondent, and completely without friends. Because Angela has shown interest in his work, he tries to cultivate her friendship, first by chatting with her in the local grocery store and next by visiting her while she practices track. However, Angela is protective of her privacy and wary of this quiet, disturbing young man. Much to Mr. Jacks's chagrin, Will has begun carving strange totemlike figures and adding them to the shop's collection kept in a storage room at school. This is a departure from his usual gnomes and whirligigs. After a local girl's death by drowning, one of these strange sculptures is found at the death scene. When the death of another teenager occurs, again one of Will's statues mysteriously appears at the scene. Will, who is subject to dreamlike states, wonders if he is responsible. On one of his encounters with Angela, Will haltingly tells her a little about himself. After the death of Will's mother, his father remarried, and scarcely a year ago both his father and his stepmother were killed in an automobile accident while his father was driving. Will won't accept the fact that his father's death was a suicide. In an act of friendship, the two take one of Will's sculptures and plant it on the sand near a rocky ocean beach. Unfortunately, this becomes the site of the deaths of two more young people, who, it is believed, had a suicide pact. Word spreads that perhaps Will has the gift of foretelling death, and his mental state, already fragile, becomes more delicate. When a reporter savagely accuses him of conducting cult activities, he strikes him so hard that he breaks a bone in his hand. Incapacitated and despondent, he takes to his bed for three days, refusing to talk to anyone. He is filled with self-doubt and feelings of guilt and hopelessness. He has no one to turn to, and, though his grandparents both try, his condition seems beyond their power to remedy.

After a visit from Angela, who accuses him of malingering and of being unwilling to face life's realities, he makes another appearance at school but, because he is treated as a freak by his classmates, is sent home for a few days by Mr. Jacks. Will and his grandparents begin receiving harassing phone calls demanding to know when the next death will occur. One of his sculptures is planted in Angela's yard, but he is able to reassure her that he was not responsible. When all of Will's sculptures suddenly appear on his grandparents' property with the word "Next?" sprayed in Day-Glo paint on the lawn, Will rouses himself into action. When the harasser next phones, Will tells him that he knows who will die next and agrees to reveal the name at a meeting on an isolated part of the beach. There, Will recognizes his tormenter as the young man who worked next to him in class. This explains his access to Will's work. He drags the boy into the ocean, letting him go only after Will tells the boy that now he will be the one responsible for the next death. When he allows the boy to escape, Will swims farther out into deep waters, intent on joining his father in suicide. But an epiphany occurs, and he suddenly regains the will to live. He returns to his grandparents' house, and the three place one of Will's sculptures on his father's grave. He hears himself saying, "It's a nice piece of work I did there. It looks good here. I'm pleased."

Suitability and Critical Comment

This is a disturbing story of a lonely, talented boy living on the fringes of both society and insanity. Although it is part mystery and part cliff-hanger, this novel is essentially a study of a boy's isolation, his inability to accept either the past or the present, and his exploration of grief, guilt, and hope. In the last scene, Will claims ownership of a piece of his sculpture and acknowledges that it makes a fitting tribute to his father, and, in so doing, he has begun to accept the past as well as himself. This complex work (even the title has many meanings) is suitable for mature readers in grades ten through twelve.

Themes and Subjects

Death, friendship, grandparents, guilt, mystery stories, school stories, sculpture, suicide, woodworking

Passages for Booktalking

Will finishes a table (pp. 1–40); he meets Angela shopping (pp. 13–17); Will discusses his woodworking with Mr. Jacks (pp. 17–20); he tells Angela about the past (pp. 70–72); and they plant a piece of sculpture in the sand (pp. 82–84).

Additional Selections

Janet Tashjian's cleverly constructed novel *The Gospel According to Larry* (Holt, 2000) is the story of seventeen-year-old Josh Swenson and his alter ego, Larry, who dispenses advice via his Web site.

Many Stones (Front Street, 2000) by Carolyn Coman is a psychologically complex novel about a teenage girl named Berry, her hostility toward her father, and the memorial services they attend in South Africa honoring Berry's dead sister.

Set in the South of the 1970s, *John Riley's Daughter* (Front Street, 2000) by Kezi Matthews is the story of young Memphis and the disappearance of her twenty-nine-year-old mentally handicapped aunt.

Brief poems written by school peers and teachers explore the life and suicide of Laura Li, a Chinese American student in Mel Glenn's *Split Image: A Story in Poems* (HarperCollins, 2000).

About the Book

Booklist, May 15, 2001, p. 1745.
Bulletin of the Center for Children's Books, March, 2001, p. 270.
Horn Book, July-Aug., 2001, p. 457.
Kirkus Reviews, Jan. 15, 2001, p. 113.
School Library Journal, Mar., 2001, p. 252.
VOYA, Aug., 2001, p. 203.

About the Author

Authors and Artists for Young Adults, vol. 19, Gale, 1996.
Children's Literature Review, vol. 58, Gale, 2000.
Continuum Encyclopedia of Children's Literature, Continuum, 2001.
Fleming, Chad. "Chris Lynch," *English Journal,* March, 1997, p. 78.
Hipple, Ted. *Writers for Young Adults,* vol. 2, Scribners, 1997, pp. 289–97.
Lives and Works: Young Adult Authors, vol. 5, Grolier, 1999, pp. 63–65.
St. James Guide to Young Adult Writers (2nd ed.), St. James, 1999.
Seventh Book of Junior Authors and Illustrators, Wilson, 1996.
Something about the Author, vol. 95, Gale, 1998.

Naylor, Phyllis. *The Grooming of Alice.* Atheneum, 2000. $16 (0-68-982633-8); pb. $4.99 (Grades 7–10).

Introduction

Phyllis Reynolds Naylor (1933–), the daughter of a salesman and a teacher, grew up during the Great Depression in an ordinary Midwestern family where books and reading were part of her everyday life. She published her first story at age sixteen and for twenty-five years wrote a humorous newspaper column for teenagers in a church newspaper. Perhaps some of Alice's escapades stem from these short pieces. Her books show an amazing diversity in subject and form, ranging from the comic to the tragic, from rural to urban settings, from the realistic to the fantastic, and from books for young children to those for mature teenagers. This is the twelfth book in the Alice saga, which began in 1985 with *The Agony of Alice* (Atheneum, 1985). It introduced the motherless Alice and her funny, poignant experiences as a sixth grader. With each book Alice grows a little older and matures as she travels through the unsettling years of adolescence. *The Grooming of Alice* takes place during the summer before high school. It is one in which Alice learns something about family relationships, friendship, and what it means to be "normal."

Principal Characters

Alice Kathleen McKinley, a fourteen-year-old about to enter high school
Dad, Alice's understanding father
Elizabeth, Alice's best friend
Lester, Alice's older brother, who lives with her and her father
Pamela, Alice's other best friend
Patrick, Alice's boyfriend
Mrs. Plotkin, Alice's former teacher

Plot Summary

Alice used to think that the summer between eighth and ninth grades, what with high school looming ahead, was going to be a rather quiet time. But then Pamela, one of her two best friends, decides that the three of them better spend the weeks toning up. Pamela declares that they must rise at seven each morning to jog for three miles. In that way, they will be in shape for high school. Alice and Elizabeth are rather dismayed by the idea, but Pamela is persuasive.

Things soon begin to get complicated. Besides the jogging, Alice has volunteered to work in the local hospital for three mornings a week. On the third day, she discovers that her sixth-grade teacher, Mrs. Plotkin, is there for a problem with her heart. Other events disrupt a calm summer. Alice's mother has been dead for some time, and lately Dad has been seeing Sylvia Summers, Alice's former English teacher. That is fine with Alice, but Dad decides to go to England for two weeks to see Sylvia, who is there as an exchange teacher. Then Lester announces he is going to Colorado to do some climbing. They won't be gone at the same time, but Alice suddenly develops a fear that she will lose them. Then she finds out that her boyfriend, Patrick, will be going away with his family for a few days. Everybody is leaving!

Things aren't going so well with Pamela and Elizabeth, either. Pamela lives with her father ever since her mother left home, but father and daughter do not get along. As for Elizabeth, she has taken this health thing so seriously that her mother, as well as Alice, fears she has developed an eating disorder.

The summer really takes a turn for the worse when Alice learns that Mrs. Plotkin has died. Alice is heartbroken because she did not know her former teacher was so ill and because she never got to tell her that she loved her. Alice goes to the funeral with her father.

More surprises are in store when the girls go to an all-day seminar, "For Girls Only." There they learn some startling—for them—facts about their own bodies.

Another big shock of the summer comes for Alice when she learns that Pamela has decided to go live with her mother and her mother's new boyfriend. Nothing seems to be the same anymore.

But things have a way of working out, even in what seems the worst of times. Elizabeth begins to realize what her bad eating habits are doing to her health and her body, and with her mother's and Alice's help seems on the way to a more normal life. And then Pamela reappears! Things did not work out with her mother, and Pamela and her father have decided to try to make it work at home together. Both Lester and Dad return safely from their respective trips. Dad has news that Alice may have a stepmother in her future. She likes that idea.

Alice figures she has learned a lot in this summer. With all the things that have happened around her, she decides that the world of grooming is important, but not important enough to spend one's life worrying about it. Life is good once again. Best of all, the Three Musketeers will be together to start high school in the fall.

Suitability and Critical Comment

An easy-to-read novel for the young teenager in grades seven through ten, with just the right emphasis on the topics of concern to this age group. It especially points up the importance of stability in the home and friendships outside.

Themes and Subjects

Boyfriends, death, dieting, family relationships, friendship, hospitals, personal grooming, volunteer work

Passages for Booktalking

Alice, Pamela, and Elizabeth go on a shape-up program (pp. 4–5); Patrick and Alice are alone for an evening (pp. 19–23); Alice sees Mrs. Plotkin at the hospital (pp. 37–40); Alice worries about losing Lester (pp. 69–72); Elizabeth stops eating (pp. 77–78); Alice hides Pamela from her father (pp. 80–87); Mrs. Plotkin dies (pp. 149–50); the Girls Only seminar (pp. 157–71).

Additional Selections

The Bad Girls of two previous Voigt novels return in *It's Not Easy Being Bad* (Atheneum, 2000) by Cynthia Voigt and are determined to increase their popularity in seventh grade.

What My Mother Doesn't Know (Simon & Schuster, 2001) by Sonya Sones is a fast, funny story about fourteen-year-old Sophie and how she fell in love.

Though often amusing, *Kissing Doorknobs* (Delacorte, 1998) by Terry Spencer Hesser is also a moving story about Tara and her struggle with her obsessive-compulsive behavior.

Set in a small southern town, Kimberly Willis Holt's *When Zachary Beaver Came to Town* (Holt, 1999) tells how Toby gets to know Zachary, who is billed as the fattest boy in the world.

About the Book

Booklist, June 1, 2000, p. 1880.
Bulletin of the Center for Children's Books, May, 2000, p. 326.
Horn Book, July-Aug., 2000, p. 463.
Kirkus Reviews, May 1, 2000, p. 637.
School Library Journal, May, 2000, p. 175.
VOYA, Oct., 2000, p. 269.

About the Author

Authors and Artists for Young Adults, vol. 4, Gale, 1990; vol. 29, Gale, 1999.
Children's Literature Review, vol. 17, Gale, 1989.
Contemporary Authors New Revision Series, vol. 24, Gale, 1988.
Drew, Bernard A. *The 100 Most Popular Young Adult Authors,* Libraries Unlimited, 1997.
Fifth Book of Junior Authors and Illustrators, Wilson, 1983.
Gallo, Donald. *Speaking for Ourselves, Too,* National Council of Teachers of English, 1993.
Graham, Joyce. "An Interview with Phyllis Reynolds Naylor," *Journal of Youth Services in Libraries,* Summer, 1993, pp. 392–98.
Hipple, Ted. *Writers for Young Adults,* vol. 2, Scribners, 1997, pp. 397–409.
Lives and Works: Young Adult Writers, vol. 6, Grolier, 1995, pp. 38–40.
Major Authors and Illustrators for Children and Young Adults, vol. 4, Gale, 1993.
McElmeel, Sharron L. *The 100 Most Popular Children's Writers,* Libraries Unlimited, 1999.

Naylor, Phyllis Reynolds. *How I Came To Be a Writer,* Macmillan, 1989.

Naylor, Res. "Phyllis Reynolds Naylor," *Horn Book,* July-Aug., 1992, pp. 412–15.

"Newbery Award Acceptance Material, 1992," *Journal of Youth Services in Libraries,* Summer, 1992, pp. 351–56.

"Newbery Medal Acceptance," *Horn Book,* July-Aug., 1992, pp. 404–11.

Rochman, Hazel. "Alice, Still Outrageous," *Booklist,* May 1, 1999, p. 1586.

St. James Guide to Young Adult Writers (2nd ed.), St. James, 1999.

Silvey, Anita. *Children's Books and Their Creators,* Houghton Mifflin, 1995.

Stover, Lois. *Presenting Phyllis Reynolds Naylor,* Twayne, 1997.

Something about the Author, vol. 12, Gale, 1977; vol. 66., Gale, 1992; vol. 102, Gale, 1999.

Something about the Author Autobiography Series, vol. 10, Gale, 1990.

Twentieth Century Children's Writers, St. James, 1995.

Twentieth Century Young Adult Writers, St. James, 1994.

West, Mark L. "Speaking of Censorship: An Interview with Phyllis Reynolds Naylor," *Journal of Youth Services in Libraries,* Winter, 1997, pp. 177–83.

Randle, Kristen D. *Breaking Rank.* Morrow, 1999. $15 (0-688-16243-6) (Grades 7–12).

Introduction

Kristen D. Randle (1952–) grew up in a family where her father moved all over the country and the family followed him. As a result, she was unable to form lasting friendships and, instead, developed a strong interest in music and reading. After marrying a fellow Mormon, she had four children and educated them at home, using her precious spare time to practice her writing skills. Her first young adult novel to gain national attention was *The Only Alien on the Planet* (Scholastic, 1995) about a lonely high-school senior, Ginny, and her love for an enigmatic young man, nicknamed "the alien," who hides a terrible secret. This novel demonstrates her unique ability to pinpoint and explore the concerns and conflicts experienced by young adults. Her second success came with *Breaking Rank,* again about a young woman who reaches out to a male outcast. Told in alternative points of view, this is a fascinating variation on the Romeo and Juliet story that also contains many insights relevant to today's readers.

Principal Characters

Thomas Fairbairn, a member of the Clan, known as Baby

Casey Willardson, a seventeen-year-old student who is asked to become Baby's tutor

Joanna, Casey's best friend

Lenny, Baby's brother and keeper of the Clan
Mrs. Fairbairn, mother of Baby and Lenny
Gene Walenski, high-school friend of Casey's who taunts the Clan
Mr. and Mrs. Willardson, Casey's supportive parents

Plot Summary

Casey, a seventeen-year-old student at Feynman High, is shocked when she is asked to become a tutor to Thomas Fairbairn. She is shocked because Thomas is a member of the Clan, a silent, enigmatic group known throughout the community. They always wear black, speak to no one, attend school only because they are compelled to, and do not participate in any activities. They don't threaten anyone or join anything. No one in the community has ever taken any action against the Clan because they have never done anything to anyone. They just exist. But one Clan member, known as Baby, did something very unusual for a member of the Clan. He agreed to take some tests to determine his intelligence. He did so well that the school has decided to put him in an honors program, with Casey as his mentor.

The relationship is strained at first. Baby is reluctant about the honors program, although he desperately wants to learn more. However, he cannot tell his family—his mother and brother—because participating in anything that smacks of formal education is against Clan rules. But Casey and Baby continue the tutoring program. Their studying hours develop into friendship and then attraction. Eventually, Baby's family discovers what he has been doing after school hours. He is surprised and pleased because his mother is delighted for him. However, his brother Lenny is outraged. Lenny, who feels that society has absolutely no redeeming qualities whatsoever, insists that Baby can remain in the Clan only if he uses Casey, that is, if Baby makes a conquest of her sexually.

Casey's family accepts her friendship with Baby, but her friends in school, except for Joanna, do not. When, at Casey's insistence, she and Baby go to a drive-in, there is a moment when Baby can take advantage of the situation to do what Lenny wants. Baby finds that he cannot do so. However, that night he is badly beaten by Gene and other high-school boys because of his relationship with Casey.

This leads to a new understanding between Baby and his brother. Lenny takes away Baby's black wardrobe and tells him that he now realizes that Baby is not meant to be a Clan member.

When Baby gets word that something is going on one night with Lenny and his friends, he and Casey discover a fight that is about to begin between the Clan and Gene and his group. Police arrive to break it up before anyone is seriously hurt. The participants are all sentenced to community service, and Casey and Thomas—ex–Clan member Baby—resume their friendship.

Suitability and Critical Comment

This is an unusual story that takes an insightful look into the meaning and value of participation in its many forms. Especially suited for the thoughtful reader in grades seven through twelve.

Themes and Subjects

Alienation, discrimination, friendship, groups, isolation, mainstreaming

Passages for Booktalking

Casey and Baby first meet (pp. 9–10); Baby tries to keep his studying from Mom and Lenny (pp. 41–45); Gene and his group first confront Baby (pp. 67–69); Baby explains the Clan to Casey (pp. 96–105); the drive-in and its aftermath (pp. 143–51); Lenny explains his feelings to Baby (pp. 174–77); the fight (pp. 193–98).

Additional Selections

Matt, whose sounding off gets him into trouble in his high school, is defended by Ursula, who calls herself "Ugly Girl" in *Big Mouth and Ugly Girl* (HarperCollins, 2002) by Joyce Carol Oates.

Fifteen-year-old Ben, growing up in a house full of women, wonders what constitutes masculinity in *Men of Stone* (Kids Can, 2000) by Gayne Freisen.

When her family doubts her dancing ability, sixteen-year-old Stephanie finds an older dancer to act as her mentor in Lorri Hewett's *Dancer* (Dutton, 1999).

While staying with her aunt, fifteen-year-old Tessa falls in love with handsome but dangerous Caleb in Jan Marino's *Searching for Atticus* (Simon & Schuster, 1997).

About the Book

Booklist, May 1, 1999, p. 1590.
Bulletin of the Center for Children's Books, June, 1999, p. 362.
Horn Book, March-April, 1999, p. 212.
Kirkus Reviews, April 15, 1999, p. 635.
School Library Journal, June, 1999, p. 130.

About the Author

Authors and Artists for Young Adults, vol. 34, Gale, 2000.
Something about the Author, vol. 92, Gale, 1997; vol. 119, Gale, 2001.
Something about the Author Autobiography Series, vol. 24, Gale, 1997.

Rennison, Louise. *Angus, Thongs and Full-Frontal Snogging.*
HarperCollins, 1999. Pb. $6.95 (0-06-447227-2) (Grades 6–9).

Introduction

For the uninitiated, the glossary in the back of this hilarious British import defines "full-frontal snogging" as "Kissing with all the trimmings, lip to lip, open mouth, tongues everything (Apart from dribble which is never acceptable)." Move over Adrian Mole, this junior version of Bridget Jones is a hysterically funny look at teenaged angst as seen through the journal articles of Georgia Nicolson. In the next installment, *On the Bright Side, I'm Now the Girlfriend of a Sex God,* Georgia is spared from going to New Zealand, her mother flirts with a George Clooney look-alike, and Georgia tries to make the sex god, Robbie, jealous by dating his younger brother. In sequel number two, *Knocked Out by My Nunga-Nungas* (HarperCollins, 2001), Georgia lands Robbie but, because he is never around, discovers that Dave the Laugh is a good substitute. Incidentally, "nunga-nungas" are bosoms. Louise Rennison has written for many British comedy stars and has had a one-woman autobiographical show. She lives in Brighton, which she claims is like San Francisco without the sun, Americans, the Golden Gate Bridge, and earthquakes.

Principal Characters

Georgia Nicolson, a fourteen-year-old English schoolgirl
Connie Nicolson, Georgia's mother
Bob Nicolson, her father
Libby, her little sister
Jas, her best friend
Angus, the Nicolsons' savage monster, masquerading as a cat
Tom, the sweet younger son of a greengrocer
Robbie, a sex god, Tom's older brother
Lindsay, Robbie's girlfriend
Peter, a kissing expert and temporary friend of Georgia's
Mark, Georgia's off-and-on ardent suitor

Plot Summary

Fourteen-year-old English live wire Georgia Nicolson is a bit larger than life, but otherwise, like most girls her age, she is preoccupied with boyfriends, her physical appearance (particularly her growing bosoms and her oversized nose), boyfriends, friendships, boyfriends, and the family that she manages barely to tolerate. It consists of Bob, a sometimes caustic but loving father (Georgia maintains he has the mentality of a Teletubby—only not so developed); Connie, her understanding but vague mother; a little sister named Libby, who still leaves her wet nappies in Georgia's bed; and a ferocious, oversized cat named Angus, who terrorizes the neighbor's poodle and secretly wants him for lunch. Still recovering from the embarrassment of a misguided appearance as a stuffed olive at a costume party, Georgia's life becomes more interesting when she and her best friend, Jas, meet a cute boy named Tom, a greengrocer's son, and his dreamy sex god of an older brother, seventeen-year-old Robbie. Unfortunately Robbie has Lindsay, a girlfriend his own age, whom Georgia immediately places on her most hated list. At school, Georgia and Jas stumble from one giddy escapade to another, often incurring the displeasure of Slim, the hugely overweight headmistress, and such teachers as Georgia's nemesis, Hawkeye, or Miss Stamp, the physical education teacher who Georgia is sure is a closet lesbian. To prepare for a party at Katie Steadman's, Georgia takes kissing lessons with an ardent snogger named Peter, but at the party Peter becomes so intent on giving Georgia some postgraduate work that she does a pratfall, an event witnessed by Lindsay. On the family front, Vati (short for *Vater,* a word Georgia learned in German class) announces that he is going to New Zealand to seek better employment and that, if successful, the family might relocate. (Georgia's reaction: *"merde!"*) As his departure approaches, her parents become lovey-dovey, much to Georgia's disgust and embarrassment. A new boy comes into Georgia's life: Mark, whom she meets on Bonfire Night. He is older than Georgia and a fast mover. Soon Georgia nicknames him "the breast molester." However, at a school dance where Robbie's band, the Stiff Dylans, is playing, Mark tries to hog the microphone and melee occurs. Before Georgia can dump Mark, she suffers the humiliation of being dumped by him. (He says she's too young.) After Mark's defection, Georgia decides to concentrate on her yoga and helping friend Jas sort out her relationship with Tom, her present boyfriend. Her advice, perhaps motivated by a teeny-weeny bit of jealousy, is to break up with Tom (after all, who wants to be a greengrocer's wife?). Pliant Jas complies, but when Sex God Robbie intervenes on his brother's behalf, Georgia becomes miffed and the two friends have a temporary estrangement. Georgia, filled with unrequited love for Robbie, persuades Jas to accompany her on a stalking expedition to discover if Lindsay has an Achilles heel. What they find is that Lindsay wears an engagement ring she claims is from Robbie. Georgia schemes to get this information to Robbie, who breaks up with Lindsay, claiming she is too possessive. It is possible that Georgia now stands a chance? Her hopes rise when, at another dance where the Stiff Dylans are playing, he gives her a big kiss but suggests that she should have a younger boyfriend. A climax is reached when Angus suddenly disappears. At first, Georgia suspects the neighbors and poisoning. Days pass, notices are posted, but no Angus. Then, one day, the phone rings. It is Robbie; he has found Angus. To make herself look older for his visit, Georgia peroxides a lock of her hair. Unfortunately this backfires. As they sit together, she runs her hand through her hair, and the dyed clump falls out. Nevertheless, he tells her how fond he is of her. Georgia is ecstatic but, at that point, her mother arrives with airplane tickets. She has heard from Vati, and they are going to New Zealand.

Suitability and Critical Comment

This is a light-hearted, hilarious look at teenage trauma and the inventive ways of coping with it devised by a basically naïve, insecure youngster. Georgia has thoughtfully appended a hilarious glossary that defines terms like "snogging." In addition to the wit, there is also some wisdom about social relationships and responsibility, but basically this is a fresh, engaging story that is, in Georgia's words, "fabbity, fab, fab." It is enjoyed by readers in grades six through nine.

Themes and Subjects

Boyfriends, dating, dogs, friendship, humorous stories, jealousy, physical appearance, school stories, teenage concerns

Passages for Booktalking

Georgia lists six things wrong with her life (pp. 3–4); she suggests dying her hair to her parents (pp. 12–14); Georgia and friends defy Slim's order on wearing the school beret (pp. 40–41); while Jas is stalking Tom, Georgia sees Sex God for the first time (pp. 47–49); and Libby causes an embarrassing situation when Georgia meets Robbie (pp. 63–64).

Additional Selections

Suspended from school for three days because he was rude to his teacher, high-schooler William has several experiences that help him reexamine his life in Susie Morgenstern's *Three Days Off* (Viking, 2001).

Myrtle looks back on her final years of high school and her friends in Rebecca O'Connell's *Myrtle of Willendorf* (Front Street, 2000), a witty and poignant look at adolescence.

Dyan Sheldon's *Confessions of a Teenage Drama Queen* (Candlewick, 1999) is the hilarious story of Lola's adjustment to life in New Jersey after growing up in exciting New York.

Great-uncle Max picks out a boyfriend for Joy with comic results in Lucy Frank's *Oy, Joy!* (DK, 1999).

About the Book
Booklist, July, 2000, p. 2033.
Bulletin of the Center for Children's Books, May, 2000, p. 329.
Horn Book, May, 2000, p. 320.
New York Times Book Review, June 4, 2000, p. 49.
School Library Journal, July, 2000, p. 109.
VOYA, June, 2000, p. 118.

About the Author
No material available.

Wittlinger, Ellen. *Hard Love.* Simon & Schuster, 1999. $16.95 (0-689-82134-4) (Grades 8–10).

Introduction
Ellen Wittlinger (1948–) had a talent in art and majored in it at college but began writing poetry while still an undergraduate. After finishing college, she began writing seriously and took a graduate degree at the University of Iowa's Writing Program. After marriage and a family, she continued writing in her free time and became interested in young adult literature. Her first success came with *Lombardo's Law* (Houghton Mifflin, 1993), about a shy, intelligent fifteen-year-old girl and her attachment to Mike, a thirteen-year-old junior high student who works with her on a writing assignment during which they form a strong attachment. Of her books, Ms. Wittlinger has said, she likes "to think of [her] books as coming-of-age stories, books that remember what it feels like to be 13, 15, or 17 and feel for the first time the tumult of adult emotions." She added, "I find I am most interested in those kids who are on the fringes . . . the slight oddballs and lovable misfits."

Principal Characters
John Gilardi, Jr., who feels he is immune to emotion since the divorce of his parents
Mr. Gilardi, John's father, who sees him every weekend but has no time for him
Mrs. Gilardi, John's mother, who is afraid to love again, even her own son
Al, Mrs. Gilardi's new boyfriend

Diana Tree, a friend who gets John to open his eyes about love

Marisol Guzman, a self-proclaimed "Puerto Rican Cuban Yankee Lesbian" and John's hard love

Brian, John's best friend

Emily, Brian's girlfriend

Plot Summary

John has proclaimed himself immune to emotion since the divorce of his parents. Part of this isolation is to become immersed in homemade zines. At a meeting of others who are interested and isolated, he meets Marisol Guzman. She is a self-proclaimed "Puerto Rican Cuban Yankee Lesbian." John has never met anyone remotely like Marisol, and he is instantly fascinated by this offbeat seventeen-year-old. They form a friendship, each trying to impress the other. More and more, John uses his friendship with Marisol to get away from his dysfunctional family.

Although John lives with his mother, she has not touched him, not hugged him or caressed him in any way since her divorce from his father. Now she has a boyfriend, Al. John doesn't know Al well, but he dislikes him anyway. Every weekend John goes to spend time with his highly successful father. Like his mother, John's father exhibits little personal interest in him except to fulfill what are obviously expected fatherly duties. At times, John feels more isolated than ever because both parents use him as a sounding board for their own problems.

Despite Marisol's insistence on her sexual preference, John feels himself attracted to her. John's friend Brian gets up the courage to ask Emily to the prom, and he insists that John ask Marisol to accompany them. John reluctantly agrees, feeling sure that Marisol will have no time for this dating scene and will turn him down. To his surprise, she accepts. Things go quite well at the dance. In fact, Marisol is so friendly to him that he misinterprets her warmth in such a way that he tries to kiss her. She immediately explodes. She is incensed that he does not understand her and threatens to break off their friendship.

John tries desperately to patch up his relationship with Marisol. Finally, she cools down and agrees to go with him to a zine conference over a weekend in Cape Cod. John tells his mother he will be visiting his father. He tells his father that he has other plans and can't make it that weekend. Cape Cod turns out to be a disaster for John. Hoping somehow that his feelings for Marisol will be resolved, he instead reaches new despair when Marisol leaves him for a lesbian relationship. She declares that she is going off to New York to lead a different life.

Added to this, John learns that his mother has discovered he is not spending the weekend with his father. He calls home and has a real conversation with Al for the first time. He begins to see that the man might not be so bad after all. And he and his mother talk about starting over when he returns. That night another zine friend, Diana Tree, sings a song to John about hard love. Sometimes you know that love is impossible, but you keep on loving just the same. John figures that maybe that's true, and maybe it's time to get back into living.

Suitability and Critical Comment

This is a realistic, although not explicit look at different lifestyles. It should be suitable for most good readers. John is presented as a thoughtful, confused young man. Some of the lesser characters are a bit zany but enjoyable. The dysfunctional relationship between John and his parents will hit home to thoughtful readers in grades eight through ten.

Themes and Subjects

Adolescence, dysfunctional families, friendship, homosexuality, romance, teenagers, writing as a release

Passages for Booktalking

John and Marisol have a conversation (pp. 21–29); John spends time with his father (pp. 70–76); John and his mother have a talk (pp. 88–91); he talks with Marisol about the prom (pp. 108–111); prom night (pp. 155–166); and Marisol tells John she is leaving (pp. 207–211).

Additional Selections

High-school junior and alcoholic Noli Brown learns about love and loneliness when she falls for the beautiful but gay T. J. Baker in Barbara Wersba's *Whistle Me Down* (Holt, 1997).

In Garret Freymann-Weyr's *My Heartbeat* (Houghton Mifflin, 2002), Ellen's love for James, her brother's best friend, becomes an emotional triangle when she discovers that both boys could be gay.

Fifteen-year-old Hannah finally gets the help she needs when everyone, including her boyfriend, rejects her because she is pregnant in Louise Plummer's *A Dance for Three* (Delacorte, 2000).

In the refreshingly original novel *When Kambia Elaine Flew in from Neptune* (Simon & Schuster, 2000) by Lori Aurelia Williams, the reader meets a host of unusual characters, including the narrator, twelve-year-old Shayla, and her sexually active older sister, Tia.

About the Book

Booklist, Oct. 1, 1999, p. 355.
Bulletin of the Center for Children's Books, July, 1999, p. 406.
Horn Book, July-Aug., 1999, p. 474.
Kirkus Reviews, June 15, 1999, p. 971.
School Library Journal, July, 1999, p. 102.
VOYA, Aug., 1999, p. 45.

About the Author

Authors and Artists for Young Adults, vol. 36, Gale, 2001.
Drew, Bernard A. *100 More Popular Young Adult Authors,* Libraries Unlimited, 2002.
"The Printz Award Revisited—Ellen Wittlinger," *Booklist,* Jan. 1–15, 2001, pp. 933–34.
Something about the Author, vol. 83, Gale, 1996; vol. 122, Gale, 2001.

2

Social and Family Problems

Bauer, Joan. *Hope Was Here.* Putnam, 2000. $16.99 (0-399-23142-0) (Grades 7–9).

Introduction

Joan Bauer (1951–) worked for ten years in marketing and advertising for a number of publishers, including *Parade* magazine, which appears as a Sunday supplement in many newspapers. In 1981, she left the security of this life to write full time as a journalist and nonfiction writer of teleplays and film scripts. This possibly explains why her novels have a strong visual appeal. As a result of an automobile accident, she was so incapacitated that she was able to hold her head up for only forty-five minutes at a time. During this period, she began her first young adult novel, *Squashed* (Putnam, 1992), the story of Ellie Morgan, an adolescent girl who has dedicated her life to growing a prize-winning pumpkin she names Mal for the Rock River Iowa Pumpkin Weigh-In. The humor and good nature that pervade her first books for young adults have, through time, given way to a darker, more sober tone. For example, *Rules of the Road* (Putnam, 1998) deals with the effects of alcoholism on a family.

Principal Characters

Hope, sixteen years old
Aunt Addie, Hope's guardian
G. T. Stoop, proprietor of the Welcome Stairways diner
Braverman, the diner's grill man
Flo, the diner floor manager
Eli Millstone, the corrupt mayor

Plot Summary

Sixteen-year-old Hope loves Aunt Addie, who is her legal guardian, and from her Hope has learned a good deal about food. Aunt Addie is a diner cook extraordinaire. Great as that is, it means that Hope doesn't get to spend much time in one place. Before long, Addie is off to straighten out another comfort food spot that needs her outstanding gifts. This particular

47

move is hard on Hope because she is especially sad at the closing of the Blue Box, the diner in Brooklyn where Hope and Addie have been working. Hope has become a first-class waitress and makes good money in tips. Now once again, she writes "Hope was here" as a way of saying good-bye to the excitement of New York City and heads for rural Mulhoney, Wisconsin, where Aunt Addie will cook and Hope will wait tables at the Welcome Stairways diner. The proprietor is G. T. Stoop. Hope likes him right away.

It may not be New York City, but Hope is slowly drawn into the lives of the people in Mulhoney, especially G. T. He is a gentle, bald man with a kind nature. He is also being treated for cancer. But G. T. has a mission. Tired of the dirty politics in town and the corrupt way Mayor Millstone has been running things, G. T. decides to run for mayor himself. No one can believe it. Millstone has been mayor in Mulhoney for eight years. He's entrenched, and he runs everything. But G. T. points out that the roads are crumbling and the Real Fresh Dairy, largest company in town, hasn't paid local taxes for five years. He thinks collecting back taxes would be a good place to start getting funds to get the town back on its feet.

Besides getting settled at the diner and introducing great food to the townspeople, Hope and Addie get caught up in the mayoral race. But it's not easy. First, they put out petitions for the people to sign. They enlist the help of the teenagers from the high school, which Hope will attend in the fall as a junior. There is trouble, of course, from the mayor's people, dirty pool and threats to G. T. and the diner. Braverman gets beaten up. In the midst of all this, Hope and Braverman are developing a warm friendship. Into all this, Hope's mother, whom she rarely sees and who never bothers with her, arrives for a visit. Hope is happy when she leaves.

When it is time for the election, after all the hard work, Hope is heartbroken because G. T. loses by 114 votes. G. T. accepts the outcome in his gentle way, and in the meantime asks Addie to marry him. Addie agrees, and Hope is delighted. She figures she'll now have a father. After the wedding, Hope gets involved in school life and her romance with Braverman. Then the unexpected occurs. Fraud by Millstone's people in the election is uncovered, and G. T. is declared the winner. He becomes the new mayor of Mulhoney.

The story shifts ahead two years. Hope has graduated, and she and Braverman are about ready to leave for college. G. T. has died of his illness. People felt badly because Hope finally got a father, only to lose him after two years. But Hope figures it's like having an extraordinary meal after eating junk food for a long, long time. It makes up for all the bad food you've ever had.

Suitability and Critical Comment

Easy to read, full of warmth, humor, and hope for the human condition, this is a novel that most teenagers will enjoy. The characters are real, everyday people. Hope is pictured as an intelligent young girl trying to deal with her mother's indifference and her father's absence. Life in the rural Midwest is nicely drawn, and G. T.'s illness is neither glossed over nor sentimentalized; for grades seven through nine.

Themes and Subjects

Elections, families, food, fraud, honesty, love, the Midwest, politics, romance

Passages for Booktalking

Hope and Addie arrive in Wisconsin and meet G. T. (pp. 23–28); G. T. runs for mayor (pp. 31–35); Braverman learns a political lesson (p. 121); Hope's mother pays a visit (pp. 138–44); G. T. becomes mayor, and Hope finds a father (pp. 167–68).

Additional Selections

Three teenage sisters who have been abandoned by their parents discover that they have inherited a run-down old house from their grandfather in Julie Johnston's *In Spite of Killer Bees* (Tundra, 2001).

Delia, an overweight, quiet high-school student falls under the manipulative influence of Amandine in *Amandine* (Hyperion, 2001) by Adele Griffin.

Jannell's life changes dramatically when her grandfather buys a 1962 Cadillac convertible and invites the trashy Pickens family to move into his empty house in the delightful *Dancing in Cadillac Light* (Putnam, 2001) by Kimberly Willis Holt.

Fourteen-year-old Mattie is determined to cause trouble when she is sent by her mother to visit a boring South Dakota town in Catherine Dexter's *Driving Lessons* (Candlewick, 2000).

About the Book

Booklist, Sept. 15, 2000, p. 231.
Book Report, Jan., 2001, p. 13.
Bulletin of the Center for Children's Books, Sept., 2000, p. 563.
Kirkus Reviews, Sept. 1, 2000, p. 1279.
New York Times Book Review, Nov. 19, 2000, p. 46.
School Library Journal, Nov., 2000, p. 150.

About the Author

Authors and Artists for Young Adults, vol. 34, Gale, 2000.
Drew, Bernard A. *100 More Popular Young Adult Authors,* Libraries Unlimited, 2002.
"Flying Starts," *Publishers Weekly,* Dec. 28, 1992, p. 260.
Lives and Works: Young Adult Authors, Grolier, 1999, vol. 1, pp. 45–47.
Something about the Author, vol. 117, Gale, 2000.

Cole, Brock. *The Facts Speak for Themselves.* Penguin, 1997. $14.41
(1-886-97014-9); pb. $5.99 (0-191-20696-3) (Grades 8–12).

Introduction

Brock Cole, who claims he was a terrible student during his public school
days, came from a family that moved frequently. Since settling down and
completing college, he has been an English instructor and a philosophy
professor as well as a prize-winning author. He is perhaps best known for
the many children's books he has written and illustrated, but his young
adult novels (which now number three) have also appeared on many "best
of the best" lists. The first is an exploration of human cruelty and redemption named *The Goats* (Farrar, 1987), in which two social outcasts who are
socially immature and vulnerable become the victims of their summer
camp colleagues and are stripped and left alone on a deserted island. The
second, *Celine* (Farrar, 1989), is the story of a confused high-school junior
who, like Holden Caulfield before her, is trying to distinguish between the
phony and artificial in life and the sincere and genuine. *The Facts Speak for
Themselves,* the third, is an equally emotional, shocking story that probes
childhood feelings and problems.

Principal Characters

Linda, thirteen years old
Jack Green, Linda's lover
Frank Perry, Linda's mother's boyfriend
Tyler and Stoppard, Linda's younger half-brothers
Linda's dysfunctional mother
Mr. Bloomberg, an older man whom Linda's mother marries

Plot Summary

As the story opens, Linda witnesses the killing of Jack Green, who is shot
by Frank Perry, her mother's boyfriend. Green was Linda's lover; she is thirteen years old. Linda is taken to the Catholic Charities center, where her
story unfolds as told to a social worker. Strangely enough, rather than being
particularly upset by the killing, Linda is far more concerned about who
will care for Stoppard and Tyler, her younger half-brothers. As she tells the
social worker, no one can rely on her often drunk, always dysfunctional
mother.

Reluctantly, Linda relates the story of her life. Her father was Charles
Taylor, a Native American who killed himself when she was very young.
After that, her mother took up with Peter Hobbs. He is the father of Stop-

pard, but he left town soon after the baby's birth. That left Linda to take over the care of Stoppard because her mother could not be depended on. Finally, the household had so deteriorated that the three of them went to Minnesota to live with her mother's parents, Dr. and Mrs. Hoeksema. As Linda remembers, that really wasn't so bad. At least Linda had her own room this time and even a little respite from the care of the baby.

But her mother became bored, so soon it was time to leave Minnesota. She became acquainted with Mr. Bloomberg, a much older and wealthy man. Her mother explained to Linda that they were getting married and the family was moving to Florida. So they did. Linda was actually not unhappy there. Mr. Bloomberg turned out to be rather nice and considerate, and she got to go to school regularly. But, unfortunately for Linda, Mr. Bloomberg was old. It wasn't long before he was boring to Linda's mother. When the old man had a stroke and the money ran out, so did Linda's mother. But Linda remained to care for him and take care of his affairs.

In time, the authorities found out that Linda was left alone to care for the old man. It was also discovered that her mother and Bloomberg had never married. After all that, there was little choice but to return Linda to her mother. So the two were back together again.

As Linda tells the social worker, it wasn't long before her mother took up with Frank Perry, by whom she had Tyler. Her mother was no better with Tyler than with Stoppard, and Linda pretty much assumed care of them both while attending school. Soon she met Jack Green, a man old enough to be her father, and they began an affair. Linda didn't particularly want the affair, she explains, but Jack did and he was nice to her. So Jack became her lover.

Eventually, Linda's mother learned of the relationship and, under the influence of alcohol, she told Frank. The result: Frank shot Jack and then himself.

Despite all the horror, the social worker thinks that in time Linda will adjust well. And she does. At the novel's end, she is doing well in school, she understands that what Jack Green did was rape, and she understands that she should not have gotten mixed up with him. She is told that she should have more therapy, and she agrees. But in her heart, she doesn't think much will come from it. Nothing can change what happened. What else is there to say?

Suitability and Critical Comment

This is a gritty, frank, unsparing view of a young girl caught on the dark side. Old beyond her years in some ways, totally naïve in others, Linda spends her days in what for most young readers would be considered despair and depression. Although the reading is easy, the book powerful and well written, it is perhaps best suited for the young reader in grades seven through twelve who can handle a strong dose of realism.

Themes and Subjects

Alcoholism, child neglect, dysfunctional families, murder, prostitution, rape

Passages for Booktalking

The murder (pp. 9–14); Linda talks about her philosophy of life (pp. 28–29); Linda's memory of her father (pp. 34–35); the move to Minnesota (pp. 52–58); the move to Florida (pp. 68–75); Linda and her mother argue (pp. 94–96); the rape (pp. 152–53).

Additional Selections

Tragedy and whimsy combine in Susanna Vance's *Sights* (Delacorte, 2001), a novel about a thirteen-year-old girl and her struggles with parental abuse, first love, and achieving self-esteem.

Recently orphaned, fifteen-year-old Ophelia reaches out from her foster home to care for ninety-two-year-old Portia McKay, who is living with a horrible memory in *When the Bough Breaks* (Walker, 2000) by Anna Myers.

In Barbara Park's *The Graduation of Jake Moon* (Atheneum, 2000), an eighth-grade boy is unable to acknowledge publicly that his grandfather suffers from Alzheimer's disease.

Homer, who is summering in an old family home in Maine, and a new friend, Roger, set out to solve the mystery of what happened to Homer's father and why he disappeared in *Following Fake Man* (Knopf, 2001) by Barbara Holmes.

About the Book

Booklist, Oct. 1, 1997, p. 318.
Bulletin of the Center for Children's Books, Oct., 1997, p. 46.
Horn Book, Nov.-Dec., 1997, p. 678.
Kirkus Reviews, Oct. 15, 1997, p. 1580.
School Library Journal, Dec., 1997, p. 24.
VOYA, Dec. 1997, p. 315.

About the Author

Authors and Artists for Young Adults, vol. 15, Gale, 1995.
Children's Literature Review, vol. 18, Gale, 1989.
Continuum Encyclopedia of Children's Literature, Continuum, 2001.
Drew, Bernard A. *100 More Popular Young Adult Authors*, Libraries Unlimited, 2002.
Gallo, Donald. *Speaking for Ourselves, Too*, National Council of Teachers of English, 1993.

Hipple, Ted. *Writers for Young Adults,* vol. 1, Scribners, 1997, pp. 249–56.
Lives and Works: Young Adult Writers, vol. 2, Grolier, 1999, pp. 53–55.
Major Authors and Illustrators for Children and Young Adults, vol. 2, Gale, 1993.
St. James Guide to Young Adult Writers (2nd ed.), St. James, 1999.
Silvey, Anita. *Children's Books and Their Creators,* Houghton Mifflin, 1995.
Sixth Book of Junior Authors and Illustrators, Wilson, 1989.
Something about the Author, vol. 72, Gale, 1995.
Twentieth Century Young Adult Writers, St. James, 1999.

Coleman, Evelyn. *Born in Sin.* Atheneum, 2001. $16 (0-689-83833-6) (Grades 7–10).

Introduction

Before *Born in Sin,* Evelyn Coleman was known for her picture books for children and her contributions to the American Girl series of "History Mysteries" for readers in grades five through eight. *Circle of Fire* (Pleasant, 2001), for example, tells of two friends—Mendy, who is black, and her white friend Jeffrey—who are growing up in a southern town in Tennessee during 1958. Because of the racial prejudice around them, they have difficulty maintaining their friendship, but after Mendy overhears men from the Ku Klux Klan plotting to kill her heroine Eleanor Roosevelt, the two work together to thwart this evil plot and get help from Jeffrey's father, who is an FBI informant. *Born in Sin,* for an older audience, also deals with racial matters, in a contemporary setting. It deals with the adjustment made by a fourteen-year-old African American girl, Keisha Wright, after she is denied entrance into a premed program at Avery College by a misguided, prejudiced high-school counselor and instead is sent to a camp for poor, at-risk kids.

Principal Characters

Keisha Wright, fourteen years old
Mrs. Wright, Keisha's hard-working mother
Betty, Keisha's best friend
Malik, Betty's brother
Jeebie, a drug dealer
Mr. Hakim, a social worker

Plot Summary

Fourteen-year-old Keisha Wright has a dream of becoming a doctor, which is not an easy thing for a black girl from a poor family. But she has the chance to enter a premed vacation school at nearby Avery University. The program is set up for kids who are smart and want to be in medicine. The summer is for orientation, which will allow her to enter a program that will permit special admission to Avery after graduation from high school. Then, she encounters a subtle form of racism in a teacher who changes her curriculum from college prep to general, which will put her in a high-minded, white-hearted urban rescue program for teens in poverty, or as Keisha says, "born in sin." Outraged, Keisha attacks the teacher; Malik, the brother of her friend Betty, tries to break up the tussle. Both of them are saved from jail by the Children-At-Risk Foundation, which takes youngsters out of the neighborhood and shows them how other children live.

Keisha is outraged to be thrown in with other girls she does not like very much. But she overcomes her anger in an effort to show she can be better than anyone, and this is especially true when it comes to swimming. Keisha takes to the water and learns to swim in an amazingly short time, so much so that the coach, Mr. Walt, is very impressed and asks her if she would like to try out for the Olympic team. Keisha realizes that she loves swimming, but she feels that any attempt to get her to excel in swimming is just another form of racism, as though all that black people can be good at is sports. She wants to be a doctor. But she becomes interested in the thought of the Olympics, especially after Walt introduces her to Sabir Muhammad, a young black who is an Olympic champion.

Since she is no longer eligible for the paid Avery program, Keisha has to pay for the chance to enter Avery. But where can she get the money? Her mother works very hard, but they have no money to spare. Keisha learns that her tuition for the program will be $6,000, and she knows there is no way she can get that kind of money. Then she begins to notice that her mother is out late at night or is not there in the morning. Fearful that somehow her mother has gotten into drugs, she tails her one night and finds that she is entering the Lion's Den, a notorious drug den and nightclub.

One night when Keisha follows her mother, she meets Jeebie, a drug dealer. He attacks her, and she would have been raped but for the interference of Mr. Hakim, a social worker. Keisha is afraid to name the attacker, but her mother gives her the courage to do so. Reluctantly, Keisha tells her mother what she was doing out so late at night and in such a neighborhood. Her mother explains that she is not on drugs or performing in a strip joint. She is earning money for Keisha's tuition to Avery by keeping the books for the Lion's Den, but she has to work at night. In addition, her mother finally talks about the mystery concerning Keisha's father. She has never wanted to talk about him before, and Keisha has always assumed that perhaps the man was dead. Her mother confesses that her father was a good man but she left him because he felt at the time that they couldn't afford children. He wanted to finish his college education. So she raised Keisha and her sister by herself. She is sorry for being so foolish, she admits, but the man has been back in Keisha's life for some time. He is Mr. Hakim, the social worker.

At first, Keisha does not want to acknowledge that this man is her father. She hates her mother for not being up front with her. But in the end, Betty convinces her that she has a good family, a mother who loves her, and a father who wants to be in her life.

At the next swim meet, Keisha wins the race. She is offered a spot on the trials team for the Olympics in Florida. The future looks good.

Suitability and Critical Comment

This is an easily read book for young teenagers, with the added interest of Olympic sports. The characters are well drawn, and there is a good relationship between Keisha and her mother. The references to racism are subtle but telling, and Keisha emerges as a teenager with a strong sense of her own personal worth who will fight for her dream. For grades seven through ten.

Themes and Subjects

Family relationships, friendship, medical school, mother-daughter relationships, physical abuse, racism, swimming, Olympics

Passages for Booktalking

Keisha learns she won't be going to the Avery program (pp. 15–16); Keisha discovers swimming (pp. 48–55); Keisha learns that her mother was smart in school (pp. 79–81); Keisha meets an Olympic champ (pp. 84–89); she is attacked by Jeebie (pp. 180–89).

Additional Selections

Raven Jefferson, a fifteen-year-old black girl who lives in the Brooklyn projects with her baby boy, is persuaded to enter a spelling bee for a college scholarship in *Spellbound* (Farrar, 2001) by Janet McDonald.

Sixteen-year-old Callisto May, whose life seems to be spent satisfying others, finds she has no one to turn to after she discovers she is pregnant in Anna Fienberg's *Borrowed Light* (Delacorte, 2000).

Francie gets help adjusting to her mother's mysterious behavior through her friendship with an African American girl and her family in *The Stones of Mourning Creek* (Winslow, 2001), by Diane Les Becquets.

Jazmin's diary entries about growing up in Harlem in the 1960s, *Jazmin's Notebook* (Dial, 1997) by Nikki Grimes, is a funny, tender, and moving story of a young girl's struggles.

About the Book
Booklist, Feb. 15, 2001, p. 1148.
Bulletin of the Center for Children's Books, Feb., 2001, p. 218.
Kirkus Reviews, Feb. 1, 2001, p. 180.
School Library Journal, March, 2001, p. 245.
VOYA, April, 2001, p. 36.

About the Author
No information available.

Cooney, Caroline B. *Driver's Ed.* Delacorte, 1994. $16.95
(0-385-45786-6); pb. Dell, $5.50 (0-440-21981-7) (Grades 7–12).

Introduction
At the age of twenty-four, Caroline B. Cooney (1947–) wrote her first novel. In 1979, the mystery *Safe As the Grave,* her first book for young adults, was published. Though many of her novels are mysteries and romances, including several titles in the Cheerleaders series and Crystal Falls series, others deal with important family and personal problems. Perhaps her most famous titles are in the trilogy that begins with *The Face on the Milk Carton* (Delacorte, 1990). In it, teenager Janie Johnson discovers, through a photograph of a missing girl on a milk carton, that the people she has known as mother and father are actually her grandparents. This identity crisis continues in *Whatever Happened to Janie?* (Delacorte, 1993), in which Janie, now Janie Spring, goes to live with her biological parents and must adjust to new parents plus four siblings. Janie's story concludes with *The Voice on the Radio* (Delacorte, 1996). Ms. Cooney is a resident of a small town in Connecticut, which, though not stated directly, appears to be the locale of this novel.

Principal Characters
Remy (Rembrandt) Marland, a sixteen-year-old high-school junior who has a wild crush on Morgan Campbell
Mr. and Mrs. Marland, Remy's unorthodox parents
Mac, Remy's often-troublesome brother who is thirteen and in the eighth grade

Morgan Campbell, a sixteen-year-old dreamboat who is Remy's love and his parents' pride

Mr. and Mrs. Campbell (Rafe and Nance), Morgan's parents, both prominent lawyers and pillars of society

Starr Campbell, Morgan's precocious twelve-year-old sister

Lark, Morgan and Remy's friend who appears to be scatterbrained but actually is quite shrewd

Mr. Fielding, the ineffective high-school teacher of driver education

Nicholas (Nickie) Budie, a high-school senior who is disliked by most but owns a car and valid license

Mr. Thompson, husband of the slain Denise Thompson and father of their two-year-old child, Bobby

Plot Summary

It began as an innocent suggestion made by bubbleheaded Lark to two of her driver's ed classmates, Remy Marland and Morgan Campbell. The suggestion is that, as a prank, the three go out one evening and steal some traffic signs. Lark would like a Thickly Populated sign for her room, and Remy has her sights on a Morgan Street sign to show how strongly she feels toward Morgan, a handsome six-footer who has just turned sixteen and with whom she is wildly in love. Remy comes from an unconventional family (for example, her younger brother was one year old before her parents finally settled on his name). In addition to her parents, Remy has an unusually pesky brother, Mac, who is almost fourteen and was named after the world-famous computer. Morgan's family is less daunting; both parents are successful lawyers (his father hopes to run for state governor next election), and his sister, twelve-year-old Starr, is a bright, disarmingly candid student now in junior high school. The high-school driver education class that these high-school juniors attend is run by the absentminded, irresponsible Mr. Fielding, a failed teacher. Lark's suggestion is accepted, and Morgan enlists the help of a former buddy who owns a car, the ill-mannered Nickie Budie, who is often referred to as a dirtbag. At the last minute, Lark, who is sensible enough to realize that the escapade might bring disaster, begs off, claiming she has to nurse her sick mother. After gathering the two signs, Nickie decides he wants a stop sign, and Remy stays in the car while Morgan reluctantly helps Nickie steal the sign. Two days later, a news bulletin on TV gives details on the death of a young motorist, Denise Thompson, whose car was crushed by a truck at the intersection that now lacks a stop sign.

Both Remy's and Morgan's lives become an agony of remorse and guilt. Afraid to reveal the truth that their misguided action has resulted in the death of an innocent mother who leaves behind a grieving husband and a two-year-old child, they try to lead normal lives though haunted and tormented by their crime. Every day becomes more painful, particularly after Mr. Thompson mounts an ad campaign in the newspapers and television, offering a reward for the arrest of the culprits. Remy's bother, Mac, stumbles on her secret after inadvertently overhearing an incriminating telephone conversation between Remy and Morgan. Mac and Lark are the only two outsiders who share their terrible secret. Surprisingly, he supports Remy and tries to ease her suffering. Both Remy and Morgan now want to confess, but Nickie's continued stubborn denial of involvement deters them. One day, when Mr. Fielding is alone with Remy, he tells her that he is about to accuse an innocent class member. She blurts out the truth and rushes home to tell her parents. At the same time, Morgan confesses his guilt to his father. Surprisingly, both fathers, though shocked and disappointed at their children's behavior, are remarkably understanding. The mothers, however, become hysterical, claiming a personal betrayal of all the ideals that they have tried to instill in their children. More torment and guilt are suffered by the two youngsters when Mr. Campbell takes them to the Thompson house, where they confess before Mr. Thompson and also meet his child. Christmas arrives and the families are still torn with misery and reproach. They attend the annual pageant that Morgan has directed at their local church. Through the message of the season and the contriteness of their children, the two sets of parents realize that, in the long run, parental love can survive crises and disappointments.

Suitability and Critical Comment

This is a realistic, poignant story of two teenagers who are on the brink of a loving relationship and who must take responsibility for an action that has produced unforeseen but horrendous results. The situation is handled candidly, and the portrayal of family relationships under severe stress is uncompromising and honest. The novel is enjoyed by readers in both junior and senior high school.

Themes and Subjects

Automobiles, driver's education, family life, family problems, friendship, guilt, love, responsibility, school stories, teachers, truthfulness

Passages for Booktalking

Mr. Fielding and driver's education (in paperback edition, pp. 3–5 and pp. 6–8); Remy at the wheel (pp. 10–12); Lark suggests the sign-stealing escapade (pp. 27–29); stealing the three signs (pp. 45–52); and the news broadcast announcing Denise Thompson's death (pp. 66–71).

Additional Selections

Fifteen-year-old Liv Trager has problems adjusting to her new coastal California home and living with her father, a professional diver, in *Tender* (Farrar, 2001) by Valerie Hobbs.

A high-school senior is consumed with guilt after he drives drunk and is responsible for his best friend's death in Sharon M. Draper's *Tears of a Tiger* (Atheneum, 1994).

Depression and guilt plague Michael after he tries to hide the fact that he has accidentally killed a man with his rifle in Joyce McDonald's *Swallowing Stones* (Delacorte, 1997).

After killing a girl while driving drunk, Brent Bishop pays for his crime by building whirligigs to her memory in the four corners of the United States in Paul Fleischman's *Whirligig* (Holt, 1998).

About the Book

Booklist, June 1, 1994, p. 1809.
Bulletin of the Center for Children's Books, Sept., 1994, p. 10.
Kirkus Reviews, Sept. 14, 1994, p. 1269.
School Library Journal, August, 1994, p. 168.
VOYA, Oct., 1994, p. 206.

About the Author

Authors and Artists for Young Adults, vol. 5, Gale, 1990; vol. 32, Gale, 2000.
Continuum Encyclopedia of Children's Literature, Continuum, 2001.
Drew, Bernard A. *The 100 Most Popular Young Adult Authors,* Libraries Unlimited, 1997.
Gallo, Donald. *Speaking for Ourselves, Too,* National Council of Teachers of English, 1993.
Hipple, Ted. *Writers for Young Adults,* vol. 1, Scribners, 1997, pp. 281–90.
Lives and Works: Young Adult Authors, vol. 2, Grolier, 1999, pp. 68–70.
Major Authors and Illustrators for Children and Young Adults, vol. 2, Gale, 1993.
St. James Guide to Young Adult Writers (2nd ed.), St. James, 1999.
Something about the Writer, vol. 48, Gale, 1987; vol. 80, Gale, 1995; vol. 113, Gale, 2000.

Koss, Amy Goldman. *The Girls.* Dial, 2000. $16.99 (0-8037-2494-2) (Grades 7–9).

Introduction

Amy Goldman Koss (1954–) was born in Detroit and of her early life has said, "I was a lousy student and never prepared for adulthood. That is, I went to lots and lots of colleges, but never graduated and I had many jobs but no career." Talented in both drawing and writing, she was persuaded by her husband to take a try at serious writing. She started with picture books and then, at the advice of an editor, began writing novels for the middle school–junior high age group. The first of these was *The Trouble with Zinny Weston* (Dial, 1998), told by Ava, a fifth-grader who becomes friends with a newcomer, Zinny Weston. Unfortunately, Zinny's mother drowns a troublesome raccoon in a garbage can, and this raises the ire of Ava's veterinarian parents. After many complications, order is restored. *The Girls*, the fourth of her novels for the middle grades, tackles the subjects of school cliques. It is interestingly told from several different points of view.

Principal Characters

Maya, one of five friends in middle school; she is being ostracized by the group
Renee, who feels badly about Maya's treatment
Darcy, who feels she must show her loyalty to Candace
Brianna, who keeps laughing at Candace's games
Candace, the leader and user of the group

Plot Summary

This novel is told in a first-person narrative by each of the five girls in middle school. The story centers on Maya, Renee, Darcy, Brianna, and Candace, who form a tight clique. The girls are dominated in no uncertain terms by Candace. She is popular and fascinating to the others, who at times hold her in awe as though spellbound by her. In varying degrees, the other four do not see her meanness and willingness to put each of them down in front of the group.

One day, Maya inadvertently finds out that she is being ostracized by the group. She innocently calls Renee to see if she wants to go to Magic Mountain on Saturday with Maya's father and her little sister. Renee, with much hesitation, says she can't go. Still not clued in, Maya calls Brianna. From Brianna's mother, Maya is shocked to learn that the group has been invited to Darcy's—all except Maya. She goes to Magic Mountain with a heavy heart.

In the meantime, the other girls react to and deal with this new situation in different ways. Renee feels decidedly uncomfortable about going to Darcy's, knowing Maya has not been invited. But, of course, she goes. She must go. How could she not go when Candace, their leader and best friend, will be there? Renee really wants to ask why the other girls suddenly all hate Maya just because Candace says they should, but she remains silent. Darcy's main concern is that if the party at her house doesn't go well, everyone—especially Candace—will want to leave. This is a disgrace she can't comprehend, so in order to make sure it doesn't happen, she has to show that she doesn't like Maya, either. Brianna sometimes feels as though the games Candace plays and the jokes she makes about all of them are tests. All of them seem to be walking on hot coals in fear that somehow they will earn the displeasure of Candace. Even so, Brianna can't stop wanting to be part of it all.

Candace finds everything beneath her, including her own family. She enjoys the power she has over the other four, and it amuses her. Yet part of her is annoyed that she can so easily bend them to her will. This kind of annoyance usually leads to boredom on Candace's part, and eventually she will find someone new to amuse her. Candace's power over the girls fills each, in turn, with self-doubt. Are they to blame for the things she says, the way she treats them? Each seems to lack the will to break away.

In the end, the other four girls tentatively get back together. As they do, Candace notices another girl in school, Nicole, whom she has not paid attention to before. Bored with the others and with the ease with which she manipulates them, Candace has found a new friend. Nicole is thrilled with the attention, and Candace is satisfied for the time being, until Nicole becomes too easy to manipulate and bores her, too. As for the others, they recognize how Candace operates, as she draws Nicole to her with flattery and attention. They realize that the spell is broken, even if they don't quite understand how or why.

Suitability and Critical Comment

This is a fast-paced, disturbing, but funny-at-times look at the phenomenon of cliques among young girls, led by a powerful leader who is charismatic but dangerous. She causes self-doubt among the others, who are unwilling or unable to face up to her put-downs. It is also a look at the dominant girl's personality. The more she forms the group to her will, the more she becomes bored with how easy it is. This leads her to drop the others and move on to the next. For grades seven through nine.

Themes and Subjects

Adolescent girls, charisma, cliques, dominant personalities, jealousy, middle school friendships, self-doubt

Passages for Booktalking

Maya finds she is left out of the group (p. 4); Renee tells her mother she feels squirmy about Maya's treatment (pp. 9–10); Darcy's concern is that everyone will enjoy her party (pp. 18–21); Candace thinks about her power over the girls (pp. 55–56); Brianna has doubts (pp. 103–107); they get together (pp. 113–16); Candace finds a new friend (pp. 119–21).

Additional Selections

Stargirl, a compulsive do-gooder, finds her perennial optimism challenged in Jerry Spinelli's light-hearted story of an outsider who triumphs, *Stargirl* (Knopf, 2000).

Eight young people narrate this novel about their concerns and the Dogwood Junior High Stardust Dance in Kathi Appett's *Kissing Tennessee and Other Stories from the Stardust Dance* (Harcourt, 2000).

When their baby sibling dies, two sisters are sent to live with their domineering Aunt Patty in *Getting Near to Baby* (Putnam, 1999) by Audrey Couloumbis.

The pain and torment of jeers and name-calling are depicted in *The Misfits* (Simon, 2001), a funny, fast, and tender novel by James Howe.

About the Book

Booklist, Aug., 2000, p. 2132.
Bulletin of the Center for Children's Books, June, 2000, p. 362.
Horn Book, July-Aug., 2000, p. 459.
Kirkus Reviews, May 15, 2000, p. 716.
School Library Journal, June, 2000, p. 148.
VOYA, Aug., 2000, p. 189.

About the Author

Contemporary Authors, vol. 186, Gale, 2000.
Something about the Author, vol. 115, Gale, 2000.

Mazer, Norma Fox. *When She Was Good.* Scholastic, 1997. $16.95 (0-590-13506-6) (Grades 8–12).

Introduction

Norma Fox Mazer (1931–) grew up in Glens Falls, New York. She was an imaginative child who lived in her own private world. She began writing early by keeping diaries and creating her first short stories. At thirteen, she joined the staff of her local school newspaper, where she obtained some valuable experience. This kindled her desire to pursue a writing career, but she didn't begin writing seriously until after her marriage to Harry Mazer, another would-be writer. They decided to write a little every day and got up at 3:30 every morning to put their idea into practice. Beginning with *I, Trissy*, a novel in diary form (Delacorte, 1971), she has written over two dozen highly acclaimed books for young adults. She writes about believable characters who are reaching maturity and facing such personal problems as lack of self-esteem and decisions about sex, as well as social concerns like alcoholism and care for the elderly. In an interview she said, "The world is . . . hard, confusing, difficult, demanding. Lies won't do. The truth will help . . . the truth about people." Her novels are explorations of this truth.

Principal Characters

Em Thurkill, a young girl left alone by her sister's death
Pamela Thurkill, Em's disturbed sister
Mr. Thurkill, Em's father
Sally, whom Mr. Thurkill marries
Louise, a woman in the apartment house

Plot Summary

After Em's sister dies at a young age of a heart problem, Em doesn't know whether to be happy or sad. Pamela was psychotic to be sure, foul-mouthed and difficult. She even slapped Em around on occasion. But she was Em's older sister and all she had left. Now Em is alone in the apartment they had shared.

Life has not been easy for Em. Her mother died four years earlier, probably from overwork and the problems of dealing with an alcoholic, abusive husband. They lived in a trailer, Em's home for fourteen years. After their mother's death, Pamela doesn't go to school anymore and no one cares, but Em likes school. She likes to write about things in her notebook, which Pamela finds one day and tears up. With their mother gone, there is barely enough to eat until Pamela takes matters into her own hands and, with Em in tow, shows up at their father's job every Friday night to demand money before he can spend it all on drink. This situation continues until Mr. Thurkill comes home with Sally, their new stepmother. Little by little, the wretched trailer is taken over by Sally. One day, Sally tells the girls that they both must go to work and give her money to run the household. Em can work part-time and go to school part-time until she is sixteen; then she has to quit and contribute fully.

Instead, Pamela packs their bags and they go to the city, where they find an apartment but are soon thrown out of it for nonpayment of rent. School is out of the question for Em, who looks for work. They try a shelter for awhile and eventually find an apartment where they can barely pay the rent. It is there that Pamela collapses one day and dies. Em is now totally alone. She thinks often of her life with her sister and even goes back to see the old trailer, surprised at how wretched it really was.

Near desperation, Em notices a Help Wanted sign in a store window. She talks herself into the job. She also becomes attracted to a middle-aged woman, named Louise, in the apartment. Em would like to be friends with her, to have someone to talk to, but the woman refuses her friendship. One day, Louise accuses Em of stalking her and blurts out that if Em is looking for a mother substitute, she is not one. Her own daughters can't stand her. Days later, after buying a new pair of shoes and experiencing a rare self-confidence, Em meets Louise on the street and, after a curt nod from the older woman, Em moves on, pleased with herself. However, Louise starts to talk to her, and the two walk to their apartment house together.

With a new job and possibly a new friend, and the possibility of a friendship with a young man she has spoken to occasionally, Em feels confident enough to allow herself to go back over the details of Pamela's death. Pamela has just thrown an iron pan at her in a rage. Then Em watches as her sister sinks to the ground, twitching. Her mouth opens and closes. Em dials 911 in the darkness. But how long did she wait to call for help? Was it hours? No, Em decides, it was only minutes before she placed the call. But was it seven minutes or seventeen or seventy? Em is sorry and not sorry. She is sorry Pamela is dead, but not sorry that she's not there.

Suitability and Critical Comment

This book is an easy read for most teenagers, but it is a realistic, gritty, often depressing look at one young girl's life. The author does not spare the harshness or the physical violence of both Em's sister and father. These realities, however, are softened by the essential sweetness and courage of Em herself, who has a remarkable sense of self-worth and the will to survive. For grades eight through twelve.

Themes and Subjects

Alcoholism, bravery, depression, family relationships, loneliness, physical and emotional violence, poverty

Passages for Booktalking

Em buys Pamela's coffin (pp. 7–16); Em returns to the trailer (pp. 47–50); Pamela gets money from their father (pp. 78–83); Louise confronts Em (pp. 180–81); Em relives Pamela's death (pp. 223–26).

Additional Selections

Callie, who has been institutionalized and is barely able to communicate, longs to solve her psychological problems, which involve her brother's near death in Patricia McCormick's *Cut* (Front Street, 2000).

In duel narratives, one by a mother and the other by a daughter, Ruth Pennebaker's *Both Sides Now* (Holt, 2000) explores the impact of breast cancer on a family.

During her senior year at high school, a lonely girl faces her mother's impending death and a future life with an unloving father in Joan Abelove's *Saying It Out Loud* (DK, 1999).

America, a survivor of sexual abuse, is a mixed-race teenager who tells his story from a hospital after a suicide attempt in E. R. Frank's *America* (Simon, 2002).

About the Book

Booklist, Sept. 1, 1997, p. 118.
Bulletin of the Center for Children's Books, Oct., 1997, p. 61.
Horn Book, Nov., 1997, p. 6982.
New York Times Book Review, Nov. 16, 1997, p. 32.
School Library Journal, Sept., 1997, p. 221.
VOYA, Oct., 1997, p. 245.

About the Author

Authors and Artists for Young Adults, vol. 5, Gale, 1991; vol. 36, Gale, 2001.
Children's Literature Review, vol. 23, Gale, 1991.
Continuum Encyclopedia of Children's Literature, Continuum, 2001.
Drew, Bernard A. *The 100 Most Popular Young Adult Authors,* Libraries Unlimited, 1997.
Fifth Book of Junior Authors and Illustrators, Wilson, 1983.
Gallo, Donald. *Speaking for Ourselves,* National Council of Teachers of English, 1990.
Hipple, Ted. *Writers for Young Adults,* vol. 2, Scribners, 1997, pp. 337–46.
Holtze, Sally Holmes. *Presenting Norma Fox Mazer,* Twayne, 1987.
Lives and Works: Young Adult Writers, vol. 5, Grolier, 1999, pp. 78–80.
Major Authors and Illustrators for Children and Young Adults, vol. 4, Gale, 1993.
Mazer, Norma Fox. "Silent Censorship," *School Library Journal,* Aug., 1996, p. 42.
St. James Guide to Young Adult Writers (2nd ed.), St. James, 1999.
Silvey, Anita. *Children's Books and Their Creators,* Houghton Mifflin, 1995.
Something about the Author, vol. 24, Gale, 1981; vol. 67, Gale, 1992; vol. 105, Gale, 1999.
Something about the Author Autobiography Series, vol. 1, Gale, 1986.
Twentieth Century Young Adult Writers, St. James, 1994.

Myers, Walter Dean. *Monster.* HarperCollins, 1999. $18.95
 (0-06-028078-6); pb. $6.95 (0-06-440731-4) (Grades 7–12).

Introduction

Although Walter Dean Myers was born in West Virginia, he spent most of his youth in Harlem and has never lost touch with the environment that helped shape his character. Harlem is the setting for this novel. It won the first Michael L. Printz Award for excellence in literature for young adults. The format is fascinating. The story is told both through the handwritten journal of Steve, a boy on trial, and through a film script of the trial also written by Steve. One describes the boy and his emotions and, in the other, Myers says in a *Booklist* interview, "he's giving himself the luxury of the distance, the film script, the wide-angle shots, what the filmmaker wants you to see." As to the genesis of the novel, the author cites two experiences. First, he recalls many interviews he conducted of prison inmates and their attitudes toward the crimes they committed. Second, "one day I was watching a trial here in Jersey City in which a seventeen-year-old boy was charged with armed robbery; and attempted murder." He heard, across the street, kids leaving their high school and realized "that these kids could go from being in high school now and not much later be faced with a life sentence."

Principal Characters

Steve Harmon, a sixteen-year-old Harlem boy accused of felony murder
Mr. and Mrs. Harmon, Steve's loving parents
Alguinaldo Nesbitt, the murdered druggist
James King, leader of the robbery scheme
Richard "Bobo" Evans, a sleazy criminal who squeals on King and the
 others
Osvaldo Cruz, a street gang member who also rats to the police
Jose Delgado, a drugstore employee
Sandra Petrocelli, the state's prosecutor
Kathy O'Brien, Steve's defense attorney
Asa Briggs, King's attorney
Lorelle Henry, a retired school librarian and key witness

Plot Summary

On July 5, the court convenes in the cast of the State of New York versus James King and Steve Harmon. Sandra Petrocelli, the prosecuting attorney, begins by summarizing the case for the judge and jury. On December 22 of last year, four people were involved in a robbery in Harlem of a drugstore owned by fifty-five-year-old Alguinaldo Nesbitt. Two of the four, King, age twenty-four, and his confederate, twenty-two-year-old Richard "Bobo" Evans, were to rob the store after Steve Harmon had checked it to make sure there were no police inside. The fourth, fourteen-year-old Osvaldo Cruz, was to impede anyone chasing the robbers. The robbery was botched. Mr. Nesbitt produced a gun and, in the ensuing struggle, it is alleged that King shot and killed the druggist. Evans and Cruz have plea-bargained, and now King and Harmon are on trial for felony murder. If convicted, each could be sentenced to twenty-five years in prison. The narrative continues in two alternating formats, both the product of one of the accused, sixteen-year-old Steve Harmon. The first is the handwritten journal he keeps while in jail, and the second is a film script for a movie starring Steve Harmon that is an adaptation of the court proceedings, complete with types of shots (for example, close-ups), flashbacks, voice-overs, and other cinematic techniques. Steve is a prize pupil in Mr. Sawicki's film club at Stuyvesant High School, and this is an opportunity to practice his craft. He has decided to title the film after the name Petrocelli called him in court, *Monster.* The journal he keeps of his prison experiences reveals Steve to be a sensitive, frightened young man appalled and terrified by the violence and cruelty that surround him and ashamed that he has caused such pain and suffering to his parents, who visit him regularly, and to his eleven-year-old brother, Jerry, who idolizes Steve. The main players in the court drama are the accused, the jury, the Judge (a sixty-year-old man who seems bored with the proceedings), Petrocelli, Asa Briggs (head counsel for King), and Kathy O'Brien, Steve's lawyer. The first witnesses called by the prosecution establish the connection between the four males and the crime. This is accomplished by tracing cartons of cigarettes stolen during the robbery to Bobo Evans, who confessed and implicated the other three. His testimony, though hardly trustworthy because he is a convicted felon and drug dealer, nevertheless confirms that King fired the fatal shot and that Steve was part of the plot. This is confirmed by Osvaldo, the other informer. In the following days, there are several other witnesses, including Jose Delgado, an articulate youth who worked at the drugstore and found the body, and Lorelle Henry, a retired school librarian who fled the store when the robbers entered but who has identified King as one of the two and does not mention Steve. The defense produces several character witnesses, including Mr. Sawicki, who vouches for Steve's integrity. In the meantime, the case is getting national attention; even Mayor Giuliani has commented on it on television. Kathy O'Brien realizes that the case against King is strong and, unless she is able to separate Steve's defense from King's, both could be convicted. She decides on a bold plan—to let Steve take the stand. Using the fact that no one saw him at the robbery and that his participation is based solely on the testimony of two unreliable witnesses, she begins coaching him on questions and answers. When he takes the stand, Steve denies any part in the robbery, admitting that he knew the participants but was completely unaware of their scheme. O'Brien's tactics work. When the jury delivers their verdict, Steve is exonerated and King is convicted of felony murder. For Steve it is an unsettling victory. In his final journal entry, he writes, "After the trial my father, with tears in his eyes, held me close and said that he was thankful that I did not have to go to jail. He moved away and the distance between us seemed to grow bigger and bigger." The entry ends, "When Miss O'Brien looked at me after we had won the case, what did she see that caused her to turn away—what did she see?"

Suitability and Critical Comment

This is an unsettling exploration of the justice system as experienced by an intelligent, sensitive young man who will spare himself the horror of a jail sentence at any cost. The dual narrative adds new dimensions to the story, and the illustrations (mostly photos of Steve), supplied by the author's son Christopher, add realism. The result is a powerful, disturbing, intense but entertaining story that is suitable for readers in grades seven through twelve.

Themes and Subjects

Courts, crime, family stories, Harlem, justice, movies, murder, prisons, robbery

Passages for Booktalking

Steve's life in prison (pp. 1–5); the trial begins (pp. 12–16); Petrocelli's opening statement, which gives the story of the crime (pp. 20–24); O'Brien addresses the jury about Steve (pp. 25–27); Jose discovers the body (pp. 28–32); and Mama visits Steve in jail (pp. 144–48).

Additional Selections

In script form, Rob relates his oral biography and his search for the father who abandoned him before birth in Paul Fleischman's *Seek* (Cricket, 2001).

Sex, drugs, violence, and family problems are featured in E. R. Frank's *Life Is Funny* (DK, 2000), the story of eleven young narrators growing up in Brooklyn over a seven-year period.

Three African American brothers living in New York City cope with the death of their parents and with problems of survival in Jaqueline Woodson's *Miracle Boys* (Putnam, 2000).

African American Benjie is growing up in Harlem, where drugs become an ever-growing temptation in *A Hero Ain't Nothin' but a Sandwich* by Alice Childress.

About the Book
Booklist, May 1, 1999, p. 99.
Book Report, Sept., 1999, p. 61.
Bulletin for the Center of Children's Books, May, 1999, p. 323.
Horn Book, May 1999, p. 337.
New York Times Book Review, June 6, 1999, p. 48.
School Library Journal, July, 1999, p. 98.
VOYA, Aug., 1999, p. 185.

About the Author
Authors and Artists for Young Adults, vol. 4, Gale, 1990; vol. 23, Gale, 1998.
Children's Literature Review, vol. 4, Gale, 1982; vol. 16, Gale, 1989; vol. 35, Gale, 1995.
Continuum Encyclopedia of Children's Literature, Continuum, 2001.
Drew, Bernard A. *The 100 Most Popular Young Adult Authors,* Libraries Unlimited, 1997.
Fifth Book of Junior Authors and Illustrators, Wilson, 1983.
Hipple, Ted. *Writers for Young Adults,* vol. 2, Scribners, 1997, pp. 387–96.
Lives and Works: Young Adult Authors, vol. 6, Grolier, 1999, pp. 32–34.
Major Authors and Illustrators for Children and Young Adults, vol. 4, Gale, 1993.
"The Printz Award Revisited—Walter Dean Myers," *Booklist,* Jan. 1 and 15, 2000, pp. 932–33.
Rochman, Hazel. "The Booklist Interview—Walter Dean Myers," *Booklist,* Feb. 15, 2000, p. 1101.
St. James Guide to Young Adult Writers (2nd ed.), St. James, 1999.
Silvey, Anita. *Children's Books and Their Creators,* Houghton Mifflin, 1995.
Something about the Author, vol. 27, Gale, 1982; vol. 41, Gale, 1985; vol. 71, Gale, 1993; vol. 109, Gale, 2000.
Something about the Author Autobiography Series, vol. 2, Gale, 1986.
Twentieth Century Young Adult Writers, St. James, 1994.

Na, An. *A Step from Heaven.* Front Street, 2001. $15.95 (1-886910-58-8) (Grades 7–9).

Introduction
A Step from Heaven is An Na's first novel. It tells the story of a Korean girl, Young Ju, from the time she leaves Korea for America as a small girl until her graduation from high school. Its main theme is the conflict between two cultures as experienced by a single child. Among the many honors heaped on this moving novel was the 2002 Michael J. Printz Award for excellence in literature for young adults. In a *Booklist* interview, the author

states that some of the story is based on her own experiences. She said, "The inspiration for the story definitely came from memory. For example, I remember being forced to get my hair permed, and being told that all American girls have curly hair." When asked if she would keep her own children in touch with their Korean roots, she said, "I hope so. But I know how difficult it is because my parents tried very hard with me. I went to a Korean school and refused to learn. . . . It will be a struggle, I think, trying to keep some of the traditions and the culture alive." This struggle is the subject of the touching and inspirational *A Step from Heaven.*

Principal Characters

Young Ju, a girl from Korea
Apa, her father
Uhmma, her mother
Joon, her American-born brother
Amanda, Young Ju's friend in America

Plot Summary

When Young Ju is four years old, she emigrates to America, known to her by the magical word Mi Gook, which must surely be a paradise where anything is possible and only wonderful things happen. At least that's what all her relatives say. Young Ju hates to leave her beloved grandmother behind, but she is very excited about the plane ride to California. However, she quickly becomes disillusioned about paradise when she and her parents begin to adjust to the realities of a new life. Young Ju discovers that Mi Gook is not paradise at all. For the next several years, as she grows up and before she goes to college, Young Ju must deal with the problems of adjusting to a new place where she cannot speak the language at first, where the customs are strange, and where she encounters pain and prejudice. In addition, her family has difficulty adjusting to America as well. Her father had problems with alcohol back in Korea, and he brought his feelings of frustration and inadequacy with him to America. Now his drinking and physical abuse of her mother become worse. Her long-suffering mother endures the abuse to keep the family together. Her brother, Joon, is born in America, and when he grows up, their father begins to abuse him as well. In addition, Joon grows to resent Young Ju because she becomes the stereotype of all Asian immigrants—she is smart and studious and at the top of her class.

Eventually, Young Ju makes friends in school. Amanda is her best friend, but her father does not want her to see American girls. He is afraid they will give her bad ideas and she will lose touch with her homeland. But Young Ju enjoys the company of her friend as she struggles to become Americanized, although she is ashamed of the poverty in which the family lives and the way in which her father acts. She does not invite Amanda to her own home. Her mother works very hard to keep them together, but her father's condition only gets worse. Trying to find a way to better their lives, Young Ju dreams of winning the lottery. She buys a ticket and is delighted to find she has a winning number, but is ashamed and surprised when she discovers that one number does not mean a winner.

Young Ju finishes the ninth grade with the highest GPA in the class, and her friend Amanda is best in literature. Her parents do not attend the graduation, and her father does not even notice the certificate of excellence when he returns home. Finally, Young Ju learns that her brother, Joon, has been skipping classes at school and is in danger of failing. She threatens to tell their parents if he does not return to school. She does not tell, but their father learns of Joon's actions and beats him. Then one day, Apa sees Young Ju at the library with Amanda. When she returns home, he begins to beat her and kick her in the stomach. Her mother tries to intervene and is savagely beaten. Young Ju gets up the courage to call 911. The police come and take away her father. Her mother is taken to the hospital.

As Young Ju prepares to leave for college, she and her mother and brother have moved into a small house without the father. She looks forward to a better life for all of them.

Suitability and Critical Comment

This is a sensitive story of growing up in a strange land in a strange culture. Some readers may have initial difficulty with the author's striking language to accentuate the process of acculturation for Young Ju. However, the fineness of detail showing the heartache and agony of a young girl trying to deal with a new life as the fabric of her own family is falling apart is well worth the effort. This book should be enjoyed by most teen readers in grades seven through nine.

Themes and Subjects

Alcoholism, California, emigration, family relationships, friendships, Korea, physical abuse, prejudice, schools

Passages for Booktalking

Young Ju emigrates to America (pp. 23–29); Young Ju meets her baby brother (pp. 38–42); the lottery incident (pp. 77–83); Young Ju talks with Joon about skipping school (pp. 132–36); Young Ju calls in the police to stop the beatings (pp. 137–41).

Additional Selections

The clash between traditional Chinese ways and American culture is explored in *Dream Soul* (HarperCollins, 2000) by Laurence Yep, a novel set is 1927 West Virginia and continuing the story of the Lee family begun in *The Star Fisher* (HarperCollins, 1991).

Breaking Through (Houghton Mifflin, 2001) by Francisco Jimenez is the story of a Mexican American teenager's struggle for survival while still dreaming of college.

Maya, who considers herself American, must return to India where she rediscovers her homeland and receives an offer of marriage in Vineeta Vijayaraghaven's *Motherland* (Soho, 2001).

Set in a Peruvian jungle in the 1970s, Joan Abelove's *Go and Come Back* (DK, 1998) tells of a culture clash between modern lifestyles and those of native tribesmen.

About the Book

Booklist, June 1, 2001, p. 1881.
Bulletin of the Center for Children's Books, July, 2001, p. 416.
Horn Book, July-Aug., 2001, p. 458.
New York Times Book Review, May 20, 2001, p. 22.
School Library Journal, May, 2001, p. 156.
VOYA, June, 2001, p. 126.

About the Author

Rochman, Hazel. "The Booklist Interview: An Na," *Booklist,* March 15, 2002, p. 1253.

Paulsen, Gary. *The Beet Fields: Memories of a Sixteenth Summer.* Delacorte, 2000. $15.95 (0-385-32647-5) (Grades 9–12).

Introduction

Gary Paulsen (1939–) is best known as a prize-winning author of such archetypal adventure/survival stories for young adults as *Hatchet* (Macmillan, 1987); its offshoots, *Brian's Winter* (Delacorte, 1996) and *Brian's Return* (Delacorte, 1999); and such gripping historical stories as those in the five-book saga about Francis Tucket's exploits in the Old West, like *Mr. Tucket* (Delacorte, 1994)—all for a slightly younger audience than *The Beet Fields.* Before turning to full-time writing, Mr. Paulsen worked in a variety of jobs, from truck driver and trapper to sailor and teacher. In this absorbing autobiographical account, the author re-creates the formative months in his life when, at age sixteen, he left home and became first a migrant farmhand and later a roustabout with a traveling carnival. Though episodic in nature, this book traces, through a series of seemingly separate incidents, a boy's sexual and emotional coming-of-age and his rapid maturation.

Principal Characters

The boy, a naïve sixteen-year-old who runs away from home to escape intolerable conditions

The older Mexican man, who befriends the boy and teaches him survival skills

Bill Flaherty, a sympathetic farmer who hires the boy

Jacobsen, a malicious deputy sheriff

The Hungarian immigrant who gives the boy a ride

Hazel, a kindly older women who offers the boy a home

Taylor, the operator of a traveling carnival

Bobby, Taylor's brother and the carnival geek

Ruby, Taylor's girlfriend and a stripper in the carnival

Plot Summary

Fed up with the squalid conditions under which he is forced to live, as well as with his parents' uncontrolled alcoholism and the unnatural advances his mother makes when she is drunk, the boy (he is never identified by name) decides to leave home and seek his fortune. He is sixteen, and it is the summer of 1955. In the nearby farmlands of North Dakota, he gets a job thinning the plants in a farmer's vast acreage of beet fields. He admires the tremendous energy and dexterity of the Mexican migrant workers who also work in the fields and, although he tries to match their performance, he achieves only bleeding blisters and total exhaustion. The leader of the Mexicans, an older man about forty, befriends the shy, quiet boy, offers him tortillas, and suggests that he contribute to the group's food supply by catching some of the pigeons that roost in the farmer's barn. After catching some pigeons by scaling the rafters, he suffers a painful fall, but the next day, he bravely rejoins the workers in the field though every bone and muscle in his body aches. When the group moves to the neighboring farm of Bill Flaherty, the boy follows them. Here, the Flaherty family takes a special interest in the boy, and Bill offers him a full-time job, which he accepts. He soon settles in with the family. One night, at the request of Alice, Bill's wife, he rescues the farmer from a poker game before Bill risks losing the handsome winnings he has amassed. The boy's stay with the Flahertys ends abruptly when the local deputy sheriff, Jacobsen, who has seen a Wanted poster picturing the runaway boy, arrests him, illegally seizes his meager savings, and takes him to the local jail. The boy escapes but now realizes that he is a fugitive from both his family and the law. A ride he has hitched with an affable, talkative Hungarian ends abruptly when a pheasant crashes into the windshield and the shards of glass kill the driver. The boy is later picked up on the highway by Hazel, a kindly elderly women who lives alone in a picture-perfect farmhouse. Hazel has never adjusted to the death of her son Robert in World War II, and still acts as though he were alive. When the boy and Hazel attend the local fair, the boy sees Jacobsen and realizes he must move on. He accepts a job offer from Taylor, the manager of the carnival, to operate one of the midway rides and also sub as a shill, or decoy, to attract gullible bystanders to the sideshows. One of these is the Wild Man of Borneo attraction, in which Bobby, Taylor's outsized brother, impersonates a scantily clad savage whose act ends with biting the head off a live chicken. The boy and Bobby, known as the carnival geek, become friends. Later, the boy becomes infatuated with another one of the carnival's attractions, the voluptuous stripper Ruby, who is Taylor's lover. One night, he watches her performance, which culminates in complete nudity. He is so visibly aroused and full of passion, that Ruby invites him to her trailer, where, under her guidance, he loses his sexual innocence. In a brief epilogue, the boy is pictured entering the army using forged permission papers from his parents. Another step toward adulthood has begun.

Suitability and Critical Comment

Paulsen's objective point of view and his spare, laconic prose remind the reader of Hemingway. The use of detached understatement increases the impact of the dramatic, often horrifying, events that are milestones in the boy's growth to maturity. Though the author avoids sensationalism, the incidents and language depict adult themes and actions, making the book best suited for mature readers in grades nine and up.

Themes and Subjects

Carnival life, coming-of-age, conquering fear, courage, family problems, farming, loss of innocence, Mexicans, migrant workers, the 1950s, North Dakota, poverty, sexual awakening, vulnerability

Passages for Booktalking

The boy leaves home (pp. 1–2); working the beet fields (pp. 5–8); the older Mexican invites the boy to join his group (pp. 14–15); catching pigeons in the barn (pp. 24–27); the boy rescues Bill Flaherty from the poker game (pp. 61–67); and Jacobsen arrests the boy and takes him to jail (pp. 74–78).

Additional Selections

After witnessing his mother's death, a boy must survive in the Oklahoma woods while trying to escape from a "patriot" group named the Soldiers of God in Barbara Snow Gilbert's *Paper Trail* (Front Street, 2000).

Fourteen-year-old runaway Chappie becomes known as Bone during his adventurous year on the road in *Rule of the Bone* (HarperCollins, 1996) by Russell Banks.

In Diana Wieler's *Drive* (Douglas and McIntyre, 1999), a mature novel for older teens, Jens and his younger brother set out on a road trip in Canada, playing gigs in small towns.

A boy who escapes from an institution finds friendship in a British Columbia forest in *Dreamspeaker* (Avon, 1981) by Cam Hubert.

About the Book

Booklist, July, 2000, p. 2033.
Bulletin of the Center for Children's Books, Oct., 2000, p. 79.
Kirkus Reviews, June 15, 2000, p. 891.
School Library Journal, Sept., 2000, p. 235.
VOYA, Dec., 2000, p. 354.

About the Author

Authors and Artists for Young Adults, vol. 2, Gale, 1989; vol. 17, Gale, 1995.
Children's Literature Review, vol. 19, Gale, 1990; vol. 54, Gale, 1999.
Continuum Encyclopedia of Children's Literature, Continuum, 2001.
Drew, Bernard A. *The 100 Most Popular Young Adult Authors,* Libraries Unlimited, 1997.
Gale, David. "The Maximum Expression of Being Human: A Talk with Gary Paulsen," *School Library Journal,* June, 1997, pp. 24–29.
Gallo, Donald. *Speaking for Ourselves,* National Council of Teachers of English, 1990.
Hipple, Ted. *Writers for Young Adults,* vol. 2, Scribners, 1997, pp. 445–63.
Lives and Works: Young Adult Authors, vol. 6, Grolier, 1999, pp. 35–37.
Major Authors and Illustrators for Children and Young Adults, vol. 5, Gale, 1993.
Mareus, Leonard S. *Author Talk,* Simon & Schuster, 2000.
McElmeel, Sharron L. *The 100 Most Popular Children's Authors,* Libraries Unlimited, 1997.
St. James Guide to Young Adult Writers (2nd ed.), St. James, 1999.
Sixth Book of Junior Authors and Illustrators, Wilson, 1989.
Something about the Author, vol. 22, Gale, 1981; vol. 54, Gale, 1989; vol. 79, Gale, 1995; vol. 111, Gale, 2000.
Twentieth Century Young Adult Writers, St. James, 1994.

Peck, Richard. *A Year Down Yonder.* Dial, 2000. $16.99
(0-8037-4618-3) (Grades 5–8).

Introduction

Although his excellent books for young adults have garnered many awards and prizes, including the Distinguished Margaret Edwards Young Adult Author Achievement award for its author in 1990, Richard Peck (1925–) had never won the Newbery Medal until, in 2001, it was given to his novel *A Year Down Yonder,* a sequel to *A Long Way from Chicago,* a Newbery Honor book in 1999. It is not necessary to be familiar with the first book to understand and appreciate the second, but the locale and principal characters are the same. *Long Way* covers seven summers from 1929 to 1935 when Joey, the narrator, and his younger sister Mary Alice visit their feisty, indomitable, and dirt-poor Grandma Dowdel, who lives in a gossipy Illinois town where life revolves about such major occurrences as the school's Christmas pageant and the community turkey shoot on Armistice Day. Its sequel is another episodic novel filled with humorous, often uproarious, incidents that capture a gentler time in American history.

Principal Characters

Mary Alice Dowdel, the fifteen-year-old narrator, who is sent in the fall of 1937 to live with her grandmother for one year

Grandmother Dowdel, an independent, indomitable, sharp-tongued woman who is larger than life both physically and temperamentally

August Fluke, the school principal, whose son is named Augie

Mildred Burdick, an overall-wearing bully who is Mary Alice's classmate and scion of the town's worst redneck family

Old Man Nyquist, the town curmudgeon

Miss Butler, one of Mary Alice's two teachers

Joey Dowdel, Mary Alice's older brother

Arnold Green, a WPA artist who stays briefly with Grandma Dowdel

Royce McNabb, an attractive high-school senior who enters Mary Alice's school late in the year

Plot Summary

Fifteen-year-old Mary Alice is not thrilled with the prospect of spending an entire year living with her eccentric grandmother in rural Illinois. In the past, she spent summers there, but always with her brother Joey to share Grandma's odd ways. Now it is the Depression, Joey is working in the Civilian Conservation Corps, and her parents can't afford to keep her at home. So, with her cat Bootsie and her radio, she arrives in Grandma's small Illinois town, where she is immediately whisked off to school. After meeting Mr. Flute, the principal, she enters the classroom of Miss Butler, a dreamy, well-intentioned teacher of many subjects, including English. Within minutes Mary Alice is being bullied by Mildred Burdick, the class hellion, who follows Mary Alice home hoping to collect. Grandma uses her usual cunning and skill to get rid of the troublemaker. Incidents follow in which Mary Alice is alternately appalled, bemused, terrified, or amazed by the unique character who is her grandmother. Right off, Grandma doesn't want Bootsie inside, and the cat is therefore relegated to the outdoor cobhouse. The cat adjusts to the situation better than Mary Alice does.

People are either terrified or in awe of Grandma, and she doesn't care which because she is obviously running the town. At Halloween, Grandma easily outwits a group of pranksters intent on upending her privy, with the result that their ringleader, Augie Fluke, has a bucket of glue poured over his head. When Grandma needs pecans for her pies, she remembers Old Man Nyquist's promise that she could have any on the ground. When she finds only a few lying around, she drives the old man's tractor smack into the tree. The impact shakes down enough pecans for a wagonload of pies! On another occasion, during the Armistice Day turkey shoot on the Abernathys' farm, Grandma makes sure that she is in charge of selling the hot stew called burgoo so she can overcharge the well-to-do and make more money to help the impoverished Abernathys. It was extortion, but for a good cause.

Mary Alice is chosen by Miss Butler to play Mary in the school's annual Christmas pageant, and Grandma helps by spending her meager resources to buy Mary Alice a needed pair of shoes. Although the pageant is a fiasco, thanks to the hilarious interference of the Burdick family, Mary Alice's holiday is made complete when her brother Joe visits. Later that winter, Grandma shows her outdoor skill by trapping wild animals like foxes and selling their pelts for provisions.

The spring also brings some noteworthy occurrences. Grandma unmasks the snooty leader of the local DAR as an imposter and acts as a matchmaker for Miss Butler and Arnold Green, a traveling artist whom Grandma takes in as a boarder. Mary Alice's days are brightened when a good-looking, well-behaved boy named Royce McNabb enters her class. However, when Mary Alice invites him over to coach her in math, the giant snake Grandma keeps in the attic to "keep down the birds" decides to make an appearance.

By the end of the year, Mary Alice has become so attached to her eccentric grandmother that she doesn't want to go, but Grandma knows better. Soon World War II comes, brother Joey joins the air force, and Mary Alice's parents get wartime jobs. Before the end of the war, Mary Alice marries soldier Royce McNabb in Grandma's house. Grandma bakes the wedding cake.

Suitability and Critical Comment

This "valentine of a book" creates a sentimental but sympathetic picture of the Depression years in a rural American community where the family values and gentler times reflect different aspects of life than found in most parts of America today. Grandma represents Yankee independence and decency, and Mary Alice is a spunky milder version of her grandmother. Their relationship is portrayed with humor, respect, and love. This book is particularly recommended for readers in grades five through eight.

Themes and Subjects

Christmas, family stories, first love, friendship, grandmothers, Great Depression, Halloween, humor, Illinois, poverty, rural life, school stories, World War II

Passages for Booktalking

Mary Alice is greeted by her grandmother (pp. 2–5); Grandma gets rid of Mildred Burdick (pp. 14–18); Grandma frightens off the Halloween pranksters (pp. 25–28); gathering the pecans (pp. 29–32); she sells the burgoo (pp. 47–54); and Royce and the snake (pp. 104–109).

Additional Suggestions

During World War II, Robert and his mom relocate to the family compound, where the boy encounters a mystery and a bullying grandfather in Janet Taylor Lisle's *The Art of Keeping Cool* (Atheneum, 2000).

Through a series of family documents, the love of a Nebraska farm is revealed in the stories of five teenaged girls from 1869 to the 1960s in Dianne E. Gray's *Holding Up the Earth* (Houghton Mifflin, 2000).

Seventeen-year-old Jenna's job in a shoe store leads to driving the crusty owner across the country to prevent a company takeover in Joan Bauer's *Rules of the Road* (Putnam, 1998).

Rizka, an orphan girl who lives by her wits, is the central character in Lloyd Alexander's humorous adventure, *Gypsy Rizka* (Dutton, 1999).

About the Book

Booklist, Oct. 15, 2000, p. 136.
Bulletin of the Center for Children's Books, Jan., 2001, p. 192.
Horn Book, Nov.-Dec., 2000, p. 761.
Kirkus Reviews, Sept. 15, 2000, p. 1361.
School Library Journal, Sept., 2000, p. 236.

VOYA, Dec., 2000, p. 354.

About the Author

Authors and Artists for Young Adults, vol. 1, Gale, 1989; vol. 24, Gale, 1998.

Children's Literature Review, vol. 15, Gale, 1988.

Continuum Encyclopedia of Children's Literature, Continuum, 2001.

Drew, Bernard A. *The 100 Most Popular Young Adult Authors,* Libraries Unlimited, 1997.

Fifth Book of Junior Authors and Illustrators, Wilson, 1983.

Gallo, Donald. *Presenting Richard Peck,* Twayne, 1989.

Gallo, Donald. *Speaking for Ourselves,* National Council of Teachers of English, 1990.

Hipple, Ted. *Writers for Young Adults,* vol. 3, Scribners, 1999, pp. 1–14.

Lives and Works: Young Adult Authors, vol. 6, Grolier, 1999, pp. 59–61.

Major Authors and Illustrators for Children and Young Adults, vol. 5, Gale, 1993.

McElmeel, Sharron L. *The 100 Most Popular Children's Authors,* Libraries Unlimited, 1997.

"Newbery Acceptance Speech," *Horn Book,* July-Aug., 2001, pp. 397–401.

"Newbery Acceptance Speech-2001," *Journal of Youth Services in Libraries,* Summer, 2001, pp. 354–61.

Peck, Richard. *Anonymously Yours,* Beach Tree, 1992.

Peck, Richard. "From Strawberry Statements to Censorship," *School Library Journal,* Jan., 1997, pp. 28–29.

Peck, Richard. "Love is Not Enough," *Journal of Youth Services in Libraries,* Fall, 1990, pp. 35–39.

St. James Guide to Young Adult Writers (2nd ed.), St. James, 1999.

Silvey, Anita. *Children's Books and Their Creators,* Houghton Mifflin, 1995.

Something about the Author, vol. 18, Gale, 1980; vol. 55, Gale, 1989; vol. 97, Gale, 1998; vol. 110, Gale, 2000.

Something about the Author Autobiography Series, vol. 2, Gale, 1986.

Sutton, Roger. "A Conversation with Richard Peck," *School Library Journal,* June, 1990, pp. 40–42.

Talbert, Marc. "Richard Peck," *Horn Book,* July-Aug., 2001, pp. 403–409.

Twentieth Century Young Adult Writers, St. James, 1994.

Strasser, Todd. *Give a Boy a Gun.* Simon & Schuster, 2000. $16 (0-689-81112-8) (Grades 7–10).

Introduction

Todd Strasser (1950–) was born in New York City and raised in suburban Long Island. In the 1960s, he became a hippie and was one of the attendees at the famous outdoor rock concert at Woodstock in 1969. After various jobs in a number of places, he settled down and studied writing in college. In 1979, his first novel, *Angel Dust Blues* (Coward, 1979), appeared and was an immediate success. It is the story of Alex Lazar, a high-school senior who is arrested for drug dealing. Based on a personal experience, his second book, *Friends till the End* (Dell, 1981), tells of a senior in high school who witnesses the slow deterioration and death of one of his friends. Speaking about his books, Strasser once said, "Most teens today want books with characters they can identify with. They want to be entertained, not preached to. I try to make my books funny, but not frivolous; readable but not patronizing. There's always an important underlying message that I want to get across."

Principal Characters

Gary Searle, high-school student who commits suicide
Brendan Lawlor, Gary's friend who also commits suicide
Ruth Hollington, Gary's fourth-grade teacher
Allison Findley, Gary's sometime girlfriend
Cynthia Searle, Gary's mother
Brett Betzig, Brendan's friend
Emily Kirsch, Brendan's friend
Sam Flach, a particular target of Brendan's rage

Plot Summary

One Friday night in February, two students at Middletown High enter the school gym where a dance featuring the school's football players is being held. The students are Gary Searle and Brendan Lawlor. They are heavily armed with semiautomatic weapons they stole from a neighbor. They have homemade bombs. Their plan is to hold their classmates hostage, but their targets are the football players and the teachers who they believe have tormented them. On this night they want revenge for their imagined torment.

After the shooting rampage that follows, Gary Searle commits suicide with a gun. Brendan is finally attacked by other students, injured so severely that he falls into a coma with irreversible brain damage.

Both Gary and Brendan leave suicide notes. They had been planning this revenge for some time. Gary's suicide note partially explains his actions by saying that he knows he can never be happy, so what is the point of living? He admits that he could have ended his life quietly, but if he takes others with him, he figures that someone will sit up and take notice and maybe some other kid won't be quite so miserable.

Gary's friends talk about him. Allison Findley can't believe that the boy she thought she knew could commit such a crime. Another friend remembers that Gary was always grumbling about the big school jocks and how he would like to kick their faces in. But no one took him seriously. Gary's elementary school teacher remembers him as a sweet-faced, polite boy whom the kids often teased about his weight. Gary's mother regrets that her son was caught in the middle of a particularly nasty divorce proceeding between herself and her husband.

Brendan's suicide note rants against parents, kids, teachers, all of those who have ruined his life. Now what he wants is to pay them back. He is tired of being ridiculed, he says.

Brendan's friends admit that he was picked on, although they point out that anyone who wasn't big and strong and on an athletic team was often picked on. It's just the way things were. Most of the kids accepted it and forgot it; some remembered and began to hate. But Brendan began to get a reputation for not backing down from this torment. He had an attitude.

Apparently Brendan never forgot these insults, particularly from Sam Flach, a jock. Sometime before the rampage, Brendan sends an e-mail to Gary in which he describes how Flach will die slowly. Brendan will start by shooting him in the knees, and then he will put the gun barrel against his forehead and blow his brains out. Brendan does shoot Flach in the knees during the carnage. Flach survives with two knees that will never be good again, and he is unforgiving toward Brendan and Gary.

After the terrible incident, schoolmates and teachers reflect on what brought these two young men to such desperate and terrible actions. Some find it impossible to forgive or even to understand; some try to reflect on what went wrong in two young lives. All blame to a large extent the ease with which Gary and Brendan were able to obtain guns to shoot others and themselves.

Suitability and Critical Comment

This timely book is easily read by high-school students. The author's use of diary-like entries throughout, with various classmates and teachers commenting on the lives and actions of the young men, adds to the stark realism and tragedy of the disaster. Strasser dwells on stress and violence among teenagers, particularly how the easy availability of guns affects the emotions and actions of young people. For grades seven through ten.

Themes and Subjects

Athletics, guns, hostages, school relationships, suicide, teenagers, violence

Passages for Booktalking

Classmates talk about Gary (pp. 6–10); classmates talk about Brendan (pp. 12–16); Brendan's e-mail to Gary (pp. 33–34); part of Brendan's suicide note (p. 41); the shooting at the gym begins (pp. 83–92).

Additional Selections

Townspeople wonder why a boy takes his father's gun and shoots an elderly storekeeper in Virginia Walter's *Making Up Megaboy* (DK, 1997).

Jamal, age twelve, struggles to survive in the inner city; then someone gives him a gun in *Scorpions* (HarperCollins, 1988) by Walter Dean Myers.

High-school dropout Zachary tries to conceal his rage and frustrations, but when his father is shot, he arms himself with a .38 in Michael Cadnum's *Edge* (Puffin, 1997).

Writers such as Chris Crutcher and Jack Gantos explore the world of the outsider in *On the Fringe* (Dial, 2001), a collection of short stories edited by Donald R. Gallo.

About the Book
Booklist, Oct. 1, 2000, p. 337.
Bulletin of the Center for Children's Books, Oct., 2000, p. 83.
Kirkus Reviews, July 1, 2000, p. 967.
School Library Journal, Sept., 2000, p. 237.
VOYA, Oct., 2000, p. 270.

About the Author
Authors and Artists for Young Adults, vol. 2, Gale, 1989; vol. 35, Gale, 2000.
Children's Literature Review, vol. 11, Gale, 1986.
Drew, Bernard A. *The 100 Most Popular Young Adult Authors,* Libraries Unlimited, 1997.
Hipple, Ted. *Writers for Young Adults,* vol. 3, Scribners, 1997, pp. 225–36.
Lives and Works: Young Adult Authors, vol. 7, Grolier, 1999, pp. 86–88.
Major Authors and Illustrators for Children and Young Adults, vol. 5, Gale, 1993.
St. James Guide to Young Adult Writers (2nd ed.), St. James, 1999.
Something about the Author, vol. 41, Gale, 1985; vol. 45, Gale, 1986; vol. 71, Gale, 1993; vol. 107, Gale, 1999.

Tan, Amy. *The Joy Luck Club.* Putnam, 1989; Pb. Vintage, 1991. $11.00 (0-679-72768-X) (Grades 10–12).

Introduction

Amy Tan (1952–) was born in Oakland, California, to immigrant Chinese parents. Her father arrived in this country in 1947, and her mother, who was one of the last people allowed out of Communist China, arrived in 1949. Amy Tan's childhood and youth were filled with constant conflict because of her demanding, possessive mother, who was overly ambitious for her daughter. The author has said, "I remember feeling the pressure from the time I was five years old." In addition to being pressured to excel in everything she tried, further conflicts arose when Amy Tan became Americanized and her mother wanted her to remain Chinese. After marriage and work as a freelance technical writer, she decided to work out some of the family conflicts by writing about these problems. The result was a series of stories like "The Rules of the Game." These were later incorporated into the full-length novel *The Joy Luck Club,* a series of interconnected stories told in the first person by four Chinese mothers and their four American-ized daughters.

Principal Characters

Jing-mei "June" Woo and her mother, Suyuan Woo
Rose Hsu Jordan and her mother, An-mei Hsu
Waverly Jong and her mother, Lindo Jong
Lena St. Clair and her mother, Ying-ying St. Clair

Plot Summary

The book is composed of sixteen interlocking stories that speak of the relationships between the members of the Joy Luck Club and their daughters. The Joy Luck Club has been meeting to play mah-jongg and eat Chinese delicacies for some forty years. Through these stories, the daughters learn of their mothers' secret lives before they left China for the United States. The lives of these women in China also help to explain their personalities and their conflicts with their Americanized daughters. It shows how alliances and affiliations are interlocked, and it emphasizes the deep love in the family relationships but also the misunderstandings between generations and cultures.

All of the stories concern the sometimes loving, sometimes rocky relationships between the mothers and daughters. Perhaps the main pairing is Jing-Mei "June" Woo and her mother, Suyuan Woo. June has been asked by her father to become the fourth corner at the Joy Luck Club to replace her mother, who died two months ago. June agrees out of love and respect for her parents, although her knowledge of mah-jongg is superficial. As she goes to attend the club meeting, June remembers her mother's story of her life in Kweilin in China. As a child, June believed that the story was a fairy tale. Then one evening she heard a completely different ending. Her mother had told of how four young women gathered at the mah-jongg table to escape the fear and horror of the forthcoming Japanese invasion. But this time, June learns that when her mother escaped, she left behind not only her homeland, but also her two babies. June learns that her own father was not her mother's first husband.

At the mah-jongg table that evening, Auntie Lin speaks of June's half sisters in China. Auntie Lin gives her a check saved from the mah-jongg winnings, with a request that she go to China to find her half sisters and tell them of her mother's death. They must know how she lived and how she died.

At the age of thirty-six, June travels with her father to a land she never knew. On this trip she begins to understand what it means to be Chinese. She also learns that a letter sent from her half sisters to America was opened by her father, which was the first time he knew that his wife had been married previously. He had given the letter to the Joy Luck Club ladies, and they had decided that instead of replying by mail, June and her father should travel to China to tell the now-grown half sisters of the woman their mother had been. The Joy Luck Club ladies insist that it is important to put on record the life of Suyuan Woo.

June meets her half sisters in China, and she learns of the bravery of her mother, who tried to save her twin daughters in the only way she knew how. She knew that if she kept the babies with her in her attempt to escape, they would have been caught and possibly put to death. Now, in this strange but joyous family reunion, June begins to understand and to appreciate in a way she had never done before, that the Chinese part of her is in her blood and in her family.

In a similar manner, the other three young women in the novel come to terms with their heritage. They cannot always understand or accept the ways of their mothers, but they come to see some of the reasons behind the actions. Through love and patience, they all try to deal with the intertwining of two different cultures in the same families.

Suitability and Critical Comment

This book is easily read by most students in junior and senior high school. The stories of the mothers' lives in China are touching and will give young readers a good understanding of the older women's concerns for their Americanized daughters. The author writes powerfully of the ways in which even the daughters are forever linked to the ancient culture of their family homeland. She also shows the struggle between two cultures in the same family; for grades seven through twelve.

Themes and Subjects

China, daughters, death, family relationships, fear, foreign culture, mothers, war

Passages for Booktalking

June's mother speaks of China (pp. 21–26); June goes to the Joy Luck Club meeting (pp. 27–41); An-mei Hsu tells her story (pp. 42–48); Lindo

Jong speaks of life in China (pp. 54–61); Ying-ying St. Clair speaks of her fears (pp. 67–83); June and her father go to China and learn her mother's story (pp. 279–86).

Additional Selections

In the nonfiction autobiography *Paper Shadow: A Memoir of the Lost and Found* (Picador, USA, 2000) by Wayson Choy, the author tells of his immigrant childhood in Vancouver's Chinatown and of the discovery of his mother's true identity.

Adeline Yen Mah's *Chinese Cinderella: The True Story of an Unwanted Daughter* (Delacorte, 1999) is the heartbreaking nonfiction account of the author's struggle with her stepmother.

Pressured by her strict Korean parents to get into Harvard, high-school senior Ellen Sung tries to lead a normal life in Marie G. Lee's *Finding My Voice* (Demco, 1994).

Kat—or "China Boy" as he is called by the neighborhood bullies—turns his life around when he learns to fight back in Gus Lee's *China Boy* (NAL, 1994).

About the Book

Booklist, March 1, 1989, p. 1093.
Kirkus Reviews, Jan. 1, 1989, p. 15.
Library Journal, Feb. 15, 1989, p. 178.
New York Times Book Review, March 19, 1989, p. 3.

About the Author

Authors and Artists for Young Adults, vol. 9, Gale, 1992.
Contemporary Authors New Revision Series, vol. 105, Gale, 2002.
Current Biography, Wilson, Feb, 1992.
Lives and Works: Young Adult Authors, vol. 7, Grolier, pp. 92–94.
St. James Guide to Young Adult Writers (2nd ed.), St. James, 1999.
Something about the Author, vol. 75, Gale, 1994.
Twentieth Century Young Adult Writers, St. James, 1994.

Trueman, Terry. *Stuck in Neutral.* HarperCollins, 2000. $15.95 (0-06-028519-2); pb. $6.95 (0-06-447213-2) (Grades 7–10).

Introduction

Terry Trueman, who has worked as a writer, teacher, and mental-health counselor, holds graduate degrees in creative writing and applied psychology and presently lives with his family in Spokane, Washington. He has cowritten two books on learning theory and young adult reading. The character, Shawn, and the basic situation in *Stuck in Neutral* are based on the author's personal experiences. He, too, has a son, Sheehan, who is a victim of cerebral palsy and cannot communicate. In an afterword to the novel, Mr. Trueman wonders if his son is like Shawn, with a rich inner life. He says "Is Sheehan a secret genius, like Shawn in this story? Inside himself is he witty and funny and wise? Is he happy to be alive? I can't say 'yes' to any of these questions. But I can't say 'no' either." Each of the sixteen brief chapters in this short (a little over 100 pages) book is preceded by a few lines excerpted from the long poem that Shawn's father wrote about his son's special condition and the family's adjustment to it.

Principal Characters

Shawn McDaniel, the fourteen-year-old narrator who is completely incapacitated physically

Lindy (Linda) McDaniel, Shawn's understanding, patient mother

Sydney E. McDaniel, Shawn's father, a successful writer and popular talk-show guest on television

Cindy, Shawn's supportive seventeen-year-old sister

Paul, Shawn's sixteen-year-old brother, who is fiercely caring of Shawn

Earl Detraux, a young man who is in prison for killing his severely handicapped young son

Plot Summary

Outwardly, it appears that fourteen-year-old Shawn McDaniel has three strikes against him. He suffered brain damage at birth and also is a victim of severe cerebral palsy. He is unable to talk, walk, or control any of his bodily functions. He experiences as many as twelve grand mal seizures per day, which produce uncontrollable twitching, unearthly laughter, and extreme exhaustion. Although the pain from these seizures is now drug-controlled, an interesting side effect is the out-of-body sensations Shawn feels during them. Unknown to everyone, Shawn has a rich inner life. He is an intelligent, sensitive youngster who has taught himself to read, has a phenomenal memory, and possesses an amazing joy for life even though he cannot communicate with anyone. As he says, "Life can be great, even for me." Shawn is cared for by his loving Seattle-based family: his mother, Lindy (for Linda), and two older siblings—sister Cindy, seventeen, and his sports-minded, fiercely protective brother, sixteen-year-old Paul. Not long ago, Paul almost killed two young thugs who were molesting his helpless brother. Shawn's father, Sydney McDaniel, is something of an enigma. He is a hugely successful poet and nonfiction writer, as well as a TV talk-show personality. His Pulitzer Prize–winning poem "Shawn" is an exploration of his feelings concerning his son's condition. He has, however, been unable to accept or cope with his son's total immobility, and when Shawn was four, he divorced Lindy. Though he visits his family regularly, he continues to dwell on Shawn's condition and believes, incorrectly, that his son is suffering endless torment with no hope for the future. Mrs. McDaniel and Cindy have adjusted to the divorce, but Paul despises his father, who he believes has deserted them. Shawn is convinced that his father harbors thoughts of euthanasia, not out of repugnance or hate, but from feelings of pity and love. This feeling is reinforced when Mr. McDaniel, on a TV assignment, visits Shawn's special ed. class, run by Mrs. Hare, and questions the rationale behind spending huge amounts of money on the severely retarded, when the humane action might be to "end their pain." Meanwhile, Shawn finds pleasure and fulfillment in a variety of ways, particularly in exploring his growing sexual awareness through watching and dreaming about his sister's girlfriends, especially the gorgeous Ally, who sometimes visits his home for a slumber party. Shawn's father has become involved with a sensational criminal case in Washington involving Earl Detraux, a sensitive young father who has been sent to prison for smothering his two-year-old severely retarded son, Colin, with a pillow. Mr. McDaniel has interviewed the prisoner for a segment on a TV talk show and, during the show, Shawn hears his father express sympathy and understanding for Detraux's action. Several days later, Shawn becomes apprehensive when he learns that his mother and Cindy will be driving on an overnight trip to Spokane to see Paul play in an important basketball tournament. Shortly after they leave, Shawn's father arrives and sends the babysitter home, telling her that he will stay overnight and care for Shawn. As he sits next to his son with a pillow cradled in his lap, he soliloquizes about the love he feels. He says, "When I think about you, Shawn, my heart breaks and when I think of you hurting, I can barely even breathe." Though filled with dread and foreboding, Shawn longs to tell his father how deeply he also loves him, but at that moment he has a seizure and sinks into oblivion.

Suitability and Critical Comment

In this poignant story, the reader is able to explore the inner feelings and thoughts of a sensitive mind trapped inside a nonfunctioning body. It is an intense reading experience that asks many questions concerning society's treatment of the severely handicapped. Though uncompromising and often grim, there are many brilliant flashes of humor and optimism throughout. It is recommended for readers in grades seven through ten.

Themes and Subjects

Cerebral palsy, death, euthanasia, family problems, family stories, physical handicaps, Seattle, Washington

Passages for Booktalking

Shawn describes his physical condition (in paperback edition, pp. 6–8); Shawn witnesses the death of a dog (pp. 13–17); Shawn is alone with his father (pp. 18–20); the first reading of the poem "Shawn" (pp. 26–30); and Shawn describes a typical seizure (pp. 32–35).

Additional Selections

Thrown out by his mother, sixteen-year-old Laker Wyatt is taken in by an elderly man and given work in *Being with Henry* (DK, 2000) by Martha Brooks.

A fourteen-year-old boy who is a social outcast and living in an abusive home begins living outside himself in *You Don't Know Me* (Farrar, 2001) by David Klass.

Benjamin, a sixteen-year-old with cerebral palsy, becomes friendly with the school's infamous druggie in Ron Koertge's *Stoner and Spaz* (Candlewick, 2002).

Rachel Anderson's *The Bus People* (Holt, 1992) focuses on six physically, emotionally, or mentally disabled passengers who ride Bertram's bus daily to a special school.

About the Book

Booklist, July, 2000, p. 2034.
Book Report, Jan. 1, 2001, p. 862.
Bulletin of the Center for Children's Books, June, 2000, p. 377.
Horn Book, May-June, 2000, p. 323.
Kirkus Reviews, June 1, 2000, p. 804.
School Library Journal, July, 2000, p. 111.
VOYA, Dec., 2000, p. 356.

About the Author

No information available.

Wolff, Virginia Euwer. *Make Lemonade.* Holt, 1993. $17.95
  (0-8050-2228-7) (Grades 7–12).

Introduction

Make Lemonade is the first of a projected trilogy by Virginia Euwer Wolff
(1937–) that features as narrator and principal character, Verna LaVaughn
(named after two aunts), a racially unidentified young girl who is growing
up in an inner-city housing project in an unidentified American city where
poverty, drugs, and violence continually hover in the background. It is told
in sixty-six brief chapters, each of which tells of a single incident or set of
impressions using a flowing stream of consciousness, free-verse style. In the
second novel, *True Believer,* LaVaughn, now fifteen, encounters some social
problems. She drifts apart from her two "born again" friends and develops
a crush on Jody, a boy who has moved back into her neighborhood. He
seems to return her attentions, but one day she sees him kissing another
boy. As in the first novel, LaVaughn learns that when life gives you lemons,
you make lemonade.

Principal Characters

Verna LaVaughn, known as LaVaughn, a bright, determined fourteen-
  year-old girl whose goals are to attend college and leave the squalid
  housing project where she lives
Mom, LaVaughn's mother, a single parent who is hardworking, resourceful, and determined to instill good values and work habits in her
  only child
Jolly, a confused and ineffective seventeen-year-old single mother of two
  children
Jeremy, Jolly's two-year-old son
Jilly, Jolly's daughter, who is at the crawling stage

Plot Outline

With her mother's constant encouragement and nagging, fourteen-year-
old LaVaughn, a ninth grader, has already set up a college fund for herself so
that one day she will be able to gain the skills and knowledge to leave the sor-
did, crime-ridden projects where she is living with Mom. Her mother is a
resourceful, no-nonsense working woman who is also head of the Tenant
Council in their sixty-four-apartment complex. When LaVaughn was still a
child, her father, whom she revered, was killed in a senseless drive-by shooting while he was playing basketball in the neighborhood park. Thinking she
might add to her bank account, LaVaughn answers an ad posted at school

that says, "Bebysitter needed bad." It leads her to a miserable, filthy apartment where seventeen-year-old Jolly (a perfect misnomer) lives with her two
young children, Jeremy and baby Jilly, along with countless cockroaches.
Jolly, a semi-illiterate without family or friends, seems so overwhelmed by life
and its responsibilities that she has become incapable of coping with the
squalor and confusion that is her life. She has taken a night job in a factory
and needs a baby-sitter. LaVaughn gets her mother's reluctant permission
and settles in. The girl tries to bring some order and sanitation into Jolly's
household. She begins potty training for Jeremy; cleans up some of the filth
that covers the floors, furniture, and walls of the apartment; and even plants
some lemon seeds, hoping to show Jeremy the miracle of life. Some progress
seems to be made when disaster strikes. Jolly loses her job after she uses force
to resist the sexual advances of her boss. Unwilling to accept welfare for fear
she will lose her children, Jolly tries to get a new job, but lacking any skills,
she is unsuccessful and sinks into lethargy and inaction. It is apparent that she
needs as much help as her children do. LaVaughn, though now without pay,
continues to offer her assistance, realizing that she must tactfully take charge
and get Jolly some direction in her life. Secretly she investigates the program
that exists in her school to educate young mothers and supply day-care facili-
ties while they are receiving training. Reluctantly, Jolly accepts LaVaughn's
help in filling out an application to join the program. After she is accepted,
she begins classes once more through the guidance of LaVaughn. Through
the program's funds, LaVaughn is hired as a home-care helper to mind
Jeremy and Jilly after school hours, to give Jolly time to do her homework.
LaVaughn and the children form strong bonds of love and understanding.
Jolly's financial problems ease somewhat when she accepts welfare payments
as well as food stamps. One competency that Jolly learns is how to administer
CPR, and this skill proves invaluable immediately when she saves Jilly's life
after the child has swallowed a plastic toy. In one of her classes, Jolly hears the
tale of the blind woman who, after being hoodwinked into accepting a
lemon instead of an orange, makes the best of things by making lemonade.
This becomes the metaphor of Jolly's new life. Through her schooling, she
begins to change her attitude, gain confidence, and plan for the future.
Gradually her life becomes more orderly—as LaVaughn's mother says, the
program has "taken hold." As the months pass, Jolly no longer needs
LaVaughn's help, and the two gradually drift apart. But one day they meet in
a school hallway, where Jolly tells LaVaughn that an amazing thing has just
happened: the lemon seeds have at last sprouted.

Suitability and Critical Comment

Without undue sentiment or didacticism, this novel shows how positive attitude, perseverance, and resourcefulness can conquer many of life's problems. In spite of the staggering everyday problems that face both LaVaughn and her mother, the two are able to face their problems with hope and common sense. This novel is suitable for readers in grades seven through twelve.

Themes and Subjects

Baby-sitting, courage, family stories, friendship, inner-city life, poverty, school life, single mothers

Passages for Booktalking

LaVaughn meets Jolly and her kids (chapters 2 and 3); Mom stresses going to college (chapter 4); LaVaughn asks her mother permission to baby-sit (chapters 5 and 6); Jeremy waits for the lemon seeds to sprout (chapter 11); Jeremy gets toilet trained (chapter 13).

Additional Selections

High-school junior Bernadette discovers that her handsome English teacher has been falsifying school records in Nan Willard Cappo's *Cheating Lessons* (Atheneum, 2002).

Lyric finds that her older sister Summer is gradually withdrawing into herself after the death of their mother in Ruth White's *Memories of Summer* (Farrar, 2000).

Kady rebels against her responsibilities, which include taking care of both a mentally handicapped boy named Rooster and her senile grandmother, in Beth Weaver's *Rooster* (Winslow, 2001).

Thirteen-year-old Raspberry Hill, who lives in the projects, obsessively tries to make money to help her hardworking mother in Sharon G. Flake's *Money Hungry* (Hyperion, 2001).

About the Book
Booklist, June 1, 1993, p. 1813.
Bulletin of the Center for Children's Books, July, 1993, p. 361.
Horn Book, Sept.-Oct., 1993, p. 606.
Kirkus Reviews, May 15, 1993, p. 303.
School Library Journal, July, 1993, p. 103.
VOYA, Oct., 1993, p. 220.

About the Author
Authors and Artists for Young Adults, vol. 26, Gale, 1999.
Children's Literature Review, vol. 62, Gale, 2000.

3

Mystery and Adventure

Clancy, Tom. *The Hunt for Red October.* Berkeley, 1985. Pb. $7.50
(0-425-13351-6) (Grades 10–12).

Introduction

Tom Clancy (1947–), one of the most successful writers about the military, espionage, and technology, has been called the "king of the techno-thrillers." Before he became the writer of a series of blockbuster adventure page-turners, he was an insurance agent. His life changed dramatically with the publication of his first novel, *The Hunt for Red October* (Naval Institute Press, 1984). The story is of a race between U.S. and Soviet forces who are vying to seize a defecting Russian submarine commander and his state-of-the art vessel. His second novel, *Red Storm Rising* (Putnam, 1986), again deals with U.S.–Soviet conflicts, which, in this story, erupt into a nonnuclear World War III.

In *Patriot Games* (Putnam, 1997), Marine officer Jack Ryan returns from *Red October* and is caught between a fanatical branch of the Irish Republican Army and the British royal family. Each of Clancy's novels has been a best-seller, selling millions of copies and pleasing countless adventure-hungry fans.

Principal Characters

Marko Ramius, captain of a Soviet sub
Jack Ryan, CIA analyst
James Greer, vice admiral and Ryan's superior
Yevgeni Petrov, doctor on board the *Red October*
Bart Mancuso, U.S. sub commander

Plot Summary

Captain Marko Ramius is the most respected man in the Soviet underwater navy. In fact, he has trained most other captains in the Russian fleet.

Now, on this day in December, he sets out in the *Red October* as commander of a submarine carrying the newest in Russian technology. It is a great advance in underwater warfare because the *Red October* has a special propulsion system that makes it all but invisible to conventional forms of detection. It has the capability of sneaking up on major cities anywhere in the world without being detected.

The United States tracks the *Red October* from the moment it leaves the Soviet shipyard. The U.S. military is concerned over the existence of such a dangerous new weapon. It is baffled when the sub almost immediately seems to disappear from any detection gear and shakes loose of the American attack submarine sent to shadow it. It is more puzzled still when the sub appears at sea and is heading toward the east coast of the United States and then disappears again. Then it looks as though the entire Soviet Navy is trying to chase the *Red October* around the Atlantic Ocean. The Russians say that Ramius has become a madman who aims at hiding the sub off the American coast and attacking New York or Washington with its nuclear missiles. Both nations become terrified with the idea of an out-of-control weapon of mass destruction aboard a submarine whose destination remains unknown.

However, Jack Ryan, a junior analyst for the CIA who specializes in naval research, has his own idea of what is happening. He has become convinced, after long studies of Ramius, that the man is not planning to attack the United States but wants to defect. He tells his superior, Admiral James Greer, that Ramius is not only planning to defect, but wants to bring the submarine intact along with him.

The top military brass at first do not agree with Ryan. Both the U.S. Navy and the Soviet Navy go on full alert. But slowly Ryan manages to convince the powers that there is some validity to his claims. The United States finds the *Red October* when the sub is about two hundred miles away. The plan is to contact the sub and then fool the Russians so that they do not believe Ramius has defected.

Meanwhile, Ramius tells the crew of a malfunction on the sub that will cause them to abandon ship. An American ship is close by, he says, and will take them aboard. Ryan boards the sub and speaks with Ramius. When the crew leaves, Ramius asks political asylum for himself and his officers. It is granted. The U.S. Navy explodes an old missile submarine about two miles away, fooling the Russians into thinking that the *Red October* has been destroyed and that Ramius and some of his officers have died. Ryan thinks they have been successful, but he discovers one of the Russian crew still aboard and ready to defend his homeland. In the fight, Ramius is shot, although not fatally, but Ryan kills the Russian sailor.

After an almost predictable confrontation between U.S. and Soviet subs, in which the *Red October* is damaged but not sunk and the United States suffers some casualties, it looks as though the Americans have accomplished their plan to have the Russians believe the nuclear sub and Ramius are lost. Ramius and his officers are promised safety in the United States, and Jack Ryan is congratulated on a job well done.

Suitability and Critical Comment

This is an exciting sea adventure that should be enjoyed and read by most competent readers. The constant action makes this a taut tale of cat and mouse under the sea. The Russian Ramius appears as an intelligent, competent officer who has thought through his plans carefully and knows what he is doing. The interplay between U.S. military and government powers heightens the suspense for readers in grades ten through twelve.

Themes and Subjects

CIA, courage, defection, honesty, international politics, loyalty, submarines, underwater technology, USSR, war

Passages for Booktalking

Ramius talks to his officers (pp. 37–43); Ryan tells the president about the defection (pp. 101–17); they find the *Red October* (pp. 293–303); Ryan boards the *Red October* (pp. 338–44); Ryan and Ramius say good-bye (pp. 461–64).

Additional Selections

A first-year game warden in Wyoming uncovers a plot involving an oil pipeline and an endangered species in *Open Season* (Putnam, 2001) by C. J. Box.

A bookstore owner investigates a lurid murder in her community and unexpectedly locates the son she gave up for adoption in *God Bless the Child* (Simon, 1998) by Ellen Feldman.

Jim Dutton, an anthropologist, and reporter Valerie Radin suspect the existence of secret genetic engineering on apes in *Dark Inheritance* (Berkeley, 2001) by W. Michael Gear and Kathleen O'Neal.

Edgar Rice Burroughs and his son solve a murder just before the bombing of Pearl Harbor on December 7, 1941, in *The Pearl Harbor Murders* (Berkeley, 2001) by Max Allan Collins.

About the Book

Booklist, Nov. 1, 1984, p. 341.
New York Times Book Review, April 21, 1985, p. 24.

About the Author

Authors and Artists for Young Adults, vol. 9, Gale, 1992.
Clancy, Tom, et al. *The Tom Clancy Companion,* Berkeley Books, 1992.
Contemporary Authors New Revision Series, vol. 105, Gale, 2002.
Contemporary Literary Criticism, vol. 45, 1987.
Current Biography, Wilson, April, 1988.

Clark, Mary Higgins. *Before I Say Goodbye.* Simon & Schuster, 2000.
$26.00 (0-684-83598-3) (Grades 9–12).

Introduction

Mary Higgins Clark (1929–), master storyteller of novels with suspenseful, tightly woven plots and believable characters, was born in New York City, where she attended school and college, graduating from Fordham University summa cum laude. She held many positions in the media world, including that of scriptwriter and producer of radio programs. Her first national best-seller was *Where Are the Children?* (Simon & Schuster, 1975). It deals with multiple-personality problems and a manipulative villain who fiendishly preys on Nancy, a likable, vulnerable mother, and makes her twice the victim of the kidnapping and abuse of her children. Since this auspicious beginning, Ms. Clark has written almost two dozen thrillers, some of her latest being collaborations with her talented daughter. Most of her novels deal with average people pursuing ordinary lives who are suddenly plunged without warning into dangerous, nightmarish situations. Another characteristic of her works is the many twists of plot that end with a last, unexpected twist that leaves the reader wanting more.

Principal Characters

Nell MacDermott, a newspaper columnist who has psychic gifts
Adam Cauliff, her architect husband
Cornelius MacDermott, Nell's grandfather and a longtime congressman
Gert, Nell's great-aunt who also has psychic gifts
Bonnie Wilson, a medium
Winifred Johnson, Adam's assistant
Jimmy Ryan, a construction foreman
Lisa Ryan, Jimmy's wife
Peter Lang, a wealthy real-estate entrepreneur
Dan Minor, a doctor who is attracted to Nell
Ben Tucker, an eight-year-old boy

Plot Summary

Ever since she was fifteen years old and nearly died when caught in a rip-tide, Nell MacDermott has known she possesses a psychic gift. As she was drowning, she heard the voices of her dead parents urging her to save herself, which she did. Nell's grandfather, the gruff but loving Cornelius MacDermott, longtime congressman, does not believe any of what he thinks is "psychic nonsense," so Nell rarely speaks of it. Now thirty-two years old and married to architect Adam Cauliff, Nell writes a successful column for a newspaper. However, Cornelius, now in his eighties, has decided to retire, and he wants Nell to run for his congressional seat. She had been interested in running some years before, but Adam opposed the idea. Now, she tells her grandfather that she has decided to run.

When she tells Adam about her decision to run, a quarrel follows. He leaves the house for a business meeting on his yacht in New York harbor. Adam is supposed to close a deal on a spectacular real-estate construction project. It partly involves land he has just purchased and that has now greatly increased in value. Adam expects to be head architect on this lucrative project. Adam; his secretary, Winifred Johnson; Sam Krause, the builder; Jimmy Ryan, construction foreman; and Peter Lang, real-estate entrepreneur, are supposed to meet on the boat and close the deal. But Lang has a car accident while driving to the meeting, so they sail out into the harbor without him. Suddenly the yacht blows up, witnessed by eight-year-old Ben Tucker, who is on a sightseeing boat.

Jack Sclafani and George Brennan, assigned to the case, soon suspect a bomb. At first, they focus on Jed Kaplan, whose mother owned the property that Adam bought for what Jed considers "a steal." Focus also falls on Peter Lang, who stands to benefit, and Jimmy Ryan, whose shady past makes him a suspect. When Ryan's wife, Lisa, finds $50,000 hidden in their home, she suspects it was money to pay him off because the construction firm was using shoddy materials, and she confides in the detectives.

With Aunt Gert's urging, Nell sees psychic Bonnie Wilson, who tells her that Adam has appeared to her. Nell feels that there is some reason for his appearance and tries to investigate the bombing on her own. In the meantime, she meets Dan Minor, a doctor who has recently moved to New York and is looking for his long-disappeared mother, who has become one of Manhattan's homeless.

The case starts to become clear when Ben Tucker, who has been having psychological problems ever since witnessing the explosion of the yacht, reveals that he saw a figure in black swimming away from the yacht and carrying a woman's handbag. Someone obviously escaped from the bombing, and Nell begins to wonder if it could have been Adam. Indeed, she begins to have doubts that she ever really knew the man she married. She also begins to have premonitions of her own danger in a fire.

When Nell visits Bonnie Wilson once again, Adam appears—in real life. He tries to kill her by burning Bonnie's apartment, but she is rescued by the detectives and by Dan Minor. Adam planned the bombing with the help of the duped Winifred Johnson and Bonnie Wilson. He had discovered that he was not going to be given the architect's job for the enormous construction project. Jimmy Ryan had been paid the $50,000 to cause a fire in the building next to Adam's property, which enhanced the project for Adam.

Nell decides to run for her grandfather's congressional seat. On election night, she accepts the congratulations of her grandfather and a new interest in her life, Dr. Dan.

Suitability and Critical Comment

This is a typical Mary Higgins Clark mystery novel, with fast-paced action and plausible characters without much depth. The reading is easy and the plot has enough twists and turns to keep readers guessing. It is enough of a mystery to keep young fans in grades nine through twelve interested.

Themes and Subjects

Extrasensory perception, family relationships, marriage, murder, New York City, politics

Passages for Booktalking

Nell has a psychic experience (pp. 15–16); Cornelius asks Nell to run for Congress (pp. 20–26); Ben sees the explosion (pp. 56–58); Lisa finds the $50,000 (pp. 85–89); Bonnie Wilson visits Aunt Gert and says she has made contact with Adam (pp. 109–12); Nell sees Bonnie Wilson (pp. 179–83); Nell goes to Wilson's apartment and sees Adam (pp. 311–13).

Additional Selections

Ute police officer Charlie Moon and his Aunt Daisy, a shaman who deals in visions, solve the mystery of the disappearance of two women in *Grandmother Spider: A Charlie Moon Mystery* (Morrow, 2001) by James D. Doss.

When her police hero husband is kidnapped by a group out to avenge murders that occurred years ago, sleuth/reporter wife swings into action in *Hocus* (Simon, 1997) by Jan Burke.

In Margaret Coel's *The Story Teller* (Prime Crime, 1998), Native American lawyer Vicky Holden begins a quest for an ancient ledger book that leads to murder.

Ann Waverly, a theology professor, is called in to conduct an undercover investigation of an international cult group in *A Darker Place* (Bantam, 1999) by Laurie R. King.

About the Book
Booklist, April 15, 2000, p. 1500.
Kirkus Reviews, April 1, 2000, p. 404.
New York Times Book Review, April 16, 2000, p. 32.

About the Author
Authors and Artists for Young Adults, vol. 10, Gale, 1993.
Contemporary Authors New Revision Series, vol. 102, Gale, 2002.
Current Biography, Wilson, Jan., 1994.
St. James Guide to Young Adult Writers (2nd ed.), St. James, 1999.
Twentieth Century Young Adult Writers, St. James, 1994.

Creech, Sharon. *The Wanderer.* HarperCollins, 2000. $15.95 (0-06-027730-0); pb. $5.99 (0-06-441032-3) (Grades 5–8).

Introduction
Sharon Creech leads a double life. For most of the year, she lives in England as the wife of the headmaster of the TASIS England American School at Thorpe, Surrey, where she also teaches literature. During the summer, she returns to a cottage on Lake Chautauqua in upstate New York, where she visits with her family and grown children. Her first American publication was *Walk Two Moons* (HarperCollins, 1994), for which she received the 1995 Newbery Medal. It tells of thirteen-year-old Salamanca Tree Hiddle—proud of the "Indian-ness in her blood"—and the car trip she takes with her grandparents, retracing the route that her missing mother took. *The Wanderer,* the name of the ship on which the main action takes place, is told through quotes from two contrasting journals. The first and most extensive is kept by Sophie, the novel's principal character. Like her, it is thoughtful, observant, and sensitive. The other is written by Cody, her irrepressible cousin and, like him, is terse, matter-of-fact, humorous, and sometimes flip.

Principal Characters
Sophie, a sensitive thirteen-year-old girl who is afraid to acknowledge her past
Uncle Dock, an understanding, easygoing, kind gentleman who is a carpenter and captain of *The Wanderer*

Uncle Stew, a distant, precise man who is pedantic and a perfectionist
Brian, Stew's quiet, serious, socially inept son
Uncle Mo, a likable, chubby man who likes to give orders
Cody, Mo's son, a loud, impulsive, charming young man
Bompie, Sophie's beloved grandfather who lives in England

Plot Summary

Thirteen-year-old Sophie is thrilled beyond belief when her parents give permission for her to leave their Kentucky home and accompany her bachelor uncle, Dock, on his two-masted sailing ship, *The Wanderer*, for a transatlantic voyage to visit her ailing seventy-two-year-old grandfather Bompie (real name Ulysses). Sophie is a sensitive but tough youngster who has always had a powerful, sometimes frightening attraction to the sea. Accompanying her and Dock as crew and passengers are Dock's two brothers (also Sophie's uncles), Stew and Mo, and Sophie's two cousins—Stew's son Brian and Mo's son Cody. Both Brian and Cody are older than Sophie. Brian is like his father: priggish, controlling, overly organized, and difficult to like. Cody is the total opposite—charming and attractive, but also flighty and irresponsible. After provisions and equipment have been stowed away, manuals read, and farewells spoken, they begin their voyage with a shakedown cruise up the Atlantic from their Connecticut port, to make sure that *The Wanderer* is really shipshape and ready for the ocean voyage. They first stop at Block Island and then move on to Martha's Vineyard, where they visit with Dock's friend Joe, who has spent the last five years rebuilding an old boat he found in a swamp. Their third and last stop is at Grand Manan Island in the Bay of Fundy, just west of Nova Scotia. Here they meet more friends of Dock's, Frank and his family, who take Sophie lobstering and clamming. Cody and Sophie also take off in a dinghy to visit a nearby island where they explore the deserted remains of a settlement they romantically like to think is haunted. Later, Sophie learns that the three stops were at places that Dock associates with Rosalie, the girlfriend he loved and lost. On the open ocean, each performs regular chores and also shares his or her special knowledge. For example, Mo teaches radio code, Cody teaches juggling skills, and Sophie tells stories about the childhood of Grandpa Bompie. Everyone is convinced that Sophie is making up these stories because, as we learn from Cody's journal, Sophie was adopted only three years ago. When Brian cruelly confronts Sophie with questions about her origins, she retreats into silence, unwilling or unable to confront her past. A wild storm hits *The Wanderer* with such severity that everyone thinks the ship will sink. It is a force-ten gale with winds at fifty knots an hour and waves like walls of water that pound them night and day even though they have no sails up. The storm lasts for several days and, though the strain is at times almost unbearable, no one cracks or shirks duties. At its climax, a gigantic fifty-foot wave almost capsizes their boat. This traumatic experience triggers Sophie's memory of another violent storm and a huge wave in which her parents drowned but from which she was saved. After weeks at sea, the ship limps into an Irish port, where, miraculously, Dock is reunited with Rosalie. The six adventurers travel to England for a joyful reunion with Bompie, and it is revealed that, through a three-year correspondence, Bompie told Sophie the stories that she narrated on the ship. As their pilgrimage ends, the six travelers realize that each has profited from the experience. The three brothers know each other better, Dock has found Rosalie, Brian has gained some social skills, Cody has gained maturity and a sense of responsibility, Sophie has come to accept her past, and all have visited with the beloved Bompie.

Suitability and Critical Comment

The voyage of *The Wanderer* is superficially a transatlantic odyssey, but it is also a journey that brings self-discovery, maturation, and greater knowledge of one's inner self to each of the participants. Each emerges a different person. One reviewer also described the book as, "a beautifully written and imaginatively constructed novel that speaks to the power of survival and the delicacy of grief." This Newbery Honor book is suitable for readers in grades five through nine.

Themes and Subjects

Courage, family stories, grandfathers, interpersonal relations, sea voyages, storms, survival

Passages for Booktalking

Sophie describes the coming voyage (pp. 4–7); anticipating the trip (pp. 8–11); the trip to Block Island (pp. 23–27); Cody's journal entry about Sophie and Brian (pp. 34–37); and Sophie tells one of Bompie's stories (pp. 60–62).

Additional Selections

Two teenagers meet after a stained glass window breaks in a church, and together they begin an odyssey that reaches into their pasts and their problems in *Stained Glass* (Tundra, 2001) by Michael Bedard.

While his newly remarried mother is on her honeymoon, teenager Martin takes off and lands without money in a small Idaho town in *Ten Miles for Winnemucca* (HarperCollins, 2002) by Thelma Hatch Wyss.

Feeling completely alone in this world, Cleo decides to run away to a desolate island that her father owns in Harry Mazer's *The Island Keeper* (Dell, 1981).

Phoebe travels from Georgia to Maine to find the father she's never met in *For the Love of Pete* (Avon, 1993) by Jan Marino.

About the Book

Booklist, April 1, 2000, pp. 145–46.
Book Report, Sept., 2000, p. 58.
Bulletin of the Center for Children's Books, April, 2000, p. 275.
Horn Book, May, 2000, p. 311.
Kirkus Reviews, March 15, 2000, p. 379.
New York Times Book Review, June 4, 2000, p. 49.
School Library Journal, April, 2000, p. 130.
VOYA, Dec., 2000, p. 346.

About the Author

Authors and Artists for Young Adults, vol. 21, Gale, 1997.
Children's Literature Review, vol. 42, Gale, 1997.
Continuum Encyclopedia of Children's Literature, Continuum, 2001.
Drew, Bernard A. *100 More Popular Young Adult Authors*, Libraries Unlimited, 2002.
Hipple, Ted. *Writers for Young Adults*, supplement 1, Scribners, 2000, pp. 29–36.
"An Interview with Sharon Creech," *Reading Teacher,* Feb., 1996, pp. 380–83.
"Newbery Award Acceptance Material, 1995," *Journal of Youth Services in Libraries*, Summer, 1995, pp. 347–53.
"Newbery Award Acceptance Speech," *Horn Book*, July-Aug., 1995, pp. 426–29.
Rigg, Lyle D. "Sharon Creech," *Horn Book*, July-Aug., 1995, pp. 426–29.
St. James Guide to Young Adult Writers (2nd ed.), St. James, 1999.
Something about the Author, vol. 94, Gale, 1998.

Cross, Gillian. *Tightrope.* Holiday House, 1999. $16.95 (0-823-41512-0); pb. Harper Trophy, $5.95 (0-06-447272-8) (Grades 7–9).

Introduction

English writer Gillian Cross (1945–) has written a number of fine historical adventure stories for children, such as *A Whisper of Lace* (Oxford, 1981), but in such young adult novels as *Tightrope, Chartbreaker* (Holiday, 1987), and *Wolf* (Holiday, 1991), this winner of the Carnegie Medal uses contemporary settings along with suspense, an exploration of social problems, and realistic characters to create riveting stories with wide appeal. Although *Tightrope* is essentially a third-person narrative told from Ashley's point of view, each chapter ends with comments on the action from various minor characters, a device that adds variety and appeal to the story. The setting is a seedy neighborhood in an unidentified city that is probably in the industrial north of England, but could just as easily be considered any decaying American urban area. The novel does not contain profanity or undue violence; nevertheless, it is a realistic portrait of teenage problems and inner-city crime.

Principal Characters

Ashley Putnam, a dutiful teenage daughter who efficiently manages her mother's household but leads a secret nocturnal life

Pauline Putnam, Ashley's arthritic mother

Vikki, Ashley's school chum

Fat Annie Galt, the disliked proprietor of a local convenience store

Geoffrey Galt, nicknamed the Hyena, Fat Annie's nerdy son who works alongside his mother

Janet, Pauline's married sister

Karen and Louise, Pauline's twin daughters, now living with Janet and Frank

Eddie Beale, the local racketeer boss and dictatorial leader of a gang of hoods

Sam, Eddie's girlfriend

Tricia, Sam's mother

Joe, one of Eddie's faithful followers who is also fond of Ashley

Plot Summary

Like an expert tightrope walker in a circus, fourteen-year-old Ashley Putnam finds that her life has become a balancing act. She is growing up in a seedy working-class neighborhood in a large city, living with her widowed mother, Pauline, an invalid crippled with arthritis. During the day, Ashley is a model teenager, a conscientious student who selflessly cares for her mother and manages their modest household. Because of her mother's illness, Ashley's two young sisters, the twins Karen and Louise, have been farmed out to Pauline's sister Janet and her husband, Frank. At night, however, Ashley assumes a new identity. She becomes a master graffiti artist who signs her creations "Cindy." One day, while shopping after school with her pal and confidant Vikki at the local convenience store, which is run by obnoxious Fat Annie Galt and her docile, pasty-faced, adult son, Geoffrey, nicknamed Hyena, Ashley discovers a new challenge, a pristine white wall above Fat Annie's store. That night, she artfully spray-paints the name "Cindy" in the space. Although Hyena, who likes Ashley because she treats him with respect, repaints the space, the following night "Cindy" strikes again. Through information gossiped by Vikki to her boyfriend, the local gang leader, Eddie Beale, learns about Ashley and invites her to party in a warehouse where she amazes everyone with her gymnastic skills. Eddie is a ruthless, egocentric, petty criminal who reigns over his hoods like a benevolent warlord. He takes care of his friends but demands absolute obedience in return. Among his minions are Joe, an uncanny mimic whom Eddie saved from an abusive household, and Sam, Eddie's girlfriend. Ashley also meets Sam's effusive mother, Tricia, who visits the Putnams regularly and becomes a close friend of Pauline's. At the same time that Ashley is introduced to Eddie and his gang, she becomes the victim of a mysterious stalker who sends her threatening letters and visits her backyard at night, leaving behind scratched messages on the drainpipes and an assortment of macabre gifts such as a goat's skull. In desperation, Ashley turns to Eddie for help and, through a series of clues, they identify the culprit as Geoffrey Galt, the Hyena. Eddie begins a whispering campaign to boycott the Galts' store and eventually force Fat Annie and her son to leave the neighborhood. After Ashley confronts the Hyena and accuses him of stalking her, she realizes that he is innocent and that the stalker menace and the clues that have incriminated Geoffrey were clever fabrications invented by Eddie to force the Galts to leave the neighborhood because they refuse to pay him protection money. Feeling betrayed and manipulated, Ashley seeks to unmask Eddie in front of the same people who are now persecuting the Galts. Through graffiti on the blank wall she painted in the past, she extends an invitation to attend a street meeting the following Monday. That day, she climbs to the roof of the movie theater across from the Galts' store. In a climactic scene, in front of everyone, including the Galts, Eddie, and his gang, she tries to unmask Eddie, but before she can, Eddie sends some of his henchmen to drag her away. Trying to escape, she falls to the street below. Her fall is partially broken by the Hyena, who has tried to save her. Recovering in the hospital with many broken bones, Ashley learns that her actions have caused the gang to revolt against Eddie and have forced him to leave the area. She also learns that the Hyena is in a neighboring ward in a deep coma caused by head injuries received while trying to catch her. She gets permission to visit him and, through her whispered messages telling him about herself and reassuring him of his worth, he regains consciousness. Through these experiences, Ashley realizes that she no longer has any need for "Cindy" and the double life she has led in the past.

Suitability and Critical Comment

The author combines both sociological and psychological truths to explore the lives of a number of three-dimensional characters caught in the drama of inner-city life. For example, Ashley evolves from a fiercely independent youngster to one who realizes the concept of interdependence. This suspenseful, fast-paced thriller has appeal for readers in grades seven through nine.

Themes and Subjects

Adventure stories, family stories, friendship, gangs, graffiti, illness, inner-city life, mystery stories, stalking

Passages for Booktalking

Ashley and Vikki see the blank wall (in paperback edition, pp.1–6); at night, Ashley paints the wall (pp. 16–22); Janet and the twins visit (pp. 37–40); Ashley repaints the wall (pp. 45–51); Ashley performs at Eddie's party (pp. 90–93); the stalker in Ashley's backyard (pp. 118–21).

Additional Selections

The ordinary and the bizarre mingle in Margaret Mahy's *24 Hours* (McElderry, 2000), in which seventeen-year-old Ellis begins a day-long frenzied adventure that resembles a roller-coaster ride.

When the old lady who is being helped by teenager Abbie is hospitalized after a suspicious attack, the young girl becomes a sleuth in *Nobody's There* (Delacorte, 2000) by Joan Lowery Nixon.

Sixteen-year-old Heidi helps rescue survivors after a 747 crashes on her family's estate in Caroline B. Cooney's *Flight #116 Is Down* (Scholastic, 1992).

Eleven-year-old Lesley discovers that her neighbor's children are hiding an illegal immigrant in their London home in Vivien Alcock's *Stranger at the Window* (Houghton Mifflin, 1998).

About the Book

Booklist, Sept. 15, 2000, p. 247.
Bulletin of the Center for Children's Books, Dec., 1999, p. 127.
Horn Book, Jan.-Feb., 2000, p. 74.
Kirkus Reviews, April 15, 1999, p. 1309.
School Library Journal, Oct., 1999, p. 148.
VOYA, April, 2000, p. 343.

About the Author

Authors and Artists for Young Adults, vol. 24, Gale, 1998.
Children's Literature Review, vol. 28, Gale, 1992.
Continuum Encyclopedia of Children's Literature, Continuum, 2001.
Drew, Bernard A. *100 More Popular Young Adult Authors,* Libraries Unlimited, 2002.
Gallo, Donald. *Speaking for Ourselves, Too,* National Council of Teachers of English, 1993.

Lives and Works: Young Adult Authors, vol. 2, Grolier, 1999, pp. 82–84.
Major Authors and Illustrators for Children and Young Adults, vol. 2, Gale, 1993.
St. James Guide to Young Adult Writers (2nd ed.), St. James, 1999.
Silvey, Anita. *Children's Books and Their Creators,* Houghton Mifflin, 1995.
Something about the Author, vol. 38, Gale, 1985; vol. 71, Gale, 1993; vol. 110, Gale, 2000.
Twentieth Century Young Adult Writers, St. James, 1994.

Dahl, Michael. *The Horizontal Man.* Archway, 2000. Pb. $3.99 (0-671-03269-0) (Grades 7–10).

Introduction

Michael Dahl is the author of a series of fast-moving, scary, amusing mysteries featuring Finnegan Zwake (look out, James Joyce) and Uncle Stoppard (maybe a relation of Tom), a mystery writer. In each of these paperback capers, thirteen-year-old Finn is searching for his parents, who are archeologists and were last seen in Iceland working on a project. In the fourth book, *The Viking Claw* (Archway, 2001), Finn and his uncle travel to Iceland to search for possible clues. Accompanying them are several people, including two guides and a business mogul named Ruben Roobick, who is searching for new flavors for his line of ice cubes, named, of course, Roobick's Cubes. As the party looks for the lost city of Tquull, one of the guides disappears, Finn and his uncle find a graveyard of Viking ships buried in the snow, and a murder occurs. As expected, Finn is successful in identifying the criminal. In *The Horizontal Man,* Finn notices that items from the storeroom of Mexican treasures left him by his parents are disappearing, and soon this mystery is made more complicated by murder.

Principal Characters

Finnegan Zwake, thirteen years old
Uncle Stoppard, a mystery writer
Pablo, a tenant in the apartment house
Ms. Pryce, the caretaker
Mr. Barrymore, a tenant
Miss Brazil and Miss Bellini, tenants and nurses
Jared, the policeman

Plot Summary

Thirteen-year-old Finnegan Zwake waits for some sign that his parents, who disappeared on an archeological expedition in Iceland some years ago, are still alive. His Aunt Verona had disappeared some time before on another expedition in Agualar, Mexico. Finnegan is convinced it is the family curse. For the time being, he lives with his Uncle Stoppard, a famous mystery writer. One day Finnegan discovers a small gold statue called the Horizontal Man in the apartment of Pablo, a neighbor who is away. Finnegan recognizes the figurine from a picture of himself and his parents taken when he was five years old. They were on the dig with Aunt Verona in Agualar and had taken Finnegan with them. The statue is Mayan. Finnegan does not understand how it could have gotten into Pablo's apartment. Finnegan and Uncle Stoppard go down to the basement, where all the tenants have space to store items. They figure out that perhaps Pablo saw the statue among things stored by Finnegan's parents and just took it because it was gold. However, they also discover the body of a man in the basement.

The police are called in to investigate the murder. Everybody in the apartment house is fingerprinted, including Ms. Pryce, the caretaker; Mr. Barrymore; and Miss Brazil and Miss Bellini, who share an apartment. Pablo returns from a computer convention, but admits nothing about the statue to Finnegan, who also sees a golden spoon, which he snatches, in Pablo's apartment. He insists to his uncle that the spoon comes from his parents' collection from the dig in Agualar. When nothing clears up the mystery, Finnegan goes down into the basement and begins to look through his father's diary of their expeditions for some clues about the statue and the spoon. He gets locked in the basement, but is finally rescued by Ms. Pryce. Then, a bike belonging to the nurses, Miss Brazil and Miss Bellini, is stolen. Strange things are happening in the apartment house. Uncle Stoppard injures his foot on a ski pole sticking up through the floorboards. Then the ski pole is found sticking out of Pablo's back. A burglar is seen fleeing the apartment house, and Finnegan chases him to no avail. As it turns out, Pablo is not dead, but he does have a punctured lung.

Things get even more complicated in the lives of the tenants, but Finnegan feels he has a clue from his father's diaries and he is going to set a trap for the murderer and thief. That plan is foiled, however, when Finnegan himself is kidnapped by a man and a woman and tossed into the trunk of a car. He cleverly manages to escape and recognizes the kidnapper. She is none other than Aunt Verona, who is not dead at all. She and her husband, Antonio Morado, whom she married in Mexico, are the kidnappers. They had traced Stoppard to his present address, figuring that with Finnegan living with him, the gold from the Mexico dig would be stored somewhere near by. Larry, a friend of Pablo's who was watering his plants while he was away, saw them in the storeroom and was killed. The nurses' bike wasn't really stolen; they just said so to get insurance money. Aunt Verona was after the gold all the time, but the plan is foiled and they are hauled off to jail. Uncle Stoppard figures he and Finnegan should go on a short vacation. He asks his nephew, "How about Agualar?"

Suitability and Critical Comment

This is a fast-paced, breezy, and funny mystery that should be suitable for all readers. Not everyone will get the amusing plays on words, such as the young hero's name, but those are not germane to the clever plot, which involves enough zany characters to keep the reader guessing and amused. Young Finnegan is a smart, likable young hero and certain to be a hit with young readers in grades seven through ten.

Themes and Subjects

Apartment houses, archeology, digs, family relationships, gold statues, kidnapping, Mayan artifacts, Minnesota, murder, mystery writers, nurses

Passages for Booktalking

Finnegan finds the body (pp. 15–17); Finnegan and Uncle Stoppard talk about the curse (pp. 40–47); Uncle Stoppard is punctured, and Pablo is stabbed (pp. 64–73); the kidnapping (pp. 146–65).

Additional Selections

Jim's investigation of his father's disappearance leads him to a girl named Rose and his mysterious stepfather, Father Fisher, in *The Boy in the Burning House* (Farrar, 2001) by Tim Wynne-Jones.

Ben's hunting expedition changes gears when he becomes the hunted one in Robb White's classic tale, *Deathwatch* (Dell, 1972).

When fourteen-year-old Alex's uncle is killed in a car crash, he suspects murder in the thriller *Stormbreaker* (Putnam, 2001) by Anthony Horowitz.

In Linda Cargill's *Pool Party* (Scholastic, 1996), Sharon's beach party at a haunted resort ends in murder.

About the Book
Booklist, March 15, 2000, p. 1371.
School Library Journal, Nov., 1999, p. 130.

About the Author
No information available.

Fleischman, Paul. *A Fate Totally Worse Than Death.* Candlewick, 1995.
$15.95 (1-56402-627-2) (Grades 7–10).

Introduction

Paul Fleischman (1952–) was born in Monterey, California, the son of
the well-respected writer of tall tales for youngsters, Sid Fleischman. As a
youngster, Paul remembers listening to his father read his stories to the
family. A graduate of the University of New Mexico, he pursued many occu-
pations, such as working as a janitor, a bookstore clerk, and a bagel maker,
before settling on writing as a full-time career. His books are unique and
defy categorizing. He has written prize-winning books of poetry and a number of unusual, haunting novels. Some are historical in nature, like the
poignant *The Borning Room* (Harper, 1991), which is told in a series of six
vignettes (and a brief epilogue) spanning a period of about seventy years
before and after the Civil War. It chronicles the fortunes of the Lott family
in Ohio. Each episode involves the special room in the Lott household
called "the borning room," where both happy and tragic events take place.
A Fate Totally Worse Than Death finds the author in a more playful, satirical
mood.

Principal Characters

    Danielle, the Al Capone of teenagers
    Helga, the new exchange student from Norway
    Drew, the rich student whom Danielle likes
    Tiffany, Danielle's friend
    Brooke, another friend
    Jonathan, the student who can get anything for a price

Plot Summary

This parody of teenage horror novels centers on Cliffside High, which is
ruled by the Huns, the cruelest of all school cliques. The Huns all come
from the exclusive Hundred Palms Estates and they run Cliffside High's
social life and student government. This year, Danielle, the Al Capone of
teenaged girls, is a senior. She is gorgeous, faultless, popular, and rich—but
not as rich as Drew, the millionaire's son who drives a BMW. Danielle has
plans for Drew. He will be her boyfriend, and they will be the Ferdinand
and Isabella of the entire school. Danielle, who is not above beating old
blind people to a seat on the bus, had plans for Drew last year, but he was
attracted to fellow student Charity Chase. There was nothing Danielle and
her friends Brooke and Tiffany could do but get rid of Charity, which they

did. They did not exactly kill her, but they did chase her toward the edge of the cliff where she just happened to fall off.

Now the path is clear to Drew's heart—until Danielle learns that Helga, a new and ravishing student from Norway, has arrived at Cliffside High to become an exchange student for a year. That in itself might be merely an annoyance, but horror of horrors, it looks as if Drew is becoming attracted to her.

Not wanting to resort to anything so drastic as with Charity, Danielle and friends try subtle warnings at first, which Helga seems not to understand. Then they come up with the idea of photographing her in some unflattering way and pasting the picture all over the boys' locker room, but that doesn't work out either. Danielle then has an idea she saw in *The Godfather* movie. When a dead fish is delivered, it means that someone has been bumped off. Danielle decides to deliver a dead fish to Helga's doorstep. The odd thing is that she cannot find the house number. It is as though it doesn't exist. Through all this, Danielle has to do voluntary work at a nursing home for a past violation. She takes great delight in tormenting the elderly woman in her care, such as blasting some rock station on the radio and eating the old woman's cherry truffles, which Danielle adores.

Things go from bad to worse. Drew has definitely become smitten. The girls now try to cut off Helga's gorgeous blond hair, but that doesn't work. However, they begin to notice strange things happening to them. Brooke starts to have trouble with her hearing. Danielle seems to be getting gray hair. Tiffany seems to be getting arthritis. How can this be? The girls decide that Helga must be the ghost of Charity Chase come back to haunt them. It is the only answer. But what to do?

As their own physical afflictions worsen and Drew continues to moon over Helga, the girls decide that Helga, the ghost of Charity, must be killed. It is the only way to get rid of the curse. But how can they get a gun? Jonathan at school can get anything. Putting their plan into action, the three girls meet up with Drew and Helga near the spot where Charity was urged to jump last year. Drew and Helga are quite stunned to be confronted with a gun and told that Helga is the ghost of Charity Chase. In the fracas that follows, Helga is wounded in the wrist.

As the horror parody ends, Danielle finds herself in the hospital, where she is recovering from pneumonia. At age seventeen, she looks as old as a great-grandmother. All sorts of tubes prevent her from talking or moving much. Into the room comes a visitor, who turns out to be Mrs. Witt from the nursing home, the old woman whom Danielle had delighted in tormenting. First, Mrs. Witt turns on the television to world news, at the highest possible volume. Then she sits down and begins to eat cherry truffles.

Suitability and Critical Comment

Although a quick and easy read, this is better suited to the older teen who can appreciate the parody of teen horror novels. It is deliciously funny and bizarre; the main character has no redeeming qualities whatsoever. The author provides an exaggerated look at all the idiosyncrasies of the high-school years, poking fun at the highs and lows of getting through life as a teenager; for grades seven through ten.

Themes and Subjects

Cruelty, exchange students, guns, health problems, high-school life, humor, jealousy, nursing homes, parody, teenagers

Passages for Booktalking

Danielle torments Mrs. Witt in the nursing home (pp. 10–14); Danielle takes the fish to Helga's home (pp. 45–49); the girls try to cut off Helga's hair (pp. 71–73); the girls discuss their ailments (pp. 84–86); they confront Drew and Helga (pp. 109–17).

Additional Selections

Steven L. Layne's thriller *This Side of Paradise* (North Star, 2001) takes place in a perfectly organized community where Jack and his grandmother rebel against the smugness and conformity.

April and her family are on the run, trying to escape a hired hit man in Lois Duncan's *Don't Look Behind You* (Bantam, 1990).

A seventeen-year-old gets involved in the murder of a favorite school counselor in Betsy Hayne's *Deadly Deception* (Dell, 1994).

For more mature readers, *We Have Always Lived in the Castle* (Amereon, 1962) by Shirley Jackson features two sisters who have become recluses after the arsenic poisoning of four members of the family.

About the Book

Booklist, Oct. 15, 1995, p. 397.
Bulletin of the Center for Children's Books, Dec., 1995, p. 126.
Horn Book, Nov.-Dec., 1995, p. 745.
Kirkus Reviews, Sept. 15, 1995, p. 1349.
New York Times Book Review, Jan. 14, 1996, p. 23.
School Library Journal, Oct., 1995, p. 152.
VOYA, April, 1996, p. 38.

About the Author

Authors and Artists for Young Adults, vol. 11, Gale, 1993; vol. 35, Gale, 2000.
Children's Literature Review, vol. 20, Gale, 1990; vol. 66, Gale, 2001.
Continuum Encyclopedia of Children's Literature, Continuum, 2001.

Drew, Bernard A. *100 More Popular Young Adult Authors,* Libraries Unlimited, 2002.

Fleischman, Paul. "The Accidental Artist (1998 Anne Carroll Moore Lecture)," *School Library Journal,* March, 1998, pp. 104–107.

Fleischman, Sid. *The Abracadabra Kid: A Writer's Life,* Greenwillow, 1996.

Fleischman, Sid. "Paul Fleischman," *Horn Book,* July-Aug., 1989, pp. 452–55.

Gallo, Donald. *Speaking for Ourselves, Too,* National Council of Teachers of English, 1993.

Hipple, Ted. *Writers for Young Adults,* supplement 1, Scribners, 2000, pp. 47–58.

Major Authors and Illustrators for Children and Young Adults, vol. 2, 1993.

McElmeel, Sharron L. *The 100 Most Popular Children's Authors,* Libraries Unlimited, 1999.

"Newbery Medal Acceptance," *Horn Book,* July-Aug., 1989, pp. 451–52.

"Newbery Award Acceptance Material," *Journal of Youth Services in Libraries,* Summer, 1989, pp. 299–306.

St. James Guide to Young Adult Writers (2nd ed.), St. James, 1999.

Silvey, Anita. *Children's Books and Their Creators,* Houghton Mifflin, 1995.

Something about the Author, vol. 39, Gale, 1985; vol. 72, Gale, 1993; vol. 110, Gale, 2001.

Something about the Author Autobiography Series, vol. 20, Gale, 1995.

Grisham, John. *The Summons.* Doubleday, 2002. $25.95 (0-385-50282-2) (Grades 10–12).

Introduction

John Grisham (1955–), the writer of many compelling legal thrillers, was born in Arkansas, but now makes his home in Oxford, Mississippi, where William Faulkner once lived. As a child, Grisham was an avid reader. His family moved many times, and the first stop in a new town would be the local library to secure a library card. He studied law as a graduate student and was admitted to the bar in 1981. He had a private practice as a lawyer for nine years. He also served in his state legislature for six years until he resigned in 1990. His first book, *A Time to Kill* (Wynwood, 1989), was a slow seller. He sold many copies himself at social functions like garden parties. After his success with *The Firm* (Doubleday, 1991), it was republished and, like his other novels, became a million-copy best-seller. Most of his novels have been turned into blockbuster movies. His novels, like *The Summons,* are characterized by taut, thrilling narratives, good dialogue, and skilled plot construction.

Principal Characters

Ray Atlee, professor of law at the University of Virginia

Judge Atlee, his father, a judge, in Mississippi

Forrest Atlee, Ray's black-sheep brother

Harry Rex, Ray's longtime friend and lawyer in Mississippi

Plot Summary

Ray Atlee, a law professor at the University of Virginia, receives a letter from his elderly father, Judge Reuben V. Atlee, in Clanton, Mississippi. The letter summons him home to be in the judge's study on May 7 at 5 P.M. That is the judge's way, dictatorial, precise, and overwhelming. Ray figures his younger brother Forrest will be there, too. Forrest is the black sheep of the family, who squanders money and time and is in and out of drug and alcohol rehab. Ray also figures that his father probably wants to talk about his will.

But Ray arrives in Clanton to find his father dead in his study. Forrest has not yet arrived, and in walking about the old house where he grew up, Ray comes upon the almost unbelievable find of $3 million stacked away in boxes. Ray cannot figure out where his father would have gotten such a sum of money and cannot believe that the old man was dishonest. Until he can decide what to do with the money, believing his brother would squander it if he knew about it, Ray hides it.

Forrest arrives, and the two men get through the ordeal of the funeral with the help of Ray's old friend, now a lawyer, Harry Rex. Ray tells Rex about the money but not the amount. He also tells Rex that someone has been trying to break into the house. Apparently someone knows about the money. Before he returns to Virginia, Ray goes to a gambling casino to try and see if his father, who, according to Rex, did a little gambling, could possibly have won all that money. When he finally returns to Virginia, Ray takes the money with him.

Ray decides he must find where the money came from. His investigating leads him to a wrongful death case a few years earlier when his father was the presiding judge. The judge's rulings were honest and courageous, and the verdict netted so much money to the attorneys who sued the drug company that, as a bonus, the Judge was given $3 million. It was money he did not want, but he was old, sick, and about to die. Apparently, not knowing what to do with it for the moment, he hid the money in the house until Ray found it. Ray also learns that the man who is after the money and after him is Gordie Priest, who had been used as a delivery boy when the cash was handed out after the drug settlement.

Ray is now on the run with Priest after him. He returns to Clanton and his father's house, but the house is attacked. Frantically, Ray returns the money to its original hiding place and runs away. Later, the house is torched. Now he tells Rex the whole story. Days later Priest is found and no longer a threat. The money is gone. Ray visits Forrest, who is now in a remote and hideously expensive rehabilitation ranch in Montana. There he learns the startling story that Forrest had arrived in Clanton a week before Ray got the message to come. Forrest rewrote the judge's will to split everything between the two of them. The old man died, with Forrest's help of morphine, before Ray arrived, but Forrest had already found the money. He put it back in its original hiding place to see what Ray would do. Now, he accuses Ray of wanting the money for himself. Did Forrest put Gordie Priest on Ray's trail and torch the house? Where is the money? Forrest just shrugs and says, "Give me a year. When I get out of here, we'll talk."

Suitability and Critical Comment

This is a taut, easily read novel of greed and money's ability to corrupt. The protagonist is pictured as an average, honest man who is tempted and very nearly corrupted by the acquisition of great wealth. The plot has clever turns with enough deceptions to intrigue the mystery fan and should keep the interest of a young reader in grades ten through twelve.

Themes and Subjects

Drug addiction, family relationships, greed, jealousy, wealth

Passages for Booktalking

Ray gets his father's summons (pp. 1–3); Ray finds the money (pp. 30–32); someone tries to break into the house (pp. 46–49); Ray goes to the casino (pp. 58–64); Ray takes the money home (pp. 92–96); Ray learns about Gordie Priest (pp. 199–201); the house is attacked (pp. 209–11) and torched (pp. 214); Ray visits Forrest (pp. 239–45).

Additional Selections

Mike's summer after high-school graduation spins out of control after his father murders his secretary and disappears in Judy Troy's *From the Black Hills* (Random, 1999).

Navaho police officers, Jim Chee and Joe Leaphorn, are featured in a puzzling, complex murder mystery set in New Mexico in Tony Hillerman's *Talking God* (HarperCollins, 1991).

Computers seem to be the only link in a series of murders by a psychopathic hacker in Jeffrey Deaver's *The Blue Nowhere* (Simon & Schuster, 2001).

John Walker, an insurance analyst, and Max Stillman, a fraud investigator, get involved in a case of phony death benefits and murder in *Death Benefits* (Random, 2001) by Thomas Perry.

About the Book
New York Times Book Review, Feb. 24, 2002, p. 7.

About the Author
Authors and Artists for Young Adults, vol. 14, Gale, 1995.
Contemporary Authors New Revision Series, vol. 69, Gale, 1999.
Contemporary Literary Criticism, vol. 84, Gale, 1995.

Hobbs, Will. *Far North.* Morrow, 1996. $15.00 (0-688-14192-7)
(Grades 7–9).

Introduction
Will Hobbs (1947–) is a born outdoorsman. By age eleven, he was back-packing and camping with the Boy Scouts and has brought into his adult life a love of both nature and adventure. Because his family moved several times while he was young, he became acquainted with many different land-scapes such as rural Virginia, Alaska, and California. As an adult, he taught English in junior and senior high schools for seventeen years in southwest Colorado until, in 1990, he decided to become a full-time writer. His first published novel was *Changes in Latitude* (Atheneum, 1988), the title coming from a Jimmy Buffet song. It tells about sixteen-year-old Travis, who accompanies his siblings and mother on a vacation to Mexico. While there, Travis sorts out family problems and helps his younger brother, Teddy, locate and preserve the nesting area of some endangered sea turtles. When Teddy is involved in a horrible accident, Travis learns the importance of his family in his life. The themes of achieving maturity and the importance of nature are also explored in *Far North.*

Principal Characters
Gabe Rogers, sixteen years old
Raymond Providence, Gabe's roommate
Mr. Rogers, Gabe's father
Johnny Raven, Raymond's uncle
Clint, bush pilot

Plot Summary
Sixteen-year-old Gabe Rogers flies up into the beauty of Canada's North-west Territories to spend his last year in high school at a boarding school in Yellowknife. He has been living with his grandparents in Texas since his mother died, but Gabe wants to be able to spend more time with his father,

who works on the drillings rigs. He is fascinated by the majestic beauty of the territory and hears stories about a river called Nahanni, which is known for its thundering plunge over Virginia Falls. Gabe's roommate turns out to be Raymond Providence. He is from a remote village, and his people are Dene, who speak an Athabaskan dialect called Slavey.

Gabe thinks he and Raymond will get along very well, and they do, but Raymond remains remote and uncommunicative most of the time. Gabe thinks he is sad about something but cannot get him to talk about it. At the end of October, Clint the bush pilot calls Gabe and tells him he is going to take him flying as his father promised. Clint is also going to passenger two people to the remote country. The people turn out to be Raymond, who says he is quitting school, and his elderly uncle Johnny Raven.

Gabe is amazed when he sees the awesome beauty of Victoria Falls, but then the trouble starts. The plane develops engine problems, and although they land safely, they are being swept toward the falls. In the desperate attempt to reach shore with supplies, Clint is lost and the two boys and the old man are left alone in the wilderness.

So begins the terrible journey. Johnny Raven is the only one who really knows something about the wilderness, but Raymond is the only one who can communicate with him. Johnny Raven thinks the best plan is to hunt for moose to give them food to survive through the winter and wait for rescue. But the boys are impatient and afraid, and they convince the old man that they should build a raft, take what supplies they can, and sail down the river. Finally, Johnny Raven agrees to help them build the raft and oars, even though he is not in favor of the idea.

The river is treacherous, and the three of them become stranded in what is known as the mysterious and terrifying Deadmen Valley. When it seems as if all has been lost and their food is nearly gone, Johnny Raven leads them to a frozen beaver pond and pulls beavers out upon the ice to save them. The old man dies soon after that.

Then it is up to the boys to muster all their skill and bravery. But Raymond hurts his foot badly. When it looks like he can no longer continue, he begs Gabe to go on without him and get help. But Gabe refuses to leave him in the wilderness and fashions a toboggan on which to pull Raymond through the ice and snow. After what seems like endless months of trekking through the desolate countryside, the boys reach a native village. They are saved.

Sometime later Gabe and his father return to Raymond's village for a celebration to honor Johnny Raven. Raymond has decided to return to school. When Raymond makes a halting speech for his uncle, he ends by repeating what Johnny Raven told him before he died: "And so I say to you:

take care of the land, take care of yourself, take care of each other." And that is just what Gabe and Raymond did.

Suitability and Critical Comment

This is a good, realistic adventure story especially aimed at teenaged boys. The beauty and hardships of this awesome land are well drawn, as is the respect that native peoples hold for nature and their understanding of its ways. The growing friendship between the two boys demonstrates how different cultures can learn to understand and respect each other. Suitable for grades seven through nine.

Themes and Subjects

Animals, bush pilots, Canada, family relationships, friendship, native cultures, respect, survival techniques, wilderness

Passages for Booktalking

Gabe meets his new roommate (pp. 9–14); the plane goes down (pp. 42–52); the trip begins on the raft (pp. 87–101); Johnny Raven dies (pp. 125–30); the boys reach the village (pp. 215–17).

Additional Selections

In Hawaii's coastal waters, thirteen-year-old Mikey works as a deckhand on his stepfather's charter fishing boat in Graham Salisbury's *Lord of the Deep* (Delacorte, 2001), an adventure novel that also explores human relationships.

A teenager becomes stranded on a world inhabited by dinosaurs in the unusual survival story *Dinosaur Summer* (Warner, 1998) by Greg Bear.

Kevin, who is doing community service in an animal rescue agency, joins fellow workers on a rescue mission during a violent flood in P. J. Peterson's *Rising Water* (Simon, 2002).

The hard, adventurous life of a lobsterman is the subject of Ethan Howland's *The Lobster War* (Front Street, 2001), the story of a teenaged boy and his dream of following his father in a life at sea.

About the Book

Booklist, April 1, 1997, p. 1272.
Horn Book, Nov.-Dec., 1996, p. 745.
School Library Journal, Sept., 1996, p. 328.
VOYA, Feb., 1997, p. 328.

About the Author

Authors and Artists for Young Adults, vol. 14, Gale, 1995; vol. 39, Gale, 2001.

Children's Literature Review, vol. 59, Gale, 2000.

Continuum Encyclopedia of Children's Literature, Continuum, 2001.

Gallo, Donald. *Speaking for Ourselves, Too,* National Council of Teachers of English, 1993.

Hipple, Ted. *Writers for Young Adults,* vol. 1, Scribners, 1997, pp. 121–30.

Lives and Works: Young Adult Authors, vol. 4, Grolier, 1999, pp. 44–46.

St. James Guide to Young Adult Writers (2nd ed.), St. James, 1999.

Seventh Book of Junior Authors and Illustrators, Wilson, 1996.

Something about the Author, vol. 72, Gale, 1993; vol. 110, Gale, 2000; vol. 127, Gale, 2002.

Thompson, Edgar H. "A Conversation with Will Hobbs," *Journal of Youth Services in Libraries,* Spring, 1995, pp. 243–49.

Thompson, Edgar H. "Interview with Will Hobbs: How His Novels Come into Being," *ALAN Review,* Fall, 1994, pp. 7–9.

Twentieth Century Young Adult Writers, St. James, 1994.

Konigsburg, E. L. *Silent to the Bone.* Atheneum, 2000. $16.00 (0-689-83601-5) (Grades 6–9).

Introduction

When Elaine L. Konigsburg (1930–) won the 1997 Newbery Medal for *The View from Saturday* (Atheneum, 1996), she became the fifth author in history to receive the award twice. Her other prize winner was *From the Mixed-Up Files of Mrs. Basil E. Frankweiler* (Atheneum, 1967), and the other authors were Joseph Krumgold, Elizabeth Speare, Katherine Paterson, and Lois Lowry. As in many of her novels, the central characters of *Silent to the Bone* are bright, likable, unconventional youngsters who are on the brink of adolescence and facing social and emotional problems that test their intelligence, values, and growing need for independence. The novel is set in a college town ironically named Epiphany and, with the exception of a few flashbacks, takes place during a little over four weeks—roughly between Thanksgiving and New Year's Eve—during which time the reader learns that sometimes "the cruelest lies are often told in silence."

Principal Characters

Branwell Zamborska, a sensitive thirteen-year-old boy noted for his bright red hair, lack of coordination, and amazing intelligence

Connor Kane, Bran's outgoing best friend, who also displays an awesome intelligence and awareness of human behavior; the novel's narrator

Margaret Kane, Connor's twenty-seven-year-old half sister from their father's first marriage

Mr. and Mrs. Roderick Kane, Connor's parents; Mr. Kane is the registrar at the local college, and Mrs. Kane is a psychologist

Dr. Stefan Zamborska, Bran's father, a world-renowned geneticist, researcher, and college professor

Tina Nquyem, Bran's stepmother and wife of Dr. Zamborska, with whom she works as part of his research team

Nicole (Nikki), the six-month-old baby of Tina and Stefan Zamborska, and Bran's half sister

Vivian Shawcurt, the attractive twenty-year-old English au pair who takes care of Nikki

Mr. and Mrs. Branwell, known as the Ancestors, Bran's ultraconservative, self-righteous grandparents

Morris Ditmar, a wisecracking young man who delivers pizza

Plot Summary

The story begins with a two-page transcript of a frantic 911 call made on November 25 in the town of Epiphany. In it, a hysterical young woman is begging someone named Branwell to speak to the operator. When Branwell remains silent, the girl blurts out that a baby has lost consciousness after Branwell dropped her. After the medics arrive, the baby is rushed to a hospital where she remains in a life-threatening coma. The baby is Nikki, the six-month-old daughter of Professor Zamborska, a noted geneticist, and his second wife, Tina. The hysterical young woman is their twenty-year-old au pair from England, Vivian Shawcurt, and Branwell, usually called Bran, is Professor Zamborska's bright, sensitive thirteen-year-old son from his first marriage to Linda Branwell, who was killed in an automobile accident when Bran was nine months old. The boy is remarkably intelligent and impressionable and, as a result of the trauma associated with Nikki's mishap, falls into a stony silence that results in his being sent as a patient to the County Juvenile Behavioral Center. Bran had always been an obedient, pliant son who managed to please even his waspy, demanding grandparents, the elder Branwells, during his annual month-long visits to their home in Florida. Unable to communicate with his son, Professor Zamborska appeals to Connor Kane, Bran's best friend, for help. Connor, another brilliant, precocious youngster, has been friends with Bran since preschool. When Bran tries to communicate with Connor through blinking his eyes, Connor devises a series of flash cards containing the alphabet and important associative words to which Bran can respond. As well, Connor seeks the help of his older half sister, Margaret, a computer expert, who has a strong affinity with Bran because she, too, is the product of a family that involved two marriages. Together, Connor and

Margaret begin their own investigation. They first conduct an interview with the seductive Vivian Shawcurt and discover that she is a manipulative tease who had naive Bran under her control. By using the flash cards, Connor discovers that Bran wants him to study the transcript tape, and, through an amplification system, Connor discovers another voice on the tape. Using the cards, Bran spells out "Morris JJ's Pizza," and at this pizza parlor, Connor and Margaret track down Morris Ditmar, a street-smart delivery boy. He later confesses that he was having afternoon trysts with Vivian at the Zamborskas' and, in time, Bran, who was infatuated with Vivian, learned of these meetings but was too confused about his own ambivalent feelings to tell his parents about Vivian's neglect of Nikki and her affair with Morris. Nikki's condition at the hospital continues to improve at the same time as the facts about that terrible Wednesday come together. On the afternoon of the catastrophe, Vivian was responsible for Nikki's fall and, after placing her in her crib, went to the neighboring bedroom where Morris awaited her. When Bran arrived home early from school, he found the baby unconscious and near death. He called out for Vivian, who, with Morris, raced into the room. At this point, Bran became so traumatized by his feelings of guilt and his involvement in Nikki's condition, that he lost the ability to speak. By New Year's Eve, Nikki has been released from the hospital; Vivian, who went into hiding, has been located and sent back to England; and Bran, now freed from his guilt and trauma, regains the power of speech.

Suitability and Critical Comment

Using mounting suspense, sophisticated humor, and a focus on two bright, savvy kids, the author explores complex human emotional responses, adolescent sexual awakening, and the problems of second-time-around families. Its piercing exploration of these themes makes it particularly suitable for better readers in grades six through nine.

Themes and Subjects

Adolescence, babies, baby-sitters, blended families, child abuse, divorce, emotional problems, families, friendship, grandparents, muteness, mystery, survivor's guilt

Passages for Booktalking

The 911 tape (pp. 1–3); Connor's first visit to Bran (pp. 5–7); Connor describes Bran's background and character (pp. 13–17); Connor devises his scheme to communicate with Bran (pp. 27–29); and Bran's first responses (pp. 33–35).

Additional Selections

A bright, witty boy uncovers fossil remains in his Kansas backyard and must find out if they are real or a forgery in *The Great Whale of Kansas* (Houghton Mifflin, 2001) by Richard Jennings.

In Jean Thesman's introspective first-person narrative *Calling the Swan* (Viking, 2000), fifteen-year-old Skylar is haunted by a crime that remains unsolved for three years.

Part historical novel and part survival story, Carol Otis Hurst's *Through the Lock* (Houghton Mifflin, 2001) tells of eleven-year-old Ella and her flight from a foster home in nineteenth-century Connecticut.

Lies, good intentions, mistakes, and honor are subjects in *The Hero* (Knopf, 2002) by Ron Woods, the story of three boys, a rafting expedition, and a fatal accident.

About the Book

Booklist, August, 2000, p. 2135.
Bulletin of the Center for Children's Books, Oct., 2000, p. 68.
Horn Book, Nov.-Dec., 2000, p. 756.
Kirkus Reviews, Oct. 1, 2000, p. 1426.
School Library Journal, Sept., 2000, p. 232.
VOYA, Dec., 2000, p. 350.

About the Author

Authors and Artists for Young Adults, vol. 3, Gale, 1990; vol. 41, Gale, 2001.
Children's Literature Review, vol. 1, Gale, 1976; vol. 47, Gale, 1998.
Continuum Encyclopedia of Children's Literature, Continuum, 2001.
Drew, Bernard A. *The 100 Most Popular Young Adult Authors,* Libraries Unlimited, 1997.
Eighth Book of Junior Authors and Illustrators, Wilson, 2000.
Gallo, Donald. *Speaking for Ourselves, Too,* National Council of Teachers of English, 1993.
Hanks, Dorrel Thomas. *E. L. Konigsburg,* Twayne, 1993.
Lives and Works: Young Adult Authors, vol. 5, Grolier, 1999, pp. 8–11.
Major Authors and Illustrators for Children and Young Adults, vol. 4, Gale, 1993.
Marcus, Leonard S. *Author Talk,* Simon, 2000.
McElmeel, Sharron L. *The 100 Most Popular Children's Authors,* Libraries Unlimited, 1999.
St. James Guide to Children's Writers, St. James, 1999.
St. James Guide to Young Adult Writers (2nd ed.), St. James, 1999.
Silvey, Anita. *Children's Books and Their Creators,* Houghton Mifflin, 1995.
Something about the Author, vol. 4, Gale, 1973; vol. 48, Gale, 1987; vol. 94, Gale, 1998; vol. 126, Gale, 2002.
Third Book of Junior Authors and Illustrators, Wilson, 1972.
Twentieth Century Children's Writers, St. James, 1995.
Twentieth Century Young Adult Writers, St. James, 1994.

Mikaelsen, Ben. *Touching Spirit Bear.* HarperCollins, 2001. $16.95
(0-380-97744-3) (Grades 6–9).

Introduction

Ben Mikaelsen (1952–) leads an adventurous life. Among his interests
he lists horseback riding, parachute jumping, motorcycle travel, sled dog
racing, flying airplanes, scuba diving, camping, and the study and raising of
bears. Born and raised in Bolivia, he returned to the United States at age
twelve. Because he was considered an outsider at school, he turned to writing as an outlet. However, adventure was always foremost in his life, and he
would get attention through his daring deeds, like jumping off cliffs. When
he married and moved to the mountains of Bozeman, Montana, he and his
wife raised a declawed black bear cub, Buffy, which they obtained from a
wild game farm. This experience formed the basis of his first published
young adult novel, *Rescue Josh McGuire* (Hyperion, 1991), about a thirteen-
year-old boy growing up in an abusive family and how he cares for an
orphaned bear cub and houses him in the family's barn. Like this first
novel, *Touching Spirit Bear* uses nature and the great outdoors as subjects.

Principal Characters

Cole Matthews, a troubled teenager
Garvey, his Indian parole officer
Edwin, a Tlingit elder
Peter Driscal, a ninth grader whom Cole badly injures
Mr. Matthews, Cole's abusive father
Mrs. Matthews, Cole's alcoholic mother
The Spirit Bear

Plot Summary

Cole Matthews is a troubled boy and a boy in trouble. Growing up in an
abusive home, he is filled with rage and hate. He has been stealing and
fighting for years and has had numerous run-ins with the law. But now he
has gone too far. In a fit of anger, he catches Peter Driscal in a parking lot
and beats him so badly—by smashing his head against the pavement—that
Peter suffers possible permanent brain damage. Cole is headed for jail
this time.

But Cole is offered an alternative. It is called Circle Justice based on traditions of Native Americans. It is aimed at providing healing for the
offender, the victim, and the community. Cole, his parents, and Peter's parents agree to accept Circle Justice. The decision is made that Cole will be

taken from his home in Minnesota to a remote Alaskan island where he will spend one year alone. Cole agrees to this simply because he figures he is smarter than anyone else and as soon as he is dropped off by Garvey, he will find a way to swim off the island and escape. No one knows that Cole is an excellent swimmer. He will just disappear, and no one will ever find him.

Garvey takes Cole to the island, builds him a cabin, and attempts to give him advice on how to survive alone and in the wilderness. Cole remains hostile. He doesn't need or want anyone's advice. He continually blames everyone else for his present situation. Soon after Garvey leaves, Cole burns the cabin in anger, tries to swim off the island and finds that it is impossible, and charges a huge white so-called Spirit Bear that Garvey spoke of. Cole is left with a broken arm and leg and other injuries. During the two days that follow until Garvey returns to check on him, Cole thinks he will die.

Cole is taken back home where he now will face a jail sentence after he heals. Instead, he asks to be sent back to the island and tries to convince Garvey and others that he is a changed boy. Finally, they agree, and Cole returns to the island with Garvey and Edwin. No one believes that he has seen the Spirit Bear. Garvey and Edwin teach Cole how to rid himself of his anger by carving and doing animal dances. Cole talks about his father's abuse and his mother's passive attitude. Before leaving Minnesota again, Cole and his mother had a reunion of sorts during which she expresses her sorrow for allowing Cole to be abused by his father. Cole's father has now been put in jail, and a divorce is pending. Garvey tells Cole that Peter is having great trouble adjusting to his life since the beating. Cole comes up with the idea of having Peter come to the island to spend some time with him so that Cole can convince the boy he has changed.

Everyone agrees so long as Garvey will be on the island with the boys. Peter is hostile at first and threatening. He attacks Cole, who does not fight back. But as the two boys come to an understanding and make the first steps toward friendship, the Spirit Bear appears in the woods. It stands for a minute and then disappears into the forest. Peter wants to know if they really did see it and asks if anyone will believe them. Cole replies that it doesn't matter what other people think or believe. What is important is what you believe, he tells Peter. Both boys seem on their way to recovery and a better life.

Suitability and Critical Comment

This is a vivid picture of a juvenile offender who, at the story's outset, has few redeeming qualities. The details of life alone on a remote island are realistic and spellbinding. Boys especially should enjoy this story of a rebellious teenager with such hatred inside that he lashes out at everything and everyone. Although the idea that Peter would be allowed to go to the island with Cole is somewhat unbelievable, the rest of the story rings true; for grades six through nine.

Themes and Subjects

Alaska, anger, animals, child abuse, loneliness, Native Americans, physical violence, survival, wilderness

Passages for Booktalking

Cole attacks Peter (pp. 7–8); Cole tries to swim off the island (pp. 41–44); the Spirit Bear attacks (pp. 65–73); Cole returns to the island (pp. 134–39); Peter and Cole see the Spirit Bear (pp. 237–38).

Additional Selections

After her father dies of a heart attack while she is traveling with him in Italy, Jackie is kidnapped by a father and son in Donna Jo Napoli's *Three Days* (Dutton, 2001).

After the Great Fire of 1899 in Dawson City, sixteen-year-old Jason and his girlfriend canoe the Yukon River in *Down the Yukon* (HarperCollins, 2000), a sequel to *Jason's Gold* (Morrow, 1999), both by Will Hobbs.

A half-breed African boy who feels rejected by both his tribes is taken up by a troop of baboons in Anton Quintana's *The Baboon King* (Walker, 1999).

In *Hatchet* (Macmillan, 1987) by Gary Paulsen, teenaged Brian survives a plane crash in the Canadian wilderness, but then must fend for himself.

About the Book

Booklist, Jan. 1, 2001, p. 940.
Book Report, Sept., 2001, p. 64.
Bulletin for the Center for Children's Books, May, 2001, p. 347.
Kirkus Reviews, Jan., 2001, p. 54.
School Library Journal, Feb., 2001, p.122.

About the Author

Authors and Artists for Young Adults, vol. 37, Gale, 2001.
Something about the Author, vol. 73, Gale, 1993; vol. 107, Gale, 1999.

Qualey, Marsha. *Close to a Killer.* Bantam, 2000. Pb. $4.99 (0-440-22763-1) (Grades 7–9).

Marsha Qualey (1953–) was born in Minnesota, a state that often figures as the locale of her novels. After marriage and starting a family, she began her writing career. Many of her stories deal with intergenerational conflicts between parents and children and with youngsters coming to terms with the past actions of their parents. Her first published novel, *Everybody's Daughter* (Houghton Mifflin, 1991), deals with these themes. The central character is the daughter of former members of a commune who still keep in touch with its residents. It also features a romantic triangle in which the girl gets involved after a fatal accident caused by commune members who are protesting at a local nuclear power plant. Ms. Qualey's first mystery was *Thin Ice* (Houghton Mifflin, 1997), in which Arden becomes convinced that the snowmobile tragedy that took her brother's life was not an accident. *Close to a Killer,* her second mystery, is a puzzler involving the murder of two prominent citizens of a Midwestern town, a beauty parlor, and a seventeen-year-old girl who harbors a troubling suspicion about these deaths.

Principal Characters
Barrie Dupre, a seventeen-year-old high-school student
Daria Dupre, Barrie's mother, an ex-con
Dean, the clerk at An Open Book
Lieutenant Henley, homicide cop who gets involved in the murders
Willa and Eric, proprietors of An Open Book
Wylie, whom Barrie meets at the bookstore

Plot Summary
Barrie, a seventeen-year-old high-school student, is not happy living with her mother in Dakota City. They have had a strained relationship ever since her mother served time in prison after she was found responsible for the death of a guard at a nuclear demonstration many years before. Barrie had been living with her father since that time, but her father remarried and went to Paris for a year. Barrie was forced to stay with her mother, Daria, who owns a hair salon called Killer Looks. This is a hair salon with a difference. All of Daria's employees have done time for murder. It is her way of helping them get a start after prison. Daria knows all of the people who work for her mother and finds them much like everyone else, even if they have all been on the other side of the law for a time. At any rate, business is booming.

But business takes a downturn when the husband of one of the salon's clients is murdered. Shortly afterward, the client herself is murdered. Homicide policeman Henley is called in to investigate the case. He not only is an experienced and thorough investigator, but he has an interest in Barrie, and especially her mother, as well.

It turns out that murder is not very good for the hair salon business. Things become more desperate and frightening when two more people are murdered. The total is now up to four, and cancellation after cancellation follows. Somehow the murders must be connected with the Killer Looks salon.

Besides the trauma of the murders and a collapsing business, Barrie tries to escape from a mother she cannot get close to by immersing herself in her writing. She makes frequent trips to her favorite bookstore, called An Open Book. She likes Willa and Eric, who own the place. In addition, Barrie is friendly with Dean, the clerk, and with Wylie, a young man who frequents the shop as much as she does.

The investigation continues, and things become even more serious. The house in which Barrie and her mother live is trashed. Killer Looks is set on fire. Lieutenant Henley is becoming increasingly fearful that Barrie and her mother are targets of the killer. Barrie confides in Henley that she has a troubling suspicion about Wylie, who seems to be acting strangely. Wylie later has a terrible accident in which he loses his foot, but he is not the murderer. In the end, when the identity of the killer is discovered, Barrie is in for a shock: Eric is the murderer. Unable to make a go of the bookstore, he has long been stealing from wealthy homes in the area. The killings are his mad attempt to cover them up.

Eric confesses to Barrie, who screams at him before he falls in front of a bus and is killed. The novel ends after Barrie returns from a visit to her father and stepmother in Paris. She finds that her friend Wylie is on the mend. He will recover from his terrible accident. Perhaps it is the appearance of Lieutenant Henley, perhaps it is the trauma of what they have gone through, but Barrie is hopeful that she and her mother now have a chance for a better relationship. Things are looking up, and Barrie is looking for a better year.

Suitability and Critical Comment

This is an easily read story of an unusual situation peopled with unusual characters such as Barrie's mother and the other ex-cons who work in the salon, as well as the ex–drug users who come into the bookstore. Realistic but not explicit and suited to grades seven through nine.

Themes and Subjects

Loneliness, mother-daughter relationships, murder, prison, rehabilitation

Passages for Booktalking

Wylie, Dean, and Barrie talk about the murder (p. 17); the second murder (pp. 48–53); Barrie spends an evening with Wylie (pp. 62–69); Barrie and her mother find the house is trashed (pp. 75–78); fire at the salon (pp. 121–25); Barrie faces the murderer (pp. 150–59).

Additional Selections

At a local prep school where her seventeen-year-old brother committed suicide, Frances wonders if the seemingly friendly façade of the school staff hides sinister motives in Nancy Werlin's *Black Mirror* (Dial, 2001).

Trying to escape the guilt related to an accidental death, a boy moves in with relatives and uncovers some horrifying family secrets in Nancy Werlin's *The Killer's Cousin* (Bantam, 2001).

Fifteen-year-old amateur sleuth P. C. Hawke investigates the mysterious death of a much-hated celebrity scientist at the Bronx Zoo in Paul Zindel's *The Lethal Gorilla* (Hyperion, 2001).

Seventeen-year-old Dina protects a child who believes she is going to be murdered in Joan Lowery Nixon's *The Specter* (Dell, 1993).

About the Book

Booklist, Feb. 1, 1999, p. 970.
Bulletin of the Center for Children's Books, Feb., 1999, p. 213.
Kirkus Reviews, Oct. 1, 1999, p. 1739.
School Library Journal, March, 1999, p. 214.
VOYA, April, 1999, p. 40.

About the Author

Authors and Artists for Young Adults, vol. 39, Gale, 2001.
Contemporary Authors, vol. 148, Gale, 1996.
St. James Guide to Young Adult Writers (2nd ed.), St. James, 1999.
Something about the Author, vol. 79, Gale, 1995; vol. 124, Gale, 2002.

Zindel, Paul. *Rats.* Hyperion, 1999. $15.99 (0-7868-0339-8)
(Grades 7–9).

Introduction

Paul Zindel (1936–) was born in Staten Island, New York, where he and his sister grew up with his single-parent mother, a nurse. His father, a policeman, left the family when Paul was a child. After graduating from Wagner College on Staten Island with a degree in chemistry, he later taught chemistry on the island for ten years at the Tottenville High School. He left to pursue a full-time career writing fiction and plays. His first book for young adults was the groundbreaking *The Pigman* (Harper, 1968), inspired by some students he taught and by Nonna Frankie, the Italian grandfather to the neighborhood. Told from two points of view, it is the story of two teenage misfits—a boy and a girl—and their friendship with a lonely old man, Mr. Pagnatti, a relationship that produces first happiness and then tragedy. Recently, Mr. Zindel has stopped writing about teenage angst and instead has produced a series of fast-moving adventure stories. *Rats* belongs to this latter genre.

Principal Characters

Sarah, fourteen years old
Michael, her brother
Mack Macafee, their father
Aunt Betty

Plot Summary

Sarah, age fourteen, and her ten-year-old brother, Michael, live in Staten Island, New York, next to a garbage dump, with their pet, Surfer, a white rat, and their father. They don't really like living there, but since their father is the dump supervisor and wants to prove to the public that it is environmentally okay to live next to a dump, they have no choice. Sometimes the smell is truly gross. But to keep the smell down, the town authorized that the dump be paved over, a plan that their father approved. And, indeed, Sarah has to admit that the smell isn't really as bad as it used to be.

But then things start happening. At first it isn't much, even if unpleasant. A rat is found in the garbage disposal, another in a hot tub, and one in a toilet. Soon, a small stream of what looks like oil or tar begins to leak out of a crack in the asphalt. However, it is not a stream of tar at all but a stream of large rats! Mutant rats are escaping from the dump and entering people's homes. What is worse, they are killing people. It seems as though the mutant rats have an organized plan to attack humans.

Soon the rats seem to be everywhere, crawling into babies' cribs, attacking animals and pets, killing people in their homes. When Sarah and Michael are attacked in their home, she decides to go to Aunt Betty's. But when they go down to the dock to row the boat across the water, they are stopped by a tide of rats. Marge Dixon in the huge compactor truck arrives and tries to save them, but the swarm of rats overtakes her, and she is killed. Sarah and Michael manage to escape to the boat and then watch in horror as the rats devour a young man out on the water.

The children arrive at Aunt Betty's, but that night they discover that the house is covered with rats. Sarah thinks they have come for Surfer, who goes with them. Michael tells Sarah that he thought Surfer had been acting strangely ever since the mound opened. Sarah thinks that perhaps the reason they escaped the rats at the dump was that Surfer talked to them. She decides to take the boat to find her father to tell him that the rats have some kind of plan. Out on the water once more, she sees the rats attack a tuna boat. She calls Aunt Betty, who discovers that Michael has taken a boat and is heading after Sarah.

Sarah locates Michael inside a huge drainage pipe at the dump. He has found Surfer, but the animal will not come to him. Sarah wonders if Surfer is the king rat. She calls Aunt Betty and tells her of their desperate situation. As the rats come after them, Sarah decides to cooperate. She will do whatever they want. Meanwhile, Betty has notified their father, and he is looking for them. Sarah, who has her laptop computer with her, notices the rats look interested, so she opens it. While the rats are engrossed, Michael snaps the collar on Surfer. They begin to move through the maze of rats with the computer open. When the rats recover and chase them, Sarah makes Michael let Surfer go. Their father arrives as a huge explosion hits the dump.

Rats are everywhere. Mack puts Sarah and Michael in a waiting helicopter, but the rats attack it. Sarah and Michael get to the control room at the landing pad, where they see the rats attacking people all over. Suddenly, Sarah has an idea and calls her father on the microphone. She tells him that rats are hypnotized by lights. That's how they were able to get away in the dump, because of the lights on the laptop computer. She tells him to turn on all the lights of the nearby amusement park. The rats stop attacking, and they are killed or driven into the sea. The terrible ordeal is over.

Suitability and Critical Comment

For the young teen, this will be a thriller. The scenes of the rats attacking individuals, which would terrorize adults, will probably delight the young reader in all their vivid detail. The images that Zindel weaves of rats swarming inside people's homes, showing up in hot tubs and garbage disposals, are mesmerizing. There is much blood-spewing and fast-paced action to keep the story rolling; for grades seven through nine.

Themes and Subjects

Courage, creativity, the environment, family relationships, garbage dumps, gore, horror, New York City, rats

Passages for Booktalking

Rats attack the Carson house (pp. 17–22); Sarah and Michael are attacked (pp. 56–62); Marge Dixon is killed (pp. 68–84); the tuna boat goes down (pp. 133–40); Sarah finds the solution (pp. 191–99).

Additional Selections

Seven truly scary stories about the unquiet dead are presented in Vivian Vande Velde's *Being Dead* (Harcourt, 2001).

Jane Yolen's *Here There Be Ghosts* (Harcourt, 1998) is a chilling collection of supernatural stories such as one that tells what happens when three friends visit a graveyard on Halloween.

After awakening from a four-year coma, Stacy becomes the target of the man who wounded her and killed her mother in Joan Lowery Nixon's *The Other Side of Dark* (Dell, 1986).

In R. L. Stine's *The Wrong Number* (Pocket, 1990), a teenager hears a murder being committed while making a crank phone call.

About the Book

School Library Journal, Oct., 1999, p. 163.

About the Author

Authors and Artists for Young Adults, vol. 2, Gale, 1989; vol. 37, Gale, 2001.
Children's Literature Review, vol. 3, Gale, 1976; vol. 45,Gale, 1998.
Continuum Encyclopedia of Children's Literature, Continuum, 2001.
Drew, Bernard A. *The 100 Most Popular Young Adult Authors,* Libraries Unlimited, 1997.
Forman, Jack. *Presenting Paul Zindel,* Twayne, 1988.
Gallo, Donald. *Speaking for Ourselves,* National Council of Teachers of English, 1990.
Hipple, Ted. *Writers for Young Adults,* vol. 3, Scribners, 1997, pp. 421–30.
Lives and Works: Young Adult Authors, vol. 8, Grolier, 1999, pp. 102–4.
Major Authors and Illustrators for Children and Young Adults, vol. 6, Gale, 1993.
St. James Guide to Young Adult Writers (2nd ed.), St. James, 1999.
Scales, Pat. "The Pigman and He," *School Library Journal,* June, 2002, p. 53.
Silvey, Anita. *Children's Books and Their Creators,* Houghton Mifflin, 1995.
Something about the Author, vol. 16, Gale, 1979; vol. 58, Gale, 1990; vol. 102, Gale, 1999.
Third Book of Junior Authors and Illustrators, Wilson, 1972.
Twentieth Century Young Adult Writers, St. James, 1994.

4

Science Fiction and Fantasy

Almond, David. *Kit's Wilderness.* Delacorte, 2000. $15.95
(0-385-32665-3) (Grades 7–10).

Introduction

David Almond grew up in the bleak, oppressive mining area of north-eastern England, the setting of *Kit's Wilderness.* His first novel for young adults, *Skellig,* won the 1998 Whitbread Children's Book Prize and the Carnegie Medal in Britain and was an honor book for the first Michael L. Printz Award in this country. It is the story of two youngsters who find in a garage a decrepit old man, Skellig, who has mystical insights and has sprouted a pair of wings. *Kit's Wilderness* shares many similarities with this first novel. It, too, contains elements of magical realism, and also deals with themes involving death, the continuity of past and present, and the healing power of love and friendship. *Kit's Wilderness* won the second annual Printz Award. About it, the author stated in an interview that, "it's very linked to the scenery of my childhood and the stories and history of the place where I grew up."

Principal Characters

Christopher "Kit" Watson, the sensitive, highly imaginative thirteen-year-old narrator who has a talent for writing

John Askew, an artistically gifted thirteen-year-old loner who, as his last name suggests, is temperamentally out of line with the people around him

Jack Askew, John's abusive, drunken father

Alison "Allie" Keenan, Kit's unconventional and untamed school friend who has a gift for the dramatic

Grandpa Watson, Kit's grandfather, a former pitman immersed in the lore and superstitions surrounding the mines

Mum and Dad Watson, Kit's loving, supportive parents

Miss Bush, also known as "Burning Bush," Kit's English teacher, who encourages his writing talents

130

Silky, a mischievous, ghostly pitboy, who becomes the subject of one of
  Kit's stories

Lak, a prehistoric teenager who is also the subject of one of Kit's stories

Plot Summary

After the death of his grandmother, thirteen-year-old Kit Watson,
together with his mother and father, relocates to the dreary former mining
town of Stoneygate in northwestern England to care for Kit's grandpa.
Below this grimy, bleak locale lies a labyrinth of deserted mineshafts, tunnels, and pits where, it is said, one can hear and see the ghostly bodies and
voices of the men and boys who worked and died in these mines. At school,
Kit, a thoughtful, likable boy who has a keen talent for writing, becomes
involved with two classmates, Allie Keenan, an independent, somewhat
rebellious girl, and John Askew, a fine artist but a troubled, introspective
youngster who is physically abused by his alcoholic father, a former miner.
In the area between the town and the river, lies the wilderness where the
mine had been. John has created a hideout in one of the pits and deco-
rated it with his grotesque pictures of animals and the names of children
who died in the mines. Here, he brings his schoolmates to play the game of
Death, in which a youngster, chosen by a spin-the-knife process, is left alone
to reenact the state of dying and death and communicate with his ghostly
counterparts. When Kit undergoes this seancelike ordeal, he emerges
shaken but convinced that he has made contact with the dead. Later, his
grandfather shows Kit a monument in a church graveyard erected in 1821
to commemorate a mining disaster in which 117 were killed, including two
thirteen-year-old boys, Christopher Watson and John Askew, ancestors of
the two friends. Grandpa, who is gradually sinking into dementia, also tells
Kit about a Puck-like spirit boy, named Silky, who supposedly lived in the
mines. This becomes the subject of a brilliant short story Kit writes for
school, which is highly praised by his English teacher, Miss Bush, nicknamed Burning Bush. Later, he writes another imaginative story about a
prehistoric boy, Lak, who is separated from his family and must care for his
baby sister.

Suspicious of Kit's growing attachment to unstable, moody Askew, Miss
Bush follows the boy to the wilderness and witnesses the game of Death.
John is expelled from school and later runs away from home. Kit regrets the
loss of his friend but is comforted and protected by the often-wild Allie,
whom Grandpa calls "the good bad lovely lass." Events reach a climax at
Christmastime during class performances of the pantomime *The Snow
Queen,* in which Allie scores a personal triumph as the wicked sister who can
make objects and people disappear and appear at will. Before the second

performance, Kit learns that John has returned and is hiding in a deserted mine tunnel. Kit visits the boy. At first John is hostile and bitter, but together they talk of life, their separate destinies, and of the ghosts of dead children that surround them. They become blood brothers in a ritual in which they cut their thumbs and mix the blood from the wounds. Kit compares John to the hero Lak, who is also on a quest, and as the night ends, Kit has won over John by the power of his love and caring. John returns to his family. In the aftermath of these events, both Allie and John have created new lives for themselves. Allie now has a goal to enter the world of the theater; John returns to school and, with his father now off alcohol, hopes to become part of his family and to develop his interest in art. Kit's grandfather dies peacefully, but for the boy, he has only joined his ancestors, the silent ghostly beings that add a different dimension to his life.

Suitability and Critical Comment

This book can be appreciated on many levels—as a supernatural ghost story, a study in the redemptive power of love, an examination of the continuity of life, or a tale of transition and coming-of-age. There will be as many interpretations of its meanings as there will be readers. Therefore, its age suitability is very flexible: from better, thoughtful readers in the junior high grades through the senior high years.

Themes and Subjects

Adolescence, allegory, coming-of-age, England, family stories, friendship, ghosts, grandfathers, magic realism, mines and mining, old age, the power of love, school stories, supernatural, surrealism, writing

Passages for Booktalking

The game of Death (pp. 5–8); Kit and his grandfather visit the mining monument (pp. 19–22); Grandpa talks about Silky (pp. 30–33); Kit plays the game of Death (pp. 48–52); Askew is expelled from school (pp. 75–77); and part of Kit's story about Lak (pp. 115–17).

Additional Selections

Lael Little's *Lake of Secrets* (Holt, 2002) is a suspenseful tale of Carlene and her mother and their visit to the lake where Carlene's elder brother disappeared eighteen years before.

Orwell's Luck (Houghton Mifflin, 2000) by Richard Jennings is an unusual novel about a middle schooler who gets communications from an injured brown rabbit she has saved.

A thirteen-year-old Irish orphan is drawn into the past when he enters a hole leading to a mass grave in James Heneghan's *The Grave* (Farrar, 2000).

A badly battered eight-year-old who has been evacuated from World War II London is taken in by a dour old man and fills a void in his life in *Goodnight Mister Tom* (HarperCollins, 1981) by Michelle Magorian.

About the Book
Booklist, Jan. 1 and 15, 2000, p. 899.
Horn Book, Mar.-Apr., 2000, p.192.
Kirkus Reviews, Dec. 15, 1999, p. 1954.
School Library Journal, March, 2000, p. 233.
VOYA, April, 2000, p. 42.

About the Author
Authors and Artists for Young Adults, vol. 38, Gale, 2001.
"The Booklist Interview—David Almond," *Booklist,* Jan. 1 and 15, 2000, pp. 898–99.
"The Booklist Interview—David Almond," *Booklist,* Apr. 1, 2001, p. 1464.
Drew, Bernard A. *100 More Popular Young Adult Authors,* Libraries Unlimited, 2002.
Odean, Kathleen. "Mystic Man (David Almond)," *School Library Journal,* April, 2001, pp. 48–52.
Something about the Author, vol. 114, Gale, 2000.

Barron, T. A. *The Lost Years of Merlin.* Putnam, 1996. $19.99 (0-399-23018-1); pb. Ace, $6.99 (0-441-00668-X) (Grades 6–9).

Introduction
After a remarkable scholastic record, including a Rhodes Scholarship to Oxford and, later, a successful business career in a venture capital business, T. A. (Tom) Barron took an early retirement in 1989 and moved back to his Colorado home with his wife and five children to devote his life to writing. Although he has written many successful nature books and picture books for children, he is best known for his fantasies for young adults, including the Saga of Young Merlin, a five-volume epic comprised of *The Lost Years of Merlin* and its four sequels: *The Seven Songs of Merlin* (Putnam, 1997), *The Fires of Merlin* (Putnam, 1998), *The Wings of Merlin* (Putnam, 1999), and *The Mirror of Merlin* (Putnam, 2000). Of the character Merlin, the wizard and mentor to King Arthur, the author has said, "He is more than just a legendary character. He is a metaphor for the idea that all of us have a heroic person somewhere down inside of ourselves, waiting to be discovered."

Principal Characters
Emrys, the twelve-year-old narrator who later becomes known as Merlin
Branwen, Emrys's mother, who is known for her healing powers
Rhita Gawr, the spirit who controls evil in the spirit world

Dagda, the spirit of good

Dinatius, the town bully who hates and fears Branwen and Emrys

Rhia, a young orphan girl who lives on the island of Fincayra

Cwen, Rhia's maid and nurse

Trouble, a spunky, fearless merlin who befriends Emrys

Shim, a small giant with hairy feet, a prominent nose, and bad grammar

King Stagmar, a follower of Rhita Gawr, who lives in the Shrouded Castle

Grand Elusa, a white spider that can change size at any time

Cairpre, a wise old man who lives underground with his books and memories

Domnu, a witch with a wrinkled, hairless head and an evil disposition

Plot Summary

Emrys's earlist remembrances are of being washed ashore during a violent storm onto the rocky coast of Gwynedd (Wales) with a woman and being saved from the tusks of an enraged wild boar by the intervention of an immense stag. The boy would later realize that this was a manifestation of the duel between the powers of evil led by Rhita Gawr and the power of good, Dagda. His rescue occurred five years ago, when he was only seven. Since then he has lived in the village of Caer Vedwyd with the woman who is named Branwen and who claims to be his mother. Branwen is both feared and scorned by the native villagers because of her miraculous herbal cures and the unusual circumstances of her arrival. Both Emrys and his mother are often tormented by the village bully, Dinatius, and his followers. One day, they try to burn Branwen as a witch. Emrys summons hidden powers and causes a flaming tree to fall on Dinatius. Horrified by his actions, Emrys tries to save his oppressor but is burned and blinded in the flames. After being nursed back to health and receiving the power of second sight, Emrys realizes that he possesses frightening magical powers. He decides to leave Wales in search of his identity and the truth behind these unusual gifts. Before he leaves, Branwen gives him a mysterious pendant called the Galator and, after weathering several violent storms on his homemade raft, Emrys lands on the island of Fincayra, halfway between the human and the spirit world. Here he meets a young leaf-draped child of nature, the orphan Rhia, who is about his age. She befriends Emrys and tells him that the far part of the island, whose capital is the rotating Shrouded Castle, is under the control of wicked King Stagmar, a liege of evil Rhita Gawr. She reveals that a spreading blight emanates from the castle and will soon kill all living things on the island. Emrys makes two other friends on the island. First, a merlin, a fierce little falcon he dubs Trouble, and then an ungrammatical small giant, named Shim. At Rhia's tree house, he also meets Cwen, the girl's nurse, who is part tree and part human. King Stagmar learns that a young stranger on his island possesses the mystical Galator and dispatches his squads of evil gremlins to find it. When Rhia is captured by the gremlins and taken to the Shrouded Castle, Emrys, Trouble, and Shim set out to rescue her. During their quest, Emrys gets sound advice from the all-knowing white spider, Grand Elusa, and learns about his childhood from a sequestered wise man named Cairpre. He is told, by Cairpre, that Branwen, then named Elen, had married a man from the spirit world of Fincayra, and eventually she and her son, Emrys, were forced from the island because her child was a half-breed. In the lair of the wrinkled, man-eating witch, Domnu, Emrys gains her help by wagering the Galator against his ability to destroy the Shrouded Castle. Domnu temporarily miniaturizes Emrys and Shim so they can ride on the wings of Trouble to the forbidden castle. There, in a series of adventures during which Emrys must again call on his awesome powers, the boy encounters both King Stagmar and the malevolent dark spirit, Rhita Gawr. By using these powers, Emrys frees Rhia, restores Shim to the stature of a full-sized giant, subdues the king, and destroys the castle. Unfortunately, when Rhita Gawr disappears into the spirit world, he takes the valiant Trouble with him. The defeated Stagmar reveals to Emrys that he is his real father, but he is still under the control of Rhita Gawr. As Emrys, together with Rhia and Shim, prepare to reclaim the Galator from Domnu, Rhia decides that the boy deserves a new name more befitting his recent deeds and names him Merlin.

Suitability and Critical Comment

This thought-provoking, action-filled novel combines Druid and Celtic folk elements, in a story that reveals a love of nature and a respect for its curative powers, while telling the story of an epic struggle between good and evil and of a young boy's search for his past, his powers, and, indeed, his soul. This book and its sequels are recommended for readers in grades six through nine.

Themes and Subjects

Adventure stories, bullies, coming-of-age, evil, fantasy, giants, goblins, heroism, magic, nature, Wales, witches

Passages for Booktalking

The prologue in which Emrys reaches Wales (in paperback edition, pp. 1–8); Emrys tells about his five years with Branwen (pp. 12–17); two encounters with the bully, Dinatius (pp. 20–24); Emrys saves Branwen from the fire (pp. 43–45); and Emrys's voyage to Fincayra (pp. 67–72).

Additional Selections

Through a magical Seeing Stone given him by Merlin, the narrator travels to thirteenth-century England and relives incidents in King Arthur's life until he draws the sword from the stone in Kevin Crossley-Holland's *The Seeing Stone: Arthur Trilogy, Book One* (Scholastic, 2001).

In the fourth book of Gerald Morris's Arthurian series, *Parsifal's Page* (Houghton Mifflin, 2001), eleven-year-old Piers becomes the servant to Parsifal, who knows nothing about being a knight and has terrible manners.

In Nancy Springer's *I Am Morgan le Fay: A Tale of Camelot* (Philomel, 2001), a companion to *I Am Mordred* (Philomel, 1998), the author again recreates the intrigues and wizardry of Arthurian England.

For better readers, Mary Stewart's *The Crystal Cave* (Fawcett, 1970) sets the stage for the birth of Arthur in this, the first of a series based on Arthur's story.

About the Book

Booklist, Sept. 1, 1996, p. 118.
New York Times Book Review, Nov. 24, 1996, p. 20.
School Library Journal, Sept., 1996, p. 201.
VOYA, Oct., 1996, p. 216.

About the Author

Authors and Artists for Young Adults, vol. 30, Gale, 1990.
Continuum Encyclopedia of Children's Literature, Continuum, 2001.
Drew, Bernard A. *100 More Popular Young Adult Authors,* Libraries Unlimited, 2002.
Estes, Sally. "The Booklist Interview—T. A. Barron," *Booklist,* April 15, 2001, p. 1560.
St. James Guide to Young Adult Writers (2nd ed.), St. James, 1999.
Something about the Author, vol. 83, Gale, 1996; vol. 126, Gale, 2002.

Card, Orson Scott. *Ender's Shadow.* Doherty, 1999. $24.95
(0-312-86869-X) (Grades 10–12).

Introduction

Orson Scott Card (1951–) was born in Richmond, Washington, to a Mormon family. While attending Brigham Young University in Provo, Utah, he began writing plays. After doing missionary work for the church in Brazil, he wanted to supplement his regular income by writing science fiction. His bibliography now contains over sixty books and includes science fiction, fantasy, religious studies, and suspense novels. In 1977, his second short story, "Ender's Game," was published. He later expanded it into a book-length novel that was published by Tor in 1985. Amazingly, it won both the

Hugo and Nebula Awards, the two top literary awards in science fiction. Several other books about Ender Wiggin have followed. They tell of Ender's search for redemption after leading his forces in a genocidal victory over alien enemies. *Ender's Shadow* is not technically a sequel because it retells the events of *Ender's Game* from the point of view of Bean, Ender's diminutive lieutenant. Bean is smarter than Ender but lacks his charismatic leadership traits. He is a fascinating character whom readers enjoy meeting.

Principal Characters

Bean, a young man of great intelligence
Ender Wiggin, hero of the previous novel
Sister Carlotta, who discovers Bean
Dimak, leader at the Battle School
Colonel Graff, commandant
Nikolai, student at the Battle School

Plot Summary

Things are not going well for Earth in its battle with an insect-like alien race known as the Buggers. Now Earth is preparing to defend itself against total destruction by this alien enemy. The focus is on developing and training any military genius who can fight and win such a war. Because of the long distances involved in an interstellar war, Earth defenders have time to take brilliant children and train them into military geniuses. They are molded into a winning force at the facility known as the Battle School.

An unlikely candidate for the Battle School is Bean. He has fought a battle just to stay alive. His childhood was spent on the streets of Rotterdam, where only his incredible genius kept him alive. He was a tiny child who soon realized he would not survive by his strength but by his wits. He used his genius to win acceptance into a tough street gang. By civilizing them, he managed to live in the mean streets. His successes get him noticed by Sister Carlotta and from her by the Battle School recruiters, who send Bean into orbit to be trained. There he meets other superintelligent children, and the battle pace is accelerated. The leaders also learn that Bean has been genetically altered. He is still the smallest and weakest, but he is so intelligent that the commanders of the International Fleet place him as backup to Ender if Ender fails for any reason. When Bean finishes Battle School and is sent out with the others, including Ender, for more tests, he realizes that the tests are actually the real war. As the "tests" go on, Ender relies more and more on others, including Bean. Ender may not know the truth of the battles, that real people are dying, but Bean knows that Ender is feeling the effects.

Eventually, the force contacts the Buggers' home planet. Surrounded by their swarming mass, there is no hope of retreat and no possibility of victory, twenty starships in the human fleet against the defenders of the queen planet. Ender seems more and more indecisive. Then, Bean realizes that Ender's indecision does not mean he has frozen up or panicked. He simply understands the situation as it really is. The leaders had kept the truth from him about the reality of the games, but now it is going to backfire because Ender wants to turn command over to Bean and simply refuse to play—as these are really the games they played at Battle School. But Bean knows he has no plan either. He knows that Ender has to try or they will all die. So, Ender sets his forces in motion through the enemy swarm with instructions to launch each Dr. Device, which sets off a chain reaction, against the planet. Finally, only two human ships are left. One of them is Bean's, but he has no way of knowing whether it is his Dr. Device or the other ship's that causes the destruction of the queen planet. The Buggers are destroyed.

The war is over, and Ender is victorious. But Bean knows that when he returns to Earth, with the shaky truce that has been forged among nations, his war may be just beginning. He also knows what Ender does not, that Ender will not be allowed to return to Earth—ever. In order to preserve peace on Earth, a truce has been worked out. Both sides in the struggle for supremacy on Earth want custody of Ender as hero of the war. Instead, all the children of the Battle School will be repatriated—except Ender. In that way, no one on Earth will be able to use Ender to gain advantage over the other.

Bean returns to Earth and to a family he never knew. He learns that Nikolai, a fellow student at Battle School, is his twin brother.

Suitability and Critical Comment

This adult novel is best suited for the good reader who is a fan of science fiction and interplanetary warfare. It is filled with so-called war games on a futuristic level in a battle school that molds children of superintelligence into a superior force that will save the world. As Bean speculates about what intrahuman wars might occur after the defeat of the Buggers, possibilities are left open for future sequels; for grades ten through twelve.

Themes and Subjects

Courage, discipline, gene altering, intelligence, interplanetary, science fiction, travel, war games

Passages for Booktalking

Bean gets his name (pp. 15–20); Bean enters Battle School (p. 101); Bean makes friends with Nikolai (pp. 125–36); Sister Carlotta discusses Bean with his family (pp. 211–16); the final battle (pp. 360–70).

Additional Selections

Nonstop action, great humor, and wonderful characters are present in the exciting fantasy *The Rover* (Tor, 2001) by Mel Odom.

Women are used only for procreation in Margaret Atwood's *Handmaid's Tale* (Houghton Mifflin, 1985), a novel set in the near future, which features Offred, a servant.

The classic battle between black and white magic is at the center of Marion Zimmer Bradley's exciting fantasy *Heartlight* (Tor, 1998).

Calrius, long-lost heir to a noble house, confronts Arioso aka Basilisk, the man who murdered his family in *Song of the Basilisk* (Ace, 1998) by Patricia A. McKillip.

About the Book

Booklist, July, 1999, p. 1892.
Kirkus Reviews, July, 1999, p. 1004
Library Journal, Sept. 15, 1999, p. 115.
School Library Journal, Dec., 1999, p. 163.
VOYA, Feb., 2000, pp. 381, 399.

About the Author

Authors and Artists for Young Adults, vol. 11, Gale, 1993; vol. 42, Gale, 2002.
Collings, Michael R. *Storyteller: The Official Orson Scott Card Bibliography and International Reader's Guide,* Overlook Connection, 2001.
Collings, Michael R., and Clarke Boden. *The Works of Orson Scott Card,* Borgo, 1995.
Contemporary Authors New Revision Series, vol. 106, Gale, 2002.
Contemporary Literary Criticism, vol. 44, Gale, 1987; vol. 47, Gale, 1988; vol. 50, Gale, 1988.
Fletcher, Marilyn P. *Reader's Guide to Twentieth Century Science Fiction Writers,* ALA, 1991.
Lives and Works: Young Adult Authors, vol. 2, Grolier, 1999, pp. 21–23.
St. James Guide to Young Adult Writers (2nd ed.), St. James, 1999.
Schellinger, Paul E. *Twentieth Century Science Fiction Writers,* St. James, 1992.
Something about the Author, vol. 127, Gale, 2002.

Colfer, Eoin. *Artemis Fowl.* Hyperion, 2001. $16.95 (0-7868-0801-2) (Grades 6–9).

Introduction

Eoin Colfer, formerly an elementary school teacher in his native Ireland, now devotes himself to full-time writing. Before *Artemis Fowl,* he wrote for the same age group two novels about Benny, a young sports fanatic. In the first, *Benny and Omar* (O'Brian Press, 2001), our young hero accompanies his family to Tunisia, where his father works, and there meets and shares several adventures with a native boy named Omar. *Artemis Fowl* is a rip-roaring, fast-paced adventure fantasy whose title character is a full-blown arch criminal, though only twelve years of age. The book has already been filmed, and it has spawned its first sequel, *Artemis Fowl: The Arctic Incident* (Hyperion, 2002). Readers should note that a pictograph code runs along the bottom of each page. Help in cracking this code can be obtained online at www.artemisfowl.com.

Principal Characters

Artemis Fowl, a twelve-year-old ingenious mastermind and seasoned criminal

Butler, a mountain of a man who is Artemis's devoted servant

Juliet Butler, Butler's teenaged sister, who is a wrestling champion

Angeline Fowl, Artemis's addle-brained mother

Holly Short, a female leprechaun whose great-grandfather was Cupid

Commander Julius Root, a blustering elf who is in charge of LEPrecon, Holly's unit

Foaly, a centaur who is in charge of the high-tech aspects of LEPrecon.

Mulch Diggums, a kleptomaniac dwarf

Plot Summary

Like his ancestors before him, twelve-year-old superintelligent Artemis Fowl has dedicated himself to a life of diabolical crime. In order to replenish some of the Fowl fortune lost by his now-missing father in nefarious dealings with the Russian Mafia, Artemis has devised a crafty plot to steal gold from the fairy folk, known as the People, who live underground and are rarely seen by humans, whom the fairies refer to as the Mud people. Artemis's fiendish plan involves traveling, with his Goliath-like manservant, Butler, from Fowl Manor, the family castle outside of Dublin, to Ho Chi Minh City, where he has located a derelict drunken fairy. Through trickery, he manages to appropriate from the fairy for a brief period (but long enough to scan it with a digital camera), a copy of the Book, the fairy bible that contains, in code, details of their commandments, magic, and high technology. Back at Fowl Manor, where his dotty mother, Angeline Fowl, dotes on her only son and grieves for her missing husband, he painstakingly cracks the code and is now in possession of all the secrets of the fairies. His plan is to kidnap a fairy and demand a ransom in the form of one ton of fairy gold. He finds a victim in Holly Short, a tough, spunky leprechaun who is the first female officer in the elite Lower Elements Police Reconnaissance (LEPrecon) unit under the direction of blustering Commander Root, a self-important elf. Holly has just distinguished herself in an operation aboveground that involved subduing a renegade troll who has terrorized a community in Italy. Her mission was made less arduous through the help of a high-tech wizard, Foaly, a paranoid centaur, who has created an amazing communication network for the underground People. Holly's magical powers are diminishing, and she must renew them by performing the Ritual, which involves burying an acorn under a full moon in a specific forest area. Artemis, who has learned about the Ritual from the Book, hides, with Butler, in the woods and captures the vulnerable fairy before she can complete the ceremony. Holly is held prisoner in Fowl Manor, and there she becomes friendly with Butler's teenaged sister, Juliet, a wrestling fanatic. Through Foaly's communication skills, Commander Root discovers the whereabouts of Holly and lays siege to the seemingly impregnable Fowl Manor. Several schemes are tried. One involves using a kleptomaniac dwarf, named Mulch Diggums, who is renowned for his skill in digging underground tunnels. Mulch eats his way into the castle and finds both Holly and the photocopy of the Book. Unable to rescue the elf, he returns with his treasure to Commander Root. A second attempt involves using a battering ram and a gigantic troll to break down the manor door. This, too, fails, but in the process of the attack, Holly is freed. As a last resort, the Commander uses Foaly's technology to create a time-stop that will eventually kill any inhabitant of Fowl Manor. Although Artemis and the Butlers use powerful sleeping pills to make them invulnerable to this fairy stratagem, Artemis realizes that his fiendish plot has been foiled and that he no longer has the knowledge to utilize fairy magic. He escapes with Butler and Juliet, vowing that he will succeed the next time.

Suitability and Critical Comment

This is a wild, rip-roaring adventure that combines fairy folklore, fantasy, and high-tech gimmicks. It is fast paced, full of action, and teeming with humor, sometimes sophisticated and sometimes earthy (for example, the excretion and flatulence of concrete-eating Mulch figure prominently). Both children and adults enjoy this outrageous tale, but it is best suited to an audience of ten- to sixteen-year-olds.

Themes and Subjects

Adventure stories, courage, crime, fairies, fantasy, Ireland, kidnapping, loyalty

Passages for Booktalking

The Prologue (pp. 1–2) introduces Artemis; he tricks the fairy into giving him the Book (pp. 9–15); Artemis visits his mother at Fowl Manor (pp. 19–23); Holly travels aboveground with Foaly's help (pp. 41–50); the fight with the troll (pp. 53–58); and Holly is caught by Artemis (pp. 70–76).

Additional Suggestions

In Kathy Mackel's *Eggs in One Basket* (HarperCollins, 2000), ● sequel to *Can of Worms* (HarperCollins, 1999), young Scott must save an alien bird and her eggs from the villainous Shards from outer space.

In Zimbabwe in 2194, a thirteen-year-old and his siblings leave their compound and embark on a series of perilous adventures in Nancy Farmer's *The Ear, the Eye and the Arm* (Orchard, 1994).

Max travels through time by using a device several people would kill to possess in William Sleator's *Strange Attractors* (Puffin, 1991).

A clever cat named the Amazing Maurice, a horde of rats, and a flute-playing kid attempt a pied piper scam in Terry Pratchett's *The Amazing Maurice and His Educated Rodents* (HarperCollins, 2001).

About the Book

Booklist, April 15, 2001, p. 1554.
Bulletin of the Center for Children's Books, July, 2001, p. 496.
Horn Book, July-Aug., 2001, p. 449.
Kirkus Reviews, April 1, 2001, p. 496.
New York Times Book Review, June 15, 2001, p. 102.
School Library Journal, May, 2001, p. 148.
VOYA, August, 2001, p. 211.

About the Author

No information available.

Cooper, Susan. *King of Shadows.* Simon & Schuster, 1999. $16.00 (0-689-82817-9) (Grades 8–12).

Introduction

Susan Cooper (1935–) spent the first eighteen years of her life about twenty miles from London in Buckinghamshire. Her other home was Aberdovey, in North Wales, where her grandmother was born. During the blitz of World War II, she found that she enjoyed writing and turned to the old tales of England and Wales for inspiration. Perhaps she is best known for the five-volume series called *The Dark Is Rising*, named after the second book in the sequence. The plots are complex and deal, as the author has stated, with such dualities in human nature as forgiveness and revenge, love and hate, kindness and cruelty, and the epic struggle between the forces of Light and Dark. These novels rely more on setting and atmosphere than on action for their appeal. Folklore, setting, and mythic atmosphere blend seamlessly. Ms. Cooper leaves the world of Welsh fantasy in *King of Shadows,* the story of Nat Field, who time travels to 1599 London in the time of Shakespeare.

Principal Characters

Nat Field, a boy from North Carolina
Arby, director of The Company of Boys
William Shakespeare
Richard Babbage/Burbage, founder of the Globe Theatre
Harry, Nat's friend in Shakespeare's time
Aunt Jen
The Fishers, Nat's foster family in London

Plot Summary

Nat Field, who lives with his aunt in North Carolina and is still suffering the effects of his father's suicide some years earlier, has joined a theater troupe. It was put together to do Shakespeare "as it was originally performed," according to the troupe's director, Arby. Nat is set to play Puck in *A Midsummer Night's Dream* and Pindarus in *Julius Caesar.* But the big excitement occurs when the troupe goes to London to perform in the Globe Theatre, which has been restored to look as it did in Shakespeare's time, four hundred years ago. Nat's Aunt Jen is not happy about his going overseas until she talks with the Fishers, who will be Nat's foster family in London.

When Nat gets to London, where members of the American Company of Boys have come from all over the United States, he begins rehearsals in the historic theater. At one rehearsal, he feels as though the backdrops are beginning to tilt and sway, and he staggers a bit. He assures everyone that he is okay, but that night after dinner he feels ill again. Mrs. Fisher thinks it's the twenty-four-hour virus. But the next morning, he awakens to find himself in a different bed, wearing different clothes. He has been transported back to the year 1599. He is still Nat Field, but this Nat is a child actor from St. Paul's School who is about to go to the Globe to rehearse *A Midsummer Night's Dream,* in which he will play the role of Puck. Still disoriented, Nat plays along and goes into the round of rehearsals as though he had always lived in that time.

The highlight of Nat's new surroundings is his meeting with William Shakespeare himself. The great playwright and the young boy grow close when Nat confesses to Shakespeare about the sorrow of losing both his parents. Shakespeare takes a special liking to Nat, who reminds him of his own lost son, Hamnet. Shakespeare treats Nat almost as a surrogate son, giving him affection, sympathy, respect, and a sonnet on the constancy of love, which is a great comfort to the boy now and later.

Nat survives well in his new world, although he does make some mistakes, such as performing the Heimlich maneuver when a young boy starts to choke. Since that was unheard of in Shakespeare's time, some people now regard him as a witch. But after the successful performance of *A Midsummer Night's Dream,* Nat gets to meet Queen Elizabeth I, who calls him a pretty boy. After that, Nat must part with Shakespeare, who must leave for Stratford but tells Nat that he can come back to him when he finishes school.

But the next morning, Nat awakens to find himself back in London in his own time. He is in the hospital, where he has been for a week. Under his pillow is the poem given him by Shakespeare. Mrs. Fisher explains that they called the doctor after he became worse, and he was taken to the hospital, where doctors were astonished to discover that he had bubonic plague, the scourge of Europe during Shakespeare's time. Aunt Jen has flown from the United States to be with him. Nat realizes that, of course, they do not know that he really was not there during his illness in the hospital. Missing Shakespeare and trying to sort out what happened to him, Nat tells his story to friends Gil and Rachel. They try to figure out what occurred in Nat's transformation. They know it really happened because of the dash of green paint on Nat's neck when he returned; he knows that came from the theater back in time. Nat still cannot be comforted until he learns the real name of his present director, whom he knows only as Arby. He is really Richard Babbage, so like the Richard Burbage of Shakespeare's time.

Suitability and Critical Comment

Although this is an easy read for most teenagers, it is best suited for those with some interest in Shakespeare or the theater. Part historical fiction and part fantasy, this book is entertaining and lively and gives a good dramatization of life in the everyday England of centuries ago. Shakespeare comes alive as a real figure, which should be attractive to readers of this age; for grades eight through twelve.

Themes and Subjects

Acting, fantasy, foster families, friendship, London, Shakespeare, suicide, time travel

Passages for Booktalking

Nat wakes up in 1599 (pp. 32–35); the doctor thinks he has bubonic plague (pp. 41–42); Nat meets Shakespeare (pp. 57–58); Nat discusses his father with Shakespeare (pp. 71–77); Nat meets Queen Elizabeth I (pp. 136–41).

Additional Suggestions

In Janet Hickman's *Ravine* (Greenwillow, 2002), a collie exists in two worlds, one realistic and the other magical, but both are linked by a mysterious ravine.

Fourteen-year-old Owl Tycho is an ordinary high schooler with a crush on her science teacher by day, but she is an owl at night in Patrice Kindl's charming *Owl in Love* (Houghton Mifflin, 1993).

Menolly and her fire lizards overcome social pressures to achieve her goal of becoming a harper on the planet Pern in Anne McCaffrey's *Dragonsinger* (Simon & Schuster, 1977).

Harry enters the Hogwarts School of Witchcraft and Wizardry in *Harry Potter and the Sorcerer's Stone* (Scholastic, 1998), the first volume of the amazing series by J. K. Rowling.

About the Book

Booklist, Oct. 15, 1999, p. 442.
Bulletin of the Center for Children's Books, Dec., 1999, p. 126.
Horn Book, Nov.-Dec., 1999, p. 735.
Kirkus Reviews, Nov. 1, 1999, p. 1740.
New York Times Book Review, Jan. 16, 2000, p. 27.
School Library Journal, Nov., 1999, p. 156.

About the Author

Authors and Artists for Young Adults, vol. 13, Gale, 1994; vol. 41, Gale, 2001.
Children's Literature Review, vol. 4, Gale, 1982; vol. 61, Gale, 2001.
Continuum Encyclopedia of Children's Literature, Continuum, 2001.
Cooper, Susan. *Dreams and Wishes: Essays on Writing for Children,* McElderry, 1996.
Cooper, Susan. "Fantasy in the Real World," *Horn Book,* May-June, 1990, pp. 304–5.
Drew, Bernard A. *The 100 Most Popular Young Adult Authors,* Libraries Unlimited, 1997.
Fourth Book of Junior Authors and Illustrators, Wilson, 1978.
Gallo, Donald. *Speaking for Ourselves,* National Council of Teachers of English, 1990.
Kingman, Lee. "Newbery and Caldecott Medal Books: 1976–1985," *Horn Book,* 1985.
Major Authors and Illustrators for Children and Young Adults, vol. 2, Gale, 1993.
"Newbery Award Acceptance Material, 1976," *Horn Book,* July-Aug., 1976, pp. 361–72.
Rochman, Hazel. "Interview with Susan Cooper," *Booklist,* Sept. 15, 1997, pp. 226–27.
St. James Guide to Young Adult Writers (2nd ed.), St. James, 1999.
Silvey, Anita. *Children's Books and Their Creators,* Houghton Mifflin, 1995.
Something about the Author, vol. 4, Gale, 1973; vol. 64, Gale, 1991; vol. 104, Gale, 1999.

Something about the Author Autobiography Series, vol. 6, Gale, 1988.
Twentieth Century Young Adult Writers, St. James, 1994.

Crichton, Michael. *Timeline.* Knopf, 1999. $26.95 (0-679-44461-5)
(Grades 10–12).

Michael Crichton has sampled many careers, including physician, teacher, film director, screenwriter, and, most prominently, the author of many best-selling techno-thrillers. He grew up in Roslyn, a suburban community on Long Island. He always wanted to write and enjoyed writing. At fourteen, his first article, an account of a family vacation, was published in the *New York Times.* Even after entering medical school, he continued a tight writing schedule. While still in school, his first novel, *The Andromeda Strain* (Knopf, 1969), became an instant best-seller. It tells of a deadly organism that arrives on Earth as a result of a NASA space probe. Because of this unexpected success, he made a tough decision to leave medicine and concentrate on writing. Another of his popular books was *Jurassic Park* (Knopf, 1990), about billionaire John Hammond and his dream of building an amusement park populated by real-life dinosaurs recreated through DNA samples and the wizardry of modern biotechnology. *Timeline* continues the fine tradition set by these suspenseful adventure stories.

Principal Characters
Robert Doniger, head of ITC
John Gordon, vice president of ITC
Edward Johnston, Yale history professor on the Dordogne project
Chris Hughes, assistant
Andre Marek, assistant
David Stern, technical expert
Kate Erickson, assistant

Plot Summary
Robert Doniger, ruthless head of ITC, is determined to use his company's newfound power for ultimate world control. ITC has found the existence of multiuniverses, or multiverses, and has devised the technology for humans to travel to these times and places. But there have been a few glitches in the operation, and Doniger is worried that they will leak to the press. When Professor Edward Johnston, who is associated with ITC only through sponsorship of the Dordogne project, which he and his assistants have been working on in France, goes to ITC to talk to Doniger, he mistak-

enly gets himself transported to the fourteenth century and is unable to get back. Assistants Chris, Andre, David, and Kate are called to ITC and asked to go back in time to fourteenth-century feudal France and get Johnston out. They know the site and time better than anyone else in the world because of their work. But they are not told of the true possibility of never returning. In the end, three of them decide to go to rescue the professor, but David Stern declines and remains behind. He is certain that something is wrong and wants to have a chance to protect his friends.

In a kind of time machine apparatus, the three historians are transported to feudal France in the fourteenth century and to the fortress of Castelgard, which they recognize from their research. They are dressed as they would be in the fourteenth century, equipped with an apparatus that translates some of the dialect of the time so that they can understand what is being said to them, and carrying a white ceramic marker, which is their ticket to return to the present time. They set out on a search for the professor, who they believe to be in the monastery, but they do not want to get too far from the apparatus that sent them back into history. Supposedly, they have two hours to do the job and rescue the professor. But almost before their adventure can begin, the unthinkable happens—their return machine is destroyed. Now they have no prospect of getting back.

The three run into more harrowing events as they are pursued by soldiers while trying to find their way to the castle. At one point, Chris is challenged to a duel and must cooperate or he will be killed. By taking a hit on his breastplate and falling down as though severely injured, he manages to survive. The three also meet Sir Oliver de Vannes, an English knight who engaged in warfare at Castelgard in 1357.

Meanwhile, back at ITC where Stern is watching the events, another disaster occurs. There is an explosion in the control room. Stern tries to get one of the original machines back in working order.

The historians endure a number of obstacles before they reach the professor, who is alive and well. But they still have the ceramic marker, and they figure they have one last shot to return to their own time. As they prepare to go, Andre tells them he will not be leaving with them. He will stay in the fourteenth century.

They return to the present time and to the head of ITC, who is furious because he is afraid his disregard for their safety and his dubious undertakings might be leaked to the press. However, Vice President Gordon knocks out Doniger and sends him back in the machine to Castelgard. Doniger is not too upset on arriving in the fourteenth century; he has the ceramic marker with him, and he can return at his will . . . or so he thinks. Then he begins to notice the people around him; they seem to be bleeding freely, and there are blackish lumps on their bodies. With horror, he realizes what year he is in—1348. The plague has struck Castelgard . . . Doniger begins to cough.

Suitability and Critical Comment

This adult novel is probably best attempted by good readers with some understanding of and a good interest in science of the future, such as the field of quantum technology. Although the novel itself is easily read with much good, lively action, the explanations of the science that transports them back to the fourteenth century are difficult to follow on any level. The novel, however, can be enjoyed without a full understanding of the technology; for grades ten through twelve.

Themes and Subjects

Fourteenth-century France, history, knights, plague, quantum technology, science, time travel

Passages for Booktalking

Edward sends a help message from the fourteenth century (pp. 90–91); Gordon explains the new technology (pp. 108–14); David Stern refuses to go (pp. 150–52); they find the professor (pp. 239–41); Doniger is sent back (pp. 439–41).

Additional Selections

Two teenage sisters must face choices about the murder of their mother in Sarah Zettel's *Kingdom of Cages* (Warner Aspect, 2001), a novel set in an Earth-colonized universe.

Richard Bachman (aka Stephen King) has written an exciting thriller in *Long Walk* (Penguin, 1979), about a grueling marathon that will claim the lives of 99 of the 100 boys who begin it.

Jack McDevitt's *Moonfall* (HarperCollins, 1998) is a gripping thriller about a comet on a collision course with the moon.

Chris Stone, who lives in darkness because of a rare disease, must explore his town's deadly secret to save his world in Dean Koontz's *Fear Nothing* (Bantam, 1998).

About the Book

Booklist, Jan. 1, 2000, p. 819.
Kirkus Reviews, Nov. 1, 1999, p. 1673.
New York Times Book Review, Nov. 21, 1999, p. 6.
School Library Journal, April, 2000, p. 158.
VOYA, Dec., 2000, p. 321.

About the Author
Authors and Artists for Young Adults, vol. 10, Gale, 1993.
Contemporary Authors New Revision Series, vol. 76, Gale, 1999.
Contemporary Literary Criticism, vol. 2, Gale, 1974; vol. 6, Gale, 1976; vol. 54, Gale, 1989.
St. James Guide to Young Adult Writers (2nd ed.), St. James, 1999.

Dickinson, Peter. *The Ropemaker.* Delacorte, 2001. $23.95 (0-385-72921-9) (Grades 7–10).

Introduction

Peter Dickinson (1927–) was born in Northern Rhodesia (now Zambia) where he spent his first seven years. Educated in England at Eton and Cambridge, he served in the British Army from 1946 to 1948. He worked for a time as reviewer and general writer at *Punch,* the British humor magazine, now defunct, before becoming a full-time writer. After his first wife died in 1988, he married the successful fantasy writer Robin McKinley (see *Rose Daughter* in this section). In the world of contemporary English literature, Peter Dickinson has a dual personality because he writes both highly acclaimed adult thriller-fantasies and equally exciting books for young adults. In this latter group, one of his most admired is *Eva* (Delacorte, 1989), a futuristic novel in which the brain of a young girl is placed into the body of a female chimpanzee after a car accident in which her parents are killed and she receives remediless bodily injuries. Its central theme is the exploitation of all forms of life by humans. *The Ropemaker* is another stunning success by this matchless storyteller.

Principal Characters

Tilja, a child of the valley
Tahl, Tilja's friend
Meena, Tilja's grandmother
Alnor, Tahl's grandfather
The Ropemaker, a mysterious stranger
Faheel, the ancient magician

Plot Summary

Tilja Urladaughter is a child of the valley. Her grandmother, Meena, can hear the whisperings of cedars in the forest. Tilja has always been jealous because Meena's magic powers have been passed to her mother and her younger sister, but not to Tilja. Tahl's grandfather, Alnor, also has the magic; he can hear the chatter of the magic streams. These families and their magic have kept the valley safe for generations. The magic keeps away barbarian marauders from the north and the greedy, powerful Empire to the south. But now comes disturbing news. The magic that has protected the families of the valley is slowly breaking down. If it goes, in time the valleys and its inhabitants will surely be destroyed. But now it is Winter Festival time, and Tilja is very excited because she thinks she may be able to see some real magic there. At the festival, however, her family meets the Ortahlsons. They learn that these new people coming are those who speak to the great ice glacier. Once again, talk turns to the fading magic of the valley.

It is decided that Tilja, Tahl, and their grandparents must set out on a quest to restore the magic. They must journey into the evil Empire to find the ancient magician Faheel, who originally cast the magic spells, but he has not been seen in many years and even to utter his name means death. Thus begins their dangerous, exciting journey over many miles of hostile, unfamiliar territory. As the quest continues, Tilja begins to learn of her own ability. She is able to neutralize magic spells, making them powerless. Since the leaders of the Empire use magic to control their subjects, Tilja's ability proves very useful and important. As she uses this magic to save them and pursue their quest, Tilja's confidence in her own abilities grows.

At one point in their dangerous journey, they are captured and tied up with ropes by thieves. But in the night a mysterious, quiet stranger comes and unties them. They call him Ropemaker. His magic is mightier than all the magicians in the Empire. Finally, they reach Talagh, the warded city. Wards of the greatest power were built into its walls by the most powerful magicians in the Empire. After many more wanderings and adventures, Tilja comes face-to-face with Faheel, creator of the original magic. He sees the hair tie that was given to her by Ropemaker and asks where she got it. Tilja replies that the man told them to call him Ropemaker. Faheel says, "Ah . . . time is a great rope." He tells Tilja that he has had to lay his magic powers aside. They are weakening as he, merely a mortal, is growing old. As Faheel's powers weaken further, he relies more and more on Tilja to surmount all the obstacles that the evildoers of the Empire put in their way. As Tilja comes of age and uses her own powers, the small group, with the help of the Ropemaker, achieves its goal of destroying the evil forces and bringing back peace to the prosperous valley.

But when Tilja and the others return from their journey, they realize that they are all better off without real magic. It belongs in the forests and the mountains, not in the valley.

Suitability and Critical Comment

This is a lengthy fantasy and mystery suited for readers who like a complex plot, a strong heroine, and constantly surprising characters and action. There are endless plot turns and high adventure, although the narrative sometimes bogs down in wordy descriptions of magical events. For the thinking reader, this is an enjoyable but challenging adventure. For grades seven through ten.

Themes and Subjects

Adventure, curses and spells, family relationships, fantasy, heredity, magic, mythology

Passages for Booktalking

Something is happening to the magic (pp. 38–45); the journey begins (pp. 71–90); Tilja meets the Ropemaker (pp. 128–40); Tilja meets Faheel (pp. 211–26); the cedars wake up (pp. 346–55).

Additional Selections

Joyce McDonald's *Shadows of Simon Gray* (Delacorte, 2001) is a combination thriller and ghost story about Simon Gray, recovering in the hospital from an automobile accident, and his counterpart who was hanged for murder in 1798.

Because of the violence and pollution, a family builds a large ship and fills it with animals just before the rains start in Barbara Cohen's *Unicorns in the Rain* (Atheneum, 1980).

Beautiful teenager Vivian, who is a werewolf, longs to share her secret with her human boyfriend in *Blood and Chocolate* (Delacorte, 1998) by Annette Curtis Klause.

In Robert Jordan's *Eye of the World* (St. Martins, 1991), three teenagers begin a fantasy quest in an epic struggle between good and evil.

About the Book

Booklist, Oct. 15, 2001, p. 394.
Bulletin of the Center for Children's Books, Jan., 2002, p. 169.
Horn Book, Nov., 2001, p. 745.
Kirkus Reviews, Nov. 1, 2001, p. 1547.
School Library Journal, Nov., 2001, p. 154.
VOYA, Dec., 2001, p. 367.

About the Author

Authors and Artists for Young Adults, vol. 9, Gale, 1992.
Children's Literature Review, vol. 29, Gale, 1993.
Continuum Encyclopedia of Children's Literature, Continuum, 2001.

Dickinson, Peter. "Fantasy: The Need for Realism in Children's Literature," *Education,* Spring, 1986, pp. 39–51.
Drew, Bernard A. *The 100 Most Popular Young Adult Authors,* Libraries Unlimited, 1997.
Fourth Book of Junior Authors and Illustrators, Wilson, 1978.
Henderson, Lesley. *Twentieth Century Crime and Mystery Writers* (3rd ed.), St. James, 1991.
Hipple, Ted. *Writers for Young Adults,* vol. 1, Scribners, 1997, pp. 373–82.
Lives and Works: Young Adult Authors, vol. 3, Grolier, 1999, pp. 9–11.
Major Authors and Illustrators for Children and Young Adults, vol. 2, Gale, 1993.
St. James Guide to Young Adult Writers (2nd ed.), St. James, 1999.
Silvey, Anita. *Children's Books and Their Creators,* Houghton Mifflin, 1995.
Something about the Author, vol. 5, Gale, 1973; vol. 62, Gale, 1991; vol. 95, Gale, 1998.
Welton, Noelle. *Twentieth Century Science Fiction Writers* (3rd ed.), St. James, 1991.

Jacques, Brian. *Redwall.* Philomel, 1987. $18.95 (0-399-21424-0); pb. Ace, $6.99 (0-441-00548-9) (Grades 5–8).

Introduction

Brian Jacques (1939–) (pronounced "Jakes") was born in Liverpool of Irish parents. He had many jobs, including seaman, longshoreman, truck driver, boxer, and member of a folk-singing group. By his early forties, he had become an entertainer with a weekly radio show. His first novel, *Redwall* was originally written for a school for the blind in Liverpool, but luckily it was picked up by a reputable author and sent it to the English publishing house of Hutchinson. In was originally intended to be part of a trilogy, but the series now numbers about twelve. Though published first, it is preceded chronologically by others in the series. The second published, *Mossflower* (Philomel, 1988), tells of the exploits of the young mouse warrior, Martin, and the building of Redwall Abbey. The third, *Mariel of Redwall* (Philomel, 1992), is the story of Mariel, the daughter of Joseph the bellmaker and how she fights the murderous pirate rat Gobool the Wild.

Principal Characters

Matthias, a courageous young novice at Redwall Abbey
Abbot Mortimer, the elderly patriarch of the abbey
Constance, the brave badger who works in the abbey compound
Methuselah, the scribe and historian of the abbey
Cornflower, the attractive daughter of Mr. and Mrs. Fieldmouse
Cluny the Scourge, the leader of a murderous band of bilge rats
Basil Stag Hare, an unusual rabbit that becomes Matthias's ally

Warbeak Sparra, a scrappy young bird that later becomes king of the
   sparrows
Asmodeus, the viper who owns Martin's magical sword

Plot Summary

Redwall Abbey is an ancient, beautiful edifice in a peaceful countryside
surrounded by many outbuildings and a high wall on four sides for protection. This idyllic institution is directed by a beatific mouse, the elderly Abbot
Mortimer. Other inhabitants include mice Matthias, an eager young novice,
and Methuselah, the wise ancient historian; and Constance the badger who
works on the grounds. While the residents of Redwall and their guests,
including Mr. and Mrs. Fieldmouse and their attractive daughter, Cornflower, are attending Mortimer's Golden Jubilee, a gang of murderous, heavily armed bilge rats, led by the one-eyed Cluny the Scourge, approach the
abbey intent on conquest. News of the impending attack reaches the abbey,
and a war council is called, during which the spirit of their great mouse
leader of yesterday, Martin, is evoked. His exploits are immortalized in a tapestry that hangs in the Great Hall. The next day, Cluny and his lieutenant
present a surrender ultimatum, which is refused. That night, one of Cluny's
henchmen, Shadow, scales the walls and steals the fragment of the tapestry
picturing Martin with brandished sword. Matthias sets off to retrieve the tapestry, and he meets in the woods a rabbit named Basil Stag Hare, who
becomes his ally. When Matthias learns that Cluny is about to attack, he
returns to the abbey with Basil but without the bit of tapestry. Through the
quick thinking of Constance, the attack is repulsed, and Cluny receives
wounds requiring three weeks of bed rest. From an inscription found under
the tapestry, Matthias and Methuselah discover that the young warrior mouse
is destined to lead his people to victory, but he requires Martin's magic
sword. Believing that the sword was used as a weathervane for the abbey,
Matthias climbs to the roof but is attacked by vicious sparrows. While being
held captive by them, he gains the friendship of a wild young sparrow named
Warbeak Sparra and learns that the sword is being held by a giant poisonous
viper, the adder Asmodeus. Matthias escapes from the sparrows by killing
their treacherous king. After bidding a tender farewell to Cornflower, who
has now become his girlfriend, he sets out to find Asmodeus. Meanwhile,
Cluny recovers and launches another attack. He tries many ploys, first the
construction of a secret siege tower, which is luckily burned by the residents
after Cornflower discovers it; next, the creation of tunnels under the walls.
Again the stratagem is discovered and the plan foiled. Luck, unfortunately,
runs out for the brave abbey dwellers. Cluny blackmails a hapless mouse into
opening the giant door in the protective wall, and the abbey is captured.

Meanwhile, Matthias finds the adder's den and, in a battle of wits and strength, kills him and seizes the sword. He learns of the abbey's fall and gathers together a great woodland army aided by Warbeak, now leader of the courageous sparrows. Together, Matthias, sword in hand, and his allies surprise the villainous rats and free their friends. Cluny attempts to escape but is pursued by Matthias. It is a fight to the death. When Cluny traps Matthias in the bell tower, the quick-thinking mouse cuts the rope holding the giant abbey bell in place. It crashes to the floor, crushing Cluny. The aged Abbot Mortimer, fearing that death is near, tells Matthias that he should remain at the abbey not as a brother but as Matthias, the Warrior Mouse of Redwall and husband to Cornflower. In a brief epilogue, we are told that that is exactly what happened and that later Matthias and Cornflower have a son, Mattimeo, who is destined to have his own thrilling adventures.

Suitability and Critical Comment

This is a full-bodied, swashbuckling adventure story filled with amazing plot twists and scary cliff-hanging situations. Although peopled with animal characters, this novel contains the ingredients of all standard epics: good versus evil and a quest involving hairbreadth escapes. Though intended for readers roughly in middle school grades, it is enjoyed by a much larger audience, including many adults.

Themes and Subjects

Adventure, animals, bravery, churches, courage, devotion, fantasy, humor, mice

Passages for Booktalking

Matthias and Abbot Mortimer are introduced (pp. 13–16); Cluny the Scourge and his rats travel toward Redwall (pp. 17–18, pp. 23–25); the inhabitants of the abbey hear about Cluny (pp. 33–38); Cluny enters the abbey with an ultimatum (pp. 49–55); and parts of the tapestry are stolen by Shadow (pp. 70–76).

Additional Selections

A Glory of Unicorns (Scholastic, 1998) edited by Bruce Coville contains thought-provoking and entertaining stories that take readers from this world to the great beyond.

After losing everything, including his life, in a dice game with King Jaya, young King Tamar tries to reclaim his honor in Lloyd Alexander's *The Iron Ring* (Dutton, 1997).

Some London mice leave their comfortable home for a terrifying life in the sewers populated by murderous rats in *The Dark Portal* (North-South, 2000) by Robin Jarvis.

A group of rabbits set out to find a new home in the classic by Richard Adams, *Watership Down* (Macmillan, 1974).

About the Book
Booklist, June 1, 1987, p. 1519.
Bulletin of the Center for Children's Books, July, 1987, p. 211.
Kirkus Reviews, June 1, 1987, p. 858.
School Library Journal, Aug. 1987, p. 96.

About the Author
Authors and Artists for Young Adults, vol. 20, Gale, 1999.
Children's Literature Review, vol. 21, Gale, 1990.
Continuum Encyclopedia of Children's Literature, Continuum, 2001.
Drew, Bernard A. *The 100 Most Popular Young Adult Authors,* Libraries Unlimited, 1997.
St. James Guide to Young Adult Writers (2nd ed.), St. James, 1999.
Silvey, Anita. *Children's Books and Their Creators,* Houghton Mifflin, 1995.
Something about the Author, vol. 62, Gale, 1990; vol. 95, Gale, 1998.
Twentieth Century Young Adult Writers, St. James, 1994.

Jones, Diana Wynne. *Dark Lord of Derkholm.* Greenwillow, 1998.
$16.00 (0-688-16004-2) (Grades 7–10).

Introduction
Diana Wynne Jones (1934–) was born in London, the daughter of two educators. Living in Northern England during World War II, she had encounters as a child with two of the legends of children's literature, Arthur Ransom and Beatrix Potter, and was shocked to discover that they both disliked children! At age eight, she announced that she was going to be a writer. She chose fantasy because she claims that she never had enough of it as a child and that books should provide more than reality. Her books combine humor, mystery, adventure, suspense, and danger in plots filled with ghosts, witches, wizards, and castles, some of which move. In the sequel to *Dark Lord of Derkholm* called *Year of the Griffin* (Greenwillow, 2000), eight years have passed since the events described in the first book, but the Wizards' University is in a shambles. Wizard Derk's griffin daughter Elda and her fellow first-year students face boring lectures, tyrannical

tutors, and awful cafeteria food. As well, a band of trained assassins and a flock of renegade griffins add to their problems in this amusing sequel.

Principal Characters
  Wizard Derk, this year's Dark Lord
  Blade, his son
  Querida, High Chancellor of Wizards' University
  Shona, Derk's daughter
  Mr. Chesney, who leads Pilgrim Parties
  Mara, Derk's wife

Plot Summary

Wizard Derk is really upset. He likes his life at Derkholm, where he lives with his wife, Mara, who is a creator of miniature universes; his son Blade, a wizard-in-training; his daughter Shona, soon to be a bard; as well as the five griffins he includes among his children: Kit, Callette, Lydda, Don, and Elda. Wizard Derk wants to be left alone to pursue his magical projects. These include flying pigs, invisible cats, horses with wings, friendly cows, and an accident or two, such as the sheep who turn out to be carnivorous. However, Querida, high chancellor of Wizards' University, has other ideas. She has received millions of letters from wizards, elves, dragons, kings, farmers, and soldiers, and they all say the same thing. Mr. Chesney's Pilgrim Parties must be stopped. Mr. Chesney sponsors tours from another world that import groups of people who want to experience a high fantasy adventure, for a high fee, of course. Also, many of the tour members are sent there by their families, who want them killed en route. This has to stop. Querida consults the Oracles about this problem, and the solution is that the job must be left to the first two people they see, who will be this year's Dark Lord and Wizard Guide. Wizard Derk is much distressed to discover that the first two people they see are himself and his son Blade. He is even more distressed to discover that in order to do the job of frightening away the tours, he must rebuild his house into an evil fortress and flatten a nearby village.

Faced with this dilemma, Derk decides to make a go of it, but the task is not easy. What follows is a madcap adventure of sturdy dwarves, smoky inns, wretched hovels, and ethereal elves. Things go badly from the start. A dragon arrives on the doorstep to offer his services against the Forces of Evil. When Derk has to explain that the Dark Lord is merely pretending to be evil for the benefit of tourists, the dragon gets quite annoyed and breathes fire at Derk, who is injured in the process. Now the whole family has to fill in. But they also have trouble. They put together an army of six hundred soldiers—actually, they are mostly murderers pretending to be soldiers. But now Blade can't get them to move, and his father is still sick. So he asks the dragon's help because it has been arranged by Mr. Chesney for the tours to have a battle, so they have to show up. The dragon agrees to help or says otherwise he'll get no peace.

Derk sleeps for five days before he is almost well again. The dragon arrives to help shape up the soldiers, and the others busy themselves with setting up the illusions for the Wild Hunts. The Friendly Cows have been transformed into great black horned things and other magic of that nature. Meanwhile, all this efficiency is beginning to annoy Querida, who had been relying on Derk's ineptitude to bring this tour business to an end. Meanwhile, the bustle goes on in preparation for the first battle. Things go from bad to worse, and Derk thinks he's lost Kit, but finds out later that that is not so. Querida is again upset because now Derk has shut the Pilgrims right out of the castle and won't open the gates. All this confusion finally ends with a plainclothes detective inquiring of Mr. Chesney why so many of his tour people never come back. Mr. Chesney says he must speak to his lawyers. But Anscher, one of the gods, appears to say that for forty years people have found it easier to do what Mr. Chesney asks than to think for themselves.

Now it will take another forty years for the wizard Querida to make the world right again. In the meantime, Mr. Chesney is transformed into a paperweight. Derk is tired of it all and is thinking of conjuring up a winged human.

Suitability and Critical Comment

This zany romp through a never-never land of improbable creatures and amusing situations is sure to delight any reader who enjoys the science fiction genre. Everything is highly unbelievable and full of twists and turns that the author describes with a wry sense of humor. Every high fantasy element imaginable is incorporated into the plot, and the author has a fine eye for details; for grades seven through ten.

Themes and Subjects

Adventure, demons, dragons, fantasy, humor, magic, other worlds, science fiction

Passages for Booktalking

Querida picks the Dark Lord (pp. 1–15); Derk goes to see Querida (pp. 62–67); Derk meets the dragon (pp. 93–103); the army is recruited (pp. 115–31); Anscher makes a judgment and sentences Mr. Chesney (pp. 340–45).

Additional Selections

In Donna Jo Napoli's *Beast* (Atheneum, 2000), a reworking of the Beauty and the Beast story, a young Persian prince assumes the shape of a lion because he has broken an ancient law.

In Patricia C. Wrede's *Magician's World* (Tor, 1997), a sequel to *Mairelon the Magician* (Tor, 1991), Kim, a former thief who is now an apprentice magician, continues her lessons and also investigates a strange burglary.

In *The Taker's Stone* (DK, 1999) by Barbara Timberlake Russell, the soul of a Georgia teenager who is psychic is fought over by forces of good and evil.

About the Book

Booklist, Sept. 1, 1998, p. 110.
Bulletin of the Center for Children's Books, Nov., 1998, p. 102.
Horn Book, Nov., 1998, p. 732.
School Library Journal, Oct., 1998, p. 136.
VOYA, Feb., 1999, p. 443.

About the Author

Authors and Artists for Young Adults, vol. 12, Gale, 1994.
Children's Literature Review, vol. 23, Gale, 1991.
Continuum Encyclopedia of Children's Literature, Continuum, 2001.
Drew, Bernard A. *The 100 Most Popular Young Adult Authors*, Libraries Unlimited, 1997.
Major Authors and Illustrators for Children and Young Adults, vol. 3, Gale, 1993.
St. James Guide to Young Adult Writers (2nd ed.), St. James, 1999.
Silvey, Anita. *Children's Books and Their Creators*, Houghton Mifflin, 1995.
Something about the Author, vol. 9, Gale, 1976; vol. 70, Gale, 1993; vol. 108, Gale, 2000.
Something about the Author Autobiography Series, vol. 7, Gale, 1989.
Twentieth Century Young Adult Writers, St. James, 1994.

King, Stephen. *Carrie.* Signet, 1974. Pb. $7.99 (0-451-15755-3) (Grades 10–12).

Introduction

Stephen King (1947–), born in Portland, Maine, had an unhappy childhood caused partly by his father's abandoning of the family when he was only two, leaving his mother to be its sole support. Stephen was an overweight, awkward child and frequently felt alone and alienated, the condition experienced by many of his characters. He had an active imagination and developed a desire to write. After graduation from college, he got married and taught English at a private high school. Several unpublished novels later, he wrote *Carrie* (Doubleday, 1974), the first success of the writer who later became America's number one author of horror and suspense stories. Of its beginnings, King says that he wrote a story about a girls' shower room and an outcast being pelted with sanitary napkins by girls who continually torment her. Unhappy with the story, he threw it away, but it was retrieved by his wife, who thought it had potential. The rest is history. Since *Carrie,* he has continued a prolific flow of best-selling books at the rate of about one a year.

Principal Characters

Carrie White, seventeen-year-old schoolgirl
Margaret White, Carrie's mother
Sue Snell, schoolmate
Christine Hargensen, schoolmate
Rita Desjardin, gym teacher
Tommy Ross, school jock
Henry Grayle, principal

Plot Summary

Seventeen-year-old Carrie, who lives in a small town in Maine, is a lonely and friendless schoolgirl who possesses a supernatural power called telekinesis. Innocent Carrie understands in a rather naïve way that this power enables her to move small objects at her will. However, her mother, who is a religious zealot and intensely domineering, keeps telling Carrie that to admit to such a power or to use it as a secret tool would be a sin.

At school, the shy and awkward Carrie is constantly taunted by her schoolmates, who are led by the insensitive Christine Hargensen. She is the pack leader of an unformed plan to "get Carrie." One day at school, Carrie is horribly disgraced and humiliated by the gang, an event that seems to stir her otherworldly powers to some degree.

Gym teacher Rita Desjardin feels both pity and shame after Carrie's humiliation. She asks principal Henry Grayle to punish the girls who participated in the terrible taunting. This leads to guilt on the part of Sue Snell. She feels so guilty over what the girls have done that she persuades her steady boyfriend, the popular jock Tommy Ross, to take Carrie to the prom. Tommy acts in a mature way and agrees to Sue's proposal. He asks Carrie to the prom and she accepts, outwardly defying her mother for the first time. In so doing, she begins to realize that her mother is actually afraid of her forbidden power, and a glimmer of defiance creeps to the surface.

At the prom, Carrie actually begins to enjoy herself, and Tommy begins to act as though he likes her. She feels a measure of self-confidence, not as though the other schoolmates accept her but at least they tolerate her. She is on the inside of a social circle for the first time, and it is a heady, intoxicating proposition. But the illusion is soon spoiled. Christine has been barred from the dance for her part in the humiliation of Carrie, and she vows revenge with the help of her roughneck boyfriend Billy Nolan. He and his gang of toughs capture and slaughter pigs. They fill buckets with the pigs' blood and hoist them to the top of the rafters. At the right time, Christine, from her hiding place, pulls the rope that drops the blood onto the dancers below.

When the blood covers Carrie and the other dancers, all the good feelings she has been experiencing leave her, and she now gains full control of her strange and terrifying power. Her humiliation on this night is so great that the genie cannot be put back in the bottle. Carrie cannot stop herself. To stop now would mean that her mother had been right all along. The only way out of the horrendous pain she is feeling is to gain revenge. For Carrie that means unleashing the restraints on her full and terrible power. As a result, the town is nearly destroyed. More than four hundred—mostly teenagers—are killed. Tommy dies quickly and without pain when one of the buckets of blood hits him squarely on the head. Later that night, Christine and Billy get away from the scene in their car. The automobile suddenly seems possessed by a strange power. They cannot stop the car, which drives on until it crashes and they are both killed.

Carrie also dies that night. She is stabbed by her mother just before she successfully wills the older woman's heart to stop. In the aftermath of this terrible disaster, it is Sue who finds Carrie's body.

Suitability and Critical Comment

This is a popular novel with teenagers and suited for most good readers. The pain and loneliness felt by Carrie are well drawn, and young readers can readily identify with her feelings of humiliation when she is taunted by her schoolmates. This is not a novel for those who are disturbed by otherworldly powers; for grades ten through twelve.

Themes and Subjects

Family relationships, friendship, guilt, humiliation, loneliness, pity, revenge, school, telekinesis

Passages for Booktalking

Carrie is taunted (pp. 6–10); Carrie and her mother talk about womanhood and sin (pp. 53–59); Tommy asks Carrie to the ball (pp. 83–87); the blood drops (pp. 166–74); Carrie and her mother have their last meeting (pp. 207–12).

Additional Selections

Using both fantasy and folklore, Neil Gaiman in *Stardust* (Avon, 1999) focuses on seventeen-year-old Tristan and his quest in Faerie to follow a falling star.

Fast paced and humorous, Robert Asprin's *Myth Conceptions* (Ace, 1985) features Skeeve, a junior magician apprenticed to a demon who has lost her powers.

Witch-hunting, greed, and madness take over a village after it has been stricken by a plague in *Year of Wonders: A Novel of the Plague* (Viking, 2001) by Geraldine Brooks.

In Arthur C. Clarke's *3001: The Final Odyssey* (Ballantine, 1997), the final volume in the Space Odyssey series, Frank Pook, revived after being frozen for a thousand years, again faces the computer, HAL.

About the Book
Booklist, July 1, 1974, p. 180.
Kirkus Reviews, Feb. 1, 1974, p. 137.
Library Journal, Feb. 15, 1974, p. 584.
New York Times Book Review, May 26, 1974, p. 17.

About the Author
Authors and Artists for Young Adults, vol. 1, Gale, 1989; vol. 17, Gale, 1995.
Beahm, George W. *The Stephen King Companion,* Andrews and McMeel, 1989.
Contemporary Authors New Revision Series, vol. 76, Gale, 1999.
Contemporary Literary Criticism, vol. 12, Gale, 1980; vol. 26, Gale, 1983; vol. 37, Gale, 1985; vol. 61, Gale, 1990.
Current Biography, Wilson, Oct., 1981.
Drew, Bernard H. *The 100 Most Popular Young Adult Authors,* Libraries Unlimited, 1997.
Hipple, Ted. *Writers for Young Adults,* supplement 1, Scribners, 2000, pp. 115–24.
Keyishian, Amy. *Stephen King,* Chelsea, 1995.
Russell, Sharon A. *Stephen King: A Critical Companion,* Greenwood, 1996.
St. James Guide to Young Adult Writers (2nd ed.), St. James, 1999.
Saidman, Anne. *Stephen King, Master of Horror,* Lerner, 1992.
Schweitzer, Darrell. *Discovering Stephen King,* Starmont, 1985.
Something about the Author, vol. 9, Gale, 1976; vol. 55, Gale, 1989.
Twentieth Century Young Adult Writers, St. James, 1994.
Underwood, Tim, and Chuck Miller. *Kingdom of Fear: The World of Stephen King,* Underwood-Miller, 1986.

Lowry, Lois. *Gathering Blue.* Houghton Mifflin, 2000. $15.00 (0-618-05812-9) (Grades 5–9).

Introduction
In her 1994 Newbery Award–winning novel, *The Giver,* Lois Lowry (1937–) created a technologically sophisticated, highly structured future world that, on the surface, appears ideal because of an absence of pain

and serious problems, but in reality has denied the essence of life: its struggles, truth, color, and a sense of the past. After twelve-year-old Jonas, the book's hero, discovers the realities of life, he makes the daring decision to leave the community and pursue the path of honesty. In *Gathering Blue,* a companion piece, the author has created a different futuristic world in which humankind, through a series of cataclysms, has changed into a primitive, brutish society similar to the Stone Age, where people survive as hunters and gatherers while living in primitive mud huts in a squalid village.

Principal Characters

Kira, a pubescent girl who possesses a magical talent for weaving threads

Matt, a disheveled street urchin of eight or nine years of age who is Kira's loyal friend

Branch, Matt's mongrel dog

Katrina and Christopher, Kira's deceased parents

Vandara, a scar-faced, vindictive women who plots to steal Kira's land after the death of Kira's mother

Jamison, a member of the ruling Council of Guardians who appears to be Kira's protector and mentor

Thomas the Carver, a young boy of Kira's age whose great talent is in wood-carving

Annabella, an old recluse who teaches Kira the art of producing dyes for threads

Jo, a six-year-old waif who possesses a remarkable singing voice

Plot Summary

After the sudden death of her beloved mother, Kira accompanies the body to the Field of Leaving on the outskirts of the village, where she keeps the customary four-day vigil until leaving the body to rot or be eaten by animals. Kira's father, Christopher, was killed while hunting before she was born, and she and her mother had made a modest living through weaving extraordinary fabrics, a craft at which Kira is amazingly gifted. Now an orphan, she is particularly vulnerable because she has a crippled leg and has, in the past, escaped the mandatory death sentence given to anyone with physical or mental handicaps only through the appeals of her mother. When she returns to her community accompanied by her friend, the tattered street ragamuffin Matt, she finds that her mud hut has been destroyed and that some of the local crones, led by vindictive Vandara, are trying to confiscate her land and have her killed because of her deformity. The case is referred to the Council of Guardians, the ruling twelve-man body that lives in the only imposing building left in the village, the Council Edifice. Here Kira's case for survival is presented by a tall, impressive-looking Guardian, named Jamison. He maintains that logically she should die, but her extraordinary weaving talent can be used by the state. Kira is taken to live in the Council Edifice and assigned the task of repairing worn patches on the ornately ornamented robe worn by the Singer at the annual Gathering, when he performs the ritual of chanting the Ruin Song, the history of humankind through the ages as depicted in the verses sung and pictures woven into the cloth of the robe. At the Edifice, she meets and becomes fast friends with another orphan, the talented wood carver Thomas, who has been brought to the Edifice to work on the staff held by the Singer during the Gathering. In order to extend her knowledge of dyeing threads with different colors, Kira begins consulting with an elderly artisan named Annabella, who lives at the edge of the village. Annabella shows Kira the intricacies of dyeing, but tells her that to dye materials blue requires leaves of the woad plant available only in a distant land. Kira is often accompanied by Matt and his dog Branch when they visit Annabella, but this friendship is cut short by Annabella's sudden death. Kira notes that it coincides with her telling Jamison that Annabella was critical of a Council proclamation. Kira and Thomas befriend a frightened six-year-old orphan named Jo, who has, like them, been brought to the Edifice to live. Jo possesses a remarkable voice and is now in training to become the next Singer. A few days before the highly anticipated Gathering, Matt and his dog disappear, but on the day of the celebration, he comes back accompanied by an elderly blind man. Matt has ventured into the distant land, where he also retrieved some blue fabrics and woad plants for Kira. The stranger reveals himself to be Christopher, Kira's supposedly dead father. Christopher tells her that he narrowly escaped death at the hands of Jamison and that she is actually a captive of wicked, ruthless ruffians who savagely protect their power and even kill the parents of gifted youngsters in order to bring them to the Edifice. Kira rejects her father's offer to accompany him back to his land where outsiders and the deformed are made welcome. Instead she will remain at the Edifice, hoping to work with Thomas and Jo to subvert the regime of Jamison and the Council.

Suitability and Critical Comment

The author has created a chilling picture of a heartless, brutal society reduced to savagery in order to survive, but she also reveals that under these horrible conditions, beauty, friendship, decency, and art can still exist albeit precariously and only through the courage of individuals. This novel is suitable for thoughtful readers in grades five through nine.

Themes and Subjects

Artistry, barbarism, corruption of power, dictatorship, embroidery, friendship, importance of memory, inhumanity, love, physical handicaps, the power of creativity, orphans

Passages for Booktalking

Kira's vigil over her mother's body (pp. 1–3); she confronts Vandara at the site of her destroyed hut (pp.13–16); before the Council of Guardians (pp. 24–30); Jamison defends Kira and shows the Council the Singer's robe (pp. 46–50); Kira meets Thomas (pp. 68–72); and Kira, along with Matt and Branch, visits Annabella (pp. 79–84).

Additional Selections

In John Herman's *Labyrinth* (Philomel, 2001), Gregory lives in the real world and the dream world of Greek mythology and the Minotaur's maze.

When global warming causes massive floods and destruction in England, social institutions crumble while young Zoe frantically searches for her missing parents in *Floodland* (Delacorte, 2001) by Marcus Sedgwick.

After a virus attack, seven surviving children living in a run-down house in a small Florida town try to reconstruct the past in *The Kindling* (Harper-Collins, 2000) by Jennifer Armstrong and Nancy Butcher.

Josh, who is beaten and robbed along the Appalachian Trail, is rescued by the inhabitants of Canara, a community that has found eternal peace in Phyllis Reynolds Naylor's *Sand Spell* (Atheneum, 1998).

About the Book

Booklist, June 1, 2000, p. 1896.
Bulletin of the Center for Children's Books, Nov., 2000, p. 111.
Horn Book, Sept., 2000, p. 573.
Kirkus Reviews, June 15, 2000, p. 887.
School Library Journal, Aug., 2000, p. 186.
VOYA, Oct. 2000, p. 276.

About the Author

Authors and Artists for Young Adults, vol. 5, Gale, 1990; vol. 32, Gale, 2000.
Children's Literature Review, vol. 6, Gale, 1984; vol. 46, Gale, 1998; vol. 72, Gale, 2002.
Continuum Encyclopedia of Children's Literature, Continuum, 2001.
Drew, Bernard A. *The 100 Most Popular Young Adult Authors,* Libraries Unlimited, 1997.
Gallo, Donald. *Speaking for Ourselves, Too,* National Council of Teachers of English, 1993.
Haley-James, Shirley. "Lois Lowry," *Horn Book,* July-Aug., 1990, pp. 422–24.
Hipple, Ted. *Writers for Young Adults,* vol. 2, Scribners, 1997, pp. 279–87.
Lives and Works: Young Adult Authors, vol. 5, Grolier, 1999, pp. 60–62.

Lorraine, Walter. "Lois Lowry," *Horn Book*, July-Aug., 1994, pp. 426.

Lowry, Lois. *Looking Back: A Book of Memories*, Houghton Mifflin, 1998.

Lowry, Lois. "The Remembered Gate and the Unopened Door," *Horn Book*, March-April, 2002, pp. 159–77.

Major Authors and Illustrators for Children and Young Adults, vol. 4, Gale, 1993.

Marcus, Leonard S. *Author Talk*, Simon & Schuster, 2000.

McElmeel, Sharron L. *The 100 Most Popular Children's Authors*, Libraries Unlimited, 1999.

"Newbery Award Acceptance," *Horn Book*, July-Aug., 1990, pp. 412–21.

"Newbery Award Acceptance Material, 1990," *Journal of Youth Services in Libraries*, Summer, 1990, pp. 281–88.

St. James Guide to Young Adult Writers (2nd ed.), St. James, 1999.

Silvey, Anita. *Children's Books and Their Creators*, Houghton Mifflin, 1995.

Something about the Author, vol. 23, Gale, 1981; vol. 70, Gale, 1993; vol. 111, Gale, 2000; vol. 127, Gale, 2002.

Something about the Author Autobiography Series, vol. 3, Gale, 1987.

Twentieth Century Young Adult Writers, St. James, 1994.

Marsden, John. *Tomorrow, When the War Began*. Houghton Mifflin, 1995. $13.95 (0-395-70673-4) (Grades 7–10).

Introduction

John Marsden (1950–) was born in Melbourne, Australia, and began writing early by creating fanciful stories about imaginary worlds. He became a teacher and head of English at the Timbertop Campus of the prestigious Geelong Grammar School. Here, the students practice survival skills as well as studying academic subjects. *Tomorrow, When the War Began* was published in 1995 and tells about a group of teenagers who return from an outdoor trip to find their country invaded by a foreign power. The youngsters must struggle to survive and begin organizing themselves to fight back. The book was originally intended to stand alone, but has now become a continuing series. In the sixth volume, *The Night Is for Hunting* (Houghton Mifflin, 2001), the five remaining teenagers, led by Ellie, find they are fighting not only the invaders but also interpersonal differences. The group rescues and tries to care for a group of feral children in this novel, which, like its predecessors, is filled with wild chases, narrow escapes, and several battles.

Principal Characters

Ellie, high-school student in Australia

Homer, Fi, Robyn, Lee, Corrie, and Kevin, schoolmates

Plot Summary

Ellie and her friends decide that what they need is a good camp out over the Christmas holiday, which is summertime in Australia. Their parents agree. Ellie will take the Land Rover because she is a good driver. There will be no smokes or drinks along. They plan to stay a week, and things go well except that Fi complains one morning that there must have been a hundred planes flying overhead during the night. They make halfhearted jokes about a nuclear war while they're away. On their last night, they decide to do this again next year.

They return, however, to find a world totally changed. Their homes are ransacked, the dogs and animals are dead or dying, and worst of all, their families are gone—just disappeared. They can think of no other explanation except that they have been invaded and there is a war. When they search everyone's homes, they find a note from Corrie's Dad telling her to "go bush" and not come out until it's safe. They decide to move only in the dark of night and scout around the town to see if they can find anyone or discover what has happened. They go to the Showground, which should have been packed up from the carnival that was there. They see an ocean of parked cars, and the place is guarded by sentries. But then they are shot at and retreat into the woods.

The teens now realize that they are at war and they have a choice to give up or fight back. They think there must have been some kind of battle in town because all the stores are smashed. They decide to round up what cars they find at the various homes, including Ellie's Land Rover, pack them full of supplies, including rifles, and take off. But when the rockets start coming, Corrie goes hysterical and they have to wait until she calms down before they can move. When they do, Lee is shot in the calf, but the wound is clean. Then they meet up with Chris, who couldn't go on the camp out with them. Chris tells them what happened. After they left, he said the Air Force jets started racing around, then the power went off and the phones, too. His parents were away, so he started to walk to find someone, but everyone was gone. Then he saw military trucks full of soldiers, but they weren't Australian.

Corrie keeps trying without success to get news on the shortwave radio. Finally, they get a voice saying that they have been invaded and the United States had better not get involved.

The teens decide that they must take a stand and fight as best they can against the invaders. In so doing, they become a tightly knit group and learn to work together. Ellie, who has always regarded herself as a tomboy, is the first of the group to kill someone. She finds she is not as tough as she thought she was. Fi, who has always been a bit ethereal, finds an inner strength that becomes an inspiration to the group. Gentle Lee hardens with a hatred for what has occurred. Robyn copes best and takes the adversity in stride. When Corrie is shot, Kevin drives her to the nearest hospital, even though neither has any idea whether they will return. Chris copes by staying stoned most of the time.

The story ends as Ellie keeps an account of their ordeal. Kevin and Corrie have not returned as yet. All she knows is that they have to stick together. She thinks they'll survive somehow. At least she hopes so.

Suitability and Critical Comment

This is a story of survival and working together as a team. It is also a story of character development as each of the teens changes and grows in his or her own way in response to the total upheaval of their lives. The enemy remains hostile and unknown. The book is probably best suited to the older reader with some knowledge of and interest in survival and guerilla warfare tactics; for grades seven through ten.

Themes and Subjects

Australia, friendship, guerilla warfare, invasion, soldiers, war

Passages for Booktalking

The campers hear planes at night (pp. 39–44); they return home to disaster (pp. 55–68); they make a plan (pp. 111–21); the voice on the radio speaks of war (pp. 168–78); Ellie wonders if they will survive (pp. 283–84).

Additional Selections

In this science fiction mystery, *A Matter of Profit* (HarperCollins, 2001) by Hilari Bell, a young man is assigned the task of tracing the origins of a plot to kill his emperor.

In 2028, sixteen-year-old Ceej, who lives on the rim of the Grand Canyon with his older sister Harryette and their uncle, survives a terrible plague that almost destroys the human race.

Bobby, fifteen, discovers he has become invisible in *Things Not Seen* (Putnam, 2002) by Andrew Clements, a thoughtful fantasy set in present-day Chicago.

In James Heneghan's *The Grave* (Farrar, 2000) fourteen-year-old Tom Mullen time travels to 1847 Ireland during the potato famine and is befriended by the Monaghans, who he also discovers are his ancestors.

About the Book

Booklist, April 15, 1995, p. 1493.
Bulletin of the Center for Children's Books, April, 1995, p. 281.

Horn Book, July-Aug., 1995, p. 467.
School Library Journal, June, 1995, p. 130.
VOYA, Aug., 1995, p. 162.

About the Author
Authors and Artists for Young Adults, vol. 20, Gale, 1997.
Children's Literature Review, vol. 34, Gale, 1995.
Lives and Works: Young Adult Authors, vol. 5, Grolier, 1999, pp. 69–71.
St. James Guide to Young Adult Writers (2nd ed.), St. James, 1999.
Twentieth Century Young Adult Writers, St. James, 1994.

McKinley, Robin. *Rose Daughter.* Greenwillow, 1997. $16.00
  (0-688-15439-5) (Grades 6–10).

Introduction

   Robin McKinley (1952–), the daughter of a sailor and a teacher, spent her childhood in many places, including Virginia, California, New York, and Japan, finally completing high school in Maine. She majored in English at Bowdoin College and after marriage began to write. She has said, "Writing has always been the other side of reading for me. It never occurred to me not to make up stories." She is an outstanding writer of fantasies, many of them reworkings of standard fairy and folk tales such as *Beauty* (Harper, 1978), a variation on the Beauty and the Beast story. It was her first published work and tells of the price Father must pay for picking a rose in the Beast's garden. The monster demands one of Father's daughters as payment. Beauty, against her father's wishes, agrees to go to the castle to live and there, gradually, learns to see beyond the beast's frightening exterior and appreciate his gentle and loving nature. This material is revisited in a startlingly new version known as *Rose Daughter.*

Principal Characters
   Beauty, youngest daughter
   The Beast, a transformed prince
   Lionheart, the eldest daughter
   Jeweltongue, the middle daughter
   Beauty's father

Plot Summary

   In this retelling of the old story of Beauty and the Beast, the characters are familiar—although some with different names—but the ending has a twist. Beauty is the youngest daughter of a wealthy businessman who falls into depression when his wife dies and his business fails. Lionheart is the oldest daughter. She is very daring and loves horses. The middle daughter is Jeweltongue, who is quite clever and has a way with words. Beauty has no particular talent as the other two do, except that she loves gardening and has a gift for making things grow, especially roses, which she loves above all flowering things.

After Beauty's father loses his business, she finds a will in his correspondence that leaves the family a small dwelling, called Rose Cottage, in the countryside. It is so small and distant that no creditors want it. Realizing that they must adapt to a lesser lifestyle, the family moves to Rose Cottage, despite the rumors that there is a mysterious curse on it. Beauty brings to life the beautiful roses of her mother, and her sisters thrive in the country and discover their own natural talents. From this point, the story proceeds along the lines of the original tale.

One day while he is away from the cottage, Beauty's father takes refuge from a blizzard in an enchanted palace. He is well treated, but when he leaves the next morning he takes a rose from the breakfast table. It is so beautiful that he wants to bring it to his youngest daughter. Instead, he is confronted by the Beast, who demands his youngest daughter in return for the theft.

Beauty feels that her father's trouble is her fault, and she goes willingly, if sadly, to live in the enchanted castle where invisible ladies-in-waiting have private conversations, mostly trying to get Beauty to wear outlandish clothes. In addition, there is the supernatural cat, the spirit of the greenwitch who left Rose Cottage to Beauty's family. There are also unicorns and preternatural Guardians wandering about. Although Beauty is greatly saddened to be far from home, she tries to adapt to her new life, including visits to the Beast's library, which has all the books in the world. She also revives the Beast's dying rose garden.

Little by little, a friendship grows between Beauty and the kind but ugly Beast. For instance, they meet for meals in the dining room, but only Beauty eats because the Beast says he cannot eat like a man. Despite their friendship, as time goes by, Beauty becomes more and more homesick. The Beast relents and tells her that she may go to see her father, but if she does not return from the visit at a certain time, he—the Beast—will die. Beauty leaves for Rose Cottage, where she is welcomed by the family. Without meaning to be, Beauty is detained. Returning late to the castle, she finds the Beast near death.

Beauty is given the choice of breaking the spell under which the Beast is confined, returning him to the handsome prince he was, or leaving him as the ugly Beast. But if she chooses to break the spell and return him to his old life, with all its wealth, she is told that the names of "Beauty" and "the Beast" will be spoken in fear and dread because of the great power they will have. And no one, Beauty is warned, can love those who have total power over them.

Beauty chooses a life with the Beast as he is. They will marry and live in happiness and love.

Suitability and Critical Comment

This is a charming and gentle story, suited for readers who like a leisurely pace filled with much description and supernatural characters with strange and sometimes amusing features. Beauty's sisters are engaging personalities, although the Beast himself is somewhat predictable. The story is deeper and darker than the original fairy tale, and although the writing style is fairly easy, it is probably best suited for more thoughtful readers in grades six through ten.

Themes and Subjects

Castles, enchantment, family relationships, good versus evil, kindness, love, mystery, physical beauty, roses

Passages for Booktalking

Beauty finds the deed to Rose Cottage (pp. 14–19); Beauty brings the Rose Garden to life (pp. 47–59); Beauty meets the Beast (pp. 93–102); Beauty describes the Beast to Jeweltongue and Lionheart (pp. 267–75); Beauty makes her choice (p. 293).

Additional Selections

Set in fictional Mediterranean lands, Megan Whalen Turner's *The Queen of Attolia* (Greenwillow, 2001) tells of Gen, whose hand has been cut off on orders of the Queen, and of his mission to kidnap her. A sequel to *The Thief* (Greenwillow, 1996).

In Meredith Ann Pierce's *Treasure at the Heart of Tanglewood* (Viking, 2001), Hannah and her talking animal friends set out to return the change of seasons to the earth.

In the first of the Magic Kingdom of Landover series by Terry Brooks, *Magic Kingdom for Sale—Sold!* (Ballantine, 1986), widower Ben buys a magic kingdom only to find he owns a run-down castle.

Transylvania is the setting of *The Sight* (Dutton, 2002) by David Clement-Davies, the story of a prophesy, a wolf pack, and an outcast she-wolf with magical powers.

About the Book

Booklist, Aug., 1997, p. 1898.
Bulletin of the Center for Children's Books, Oct., 1997, p. 58.
Horn Book, Sept.-Oct., 1997, p. 574.
Kirkus Reviews, June 1, 1997, p. 877.
School Library Journal, Sept., 1997, p. 219.
VOYA, Feb., 1998, p. 366.

About the Author

Authors and Artists for Young Adults, vol. 4, Gale, 1990; vol. 33, Gale, 2000.
Children's Literature Review, vol. 19, Gale, 1986.
Continuum Encyclopedia of Children's Literature, Continuum, 2001.
Drew, Bernard A. *The 100 Most Popular Young Adult Authors*, Libraries Unlimited, 1997.
Lives and Works: Young Adult Authors, vol. 5, Grolier, 1999, pp. 88–90.
Major Authors and Illustrators for Children and Young Adults, vol. 4, Gale, 1993.
"Newbery Award Acceptance Material, 1985," *Horn Book*, July-Aug., 1985, pp. 395–409.
"Newbery Award Acceptance Material, 1985," *Top of the News*, Summer, 1985, pp. 386–96.
St. James Guide to Young Adult Writers (2nd ed.), St. James, 1999.
Sanders, Lynn Moss. "Girls Who Do Things: The Protagonists of Robin McKinley's Fantasy Fiction," *The ALAN Review*, Fall, 1996, pp. 38–42.
Silvey, Anita. *Children's Books and Their Creators*, Houghton Mifflin, 1995.
Something about the Author, vol. 32, Gale, 1983; vol. 50, Gale, 1988; vol. 89, Gale, 1997.
Twentieth Century Young Adult Writers, St. James, 1994.

Nix, Garth. *Sabriel.* Harper, 1995. $15.95 (0-06-027323-2) (Grades 7–10).

Garth Nix (1963–) was born in Melbourne, Australia, and raised in Canberra, where he first enjoyed fantasy novels as a young reader. His parents were both readers and writers, and the author has said, "Our house was always full of books and there was a culture of reading." After trying many careers, such as marketing consultant and publicist, he settled on editing and writing. He has written many books for children, and in the late 1990s began work on The Old Kingdom Trilogy, which begins with *Sabriel*. It tells the story of Sabriel, the daughter of the necromancer Abhorsen, and her journey into the mysterious and magical Old Kingdom to rescue her father from the Land of the Dead. It is followed by *Lirael* (HarperCollins, 2001). This novel centers around the Clayr, who are a group of women known for their ability to see into the future, and the young novice, Lirael, who has yet to receive the gift of the Sight. In the library with her magical pet, the disreputable Dog, she discovers her fate and is sent out on a mission. The third volume is *Abhorsen* (HarperCollins, 2003), another complex but rewarding fantasy.

Principal Characters

Sabriel, a necromancer's daughter
Mage Abhorsen, Sabriel's father
Moggett, a Free Magic spirit
Touchstone, a Charter Mage

Plot Summary

Ever since she can remember, Sabriel has lived in Ancelstiere, a safe and friendly land outside the walls of the Old Kingdom, away from its sorcery and walking Dead. But when she is eighteen, Sabriel receives a message from her missing father, the Mage Abhorsen. It is delivered by a strange creature who gives her a sack. She hears her father's voice telling her to take it. Inside the sack is a sword with the Charter symbols on it. Sabriel realizes her father must be trapped in the Kingdom and cannot return to the land of the living. She knows he would not call for her unless his life was in danger. She must face the mysteries beyond the walls of the Old Kingdom and rescue him.

Armed with her father's bandolier and sword, Sabriel enters the Old Kingdom and immediately encounters a great force of evil that is everywhere. She must overcome this force if she is to rescue her father and return alive. All around her, grotesque "undead" creatures roam the countryside. They eat humans in order to survive. But they can be vanished by the peals of bells. Villages and cities are abandoned. Great stones of power guard the land and keep the barrier between life and death.

Frightened and alone, Sabriel nevertheless takes her father's title of Abhorsen, signifying that she is one of the most powerful of necromancers. She makes her way to his house in the Old Kingdom. There she meets Mogget, a Free Magic spirit trapped in a feline body. With Mogget's help, she will search for her father. But nothing goes right from the beginning. When she starts the search in an enchanted plane, called a Paperwing, it crashes, which frees the spirit in Mogget. Sabriel is knocked unconscious and, when she wakes, the Free Magic is all about her in the form of a menacing blue-white creature. Mogget's voice is lost in this menace. But in a fight with the creature, Sabriel throws a silver ring over its neck. It is defeated, and Mogget returns to her.

They continue the search, encountering many strange characters on the way. One of them is a young man who has been trapped inside a wooden figurehead for hundreds of years. She rescues him and asks for the best directions to the castle at Belisaere. Touchstone accompanies them on their journey. They arrive in Belisaere after more adventures and finally come to the Royal Palace, where they find Sabriel's father entrapped in a diamond of protection. She must cross into Death to rescue him. In so doing, she loses her physical body, trapped in the reservoir next to her father. But their voices communicate, and Sabriel learns that the evil Kerrigor is the cause of this imprisonment and, as he grows stronger, her father's magic grows weaker. Sabriel finds and confronts Kerrigor. In the battle that follows, Kerrigor is dispatched, but Sabriel knows he will return until his real body is destroyed. Her father is dead. And once again, Sabriel must face the evil Kerrigor. This time, in the terrible battle that follows, Sabriel is mortally wounded. But as she is ready to go, to pass beyond the Ninth Gate, a voice tells her that it is not her time yet. She is urged to go back and live. Suddenly, she finds the strength. As she enters the hall, she discovers Touchstone weeping at her death. He is astonished to see that she is alive. Sabriel, quite surprised to find that it is so, only says, "Yes, I am." This leaves an opening for a sequel in this strange land where death is divided by gates and the undead can be vanished by a peal of bells.

Suitability and Critical Comment

For the young reader who delights in strange creatures, twist and turns, enchanted beings, and the undead, *Sabriel* will be much enjoyed. The action is fast with many changes in plot, blending suspense, humor, and romance. There are some especially enchanting scenes concerning Mogget, the enchanted feline. Marketed as young adult, it is best suited for teens in grades seven through ten.

Themes and Subjects

Enchanted beings, fantasy, machines, magic, sorcery, the undead

Passages for Booktalking

Sabriel gets a message from her father (pp. 8–11); she meets Mogget (pp. 66–75); the flight in the Paperwing (pp. 93–103); they meet Touchstone (pp. 126–36); Sabriel finds her father (pp. 189–98).

Additional Selections

Shade, the young bat of *Silverwing* (Simon & Schuster, 1997), sets off to find his missing father in the sequel, *Sunwing* (Simon & Schuster, 2000), by Kenneth Oppel.

Ged, a student of wizardry, unleashes a wicked creature that threatens himself and his world in Ursula K. Le Guin's *A Wizard of Earthsea* (Bantam, 1968).

In the moody, mysterious *Clockwork* (Scholastic, 1998) by Philip Pullman, the reader meets an apprentice clockmaker, a menacing magician, a generous serving girl, and the great clock of Glockenheim.

In Edith Pattou's *Fire Arrow,* a sequel to *Hero's Song* (Harcourt, 1997), Brie takes a magical arrow and sets out to avenge her father's murder.

About the Book
Booklist, Oct. 1, 1996, p. 63.
Bulletin of the Center for Children's Books, Dec., 1996, p. 146.
Horn Book, Jan.-Feb., 1997, p. 64.
School Library Journal, Sept., 1996, p. 228.
VOYA, April, 1997, p. 44.

About the Author
Authors and Artists for Young Adults, vol. 29, Gale, 1999.
Children's Literature Review, vol. 68, Gale, 2001.
Drew, Bernard A. *100 More Popular Young Adult Authors,* Libraries Unlimited, 2002.
St. James Guide to Young Adult Writers (2nd ed.), St. James, 1999.
Something about the Author, vol. 97, Gale, 1998.

Pierce, Tamora. *Daja's Book.* Scholastic, 1998. $15.95
(0-590-55358-5) (Grades 7–9).

Introduction
Tamora Pierce (1954–) once said, "I enjoy writing for teenagers because I feel I help to make life easier for kids who are like I was." She was the child of divorced parents and attended eleven different schools by the time she graduated from high school. During this time she found solace and comfort in books. She writes interesting fantasies, most of which contain strong female characters. Her books are usually in series format of four books each. For example, the Song of the Lioness series contains four books beginning with *Alanna: The First Adventure* (Random, 1997). It tells of a young woman who disguises herself as a man to train as a knight under the tutelage of Prince Jonathan, who, when he discovers the deception, continues to support her. Circle of Magic also contains four books and deals with four girls from different backgrounds who become friends in a temple community where they learn various magical crafts. The four girls—Sandry,

Daja, Briar, and Tris—each have their own book that tells about their backgrounds and special gifts.

Principal Characters
Daja Kisubo, an outcast Trader
Her friends, Sandry, Tris, and Briar
Duke Vedris, Sandry's uncle
Yarrun Firetamer, chief mage
Frostpine, the smith-mage

Plot Summary
Book three of the author's Circle of Magic quartet centers on Daja Kisubo. She is a Trader, but a *trangshi,* an outcast and an image of bad luck because she is the sole survivor of a shipwreck that destroyed her family and their ships. Daja and three mage-in-training friends, Sandry, Tris, and Briar, are on a journey to the Gold Mountains, north of Winding Circle Temple. Each of the four young people has a special talent. Sandry, an aristocrat, has a talent for spinning and weaving. Tris, of a merchant family, can control weather and water. Briar is a talented gardener, and Daja is a gifted smithy with a special talent for making fire.

Heading the journey is Sandry's uncle, Duke Vedris, who is the ruler of Emelan. He is going to survey the impact of a drought on the region; the entire area seems like a huge pile of twigs waiting for a spark to ignite them. Daja is bored on the journey and begins to make nails to occupy her time. But accidentally she creates a most unusual living metal vine. Tris and Daja become trapped in the vine. Frostpine, the smith-mage, is able to free them.

This unusual vine gets the attention of a nearby Trader caravan. However, they are reluctant to talk to Daja about it because she is an outcast. A way around the taboo is found, and the Traders begin negotiations with Daja about the vine. Through these talks, Daja discovers that she has mixed feelings about the Traders. She has long been bitter about being an outcast, but she also has longings for her people and their traditions. Daja is torn between her anger and her sadness.

Through the journey, the four young people are learning not only to combat evil, but to combine their talents to make them work effectively. All four come from different backgrounds, and they are initially hostile to each other. It is this learning to cooperate that permeates the story of the journey.

A grass fire begins to smolder all about them, and the folk of Winding Circle wonder if the chief mage, Yarrun Firetamer, has enough magic to save them. He insists that he does and, refusing help, puts out the fires. But others feel that the fire has gotten into the piled-up leavings on the forest floor and is smoldering. Yarrun will not listen, and he will accept no more help. But in his final battle to save his people, Yarrun dies. Briar, Tris, and Sandry watch in horror as the fire spreads once again, catching the tree-tops. They realize that on the other side of the blaze, Daja may be trapped with the caravan.

On the other side, Daja becomes aware of the blaze. Somehow she has to stop the fire's advance. With the help that she has learned to accept from her friends and with Frostpine's aid as well, Daja is able to pinch the fire into a small channel and make it bend to her will. Although she has saved the region, the fire has encircled Daja and the caravan, which is full of Traders, the people who have branded her an outcast. It takes all of Daja's courage and talent, but she uses the fire to melt a glacier, which also relieves the drought. The Traders tell her she will be honored among her people.

Suitability and Critical Comment

For the young teenager who is enchanted by magic, this is a must read. The author treats magic as a science that must be studied and worked at. There are fanciful events such as the fire that melts a glacier or the plant of living iron that eats a copper bowl. The personal bonds among the young people who must learn to use their magic to work together is nicely drawn; grades seven through nine.

Themes and Subjects

Drought, fantasy, fire, friendship, loyalty, magic, poverty, storms, taboos

Passages for Booktalking

Daja creates a living metal vine (pp. 23–26); Daja talks to a Trader (pp. 69–76); the young people ride to see the glacier (pp. 131–34); Yarrun is killed (pp. 191–94); Daja saves the Trader caravan (pp. 207–19).

Additional Selections

Born into a family where magic is part of her inheritance, Georgie, age fifteen, is preparing for her first solo flight in Rita Murphy's *Night Flying* (Delacorte, 2000).

Gabriel becomes disenchanted with the misuse of power in the Navorran Empire and tries to become a healer in the Citadel in *Secret Sacrament* (HarperCollins, 2000) by Sherryl Jordan.

In fourteenth-century England, a young illiterate peasant named Jude must kill the last dragon, which has been terrorizing the area in another of Sherryl Jordan's fantasies, *The Hunting of the Last Dragon* (HarperCollins, 2002).

Annie accidentally sets free a swarm of telepathic creatures that can slow down time in William Sleator's *The Boxes* (Dutton, 1998).

About the Book
Booklist, Dec.1, 1998, p. 662.
Bulletin of the Center for Children's Books, Dec., 1998, p. 142.
School Library Journal, Dec., 1998, p. 129.

About the Author
Authors and Artists for Young Adults, vol. 26, Gale, 1999.
Drew, Bernard A. *100 More Popular Young Adult Authors,* Libraries Unlimited, 2002.
Gallo, Donald. *Speaking for Ourselves, Too,* National Council of Teachers of English, 1993.
St. James Guide to Young Adult Writers (2nd ed.), St. James, 1999.
Something about the Author, vol. 51, Gale, 1988; vol. 96, Gale, 1997.
Twentieth Century Young Adult Writers, St. James, 1994.

Pullman, Philip. *The Golden Compass.* Knopf, 1995. $20.00 (0-629-87924-2) (Grades 7–12).

Introduction
The Golden Compass (published in Britain as *Northern Lights*) is the first volume in the trilogy, *His Dark Materials,* by Philip Pullman (1946–). In the second volume, *The Subtle Knife* (Knopf, 1997), our heroine, Lyra, teams up with Will Perry, a twelve-year-old boy who is searching for his missing father, an Arctic explorer. Will has learned the secret of invisibility and also gains possession of a subtle knife, a deadly, ancient tool that can cut through anything, even space. Together the youngsters explore another world while Lyra continues her quest for the mysterious element known as Dust. The last volume, *The Amber Spyglass* (Knopf, 2000), is named after a magical scientific instrument constructed by Lyra's ally, Dr. Mary Malone. This book, the most metaphysical of the three, contains a climactic battle between the corrupting influences of the organized Church and the liberating forces of wisdom and good. In the end, Lyra emerges as the new Eve, and Will becomes her Adam. In the broadness of its scope and religious overtones, the trilogy has been compared to Milton's *Paradise Lost.*

Principal Characters

Lyra Belacqua (also called Lyra Silvertongue), a precocious, self-reliant eleven-year-old girl who is growing up in Oxford

Daemons (pronounced "demons"), animal manifestations of the human soul or one's alter ego. Each human is born with its own daemon, which remains with him or her until death. Until humans reach puberty, their daemons can change shape at will, but once an individual reaches maturity, the daemon must decide on a fixed identity. For example, Lord Astril's daemon is a snow leopard, and Mrs. Coulter's, a golden monkey.

Pantalaimon, or Pan, Lyra's daemon who can still change shape at will, though he often is a moth or bird

Master, the chief administrator at Jordan College

Lord Asriel, a brusque, dictatorial, but brilliant scientist who Lyra believes is her uncle

Mrs. Coulter, a beautiful, brilliant woman who is unscrupulous in her pursuit of power

Roger Parslow, a kitchen boy who is Lyra's best friend

The Costas, a lowly, honest gyptian family who befriend and protect Lyra

John Faa, king of the gyptians

Farder Coram, an ancient, highly respected gyptian who was once Serefina Pekkala's lover

Serefina Pekkala, the leader of a band of witches dedicated to fighting for justice

Lee Scoresby, an adventurer from Texas who operates a hot-air balloon

Iorek Byrnison, a massive renegade armored bear who becomes Lyra's protector

Irfur Raknison, a vain, powerful bear who has become king of Svalbard, the bear's headquarters

Plot Summary

Although eleven-year-old Lyra is being reared and educated by the Scholars at Jordan College, she spends most of her time accompanied by her shape-changing daemon Pan, roaming the streets of Oxford and scaling its rooftops, usually with her best friend, Roger, a kitchen boy. One day the testy Lord Asriel, whom Lyra believes to be her uncle, revisits the college where he has an affiliation, after spending a year in the far North. He makes a presentation to the Scholars to solicit funds and support for his study of a mysterious substance known as Dust, which enables one to bridge universes. Eventually he hopes to explore an alternate world that has become visible in the Aurora or northern lights. Before he leaves Oxford,

Lyra saves him from a plot to kill him perpetrated by the Master and his ally, the Librarian. At this time (somewhere in the vague past), England is terrorized by the mysterious disappearance of children of Lyra's age. Billy Costa, a young boy from a gyptian (lower class) family, as well as Roger, her dear friend, become victims of this group of kidnappers known as the Gobblers. Before Lyra can investigate, the Master decides to send her to London, where she will become the charge of Mrs. Coulter, a brilliant, beautiful scientist who has taken an unusual interest in Lyra's upbringing. Before leaving Oxford, the Master, in confidence, gives Lyra a strange instrument called an alethiometer. It resembles a golden compass, but with dials and needles that point to a series of symbols. After much experimenting, Lyra is able to discover its secret—it can answer any question posed to it, regardless of subject, time, or place. In London, Lyra is captivated by the suave, aggressive Mrs. Coulter, but when she accidentally learns that her guardian is the leader of the Gobblers, she flees for her life. She is saved by the Costa family, whom she knew in Oxford. They are now part of a large group of gyptians, led by John Faa and their seer, Farder Coram, who are outfitting a ship to sail into the North, where, they have learned, the kidnapped children are being held in a prison camp. The Costas tell the girl the truth about her family origins—Lord Asriel is actually her father, and Mrs. Coulter, her mother. The two had married but separated after they began a fierce competition in the pursuit of Dust. Through the use of the alethiometer, Lyra learns that her father is being held captive, under Mrs. Coulter's orders, in another stronghold in the North commanded by massive armed bears. Their leader is Irfur Raknison, a wily creature who has gained power by murdering his father. Lyra is allowed to become a member of the expedition because she alone can manipulate the valuable truth-divining compass. Along the way, the band gathers a number of unusual allies: Lee Scoresby, a good-hearted adventurer and mercenary from Texas who contributes his hot-air balloon to the cause; Serefina Pekkala, a wise witch whose band of warriors helps the gyptians; and lastly, Irfur Raknison, an exiled warrior bear and the rightful leader of the warrior bears who hold Lord Asriel captive. Through a series of extraordinary encounters, Lyra and her friends are able to free the young captives, including Billy Costa and Roger. Mrs. Coulter and her minions were performing experiments on them, separating them from their daemons, hoping to capture their inner selves and Dust, this powerful force of energy that has been found particularly around prepubescent children. Lyra cleverly goads Iofur Raknison into a deadly battle with Iorek Byrnison from which Iorek emerges victorious to become the rightful leader of the fierce armored bears. However, after her father, Lord Asriel, is freed, he is so obsessed with his scientific quest that he subjects Roger to deadly experiments hoping to capture his Dust and use it to bridge the gap between the earth and the new universe revealed in the Aurora. He succeeds. As Lord Asriel leaves the earth, Roger dies before Lyra can save him. She vows that she will find a way to follow her father, avenge Roger's death, and discover the secret of Dust.

Suitability and Critical Comment

This is the beginning of a massive, compelling trilogy that will surely take its place alongside Lewis's Narnia series. The provocative mixture of science, religion, symbolism, and fantasy with a complex but exciting plot allows for appreciation at different levels. The touching depiction of such human emotions as loss, heartbreak, and loyalty supplies an additional dimension. It has appeal for both young readers, from about age twelve and up, as well as adults.

Themes and Subjects

Adventure, Arctic regions, bears, fantasy, friendship, good versus evil, magic, Oxford (England), religion, science, witches

Passages for Booktalking

Lyra witnesses the poisoning of wine intended for Lord Asriel (pp. 4–8); Lyra prevents his murder (pp. 10–15); Lord Asriel makes a presentation about Dust and another world revealed in the Aurora (pp. 19–23); Mrs. Coulter kidnaps a young boy named Tony (pp. 40–44); and Lyra receives the golden compass (pp. 72–74).

Additional Selections

In Beth Goobie's *Before Wings* (Orca, 2001), a fifteen-year-old girl who is able to see spirits uses her power and a friendship to unravel a dark mystery surrounding her aunt.

Fire Bringer (Dutton, 2000) by David Clement-Davies is an outstanding animal fantasy about a deer hero and a fawn named Rannock who is destined to overthrow the harsh dictatorship of the evil Drail.

Fantasy, adventure, and reaching maturity are themes explored in Dia Calhoun's *Firegold* (Winslow, 1999), which is about a blue-eyed boy who threatens the stability of a conformist community where everyone's eyes are brown.

In *Spirit Fox* (DAW, 1998) by Mickey Zucker Reichet and Jennifer Wingert, Kiardo is born at the moment that an orphaned fox is killed and, in later life, the animal's spirit gradually turns her into a fox.

About the Book

Booklist, March 1, 1996, p. 1179.
Bulletin of the Center for Children's Books, April, 1996, p. 279.
Horn Book, July-Aug., 1996, p. 464.
Kirkus Reviews, March 1, 1996, p. 379.
School Library Journal, April, 1996, p. 158.

About the Author

Authors and Artists for Young Adults, vol. 15, Gale, 1995.
Children's Literature Review, vol. 20, Gale, 1990; vol. 62, Gale, 2000.
Cooper, Ilene. "Darkness Visible—Philip Pullman's *Amber Spyglass*," *Booklist*, Oct., 2000, pp. 354–55.
Hipple, Ted. *Writers for Young Adults*, supplement 1, Scribners, 1999, pp. 249–55.
Lives and Works: Young Adult Authors, vol. 5, Grolier, 1999, pp. 81–83.
Major Authors and Illustrators for Children and Young Adults, vol. 5, Gale, 1993.
Odean, Kathleen. "The Story Master—Philip Pullman," *School Library Journal*, Oct., 2000, pp. 50–54.
Pullman, Philip. "Gotterdammerung or Bust," *Horn Book*, Jan.-Feb., 1999, pp. 31–33.
Pullman, Philip. "The Republic of Heaven," *Horn Book*, Nov.-Dec., 2001, pp. 655–67.
St. James Guide to Young Adult Writers (2nd ed.), St. James, 1999.
Sixth Book of Junior Authors and Illustrators, Wilson, 1989.
Something about the Author, vol. 65, Gale, 1991; vol. 103, Gale, 1999.
Something about the Author Autobiography Series, vol. 17, Gale, 1994.
Twentieth Century Young Adult Writers, St. James, 1994.

Voight, Cynthia. *Elske.* New York: Atheneum, 1999. $18.00 (0-689-82472-6) (Grades 7–10).

Introduction

Cynthia Voigt (1942–) was born in southern Connecticut, where she attended private schools. After graduating from Smith College, she worked at an advertising agency and then gravitated to teaching English principally at the Key School in Annapolis, Maryland. As a writer, she is perhaps best known for the seven-book cycle involving the Tillerman family, featuring with particular emphasis on Dicey, the courageous, resourceful central character in many of these books. In the first, *Homecoming* (Atheneum, 1981), Dicey, without money, leads her three siblings as the four travel from Provincetown, Massachusetts, to Crisfield, a town on Maryland's eastern shore where they hope to find a home with their maternal grandmother. From the early 1980s through the 1990s, Ms. Voigt was involved in a four-book cycle about the Kingdom, an imaginary medieval land. The quartet begins with *Jackaroo* (Macmillan, 1985) and ends with *Elske*. Each can be read separately. Coincidentally, its dust jacket illustration is Vermeer's *Head of a Girl*, the subject of Tracy Chevalier's *Girl with a Pearl Earring* featured later in this book.

Principal Characters

Elske, a twelve-year-old girl raised in the realm of the Wolfers
Mirkle, Elske's grandmother
Beriel, a princess denied her throne
Guerric, Beriel's brother
Lord Dugald, whom Elske will marry
Win, whom Beriel will marry

Plot Summary

This is the fourth title in the Kingdom cycle, which began with *Jackaroo*, about a mythical Robin Hood–type outlaw, followed by *The Wings of a Falcon* and *On Fortune's Wheel*, which are set in an imaginary land known as the Kingdom with the flavor of medieval times. In this final book in the series, Elske is a twelve-year-old girl who has been raised in the brutal realm of the Wolfers on a continent that resembles medieval Europe. The Wolfers are ruthless people with barbaric customs. Elske has been raised for a sacrificial death. She was chosen at birth to be a death maiden. This means that as she nears the time of her womanhood, she will be ravaged and then killed to please the Volkking.

But Elske is saved from this horrible fate by the cleverness of her grandmother, Mirkle, who sacrifices her own life for that of her granddaughter, whom she has raised since infancy. In this manner, Elske is able to escape both her fate and the terrible Wolfers, who do not notice the trickery.

Elske makes her way to the more civilized city of Trastad. She begins work as a servant in the home of Var Jarrol. Quickly Elske begins to show her bravery and faithfulness, as when she defends her mistress against a group of drunken men. When she screams to frighten them away, her voice sounds like that of a wolf howling—the war cry of the Volkaric. After that, the other citizens of Trastad give her careful respect. Elske is also very intelligent, and Var Jarrol is fascinated when he learns she can speak not only her native tongue of Volkaric but also the language of Trastad. Var Jarrol puts her to work as a spy against foreign merchants. She works at the serving table for the merchants and overhears their conversations. Then she reports to Var Jarrol.

Because Elske is from the brutal Wolfers, she is not trusted at first by the people. However, they soon respond to her friendliness and intelligent manner. She learns that Var Jarrol is interested in the formula for black powder to be used in warfare.

Soon Beriel arrives in Trastad. She is a difficult young woman in search of a husband during the Winter Courting season. Elske becomes her hand-maiden, and the two young women soon respond to each other and form a friendship. Elske learns that Beriel is with child, a secret that both women try to hide. Elske not only helps Beriel to deliver a daughter, but finds a home for the child.

Beriel is the rightful heir to the Kingdom. A new law has decreed that a female may take the throne if she is the firstborn. Beriel is indeed the first-born, but neither her father nor her mother wish her to be crowned. They want her brother, Guerric, to be king. Guerric has forced her into exile so that he can have the throne for himself.

Beriel and Elske travel to the Kingdom to raise an army so that she can defeat her brother and take her rightful place on the throne. Beriel challenges her brother to a duel for the Kingdom, which he refuses on the grounds that she is a woman. In the battle that follows, Beriel is victorious. She becomes queen of the realm, and the Kingdom enjoys a golden age.

Suitability and Critical Comment

Teenaged girls, twelve and up, will enjoy this tale of adventure and dar-ing. The character of Elske is well developed throughout the novel. Com-ing from a land where cruelty toward others is the norm, Elske slowly grows into a kinder, more knowledgeable person. Her quick mind allows her to adapt to a new environment and enables her to achieve personal growth. For grades seven through ten.

Themes and Subjects

Bravery, childbirth, cruelty, friendship, mythical kingdoms, rape, valor, war

Passages for Booktalking

Elske escapes her fate (pp. 1–4); Elske defends her mistress (pp. 42–47); Elske meets Beriel (pp. 77–90); Beriel's child is born (123–126); Beriel is victorious in battle (pp. 229–237).

Additional Selections

Set in 2154, this science fiction survival story, *Invitation to the Game* (Simon, 1993), by Monica Hughes tells about eight bored school graduates and the game that transports them to a frightening future.

In the aftermath of a post-atomic holocaust, a teenaged survivor finds she is not alone in the valley in Robert C. O'Brien's *Z for Zachariah* (Aladdin, 1974).

Nola, a teenaged witch, must take on the appearance of Brinna, a beautiful household servant to solve a mystery in *Magic Can Be Murder* (Harcourt, 2000) by Vivian Vande Velde.

When she visits Glastonbury Tor, sixteen-year-old Felicity discovers she has the power to see into an alternate world in *The Last Grail Keeper* (Holiday, 2001) by Pamela Smith Hill.

About the Book
Booklist, Sept. 1, 1999, p. 125
Bulletin of the Center for Children's Books, Dec., 1999, p. 152.
Horn Book, Jan.-Feb., 2000, p. 85.
Kirkus Reviews, Oct. 15, 1999, p. 1653.
School Library Journal, Oct., 1999, p. 160.
VOYA, April, 2000, p. 14.

About the Author
Authors and Artists for Young Adults, vol. 3, Gale, 1990; vol. 30, Gale, 1999.
Children's Literature Review, vol. 13, Gale, 1987; vol. 48, Gale, 1998.
Continuum Encyclopedia of Children's Literature, Continuum, 2001.
Drew, Bernard A. *The 100 Most Popular Young Adult Authors,* Libraries Unlimited, 1997.
Gallo, Donald. *Speaking for Ourselves,* National Council of Teachers of English, 1990.
Hipple, Ted. *Writers for Young Adults,* vol. 3, Scribners, 1997, pp. 329–38.
Lives and Works: Young Adult Authors, vol. 8, Grolier, 1999, pp. 36–38.
Major Authors and Illustrators for Children and Young Adults, vol. 6, Gale, 1993.
McElmeel, Sharron L. *The 100 Most Popular Young Adult Authors,* Libraries Unlimited, 1999.
"Newbery Award Acceptance Material-1983," *Horn Book,* Aug.-Sept., 1983, pp. 401–13.
"Newbery Award Acceptance Material-1983," *Top of the News,* Summer, 1983, pp. 360–65.
Reid, Suzanne. *Presenting Cynthia Voigt,* Twayne, 1995.
St. James Guide to Young Adult Writers, (2nd ed.), St. James, 1999.
Silvey, Anita. *Children's Books and Their Creators,* Houghton Mifflin, 1995.
Something about the Author, vol. 33, Gale, 1983; vol. 48, Gale, 1987; vol. 79, Gale, 1995; vol. 116, Gale, 2000.
Sutton, Roger. "A Solitary View—Talking with Cynthia Voigt," *School Library Journal,* June, 1995, pp. 28–32.
Twentieth Century Children's Writers, St. James, 1995.
Twentieth Century Young Adult Writers, St. James, 1994.
Voigt, Cynthia. "1995 Margaret A. Edwards Award Acceptance Speech: Thirteen Stray Thoughts about Failure," *Journal of Youth Services in Libraries,* Fall, 1995, pp. 23–32.

5

Historical Fiction
and Other Lands

Avi. *Beyond the Western Sea. Book One: Escape from Home.* Orchard,
1996. $18.95 (0-531-09520-7) (Grades 5–8).

Introduction
Avi Wortis (1937–), the son of a psychiatrist and a social worker, was
nicknamed Avi because that is how his young sister pronounced his given
name. He loved reading as a child, with a preference for Thornton W.
Burgess's books and *The Wind in the Willows* by Kenneth Grahame. He
worked as a librarian for many years, but when he began telling stories to
his sons, he became inspired to write books for young people. He has written about thirty books in various genres, from historical fiction to contemporary realism, but he is probably best known and respected for his
historical novels, most of which take place in the United States. *Escape from
Home,* the first part of *Beyond the Western Sea,* tells about three immigrant
youngsters and the dangers and hardships they face on their journey to
America in the 1850s. The second part, *Lord Kirkle's Money,* continues their
odyssey to the mill town of Lowell, Massachusetts, where they again
encounter the villains who pursued them in the first book.

Principal Characters
Patrick O'Connell, twelve-year-old Irish boy
Maura O'Connell, Patrick's fifteen-year-old sister
Laurence Kirkle, eleven, the O'Connell landlord's runaway son
Assorted characters, including: Mr. Pickler, an investigator; Horatio
    Drabble, an actor
Fred Noname and Sergeant Rumpkin, Lime Street Runners Association

Plot Summary
The story begins in 1851, when Maura and Patrick O'Connell abandon
the poverty, famine, and disease of their Irish home. They have received a
message from their father in America. He has saved enough money so that

the family can journey to Liverpool, where they will board a ship to America to join him. Their mother does not want to leave at first, but they persuade her. However, once they start out, she turns back. She cannot leave Ireland, where the body of her other child is buried, but she insists that they go on without her. Maura and Patrick must travel on alone.

When the children reach Liverpool, they join the many other unfortunate and malcontented characters who roam the streets. Among them is Laurence Kirkle, a young English lord who is also running away to America. Penniless and confused, Laurence left his home in a rage to escape the cruelty of his brother and to hide his shame at committing a theft.

In the back streets and alleys of Liverpool, these three children struggle to keep themselves alive and their wits about them until they can board the ship that will take them to a new life in America. These three major characters run into a range of Dickensian characters, from the kind and helping to the devious. How they manage to keep together is a challenging maze of action and suspense, as in short, brisk chapters the author leaps from one situation and character to another.

From the time he runs away until he manages to board the ship for America, Laurence is pursed by Mr. Pickler, who is searching for the runaway. When Laurence boards a train for Liverpool, Pickler spies him and pursues. It is only by the kindness of a stranger, Mr. Clemspool, who yanks him aboard a third-class car, that Laurence escapes.

Patrick and Maura are in awe when they first see the jumble of brick, stone, and marble that is the city of Liverpool. When they lose what little belongings they carry, they are befriended by one Ralph Toggs, who offers to take them to a place to spend the night. He belongs to the Lime Street Runners Association. It is a place to stay, but it is wretched, and both children fear for their safety.

In the meantime, Laurence soon discovers that his helpful benefactor, Mr. Clemspool, knows that he is from a wealthy family and is holding him prisoner. He escapes through a second-story window. On the run, Laurence meets Ralph Toggs and then meets briefly with Patrick, and a friendship is formed.

With Clemspool and Mr. Pickler in hot pursuit and the O'Connell children often not knowing whether people like Toggs are intending to help them or hurt them, the last days wind down for the sailing of the ship to America. The ending is a lead-in to the sequel, *Lord Kirkle's Money.* In this action-packed, cliff-hanging novel, book one ends as a distraught Laurence is hiding in the bottom hold of the *Robert Peel.* Feeling more alone than he ever has in his life, he feels the crates swaying in the hold and thinks that the ship must be under way. Now he wonders if his friend Patrick will come and find him. If Patrick does not come, Laurence feels he will die.

Suitability and Critical Comment

This is a good, action-packed adventure tale much in the style of serialized Victorian novels. Some young readers may find the shifting scenes and constantly changing assortment of characters to be challenging, but most should enjoy this engrossing read that is a twisting page-turner with lots of suspense and a dash of melodrama.

Themes and Subjects

Bravery, cruelty, death, England, family love, fear, friendship, immigration, Ireland, poverty, suspense, thievery

Passages for Booktalking

Patrick and Maura hear from their father about going to America (pp. 4–7); Mrs. O'Connell refuses to go with them (pp. 26–29); Laurence runs away (pp. 41–44); Laurence makes the train (pp. 70–76); Patrick and Maura reach Liverpool (pp. 86–92); Laurence gets away from Mr. Clemspool (pp. 123–26); Mr. Pickler gets to Liverpool in pursuit of Laurence (pp. 146–52); Laurence and Patrick meet (pp. 160–66); Maura searches for Patrick (pp. 192–95); Maura and Patrick get ready to board (pp. 265–70).

Additional Selections

In Sonia Levitin's historical adventure *Clem's Chances* (Scholastic, 2001), young Clem sets out in the 1860s to find his father in the California goldfields.

After Mary's grandmother is hanged as a witch, the young girl, really a witch, is sent to America disguised as a Puritan in the supernatural historical novel *Witch Child* (Candlewick, 2001) by Celia Rees.

In Elizabethan England, young Richard Malory, who is in London searching for his father, gets involved in the theater of Shakespeare's time in J. B. Cheaney's *The Playmaker* (Knopf, 2000).

In *Nora Ryan's Song* (Delacorte, 2000) by Patricia Reilly Giff, the tragic days of the mid-nineteenth century Irish potato famine are seen through the eyes of young Nora Ryan.

About the Book

Booklist, Feb. 1, 1996, p. 930.
Bulletin of the Center for Children's Books, Feb., 1996, p. 82.
Horn Book, July-Aug., 1996, p. 461.

Kirkus Reviews, Jan. 15, 1996, p. 132.
School Library Journal, June, 1996, p. 150.
VOYA, June, 1996, p. 92.

About the Author

Authors and Artists for Young Adults, vol. 10, Gale, 1993; vol. 37, Gale, 2001.
Avi. "The True Confessions of Charlotte Doyle—Acceptance Speech," *Horn Book,* Jan.-Feb., 1992, pp. 24–27.
Bloom, S. P., and C. M. Mercier. *Presenting Avi,* Twayne, 1997.
Children's Literature Review, vol. 24, Gale, 1991; vol. 68, Gale, 2001.
Continuum Encyclopedia of Children's Literature, Continuum, 2001.
Cooper, Ilene. "The Booklist Interview—Avi," *Booklist,* May 15, 2002, p. 1609.
Drew, Bernard A. *The 100 Most Popular Young Adult Authors,* Libraries Unlimited, 1997.
Fifth Book of Junior Authors and Illustrators, Wilson, 1983.
Gallo, Donald. *Speaking for Ourselves,* National Council of Teachers of English, 1990.
Hipple, Ted. *Writers for Young Adults,* vol. 1, Scribners, 1997, pp. 73–76.
Lives and Works: Young Adult Authors, vol. 1, Grolier, 1999, pp. 34–36.
Major Authors and Illustrators for Children and Young Adults, vol. 6, Gale, 1993.
McElmeel, Sharron L. *The 100 Most Popular Children's Authors,* Libraries Unlimited, 1999.
St. James Guide to Young Adult Writers (2nd ed.), St. James, 1999.
Silvey, Anita. *Children's Books and Their Creators,* Houghton Mifflin, 1995.
Something about the Author, vol. 14, Gale, 1978; vol. 71, Gale, 1993; vol. 108, Gale, 2000.
Twentieth Century Young Adult Writers, St. James, 1994.

Bagdasarian, Adam. *Forgotten Fire.* Dorling Kindersley, 2000. $17.95 (0-7894-2627-7) (Grades 10–12).

Introduction

In 1915, during World War I, the Turkish government and its military used a false accusation that Turkish Armenians were aiding the Russian enemy, as a pretext to wage a genocidal attack on the Armenian population. The purpose of the inhuman slaughter that resulted was really to rid the country of this non-Turkish Christian minority and create a new country inhabited solely by Turkish Muslims. The Armenian holocaust lasted until after the war ended in 1918, when a new regime came to power in a defeated Turkey. By this time over 1.5 million Armenians had died. This represented approximately three-quarters of their original population. Although some of the key perpetrators were executed or assassinated, most went unpunished. The Armenian massacres remain one of the darkest chapters in the history of humanity. This first-person narrative is based on the recorded memoirs of the author's great-uncle, who survived the genocide and managed to escape to the United States. It is Mr. Bagdasarian's first book.

Principal Characters

Vahan, the youngest child in the prosperous Kenderian family of Biltis, Turkey

Sisak, Vahan's next oldest brother and close companion

Pattoo Altoomian, Vahan's classmate whose mother shelters him and finds him a position with Selim Bey

Selim Bey, the hated Turkish official known as "The butcher of Armenians" and "Horseshoer of Bashkale" because he nailed horseshoes to the feet of his victims

General Khalil, a fierce, terrifying retired army officer who is Selim Bey's father

Dr. Tashian, an Armenian physician, doctor to the local German consul and who, with his wife, shelters Vahan

Werner, the hated, pompous consul

Seta, a beautiful Armenian girl whom Vahan loves and who is enslaved by Werner

Plot Summary

Vahan Kenderian, age twelve, is the seventh and last child in a wealthy, highly respected Armenian family living in the township of Bitlis in southeastern Turkey. It is 1915, and Turkey has joined forces in the World War with Germany, against the Western allies and Russia. Vahan's privileged childhood within a loving family ends abruptly when news arrives of massacres of Armenians in neighboring townships. Soon a disbelieving family sees their father being arrested and taken off by the gendarmes. A few days later, seven soldiers question the family and take Vahan's two eldest brothers, both in their late teens, into the garden where they are shot. The rest of the family—Vahan; his two sisters, Armenouhi and Oskina; Sisak, Vahan's fourteen-year-old brother; their mother, Meera; and Toumia, their grandmother, are rounded up and forced to join other refugees in a death march. The weak and sick are shot or bayoneted, and many of the women are raped. They pass stacks of corpses by the wayside. Despairing of the future, Armenouhi drinks poison, and later, Vahan witnesses the death of his grandmother, killed by soldiers after she stops to drink water from a corpse-clogged river. At the insistence of their mother, Vahan and Sisak escape at night, but in their flight they become separated. Vahan returns to Bitlis and seeks refuge at the home of his former schoolmate Pattoo Altoomian. Pattoo's mother feeds and nurses Vahan back to health but, after a week, she is so fearful of being discovered harboring a fugitive, that she reluctantly tells Vahan that he must leave. Vahan finds a deserted house in which to live and discovers his brother Sisak near death, lying in a street littered with dead bodies. A few days later, Sisak dies in his arms. Captured by gendarmes, Vahan is dragged to a holding pen, his former school. Here he is able to escape by forcing his body though one of the toilet holes in the boy's washroom. He returns to the Altoomians, where Pattoo's mother arranges for Vahan to become the stable boy of the hated Selim Bey, the ex-governor of Van, known throughout the district for the atrocities he has committed against the Armenians. Selim Bey is now living in the Kenderian house and, because he remembers Vahan's father fondly, is willing to allow the boy to live. Vahan learns that cold-blooded murderers can present a charming, caring exterior. At one point, Vahan shares the barn with a fearful Armenian girl, named Seranoush, who is not quite his age. At night, she is repeatedly raped by Turkish soldiers and, after a few days, she dies. Vahan's horrifying odyssey continues as he wanders through Turkey eluding the authorities and seeking a safe haven. For a time he is the stable boy of Selim Bey's father, the terrifying General Khalil. Later he feigns being deaf and dumb to disguise his Armenian accent from a group of Turkish refugees with whom he stays for a time, and still later, in the northern town of Sivas, he becomes the ward of Dr. Tashian, who is protected from the Turks because he is the personal physician of Werner, the conceited, hateful German consul. Here, Vahan falls in love with Seta, a fifteen-year-old girl who has been coerced into being Werner's mistress. When the girl dies in childbirth, Vahan is heartbroken. He again takes up his wandering and eventually, through amazing courage and ingenuity, arrives at the Black Sea port of Samsun, where he is able to book passage on a freighter bound for Constantinople. Here, at war's end and after three years of wandering, he is able to look toward the future with a tiny ray of hope.

Suitability and Critical Comment

This harrowing tale of tragedy and human catastrophe is told with amazing objectivity. Its matter-of-fact prose and lack of sentiment increase the power and heartbreak of the narrative. Because of the graphic, disturbing nature of the atrocities depicted, this book is best suited to an older teenaged audience roughly in the senior high-school years.

Themes and Subjects

Armenia, Armenian holocaust, coming-of-age, courage, death, determination, family, fortitude, friendship, genocide, ingenuity, inhumanity toward others, self-reliance, sexual awakening, survival, Turkey, World War I

Passages for Booktalking

Vahan talks about his childhood and family (pp. 4–7); he describes his attitude toward Turks (pp. 9–10); Vahan's brothers are shot (pp. 24–28); his grandmother is killed (pp. 46–48); Mrs. Altoonian gives Vahan shelter and food (pp. 69–74); he escapes via the toilet (pp. 95–99).

Additional Selections

Gaye Hicyilmaz's *Smiling for Strangers* (Farrar, 2000) is the harrowing story of a fourteen-year-old war refugee and her journey from war-torn Yugoslavia to Sussex, England.

Kiss the Dust (Puffin, 1993) by Elizabeth Laird is a docu-novel about a teenaged Kurdish refugee caught up in the 1984 Iran-Iraq war.

The nonfiction *Why Do They Hate Me? Young Lives Caught in War and Conflict* (Pocket, 1999) edited by Laurel Holiday focuses on the diaries of three youngsters, one in the Holocaust, another in Northern Ireland, and a third that involves the Palestinians and Israel.

Set during World War II at home, Miriam Bat-Ami's *Two Suns in the Sky* (Front Street, 1999) tells of the love between a Catholic American and a Jewish Holocaust survivor from Yugoslavia.

About the Book

Booklist, July, 2000, p. 2024.
Bulletin of the Center for Children's Books, Jan., 2001, p. 175.
Horn Book, Nov.-Dec., 2000, p. 752.
Kirkus Reviews, Oct. 1, 2000, p. 1418.
School Library Journal, Dec., 2000, p. 138.
VOYA, Dec., 2000, p. 344.

About the Author

No information available.

Frazier, Charles. *Cold Mountain.* Vintage, 1998. Pb. $13.00 (0-375-70075-7) (Grades 10–12).

Introduction

Charles Frazier (1950–), the son of a high-school principal and a librarian, always had a love of reading. He majored in English at college and taught literature at the University of Colorado for fifteen years. After traveling extensively in South America, he and his coauthor Donald Secreast wrote *Adventuring in the Andes* (Sierra Club, 1985). In the mid-1980s,

Frazier began visiting the old family haunts in rural North Carolina, studying family history, observing the flora and fauna, and taking notes on what he found. Through research, he also learned about an ancestor, W. P. Inman, a Confederate soldier during the Civil War, who was wounded in battle, deserted his company, and walked back to his home on Cold Mountain. Using this as a framework, he began writing and, with his wife's encouragement, left his teaching position to write full time. Seven years of research and writing produced the final product, which became a bestseller and a National Book Award winner.

Principal Characters

Inman, a wounded Confederate soldier
Ada, whom Inman loves
Ada's ill father
Ruby Thewes, a mountain woman
Veasey, a defrocked preacher
Odell, heir to a Georgia planter
Junior, a noisy hillbilly
Stobrod, Ruby's long-lost father

Plot Summary

Inman is a severely wounded and badly disillusioned Confederate soldier, weary of what he has seen in the battle at Petersburg. He is so badly wounded that he is put on a cot along with the others who are waiting to die. But Inman does not die at Petersburg. Instead, he is sent farther south to a hospital where it is expected that eventually he will die. But still he does not. Slowly it seems as though his body heals itself. Through his long months of convalescing, he becomes further depressed as he relives the horror of Sharpsburg and Fredericksburg and Petersburg. The only peace he finds in his mind is recollections of his childhood friend Swimmer and his Cherokee folk tales. He remembers that Swimmer spoke of a high land above the blue vault of heaven where the spirit could be reborn. Cold Mountain becomes his idea of a better place where he can heal his broken spirit.

Knowing he will be returned to active duty in a war that the South is soon to lose, Inman slips out of the hospital at night armed with a revolver. So begins his long walk home to a place in the Blue Ridge Mountains and to Ada, the girl he loved there so many years ago.

Meanwhile, Ada has moved from Charleston with her missionary father, who is suffering from tuberculosis, to a new home in the healthy air of North Carolina. But his death leaves her penniless and alone without the slightest sense of how to survive. In the prewar South, she could play the piano well and had a literary turn of mind, considered fine talents for young ladies. Members of her father's congregation fully expect her to return to Charleston, but she refuses to beg for charity to get there. She is saved by the appearance of Ruby Thewes, a solitary mountain woman who begins to teach Ada self-reliance and a love of physical labor as well as a love of the land. At one point, Ruby's long-lost wastrel father, Stobrod, turns up. He had spent his life drinking and making moonshine. But here on Cold Mountain, he transforms himself once again through his music.

As Inman walks a perilous journey through the bruised land that is the South, he encounters brutal bands of vigilantes who patrol the highways searching for runaway slaves to return to their owners for money. He also meets up with a strange group of misfits who are also wandering the countryside. Among them are Veasey, a defrocked preacher who names Inman as his personal confessor; Odell, a former heir to a Georgia plantation, and now wandering the countryside in search of his slave lover; and Junior, a treacherous hillbilly.

When Inman and Ada are finally reunited, they are touched with a kind of awkwardness, for they were neither married nor lovers before the war. Now they are confronted not only with their feelings for one another, but with the different people they have become since their last meeting. Inman has lost his innocence in the horror of war; Ada is no longer the artless young woman who knew nothing of life but the piano and parties. Living in a tragic land in this tragic time, how will they find their life together?

Suitability and Critical Comment

This book is best recommended for the older teenager who has an appreciation of history and the effect that the devastation of war has on Inman and his desire to find a place that will heal his tortured spirit. It is a panorama of a special time, with richly developed characters and beautiful descriptions of the both tortured and lovely landscape. Intertwined with battle and romance is a satisfying story for grades ten through twelve.

Themes and Subjects

Brutality, depression, desertion, friendship, romance, slavery, war

Passages for Booktalking

Inman remembers Swimmer's stories (pp. 23–24); Ada meets Ruby (pp. 66–68); Inman meets the gypsies (pp. 124–32); Inman is captured and escapes (pp. 225–33); Inman and Ada meet again (pp. 402–6).

Additional Selections

Newly married Alice is left to manage the family farm when her husband enlists in the Union Army in *Alice's Tulips* (St. Martin's, 2000) by Sandra Dallas.

For younger readers, the nonfiction *When Johnny Went Marching: Young Americans Fight the Civil War* (HarperCollins, 2001) by G. Clifton Wister tells the true stories of several young soldiers, including Willie Johnston of Vermont, who received the Medal of Honor when he was thirteen.

Also for a younger audience, Gary Paulsen's *Soldier's Heart* (Delacorte, 1998) is a novel based on fact about a fifteen-year-old Union soldier and the brutality of war.

Paul Fleischman's *Bull Run* (HarperCollins, 1993) highlights the diary entries of sixteen fictional characters—eight each from the South and the North—in which they express their hopes, fears, and attitudes about the battle.

About the Book

Library Journal, May 15, 1997, p. 100.
New York Times Book Review, July 13, 1997, p. 14.
School Library Journal, Nov., 1997, p. 146.

About the Author

Authors and Artists for Young Adults, vol. 34, Gale, 2000.
Contemporary Authors, vol. 161, Gale, 1998.

Hesse, Karen. *Stowaway.* Simon & Schuster, 2000. $17.95 (0-689-83987-1) (Grades 7–9).

Introduction

Karen Hesse (1952–) loved reading as a child and, as an adult, took many book-related jobs—librarian, reviewer, and freelance editor—before she became a full-time writer. She has written a number of historical novels, perhaps the best known being *Out of the Dust* (Scholastic, 1997), the winner of the 1998 Newbery Prize. Told in the form of free verse diary entries, it covers two years, 1935 and 1936, in the life of teenaged Billie Jo, who is growing up on a wretched farm in the Oklahoma Panhandle. In speaking about her work in her Newbery acceptance speech, the author said, "Young readers are asking for books that challenge, and confirm, and console. They are asking for us to listen to their questions and to help them find their own answers." *Stowaway* is in a slightly lighter vein than her other books. In it, the author has taken the few facts we know about Nicholas Young, an eleven-year-old stowaway, and woven them into a fictional diary that will transport readers back to the fantastic voyage of Captain Cook on the *Endeavour.*

Principal Characters

Nicholas Young, an eleven-year-old stowaway
James Cook, captain of the *Endeavor*
Bootie, a midshipman
Mr. Banks, a botanist

Plot Summary

The story of eleven-year-old Nicholas Young told in this book is the fictionalized account of the real-life Nicholas Young. The adventures aboard the *Endeavor* are told as the boy might have experienced them. The adventures themselves actually happened from 1768 to 1771.

Young is an educated boy who can read and write, but he runs away from a school headed by the Reverend Smythe, who is a cruel man. When his father apprentices him to a butcher who beats him, the boy runs away again. He bribes three seamen—Francis Haite, John Ramsay, and Samuel Evans—to sneak him aboard the ship *Endeavor* anchored in Plymouth but ready to set sail. It is captained by English explorer and navigator James Cook, and this will be the first of his three expeditions to the South Pacific, unknown to the boy. The seamen smuggle food to him as he hides in a small landing boat aboard ship. It is cramped, cold, and has no cover, so he is constantly wet from the sea and the rain. It is also smelly because the goats, pigs, and chickens are penned up nearby. But Nicholas cannot make his presence known until they are well out to sea, for fear he will be returned to England.

Eventually, the presence of the stowaway is made known to Captain Cook. A reasonably fair and just man, Cook accepts the boy into the crew and makes him assistant to the ship's surgeon. But life is not easy on board the *Endeavor,* especially because Nicholas is the lowest of the low in the pecking order. When midshipman Bootie is blamed because the boy's hiding place was not discovered sooner, Bootie takes out his anger by beating Nicholas. However, the boy does not complain, even though Bootie again beats him when he finds out that Nicholas is teaching one of the crew to read. Nicholas continues to work hard and, as the ship sails on, he begins to enjoy the adventure. The ship's surgeon is pleased with his work, and Mr. Joseph Banks, the botanist on board, takes an interest in him, too. Banks and his assistants study and paint every fish and plant they can find in their frequent stopping places.

Over the next three years, Nicholas's life is filled with more adventure than he could have dreamed. On an island that the English called King George's Land, he becomes friends with a native boy who calls the island Otahiti. Cook keeps careful charts of everywhere they go for the benefit of those who will sail after him. At Batavia the crew contracts an illness that spreads throughout the ship. Nicholas helps the surgeon to care for the sick and dying and watches as sailor after sailor is buried at sea.

Nicholas gives an eyewitness account to history in the making over this three-year journey. He is the first person of the crew to spot New Zealand. Many of his adventures are frightening, however, as when the crew encounters hostile natives or when the ship is going through harrowing storms. In the process, young Nicholas grows into a young man with a wealth of experience behind him.

Nicholas returns home on the *Endeavor* and is the first to spot English soil. After he says good-bye to the crew, he has to talk to his father and the butcher, and then he will keep an appointment with Mr. Banks. The real Nicholas Young never sailed again with James Cook, but he did make one journey with Mr. Banks in 1772.

Suitability and Critical Comment

This is an ideal story for young readers who like adventure and the sea. Told in the first-person narrative, it is easily read by most readers. Life aboard a ship in the eighteenth century is vividly depicted. The enthusiasm of young Nicholas makes history come alive as the *Endeavor* charts its historic three-year voyage. The end pages feature a world map showing the ship's journey. For grades seven through nine.

Themes and Subjects

Apprenticeship, botany, cruelty, family relationships, friendship, islands, sailing, seamanship, ships, South Pacific, stowaways

Passages for Booktalking

Nicholas meets Captain Cook (p. 15); rounding Cape Horn (pp. 57–58); the crew battles the natives (pp. 120–27); Bootie catches Nicholas teaching one of the crew to read (pp. 173–75); on the Great Barrier Reef (pp. 227–31).

Additional Selections

Disguised as a Christian ship's boy, a sixteen-year-old Jewish girl comes aboard the *Santa Maria* for Columbus's first voyage to the New World in Waldtraut Lewin's *Freedom Beyond the Sea* (Delacorte, 2001).

The life of prim sixteen-year-old Jane, a graduate of a young ladies' academy, changes dramatically when she takes a sea journey to join her fiance in *Boston Jane: An Adventure* (HarperCollins, 2000) by Jennifer Holm.

Set in the eighteenth century, *Anson's Way* (Clarion, 1999) by Gary D. Schmidt tells about a young drummer boy who is sent to Ireland to prevent uprisings.

An Ojibwa child experiences the invasion of the land and the customs of the tribe when white settlers arrive in Louise Erdrich's *The Birchbark House* (Hyperion, 1999).

About the Book

Booklist, Dec. 15, 2000, p. 820.
Bulletin of the Center for Children's Books, Oct., 2000, p. 65.
Horn Book, Jan.-Feb., 2001, p. 91.
Kirkus Reviews, Nov. 1, 2000, p. 1545.
School Library Journal, Nov., 2000, p. 156.
VOYA, April, 2001, p. 40.

About the Author

Authors and Artists for Young Adults, vol. 27, Gale, 1999.
Bowen, Brenda. "Karen Hesse," *Horn Book,* July-Aug., 1998, pp. 428–32.
Children's Literature Review, vol. 54, Gale, 1999.
Continuum Encyclopedia of Children's Literature, Continuum, 2001.
Drew, Bernard A. *100 More Popular Young Adult Authors,* Libraries Unlimited, 2002.
Eighth Book of Junior Authors and Illustrators, Wilson, 2000.
Hipple, Ted. *Writers for Young Adults,* supplement 1, Scribners, 2000, pp. 93–102.
Lives and Works: Young Adult Authors, vol. 4, Grolier, 1999, pp. 38–42.
"Newbery Award Acceptance Material, 1998," *Horn Book,* July-Aug., 1998, pp. 422–27.
"Newbery Award Acceptance Speech, 1998," *Journal of Youth Services in Libraries,* Summer, 1998, pp. 341–45.
St. James Guide to Young Adult Writers (2nd ed.), St. James, 1999.
Something about the Author, vol. 74, Gale, 1993; vol. 103, Gale, 1999; vol. 113, Gale, 2000.
Something about the Author Autobiography Series, vol. 25, Gale, 1998.

Karr, Kathleen. *The Boxer.* Farrar Straus, 2000. $16.00 (0-374-30921-3) (Grades 7–9).

Introduction

Kathleen Karr (1946–) grew up on a chicken farm in rural New Jersey. Because there were few playmates around, she developed a love of books and reading. By age seventeen, she was contributing articles to local publications, and in college wrote extensively about her interest in films and movie history. She also developed an interest in boxing. At the prompting of her children, she began writing books for children and young adults, most of them historical novels. These stories, about two dozen in number, use a variety of settings and a number of different historical periods as their subjects. She has said, "I love trying to recreate a time period, to take readers to the past like a time machine. . . . I love the little stories behind the sweep of history." *The Boxer* is about a boy who makes his way in the ring and on the rough streets of New York City in 1881. Of this novel, Ms. Karr said, "I am really proud of *The Boxer*. . . . I have to admit that it is one of my favorites because I was able to use all the ring lore I have."

Principal Characters

Johnny Woods, a fifteen-year-old boxer
Michael O'Shaunnessey, who recognizes the boy's talent
Ma, Johnny's mother
Pa, his father

Plot Summary

Fifteen-year-old Johnny Woods lives in the tough tenement world of New York City's Lower East Side in 1885. He likes to box. He is small but fast. Everyone says he is fast. One day he reads the sign outside Brodie's saloon, calling for barefisted fighters, $5 if they can go four rounds. Johnny figures he is fast enough to go four rounds, and he certainly can use the money. He doesn't make $5 in two weeks at the sweatshop. The money will mean food for Ma and the kids. Johnny gets in the ring and is still standing during round three when the police come in, stop the fight, and arrest Johnny. He gets six months for boxing in the saloon.

Right away he gets into a fight in jail. But he is befriended by Michael O'Shaunnessey, also in jail for boxing. O'Shaunnessey is known as Perfessor Mike. The Perfessor thinks Johnny has the best natural uppercut he's ever seen. So the Perfessor takes Johnny under his wing and begins to teach him the fundamentals. He even gives him a new name, the Chopper. Once in training, Johnny hits the Perfessor and apologizes. He is told never to apologize for hitting an opponent. That is just one of the many lessons he learns from the Perfessor as Johnny is transformed in jail into a boxer with smarts, determination, and an explosive uppercut. He has his first real test of sorts while still in jail, when he defeats Tommy "Tough Boy" Skelly.

Six months go by, and Johnny gets out of jail. He knows he can't go back to the sweatshop. He tries to get a construction job but can't afford paying the dues to get it. Johnny ends up back at Brodie's Saloon. This time it's called a club, which makes boxing legal. He begins to fight at Brodie's, but he soon wonders how many $5 fights he can survive to help keep Ma and the kids in food. Johnny's father has long since taken off.

Johnny keeps on fighting because the money he makes is so important at home. He is becoming a name at Brodie's, and soon he is offered double the money for his fights. With the dream of a home in Brooklyn for the family, he saves some money from each of his fights. One day, Brodie offers him real money to fight—only this time he is to lose. Johnny agrees because of the money, but in the ring he cannot throw the fight. He is thrown out of Brodie's for good.

Luckily for Johnny, the Perfessor is now out of jail himself and, as a former champion with a good reputation, has landed a fine job at the New York Athletic Club. He hires Johnny for exhibition bouts and gets him part-time work in construction as well. This will enable Johnny to help the family and will also let him continue high school. He even earns enough to buy his mother a sewing machine so she can work at home instead of in the sweatshops. He sees to it that his younger brothers and sisters are well fed and clothed, and he prompts them to pay attention to their lessons.

Johnny—alias Chopper—becomes a big draw at the Athletic Club. Then the Perfessor gets him the chance to be the opener for a middleweight fight, but the fight has to be held out of the city. About this time, Johnny's long-lost father, having heard about his success, tries to come back to the family, but his mother says no. Johnny and the Perfessor take a day of relaxation before the fight in Niagara Falls. Johnny wins his fight—the undefeated Chopper Woods. He returns home with his purse money and an eye on a house in Brooklyn.

Suitability and Critical Comment

This is a book easily read by most reading levels. Johnny is a sympathetic, likable young man who takes his duties to his family seriously and seems older than his years. Readers interested in sports will like the boxing sequences. Life in a Lower East Side tenement in the late 1880s is described with rich flavor; for grades seven through nine.

Themes and Subjects

Boxing, courage, desertion, family relationships, friendship, honesty, jail, New York City, Niagara Falls

Passages for Booktalking

Johnny gets thrown in jail (pp. 7–12); the Perfessor starts his training (pp. 22–31); he goes back to Brodie's (pp. 51–58); Johnny is asked to throw a fight (pp. 74–77); Johnny wins the big fight (pp. 158–65).

Additional Selections

Set in Corvallis, Oregon, in 1903, Linda Crew's *Brides of Eden: A True Story Imagined* (HarperCollins, 2001) tells about a sixteen-year-old girl and a charismatic cult leader who makes increasingly outrageous demands of his followers.

Two young men named Melvin share adventures and friendship when they travel along the Chisholm Trail shortly after the Civil War in *Stick and Whittle* (Scholastic, 2000) by Sid Hite.

Set in New York City in 1911, the novel *Ashes of Roses* (Holt, 2002) by Mary Jane Auch tells of the harsh, cruel life of Irish immigrants through the experiences of sixteen-year-old Rose.

Robert Newton Peck's *Horse Thief* (HarperCollins, 2002) takes place in the West during the Depression and tells of a teenaged orphan who rescues thirteen horses from a slaughterhouse.

About the Book

Booklist, Sept. 1, 2000, p. 116.
Horn Book, Sept.-Oct., 2000, p. 573.
Kirkus Reviews, Sept. 15, 2000, p. 1357.
School Library Journal, Nov., 2000, p. 157.
VOYA, Oct., 2000, p. 266.

About the Author

Authors and Artists for Young Adults, vol. 44, Gale, 2002.
Contemporary Authors New Revision Series, vol. 106, Gale, 2002.
Something about the Author, vol. 82, Gale, 1995; vol. 127, Gale, 2002.

Lawrence, Iain. *The Smugglers.* Bantam, 1999. $15.95 (0-385-32663-7); pb. $4.99 (0-440-41596-9) (Grades 7–10).

Introduction

Iain Lawrence, a journalist, travel writer, and avid sailor, has written a series of exciting page-turners known as the High Seas trilogy. The first book of the trilogy, *The Wreckers* (Delacorte, 1998), takes place some two hundred years ago on the coast of Cornwall, where there exists a community that gains its livelihood by luring ships during storms to crash on their rocky shores and then living off the loot the residents salvage. *The Isle of Skye* is one of these doomed ships. One of the survivors is the youngest crew member and narrator, John Spencer, who experiences a number of wild adventures before eluding his captors. In the second, *The Smugglers,* John, now sixteen, is aboard his father's ship under the command of an unscrupulous, deranged captain. Pirates, violence, and murders are present in this well-written period adventure. The last, *The Buccaneers* (Delacorte, 2001), again has John at sea, this time on an ill-fated voyage from England to the Caribbean aboard a trading ship that experiences a string of disasters, including an encounter with the most feared pirate of all, Bartholomew Grace. They are a trio of edge-of-the-seat thrillers.

Principal Characters

John Spencer, a boy of sixteen
John's father, an English merchant
Mrs. Pye, a blind woman who tends an inn
Captain Turner Crowe, who sails with John on the *Dragon*
Tommy Dusker, known as Dasher, a seaman on the *Dragon*

Plot Summary

John Spencer and his father are traveling from London to Dover in a coach. They are off on an exciting business adventure. John's father is going to buy a schooner, the *Dragon*. His father is a merchant, and the *Dragon* will be used to ship wool. However, the *Dragon* has a jaded history behind it, as Mr. Spencer explains, for it was once involved in the smuggling trade. On the coach trip to Dover, a stranger traveling with them warns John's father that the ship will only bring death to them. Trouble starts soon after. Before they can reach the ship, they are robbed by a highwayman and must spend the night in Mrs. Pye's inn.

At the inn they meet Captain Turner Crowe, and John's father hires him to pilot the ship across the treacherous Goodwin Sands to get it to London. After they reach Dover and see the ship, John's father returns to London. John stays behind to wait for the arrival of Captain Dawson, whom Mr. Spencer has hired to command the schooner. But John receives a letter from his father saying that Dawson was killed by thieves on his way from London, and he has asked Crowe to sail the schooner. John, in nominal command, will sail with him.

Trouble overtakes them once more. While Crowe and John must wait for the wind to pick up, the crew of the *Dragon* discovers a dead man in the water. On his body is a list naming the largest smuggling gang in England. From all indications, a smuggling ship left for France that morning. John argues with Crowe and commands him to sail for France to get the smuggled rum first and then take it back to Dover to set a trap for the smugglers.

The trip is filled with tension for young John. After careful observation, he begins to wonder if Tommy Dusker, who is known as Dasher, could be the highwayman who robbed his father. But the *Dragon* arrives in France without further incident. After loading the rum, they set sail once again for England. When the revenue boat tries to overtake them, Crowe threatens John's life if he tells the revenuers what they have on board. In turn, John warns Crowe that he has the list of smugglers taken from the dead man and he has hidden it.

John finally realizes that there never was a smuggler's boat going to France to pick up the rum. It was the *Dragon* that was supposed to be going all the time. Crowe is, indeed, a smuggler. Dasher tells John that his only escape is to run away when the boat docks. John manages to escape, and he makes his way to Mrs. Pye's inn. He takes the revenue men to the *Dragon,* and they catch the smugglers trying to unload the cargo of rum.

The *Dragon* is saved. John's father joins him from London. Despite all the danger, John decides that he loves the sea, and he is delighted when his father tells him that he will soon be off on another sailing venture, this time to the Indies. As the two travel together in a coach to Canterbury, they are once again stopped by the highwayman who had robbed them before. It is, indeed, Dasher, but this time he spares the two and hopes to sail with John again.

Suitability and Critical Comment

A fast-paced, easy-to-read swashbuckling adventure at sea, with well-drawn characters and a good mystery. For grades seven through ten.

Themes and Subjects

Adventure, England, France, historical fiction, mystery, sea tales, smuggling

Passages for Booktalking

John and his father first meet the highwayman (pp. 5–9); they meet Captain Crowe (pp. 17–26); the crew takes a dead man aboard, and John finds the list (pp. 47–56); the landing in France (pp. 78–83); they are chased by the revenue boat (pp. 94–99); John escapes from the schooner (pp. 133–40).

Additional Selections

Told from various points of view, Michael Cadnum's novel *Raven of the Waves* (Orchard, 2001) tells of the brutal raids by the Norse on Anglo-Saxon villages in Northumberland during the eighth century.

In order to protect her inheritance, Meg tries to sabotage her father's new marriage in Katherine Sturtevant's novel set in Restoration London, *At the Sign of the Star* (Farrar, 2000).

In Joan E. Goodman's *The Winter Hare* (Houghton Mifflin, 1996), Will becomes a page to the wicked Earl Aubrey in twelfth-century England.

Mollie Hunter's *The King's Swift Rider* (HarperCollins, 1998) tells the story of a young Scot, Martin Crawford, who becomes a page and spy for Robert the Bruce.

About the Book
Booklist, April 1, 1999, p. 1424.
Book Report, Nov., 1999, p. 62.
Bulletin of the Center for Children's Books, July, 1999, p. 391.
Horn Book, May-June, 1999, p. 331.
Kirkus Reviews, May 1, 1999, p. 724.
School Library Journal, June, 1999, p. 132.

About the Author
No information available.

Levitin, Sonia. *Escape from Egypt.* Little, Brown, 1994. $16.95 (0-316-52273-2) (Grades 7–10).

Introduction
Sonia Levitin was born in Germany to an upper-middle-class family who fled the Nazi Holocaust to the United States in 1938. This was the subject of her first book for young adults, *Journey to America* (Atheneum, 1987). Because her family left everything behind, she grew up in poverty and was beset with many related family problems. After college and some years as a schoolteacher, she married and turned to full-time writing. She is a very versatile writer, equally at home with historical and contemporary subjects and locales. One of her most moving novels is *The Return* (Atheneum, 1987), about Desta, a poor, black, little-educated Ethiopian Jewish girl, and her long journey to join Operation Moses, the secret maneuver in 1984 and 1985 that enabled Jews to flee the oppression and genocide in the Sudan to freedom in Israel. *Escape from Egypt* tells of the original Operation Moses and the exodus of the Hebrews from Egypt in biblical times. It is personalized by telling the story from the standpoint of Jesse, a young Hebrew slave who becomes a follower of Moses.

Principal Characters
Jesse, a Hebrew slave
Jennat, a half-Egyptian, half-Syrian girl

Mamnet, Jennat's wealthy mistress
Uncle Rimon, Hebrew clan leader
Talia, Jesse's cousin
Avi, Jesse's best friend
Shepset, Jennat's best friend

Plot Summary

Jesse is a young Hebrew slave in a time centuries ago when the Jews were enslaved in Egypt. He is subjected to cruel treatment by his masters. At home he hears conflicting views on the fate of the Jews. His mother is certain that God will send a rescuer into Egypt to lead them to freedom. Already there is talk of such a leader called Moses. However, Jesse's father has no such fantasies. His concern is to survive and, toward that end, he curries favor with the powerful Egyptians.

Jennat is a half-Egyptian, half-Syrian girl in the employ of wealthy and spoiled Mamnet. Although she, too, is a slave, she is content to enjoy the riches of the household she serves. She also participates in Egyptian idol worship.

When Jesse and Jennat chance to work in the same household, they are attracted to each other despite the differences in their outlooks and beliefs. Soon they become embroiled first in the terrible plagues inflicted on Egypt and then in the exodus from Egypt as Moses leads his people out of slavery.

Jesse is soon conflicted by his growing belief in God and his growing love for Jennat. His family disapproves of her because of her idol worship and the fact that she was to become the concubine of the wealthy Egyptian In-hop-tep, whom she does not love. Jesse's family promises him to his cousin, Talia, whom he does not love.

As the Hebrews leave Egypt, Jennat goes with them. But this only causes Jesse to become more conflicted. He knows that his desire for Jennat is wrong because he is betrothed to another. The death of his baby sister breaks his mother's faith. His father becomes ever more hateful. His best friend, Avi, is the son of the Hebrew clan leader Rimon, who begins to question the leadership of Moses. Even the miracles performed by Moses become subjects of doubt to the clan.

Jennat has doubts of her own. Despite her worship of Egyptian idols, they seem not to hear her cries. She does not want to become the mother of In-hop-tep's children. Even her best friend Shepset, who is the loved temple dancer, does not bring her solace. She finds this only in the company of Jesse.

During the wanderings in the desert, Jennat throws away her Egyptian idols of worship and begins to worship Jesse's God. Still, Jesse is torn. Will their different backgrounds and lifestyles tear them apart? What can he do about Talia, who is jealous of his obvious feelings for Jennat?

In the end, the two teenagers come to terms with their faith and their love for each other. The novel ends long after Jesse and Jennat are married, and Jesse tells the story of their heritage to his two youngest sons. Their other seven children are already grown. He tells them how their aunt Talia interceded when Jennat was put on trial for being a temptress of the Hebrews and how their father spoke compassionately on her behalf and was heard by Moses. Jennat was freed, and the two were married. Now the family looks forward to their lives in Canaan.

Suitability and Critical Comment

Some knowledge of the story of the Israelites in Egypt and their escape to wander in the desert might be helpful, but is not necessary to understand the conflicts of the characters in the story. Young teens will enjoy this tale that interweaves romance, religion, and adventure as the young characters struggle within themselves to follow the desires of their hearts and the dictates of their faith; for grades seven through ten.

Themes and Subjects

Abuse, adventure, death, family conflict, idol worship, religion, romance, slavery

Passages for Booktalking

Jesse fights his growing attraction to Jennat (pp. 4–5); Jesse and his family talk about their confinement (pp. 10–14); Jennat learns of her future (pp. 25–26); Jesse recovers from his punishment (pp. 33–36); the plagues (pp. 63–70); Jesse meets Moses (pp. 82–86); Jennat leaves with the Israelites (pp. 108–13); Jesse's baby sister dies (pp. 139–45); Jesse and Jennat argue (pp. 178–82); Jesse talks to his children (pp. 260–67).

Additional Selections

In *Troy* (Harcourt, 2001) by Adele Geras, the major events of the Trojan War are interwoven into the story of two young Trojan sisters, one of whom is maid to Helen of Troy.

Julius Lester's *Pharaoh's Daughter: A Novel of Ancient Egypt* (Harcourt, 2000) is an imaginative retelling of the story of Moses and of the Hebrews in Egypt from differing points of view.

The story of Moses' older sister, Miriam, who saved her young brother's life, is told in Beatrice Gormley's *Miriam* (Eerdmans, 1999).

The story of the fall of Masada as seen through the eyes of a young Jewish man and a Roman commander is told in Gloria D. Miklowitz's *Masada: The Last Fortress* (Eerdmans, 1998).

About the Book
Booklist, May 1, 1994, p. 1595.
Bulletin of the Center for Children's Books, July, 1994, p. 365.
Kirkus Reviews, March 15, 1994, p. 365.
School Library Journal, April, 1994, p. 152.
VOYA, April, 1994, p. 28.

About the Author
Authors and Artists for Young Adults, vol. 13, Gale, 1994.
Children's Literature Review, vol. 53, Gale, 1999.
Continuum Encyclopedia of Children's Literature, Continuum, 2001.
Drew, Bernard A. *100 More Popular Young Adult Authors*, Libraries Unlimited, 2002.
Gallo, Donald. *Speaking for Ourselves, Too*, National Council of Teachers of English, 1993.
Lives and Works: Young Adult Authors, vol. 5, Grolier, 1999, pp. 38–40.
Major Authors and Illustrators for Children and Young Adults, vol. 4, Gale, 1993.
St. James Guide to Young Adult Writers (2nd ed.), St. James, 1999.
Something about the Author, vol. 4, Gale, 1973; vol. 68, Gale, 1992; vol. 119, Gale, 2001.
Something about the Author Autobiography Series, vol. 2, Gale, 1986.
Twentieth Century Young Adult Writers, St. James, 1994.

Mazer, Harry. *A Boy at War: A Novel of Pearl Harbor.*
Simon & Schuster, 2001. $15.00 (0-689-84161-2) (Grades 7–9).

Introduction
Harry Mazer (1925–) was born in New York City, the son of Polish-Jewish parents. He served in the Air Force during World War II and attended Union College in Albany, New York. He married Norma Fox in 1950 and had several different jobs before he and his wife decided to write full time. His first success came with the survival story *Snowbound* (Delacorte, 1973), the story of two teenagers who are stranded in a blizzard in upstate New York. Tony Laporte, a fifteen-year-old, runs off with his mother's car and picks up young Cindy Reichart, who is hitchhiking home. Tony wrecks the car, and the two are stranded in a desolate area far from the main highway as a dangerous snowstorm rages outside. They survive eleven days before rescue comes. During that time they have faced death, but they emerge stronger, wiser youngsters. Like Tony, fourteen-year-old Adam Pelko is a callow, thrill-seeking boy at the beginning of *A Boy at War*, but the harrow-

ing experience of seeing and participating in the Japanese destruction of Pearl Harbor changes him overnight. As Harry Mazer says in an epigraph, "Nobody, however young, returns from war still a boy."

Principal Characters

Adam Pelko, high-school student
Adam's mother
Lt. Emory Pelko, Adam's father
Davi Mori, Adam's friend of Japanese ancestry
Martin, a Hawaiian friend

Plot Summary

Adam is a military boy. His father is a U.S. Navy lieutenant, newly stationed at Pearl Harbor in Hawaii in 1941. Adam is used to living all over, without even a hometown to call his own. His father says it's important to adjust. Adam's father is very military. Actually, Adam finds that he likes Hawaii. He becomes friends with Davi, a schoolmate of Japanese ancestry. At least, he thinks they are friends. They call each other names and try to beat each other up a lot. Adam's father is not so pleased, however, when Adam tells him about Davi. His father thinks he should find friends of his own kind. He shouldn't be friends at this time with anyone who is Japanese. Adam says Davi is Nisei; he was born in the United States.

On Sunday morning, December 7, 1941, without his father knowing, Adam joins Davi and Martin, a Hawaiian kid, to go fishing in Pearl Harbor. They soon find themselves in the midst of the Japanese surprise attack on the island that drew the United States into World War II. At first the boys think they must be making a movie, but it soon becomes all too real. But when Davi stands up in the boat cheering as though at a movie, Adam starts to beat him. Then Martin gets a splinter in his chest the size of a pencil. They manage to get Martin taken to a hospital. Adam wants to apologize for beating Davi and to tell him it had something to do with being scared and afraid for his father, but Davi will not listen. Davi leaves, and Adam is alone with the boat. An officer, mistaking Adam for a sailor, orders him to row the boat out to the *Westy*. When they get there, Adam tries to find news about his father. He learns that the *Arizona*, his father's ship, has been sunk in the harbor.

Adam spends the rest of the day helping out where he can and is finally able to return to his home. His mother tells him that his father's ship is gone, but Adam holds out hope that there are survivors. The next few days are agonizing as they try to get some information, but the losses at Pearl Harbor are staggering, and confusion is rampant. The president of the United States declares war on the Japanese.

About a week later, Adam goes to see Davi to apologize. He finds out that Martin is okay, and he learns that Davi's father has been taken away because he is Japanese. Both boys are friends again, and they go to the hospital to see Martin.

When he can stand the waiting no longer, Adam decides to go back to the base to find out what he can about his father. It is the first time he has seen the harbor since the attack. He sees the *Arizona* and the bodies floating in the bay. He knows that many of the crew are buried with the ship. Soon a telegram arrives announcing that Lt. Emory J. Pelko is missing in action. That could mean hope, but Adam knows there is no hope.

Although he at first rebels, Adam knows he must return to the mainland with his mother when the government decides to send all dependent families back. As they pass Diamond Head, he drops a lei into the water to say good-bye.

As the author notes, the USS *Arizona* was never raised, and the bodies it contains are still there. Today, it remains as a memorial.

Suitability and Critical Comment

This is a well-written lesson in history for all readers. The terror and devastation at Pearl Harbor as seen through the eyes of Adam, more than a boy and not yet a man, are vivid and moving. It shows the impact that war can have on the lives of young people and how it changes them forever. It also shows how easily one can fall victim to the impact of racism; for grades seven through nine.

Themes and Subjects

Family relationships, friendship, Hawaii, Japan, military life, Nisei, Pearl Harbor, World War II

Passages for Booktalking

Adam discusses Davi with his father (pp. 30–33); the Japanese attack (pp. 42–45); Adam reaches the *Westy* (pp. 54–58); war is declared (pp. 78–80); Davi and Adam reunite (pp. 85–89); the telegram arrives (pp. 94–95).

Additional Selections

Dean Hughes's novel *Soldier Boys* (Atheneum, 2001), set during World War II, tells parallel stories, one of a sixteen-year-old American training to be a paratrooper, and the other of a fifteen-year-old German soldier who believes in Hitler.

In World War II, Pennsylvania, the brother of a Quaker conscientious objector, forms a friendship with the daughter of a patriotic war supporter in M. E. Kerr's *Slap Your Sides* (HarperCollins, 2001).

The story of a sixteen-year-old German soldier during World War II and his adventures after being captured by the Russians are the subject of Don Wulffson's *Soldier X* (Viking, 2001).

A Navajo boy joins the Marines after Pearl Harbor and becomes one of the celebrated "code talkers" in *To Be a Warrior* (Sunstone, 1997) by Robert Barlow Fox.

About the Book
Booklist, April 1, 2001, p. 1481.
Horn Book, May-June, 2001, p. 331.
Kirkus Reviews, April 15, 2001, p. 589.
New York Times Book Review, August 12, 2001, p. 24.
School Library Journal, May, 2001, p. 156.
VOYA, June, 2001, p. 124.

About the Author
Authors and Artists for Young Adults, vol. 5, Gale, 1990; vol. 36, Gale, 2001.
Children's Literature Review, vol. 16, Gale, 1968.
Continuum Encyclopedia of Children's Literature, Continuum, 2001.
Drew, Bernard A. *The 100 Most Popular Young Adult Authors,* Libraries Unlimited, 1997.
Fifth Book of Junior Authors and Illustrators, Wilson, 1983.
Gallo, Donald. *Speaking for Ourselves,* National Council of Teachers of English, 1990.
Hipple, Ted. *Writers for Young Adults,* vol. 2, Scribners, 1997, pp. 327–36.
Lives and Works: Young Adult Authors, vol. 5, Grolier, 1999, pp. 75–77.
Major Authors and Illustrators for Children and Young Adults, vol. 4, Gale, 1993.
Reed, J. S. *Presenting Harry Mazer,* Twayne, 1996.
St. James Guide to Young Adult Writers (2nd ed.), St. James, 1999.
Something about the Author, vol. 31, Gale, 1983; vol. 67, Gale, 1992; vol. 105, Gale, 1999.
Something about the Author Autobiography Series, vol. 11, Gale, 1991.
Twentieth Century Young Adult Writers, St. James, 1994.

Park, Linda Sue. *A Single Shard.* Clarion, 2001. $15.00 (0-395-97827-0) (Grades 7–9).

Introduction

Linda Sue Park (1960–), a Korean American, was born in Urbana, Illinois. Her father was a computer specialist and her mother a teacher. After college she taught English as a second language in both England and the United States and was a food journalist in London. She has always been interested in writing, particularly poetry and fiction for adults, as well as books for young people. On her writing, she said, "I have been writing all my life, but only when I had children of my own, did I feel the desire to explore my ethnic heritage through writing." *A Single Shard* was preceded by *The Kite Fighters* (Clarion, 2000), a novel for young people that takes place in fifteenth-century Korea and tells how the young king asks Kee-sup to design a majestic kite for him. He does, and the king eventually allows Kee-sup's younger brother Young-sup to fly it. *A Single Shard,* which was awarded the 2002 Newbery Medal, is set in Korea during the twelfth century and is equally rich in historic detail, believable characters, and an inspiring plot.

Principal Characters

Tree-Ear, an orphan in twelfth-century Korea
Crane-Man, an elderly man
Min, a potter
Ajima, Min's wife

Plot Summary

Ten-year-old Tree-Ear, who is named for a mushroom that grows "without benefit of parent seed," is an orphan in twelfth-century Korea. He lives with elderly and lame Crane-Man, also an outcast, and the two share a loving bond. But they are very poor and must forage in the castoff garbage for food. They sleep under a bridge in summer and in a pit in winter. They both live in Ch'ulp'o, a small village that is known throughout Korea for the celadon green glaze of the pottery created there. The art of pottery making fascinates Tree-Ear, especially the work of the finest potter in the village, Min. One day Tree-Ear is so engrossed in watching the potter at work that he accidentally breaks one of Min's creations.

To compensate the potter for his loss, Tree-Ear goes to work for Min until the debt is paid. The work is very hard, and Tree-Ear suffers physically for some time until he gradually becomes accustomed to his duties and begins to enjoy them. Min is very gruff and taciturn, but once the debt is paid, Tree-Ear continues to work for him because he wants to learn the craft and he also hopes that one day he will get a chance at the potter's wheel. In the meantime, he is grateful for Min's kind wife, Ajima, who provides him with daily lunches, which after some ethical soul-searching, Tree-Ear shares with Crane-Man. He hides half of his lunch each day to share, but Min's wife notices and quietly fills his bowl again.

The emperor's assistant comes to the small village to assign a commission. All the potters work desperately, but Tree-Ear spies on one of the other potters and sees that he has a new technique for making inlaid designs. He wants to tell Min of this new technique because he wants him to win the commission, but Crane-Man advises him that this would be stealing. The potter Kang wins the commission. However, the emperor's assistant, impressed with the mastery of Min, gives him the opportunity to show that he, too, can create pottery with the new technique.

When the pots are finished, Min now trusts the boy enough to deliver two precious pots to the royal court at Songdo. Tree-Ear must travel over miles of unknown territory. In so doing, he is attacked by thieves, who smash the pots, leaving the boy with a single shard. Tree-Ear must consider whether to turn back or to go ahead to the royal court with only a single shard to show of Min's work.

Tree-Ear goes on to the royal palace. At the palace, Tree-Ear talks his way into a visit with the emissary to the emperor. He shows him the single shard, and Min receives the commission. He returns home to find that Crane-Man has died in his absence. Min and Ajima ask Tree-Ear to live with them, but he must have a new name. He will be called Hyun-pil, a name that shared a syllable with Hyun-gu, who had been their son. Hyun-pil is no longer an orphan and now he will learn a craft. He does not know how long it will take him to learn to be a master craftsman, but he knows that he will work long and hard at the side of Min and that, one day at a time, he will keep on learning and working until he has found the perfect design.

Suitability and Critical Comment

This is a quiet, sensitive story of love, honesty, and courage that should delight all teen readers. The author brings the details of pottery making to life, as do the sincerity and loyalty of the young orphan as he struggles with ethical questions of truthfulness and honor. Readers in grades seven through nine will enjoy watching the young Tree-Ear grow from hardworking apprentice to a young man on the path to artisan.

Themes and Subjects

Courage, dedication, friendship, honor, Korea, pottery making, thievery, truthfulness

Passages for Booktalking

Tree-Ear breaks Min's pot (pp. 16–19); Tree-Ear asks to continue to work for Min (pp. 30–31); Tree-Ear speaks with Crane-Man about telling Min of the new technique (pp. 60–64); the thieves attack (pp. 120–25); he shows the emissary the single shard (pp. 136–39).

Additional Selections

Because she can't pay the debt on the family farm, young Lyddie is forced to work in the textile mills in Massachusetts during the 1840s in Katherine Paterson's *Lyddie* (Lodesar, 1991).

The culture and lore of the ancient Chinese and Mongols are used as a backdrop in Geraldine McCaughrean's *The Kite Rider* (HarperCollins, 2002), the story of twelve-year-old Haoyou, who becomes a kite rider for a traveling circus.

A Turkish boy is accused of blasphemy when he states that a man has walked on the moon in *No One Walks on My Father's Moon* (Voyage, 1996) by Chara M. Curtis.

In post–World War II Korea, two children become separated from their mother when they attempt to cross the border into South Korea in Sook N. Choi's *Year of Impossible Goodbyes* (Harcourt, 1991).

About the Book

Booklist, April 1, 1001, p. 1483.
Bulletin of the Center for Children's Books, March, 1001, p. 275.
School Library Journal, May, 2001, p. 158.

About the Author

Contemporary Authors, vol. 197, Gale, 2002.
Something about the Author, vol. 127, Gale, 2002.

Rinaldi, Ann. *Hang a Thousand Trees with Ribbons: The Story of Phillis Wheatley.* Harcourt, 1996. $12.00 (0-15-200876-4) (Grades 7–9).

Introduction

Ann Rinaldi (1934–) was born in New York City. Her mother died when she was born, and she spent her first two years with an aunt and uncle in Brooklyn, who happily spoiled her. Unfortunately, her father took her to New Jersey, where she spent an unhappy childhood with her siblings and stepmother. After high school, she married and began a career in journalism, writing prize-winning columns for New Jersey papers. She also wrote several young adult novels that addressed adolescent problems of growing up in contemporary times. When her son Robert at age fourteen became part of a historical reenactment group, Ms. Rinaldi also became interested in history, particularly the story of our nation's past. Her first of a long list of distinguished historical novels was *Time Enough for Drums* (Holiday House, 1986), a story set in Trenton during Revolutionary times. It raised the issue of slavery, a subject that Ms. Rinaldi explores in several of her novels, including *Hang a Thousand Trees with Ribbons,* a well-researched story about the life of Phillis Wheatley.

Principal Characters
Phillis Wheatley, a young slave girl from Africa
Captain Quinn, master of the slave ship
Nathaniel Wheatley, son of the family who has bought her
Mr. and Mrs. Wheatley
Aunt Cumsee, servant in the Wheatley home
John Peters, a free black man whom Phillis marries

Plot Summary
Told in the first person, this is the story of Phillis Wheatley, a slave who became the first black woman poet of note in the United States. Born about 1753 in Senegal, West Africa, she is captured and sent to America in 1761 on a slave ship under the command of Captain Quinn. Terrified and lonely, she soon learns to keep her wits about her to survive in a cruel and brutal world. She remembers the words of her mother, who told her to "keep yourself small, eat what you are given, and never make a sound." On the journey she is branded on her hip with the initials "T. F." for Timothy Fitch, who owned the slave ship. Ten years will pass before she can bring herself to look at the mark on her body that brands her as the property of someone else.

The young girl is sold from the slave ship in Boston Harbor to John Wheatley, a Boston merchant. The family consists of John and his wife; their daughter, Mary; and their son, Nathaniel, who is ten years her senior and whom she almost instantly—if secretly—adores. The Wheatleys name her Phillis. She is not long in the household when the Wheatleys recognize her obvious intelligence. They act in a most unusual manner for the times. Nathaniel Wheatley decides to take the young slave girl under his wing and educate her.

At the age of fourteen, Phillis begins to write poetry. When the Wheatleys discover this, she is encouraged to continue. In fact, they urge her to perform her works for their guests. This is a first step to having her works published. With the encouragement and aid of the Wheatleys, her first published work, "An Elegiac Poem, on the Death of the Celebrated Divine . . . George Whitefield," dated 1770, receives some attention. However, no major publisher in America is bold enough to publish poems by a black slave woman. So, three years later, in 1773, Phillis and Nathaniel sail to England. She becomes the toast of London society, and *Poems on Various*

Subjects, Religious and Moral is published in England under the sponsorship of the countess of Huntingdon. It is the first book of poetry by an American black woman. This spreads the young poet's reputation in England as well as in America. In 1776, she dedicates a well-received poem to George Washington.

Fame has its price, and Phillis Wheatley struggles to make a place for herself in a white world. Then, little by little, her world falls apart as Mrs. Wheatley and Aunt Cumsee die, then John Wheatley in 1778. That same year, Phillis marries John Peters, a free man and the greengrocer from down the street. Although the marriage is happy at first and they have children, Peters soon proves unable or unwilling to support his family and goes to debtors prison. Nathaniel Wheatley dies in London in 1783. Neither he nor his father left Phillis anything in their wills.

Phillis Wheatley, in poverty and poor health, went back to working as a servant. She died in Boston on December 5, 1784, at the age of thirty. Her poetry was largely concerned with morality and was conventional for its time. Her poems were reissued in the 1830s by abolitionists who wanted to show that blacks were capable of such endeavors.

Suitability and Critical Comment

This first-person narrative is a compelling story of courage, cruelty, and kindness by an author who is both avid researcher and history buff. Told without sentimentality, it draws a chilling picture of what life must have been like, especially for the young slaves, who were torn away from the only world they knew and placed in the hands of strangers who could be as cruel as they could, in Wheatley's case, be kind. Suitable for all young readers in grades seven through nine who like a good story and are fascinated by the details of history.

Themes and Subjects

Bigotry, compassion, cruelty, fear, friendship, intelligence, poverty, slavery

Passages for Booktalking

Phillis meets John Hancock (pp. 19–23); the capture (pp. 27–28); Phillis confronts Captain Quinn (pp. 35–36); Phillis is sold (pp. 47–51); Phillis meets Nathaniel (pp. 54–56); the fear of smallpox (pp. 95–98); Phillis begins to write (pp. 124–25); Phillis and Nathaniel go to England (pp. 218–26).

Additional Selections

In Andrea Davis Pickney's nonfiction *Let It Shine: Stories of Black Women Freedom Fighters* (Harcourt, 2000), there are exciting profiles of eighteen indomitable women, including Sojourner Truth, Harriet Tubman, and Rosa Parks.

Based on fact, *Send One Angel Down* (Holiday, 2000) by Virginia Frances Schwartz is the story of Eliza and her life growing up as a slave in the pre–Civil War South.

Though only fourteen, Evvy, who is growing up in Virginia during the 1860s, must take charge of the household when her father joins the Confederate forces and her mother sinks into depression in *Evvy's Civil War* (Putnam, 2002) by Miriam Brenaman.

In Shelley Pearsall's *Trouble Don't Last* (Knopf, 2002), a story of the Underground Railroad, eleven-year-old Samuel and an aging slave flee from their Kentucky plantation.

About the Book
Booklist, Sept. 1, 1996, p. 119.
Kirkus Reviews, Oct. 15, 1996, p. 1538.
School Library Journal, Nov., 1996, p. 126.
VOYA, Dec., 1996, p. 273.

About the Author
Authors and Artists for Young Adults, vol. 15, Gale, 1995.
Children's Literature Review, vol. 46, Gale, 1998.
Continuum Encyclopedia of Children's Literature, Continuum, 2001.
Drew, Bernard A. *The 100 Most Popular Young Adult Authors,* Libraries Unlimited, 1997.
Gallo, Donald. *Speaking for Ourselves, Too,* National Council of Teachers of English, 1993.
Hipple, Ted. *Writers for Young Adults,* vol. 3, Scribners, 1997, pp. 75–86.
Lives and Works: Young Adult Authors, vol. 6, Grolier, 1999, pp. 99–101.
St. James Guide to Young Adult Writers (2nd ed.), St. James, 1999.
Something about the Author, vol. 51, Gale, 1988; vol. 78, Gale, 1994; vol. 117, Gale, 2000.
Twentieth Century Young Adult Writers, St. James, 1994.

Staples, Suzanne Fisher. *Shiva's Fire.* Farrar Straus, 2000. $17.00 (0-374-36824-4); pb. Harper Trophy, $5.95 (0-06-440979-1) (Grades 7–10).

Introduction
Suzanne Fisher Staples (1945–) has spent much of her adult life as a writer working in Asian countries like China and India. In 1985, she went to Pakistan to conduct a study on rural women. There she began work on her first novel for young adults, which became *Shabanu: Daughter of the Wind*

(Knopf, 1989), the Newbery Honor Book that is set in the Cholistan Desert of present-day Pakistan and tells of an eleven-year-old girl, Shabanu; her coming-of-age with her nomadic family of camel raisers; and her struggles to adjust to the crushing restrictions placed on women by Muslim traditions, particularly in accepting arranged marriages. In its sequel, *Haveli* (Knopf, 1993), Shabanu, now one of a wealthy landowner's four wives, fights to protect her young daughter and herself from the intrigues and jealousy of the other members of her husband's family. By contrast, *Shiva's Fire* deals with Hindu culture in southern India and covers a period of about fourteen years—from the birth of the heroine, Parvati, in 1987, to the year 2001. A glossary of unfamiliar Indian words follows the main text.

Principal Characters

Parvati, the unusually gifted daughter of Meenakshi, who possesses unusual communicative powers, particularly through dance

Meenakshi, Parvati's courageous and devoted mother

Sundar, Parvati's father and chief of Maharaja Naraimha Deva's mahouts or elephant keepers

Venu and Vencat, Parvati's brothers, who are respectively two and four years older than she

Uncle Sathya, Sundar's devoted older brother

Auntie, Sathya's vindictive wife

Maharaja Naraimha Deva, the highly respected, wealthy landowner and former ruler of a small kingdom in southern India

Rama, the Yuraraja, or son and heir of Maharaja Naraimha Deva

Guru Pazhayanur Mutha Kumara Pillai, the principal of a gurukulam outside Madras, an ashramlike school for girls devoted to dancing and spiritual development

Indira, the stern but even-handed house mistress of the gurukulam

Kalpana, the Guru's daughter and principal teacher at the gurukulam

Nalini, an older student at the gurukulam and friend of Parvati's

Plot Summary

On the day in 1987 when Parvati was born in the village of Anandanagar in the tiny state of Nandipuram in southern India, the forces of Nature unleashed a giant cyclone that destroyed her village and killed many of its residents, including her father, Sundar, who was trampled to death by the frightened elephants that he cared for as an employee of the resident maharaja, Naraimha Deva. Sundar was also a talented woodcarver and, among the few possessions that were saved from their demolished home, was a delicately modeled sandalwood statue of Nataraja, the dancing incarnation of Lord Shiva, god of destruction and re-creation. Now homeless, Meenakshi, Parvati's mother, takes her daughter and two older boys, Venu and Vencat, to live with Uncle Sathya, Sundar's older brother, and his wife, a vindictive and unpleasant woman known as Auntie. From an early age, Parvati shows remarkable gifts and an amazing ability to dance by copying the movements of the god Shiva, who appears to come to life to perform for her. At age six she dances unharmed through the flames of a cooking fire, and later she displays the ability to charm fish, birds, and other animals, including a giant cobra that had been hiding in their woodpile. She is shunned by the residents of the village, who believe that her unearthly powers caused the cyclone and the ensuing floods, famine, and disease. A renowned guru, Pazhayanur Mutha Kumara Pillai, hears of Parvati's great talent and invites her to study at his gurukulam, a school for girls outside Madras where classic dance is the specialty. Parvati, who is only twelve, accepts, knowing that it will mean complete separation from her family but also knowing that the guru will give her mother a much-needed stipend. At the gurukulam, Parvati meets Indira, the tough but just house mistress, and Kalpana, the guru's daughter, who is the principal teacher. Because of her unusual talents and abilities, many of her classmates shun Parvati. Her only friend is an older student, a favorite of the guru, named Nalini, who secretly longs to leave the sheltered, stifling life of the conventlike school. She gets her wish in an unusual way. After innocently flirting with a man she often sees while shopping in the market, she discovers that he is the notorious local Robin Hood–type robber (dacoit) named Mayappan, who, later, stages a daring kidnapping raid and abducts Nalini while she is on a school outing. Parvati never hears from her friend again. Parvati progresses so quickly in her studies that she is allowed to give her first *arangetram,* or dance recital, before the guru and a select audience. It is a great, outstanding success, and Parvati is invited to dance before the Maharaja of Nandipuram, her father's former employer. With Indira and Kalpana, she travels to the Raja's palace and, before the dance festival, spends a few joyful days reunited with her family and meeting her older brother's new wife. At the palace, Parvati meets Rama, the Yuraraja or son and heir of the Raja. He and Parvati are instantly attracted to one another. Coincidentally, they share not only the same birthday, but also many of the same occult gifts. Rama is adament in his pursuit of Parvati. He begs her to escape the palace with him and start a new life in America where he plans to study medicine. Parvati is torn between this blossoming romance and fulfilling the dharma she knows she is destined to fulfill. After painful introspection, she decides that her future lies not with Rama but with the dance.

Suitability and Critical Comment

The author has captured the sounds and smells of India, its beauty and squalor, and the strong family units that holds its society together. Though the settings and events are often exotic, the characters, emotions, and sufferings depicted are universal and can be shared by readers anywhere. The injection of elements of magic realism (reminiscent of Salman Rushdie's adult novels) adds a unique dimension. This spellbinding novel is enjoyed particularly by girls in grades seven through ten.

Themes and Subjects

Dance, death, destiny, disease, duty, family life, friendship, India, poverty, responsibility, romance, storms

Passages for Booktalking

Sundar is killed by the elephants during the cyclone (pp. 19–21); Meenakshi flees with her family to Sathya's house during the storm (pp. 23–26); the funeral of Sundar (pp. 35–37); the Maharaja organizes a tiger hunt (pp. 53–56); Parvati dances in the fire (pp. 71–74) and encounters a cobra (pp. 79–82); and the guru offers Parvati a place in his school (pp. 86–91).

Additional Selections

In ninth-century Britain, the fifteen-year-old daughter of King Alfred must assume adult responsibilities to combat the Danish invaders in *The Edge of the Sword* (Putnam, 2001) by Rebecca Tingle.

Gloria Whelan's *Homeless Bird* (HarperCollins, 2000) is a moving story set in India about a thirteen-year-old girl, her arranged marriage, and her struggle for independence.

During the Ming Dynasty, two very different Chinese brothers travel to Beijing in *The Examination* (Farrar, 1994) by Malcolm Bosse.

An Amerasian teenager wants to escape the prejudices of a Vietnam village and tries to find her father in Sherry Garland's *Song of the Buffalo Boy* (Harcourt, 1992).

About the Book

Booklist, March 15, 2000, p. 1375.
Bulletin of the Center for Children's Books, Sept., 2000, p. 38.
Horn Book, May-June, 2000, p. 321.
Kirkus Reviews, Feb. 15, 2000, p. 246.
School Library Journal, April, 2000, p. 142.
VOYA, June, 2000, p. 1119.

About the Author
Authors and Artists for Young Adults, vol. 26, Gale, 1999.
Children's Literature Review, vol. 60, Gale, 2000.
Continuum Encyclopedia of Children's Literature, Continuum, 2001.
Drew, Bernard A. *100 More Popular Young Adult Authors,* Libraries Unlimited, 2002.
Hipple, Ted. *Writers for Young Adults,* supplement 1, Scribners, 2000, pp. 279–86.
Lives and Works: Young Adult Authors, vol. 7, Grolier, 1999, pp. 67–69.
St. James Guide to Young Adult Writers (2nd ed.), St. James, 1999.
Seventh Book of Junior Authors and Illustrators, Wilson, 1996.
Silvey, Anita. *Children's Books and Their Creators,* Houghton Mifflin, 1995.
Something about the Author, vol. 70, Gale, 1993; vol. 105, Gale, 1999.

Taylor, Mildred D. *The Land.* Penguin, 2001. $17.99 (0-8037-1950-7)
(Grades 6–9).

Introduction

Mildred D. Taylor (1943–) is a black American who was born in segregated Jackson, Mississippi. Her family moved north to Ohio when she was ten, and there she attended school as the only black child in the class. After college, she spent time in the Peace Corps in Ethiopia and later taught English. Her major contribution to literature for young people is the moving saga of the valiant black Logan family and their struggle for survival and acceptance in the 1930s through the 1950s. In these books, like *Roll of Thunder, Hear My Cry* (Dial, 1976), the central characters are young Cassie, the spunky, courageous youngster who possesses an indomitable spirit, and her father, the strong, high-spirited David Logan. Ms. Taylor has said that she modeled David Logan on her father, an accomplished storyteller whom she loved and admired. *The Land* is a prequel to these novels. It takes place in the South of Reconstruction times and tells how Paul Logan, half white and half black, rejects his white roots and purchases land for his future family.

Principal Characters

Paul-Edward, born to a black mother and white father in the South
Cassie, Paul's sister
Deborah, Paul's mother
Edward Logan, Paul's father
Robert, Paul's white brother
Mitchell, his friend

Plot Summary

Paul is the son of a white plantation owner and a black slave in the South. When he was still a very young boy, slavery ended, but Paul, his mother, and his sister Cassie have stayed on at the plantation. His mother, Deborah, is the cook and housekeeper. Paul's father, Edward Logan, acknowledges that he has black children and treats them much as part of the family except that they are not allowed to sit at the dinner table with them if there are white guests on the plantation. Despite this, Paul is fairly content with his life. Although he is a colored boy, he looks almost white. He is sent to school in Macon to learn furniture making at a colored school. Paul is also very close to his white brothers, especially Robert. Paul loves his daddy, and he grows to love the land as well and has a dream of one day owning land that is as good as his father's.

Life changes for Paul when he is thirteen and is picked on by some white boys, taunted for being half black, half white. Robert sides with the boys. Then Paul's father takes his brother's side and whips Paul in public. It is the public disgrace and humiliation that starts Paul on his quest to find a land of his own. At the age of fourteen, he leaves the plantation and vows to make it on his own.

With his friend Mitchell, Paul goes off into the world to find work. Their first job is in a turpentine camp. After that, Paul gets teaching jobs and carpentry work and sometimes trains and races horses, at which he is very skilled. Mostly, however, the work is in lumbering—long, hard hours in the Louisiana and Mississippi lumber camps. Paul hears of a man named Luke Sawyer near Vicksburg and figures he will see if he can make furniture for him to sell. Paul begins work for Sawyer. When Sawyer learns that Paul has an eye for horses, he hires him to select some horses. Later, Paul races a few and makes money for both himself and Sawyer.

Finally, Paul decides it is time for him to buy land of his own. He rides to Vicksburg to see if he can get a loan to buy his forty acres. All the banks turn him down. So, he makes a shrewd deal with landowner J. T. Hollenbeck that will bring him the land in seven months if he can earn the money in that time.

Paul returns home to find that Mitchell, who has married Caroline Perry, has been shot in the back while clearing land. Mitchell dies after exacting a promise from Paul to take care of Caroline. When it seems as though Paul cannot make good on his promise of delivering the money for the land in time, Robert arrives with an envelope from Paul's sister Cassie. Their mother had owned ten acres of land, which Cassie sold, and part of the money is now Paul's. It is enough to buy his land.

Paul gets his forty acres and asks Caroline to marry him. She refuses at first because he is just fulfilling a promise he made to Mitchell to take care of her. But love grows between the two, and they marry. On Paul's beloved land, they will raise a family of four boys. Although Paul buys the land clear in 1887, he mortgages it some years later so that he can build a proper house for his family. Later still, he will mortgage it to buy 200 more acres.

Suitability and Critical Comment

The Land is not a story of slave owners or racial cruelty, but rather a tale of trying to raise children of mixed races in a violently racist world. The characters of the mother and father are especially human as they deal with their own prejudices and feelings in the South of the nineteenth century. The author deftly describes Paul's love of the land in a gritty and realistic look at how it was then. Suitable for teen readers in grades six through nine.

Themes and Subjects

Bigotry, family relationships, friendship, horseracing, mixed ancestry, slavery, the South, woodworking

Passages for Booktalking

Paul is beaten (pp. 77–81); Paul meets Caroline (pp. 167–69); Paul checks out horses for Sawyer (pp. 181–86); Paul makes a deal with Hollenbeck (pp. 299–302); Mitchell is shot (pp. 302–7).

Additional Selections

Told from the viewpoint of a fifteen-year-old Mexican recruit, Sherry Garland's *In the Shadow of the Alamo* (Harcourt, 2001) tells the story of the march through Texas by a boy and his family and the Battle of the Alamo.

Twelve-year-old Anna Rosa and her family get involved in the struggle for free speech in her native Dominican Republic in Lynn Joseph's *The Color of My Words* (HarperCollins, 2000).

Lois Ruby's *Soon Be Free* (Simon & Schuster, 2001) continues the tale begun in *Steal Away Home* (Simon & Schuster, 1995) and intertwines past and present in a tale about the Underground Railroad.

In 1886, young Lisa hides a Chinese boy when a coastal town in California expels its Chinese residents in Susan Fletcher's *Walk Across the Sea* (Atheneum, 2001).

About the Book

Booklist, August, 2001, p. 2108.
Bulletin of the Center for Children's Books, Oct., 2001, p. 78.
Horn Book, Sept.-Oct., 2001, p. 596.
School Library Journal, August, 2001, p. 190.
VOYA, Oct., 2001, p. 36.

About the Author

Authors and Artists for Young Adults, vol. 10, Gale, 1993.
Children's Literature Review, vol. 9, Gale, 1985; vol. 59, Gale, 2000.
Continuum Encyclopedia of Children's Literature, Continuum, 2001.
Drew, Bernard A. *The 100 Most Popular Young Adult Authors,* Libraries Unlimited, 1997.
Fifth Book of Junior Authors and Illustrators, Wilson, 1983.
Hipple, Ted. *Writers for Young Adults,* vol. 3, Scribners, 1997, pp. 273–82.
Lives and Works: Young Adult Authors, vol. 7, Grolier, 1999, pp. 96–98.
Major Authors and Illustrators for Children and Young Adults, vol. 6, Gale, 1993.
McElmeel, Sharron L. *The 100 Most Popular Children's Authors,* Libraries Unlimited, 1999.
St. James Guide to Young Adult Writers (2nd ed.), St. James, 1999.
Silvey, Anita. *Children's Books and Their Creators,* Houghton Mifflin, 1995.
Something about the Author, vol. 15, Gale, 1979; vol. 70, Gale, 1993.
Something about the Author Autobiography Series, vol. 5, Gale, 1988.
Twentieth Century Young Adult Writers, St. James, 1994.

Temple, Frances. *The Ramsay Scallop.* Orchard, 1994. $17.95 (0-531-06836-6) (Grades 7–9).

Introduction

Frances Temple (1945–1995) was born in Washington, D.C., but spent her early childhood on a farm in Virginia. When her father, a diplomat, was posted to Paris, she and her family lived there for five years. In the early 1960s, the family moved to Vietnam, but she returned before the outbreak of war to attend college. She became a teacher and began writing while teaching primary grades. In 1987, she wrote *The Ramsay Scallop* but was unable to find a publisher because each said the subject would not appeal to young readers. Seven years later, it was published, to glowing reviews. It is set in 1299 in Europe and tells of the pilgrimage made by fourteen-year-old Elenor and her betrothed. This novel was followed by *A Taste of Salt* (Orchard, 1992), inspired by information gained about Haiti during a work-study semester the author spent with her husband in the Dominican Republic. It begins with a young street urchin being beaten up and left to die by thugs who support the dictatorship. Ms. Temple died suddenly of a heart attack in 1995.

Principal Characters

Elenor, a fourteen-year-old orphan
Lord Thomas, Elenor's betrothed
Robert of Thornham, Thomas's father

Etienne, a pilgrim
Martin McFeery, a pilgrim
Father Gregory, village priest

Plot Summary

The title of the book refers to the scallop shells that pilgrims bought at their destinations and pinned to their caps. In the year 1299, fourteen-year-old Elenor lives in Ramsay castle, a small English village that was once the domain of her family. Now Elenor is an orphan, and the village is ruled by Robert of Thornham, who not only bought the land after the death of her parents but became Elenor's ward as well. Elenor is not happy about the fact that she is betrothed to Robert's son, Lord Thomas, who is five years older than she. She has no interest in marriage in the first place, and she does not know Thomas very well since he has spent the last eight years off fighting for the holy lands in the Crusades. Elenor secretly hopes Thomas will not return from the Crusades to claim her as his bride.

Thomas, however, does return to the village, but he has no interest in Elenor, either. He also has no interest in marriage. Eight years enduring the misery and death of the Crusades, which began for him as a joyful fight in the name of Christianity, now fills him with shame and humiliation. When Thomas and Elenor meet once again, they are awkward and uncomfortable around each other because of the betrothal. Elenor's memory of Thomas is his boisterous youthful behavior, so she thinks of him as a bully. He remembers her only as a young child and regards her as a brat.

Into this unpleasant situation steps the village priest, Father Gregory. He is also a good friend to Elenor. Father Gregory decides that the two young people should go on a pilgrimage to Spain, to Santiago de Compostela, to atone for the sins of the village.

Although Elenor and Thomas are not pleased to be traveling in each other's company, they are only too happy to find an excuse to put off their marriage. The priest also cautions that they must be chaste during the pilgrimage, which is a relief for Elenor.

Joining hundreds of other pilgrims dressed in brown, wearing black hats, and carrying little else with them, the two young people set out across the English Channel, through the French cathedral towns of Amiens, Paris, and Chartres, down through France and over the Pyrenees on the road to Spain. They meet many interesting characters along the way, each with a story to tell of the reason for the pilgrimage. The most interesting is Etienne, who becomes a good friend to them both.

As these three young people become friends, they learn more of themselves and of the teachings that they have always accepted through the years. All their lives they have believed without question; now they begin to wonder if all they have been taught is true. Thomas is especially doubtful about the Crusades, which were called religious wars to convert or kill infidels, or nonbelievers. Elenor has questions about her own limited choices in this world that allows only two pathways for women—marriage or the nunnery.

As Elenor and Thomas question their world, they begin to know themselves and they begin to care genuinely for each other. When Thomas is injured near the end of their journey, Elenor realizes that she wants to spend her life with him.

Suitability and Critical Comment

With its detailed descriptions of life and times in thirteenth-century Europe, *The Ramsay Scallop* is best suited for good readers with an interest in other times and lands. The intellectual growth of the young people is nicely drawn and blended with the history of the times. The questions that the young pilgrims raise among themselves are interesting discussions for classroom groups; grades seven through nine.

Themes and Subjects

The Crusades, England, Europe, love, marriage, religion, Spain, thirteenth century, war

Passages for Booktalking

Thomas returns to the village (pp. 23–28); they leave on the pilgrimage (pp. 48–50); they meet Etienne (pp. 95–101); they meet Martin McFeery (pp. 192–200); Thomas is injured (pp. 283–86).

Additional Selections

In Tamora Pierce's *Squire* (Random, 2001), the third volume in the Protector of the Small series set in the Middle Ages, Kel, now a squire, fights in many tournaments and satisfies her most vocal critics.

Queen's Own Fool (Philomel, 2000) by Jane Yolen and Robert Harris is the story of Mary, Queen of Scots, as witnessed by one of the queen's female fools.

In twelfth-century Europe, Edmund, an English lad, is taken on as a squire by a crusader who is setting off to join Richard the Lion-Hearted in Michael Cadnum's *The Book of the Lion* (Viking, 2000).

An eleventh-century princess fights for her throne when her brother tries to seize it in Tracy Barrett's *Anna of Byzantium* (Delacorte, 1999).

About the Book

Booklist, March 15, 1994, p. 1348.
Book Report, Sept., 1994, p. 27.
Bulletin for the Center for Children's Books, April, 1994, p. 271.
Kirkus Reviews, March 15, 1994, p. 405.
School Library Journal, May, 1994, p. 135.
VOYA, April, 1994, p. 31.

About the Author

Authors and Artists for Young Adults, vol. 19, Gale, 1996.
Lives and Works: Young Adult Authors, vol. 7, Grolier, 1999, pp. 102–4.
St. James Guide to Young Adult Writers (2nd ed.), St. James, 1999.
Seventh Book of Junior Authors and Illustrators, Wilson, 1996.
Something about the Author, vol. 85, Gale, 1996.

6

Sports in Fact and Fiction

Bachrach, Susan D. *The Nazi Olympics.* Little, Brown, 2000. $21.95
(0-316-07086-6) (Grades 9–12).

Introduction

Susan D. Bachrach has been a member of education department staff of
the U.S. Holocaust Memorial Museum for many years. Since it opened its
doors in 1993, the museum has been visited by over 1.5 million people. In
the author's earlier *Tell Them We Remember: The Story of the Holocaust* (Little,
Brown, 1994), artifacts, photographs, maps, and taped oral histories from
this museum and others in Europe are used to chronicle this terrible
period in history. It is divided into three parts—Germany before and during the Nazi regime; the final solution, including the ghettos; and rescue,
resistance, and liberation. This is a personal, extremely effective approach
to the Holocaust that is duplicated in *The Nazi Olympics,* a book based on a
special exhibit developed by the museum to tour the country. Illustrated
with archival photographs, posters, and cartoons, this account presents
both the history of the games and controversial questions such as: Should
the United States have boycotted the 1936 Olympics?

Principal Characters

Adolf Hitler, head of Nazi Germany
Athletes of the 1936 Olympic Games

Plot Summary

The 1936 Olympic Games were held in Berlin, the capital of Germany.
The choice of Berlin as the site was made in 1931, two years before Adolf
Hitler came to power in Germany, putting his National Socialist German
Workers (Nazi) party in control. Speaking to a nation that had been suffering since the end of World War I, Hitler vowed to give the Germans a new
nation. By 1936, it was clear that Hitler planned to use the Olympic Games
as a showcase for his new police state for "Aryans only." Other countries
began to question whether it was proper to hold the games in a place that

was so obviously contradictory to Olympic ideals. Athletes themselves questioned whether they should participate.

But the Games were held in Berlin. Hitler was anxious to showcase German athletes to spread the myth of "Aryan" racial superiority and physical power. Jewish or part-Jewish athletes were excluded from German sports associations. Daniel Prenn, who was one of Germany's top-ranked tennis players and number six in the world, was removed from the German Davis Cup team because he was Jewish. But Germany assured the world that all would be treated equally and pledged that black athletes would be treated well in Berlin. Thus assured, nineteen male athletes, including two black men, from the United States went to Berlin. This was a special opportunity for these athletes who had suffered from discrimination, which often prevented them from gaining opportunities for sports at the college and professional levels.

One of the Americans was track star Jesse Owens (1913–1980), a native of Alabama who had already broken five world records at a Big Ten track meet in Ann Arbor, Michigan, in 1935. Owens and other black athletes especially wanted to compete in Berlin to disprove Nazi theories of racial superiority. They won eight of twelve track and field events. Jesse Owens was the hero of the Games, with four gold medals. He set a new world record in the 100-meter run at 10.3 seconds and was called the "fastest human being." Other African Americans did well, too, although there was much discrimination against Jewish athletes.

Germany was victorious in the Games in that its athletes won the most medals in total count. But Owens went home the single top winner and a hero. This made many people believe that the myth of the superiority of the German race had been dispelled, and they began to feel good about participating in the German Games. In fact, the performance by Owens and the many other black and Jewish athletes had little effect on racism—at home or in Germany. Hitler made big plans for taking over the Games forever. He ordered a new sports stadium built at Nuremberg. It would seat 400,000, which greatly pleased Hitler. But the new stadium would not conform to the Olympic standards. This did not bother Hitler, who said that after the scheduled Olympic Games in Tokyo in 1940, the Games would be held in Germany from then on.

In 1939, German troops marched into Czechoslovakia and five months later into Poland. World War II had begun. Millions of people would die in the war and concentration camps before the Aryan myth was dispelled.

Suitability and Critical Comment

This is an easily read book and suitable for all teens with an interest in sports and history. It discusses Germany's plans for the Games as an integral part of Hitler's plans for the country. It shows how Germany planned to use the Games as a showcase for its claims of racial superiority. It also documents the accomplishments of many Jewish and African American athletes; for grades nine through twelve.

Themes and Subjects

Athletics, competition, concentration camps, Nazi Germany, Olympic Games, racism, World War II

Passages for Booktalking

Hitler's rise to power (pp. 16–20); Nazification of German sport and takeover of the Olympics (pp. 28–34); opening of the Games (pp. 90–91); Jewish athletes and the Games (pp. 100–105).

Additional Selections

James Cross Giblin's *The Life and Death of Hitler* (Clarion, 2002) is a well-documented biography that covers Hitler's life from his youth to his death in a Berlin bunker.

In spite of pervasive racism and a frail constitution, Jesse Owens became the gold medal hero of the 1936 Olympics, described in *The Legend of Jesse Owens* (Watts, 1998) by Hank Nuwer. For a slightly younger audience, use Tony Gentry's *Jesse Owens: Champion Athlete* (Chelsea House, 1990).

Past and present controversies surrounding the Olympic Games are covered in Stephen Currie's *The Olympic Games* (Lucent, 1999).

About the Book

Booklist, Feb. 15, 2000, p. 1093.
Bulletin of the Center for Children's Books, March, 2000, p. 237.
New York Times Book Review, Aug. 13, 2000, p. 16.
School Library Journal, June, 2000, p. 157.
VOYA, Aug., 2000, p. 201.

About the Author

No information available.

Colton, Larry. *Counting Coup: A True Story of Basketball and Honor on the Little Big Horn.* Warner, 2000. $24.95 (0-446-52683-5) (Grades 9–12).

Introduction

Larry Colton is an ex–professional baseball player and a regular contributor to *Sports Illustrated.* In a previous book, *Goat Brothers* (op), he chronicled the lives of five members of the Pi Kappa Alpha fraternity at Berkeley who are about average in their responsible and not-so-responsible actions. The book follows their lives from the late 1960s into the 1990s. Readers share their campus activities such as keg parties, football games, and protests, and follow them as they leave college to make their way in the world, with painful steps to maturity, tentative romances, some victories, and also some defeats. It is an excellent introduction to the culture of the United States during the 1960s and beyond. Concerning *Counting Coup*, Colton arrived in Crow, Montana, to write a book about a season of boy's high-school basketball in the Crow Indian community and, after seeing Sharon LaForge play, decided to write about her team instead. He stayed a year gathering material. "Counting coup" literally means touching one's enemy on the chest in battle, an act considered the bravest a young Plains Indian could perform.

Principal Characters
Sharon LaForge, cocaptain of the Hardin High team
Coach Mac, girls' basketball coach
Tiffany Hopfauf, a player
Holly Johnson, Sharon's best friend
Randy, her boyfriend
Sharon's grandmother

Plot Summary
Author Colton arrives on the Crow Indian Reservation in Montana to write about young Native American athletes, especially about the boys' basketball team at Hardin High School, which is located just north of the reservation. Instead, he encounters Sharon LaForge, senior cocaptain of the Hardin girls' basketball team. They are on a journey toward the state championship game. Intrigued with Sharon and the team, Colton instead focuses on their story, especially Sharon's.

Girls play basketball in Montana in the fall and boys in the winter. Coulton arrived several days before the first practice of the girls' team. Thus begins the stark, sad, almost unrelenting depiction of the effects of the deteriorated Indian culture on potential careers.

Sharon LaForge is bright, talented, and brash. She has not had an easy life, like so many of her classmates on the reservation. During this senior year in high school and the summer before, she lives at times with her aunt, her grandmother, and sometimes the family of a friend. Her father is gone from the family, and her mother lives off the reservation, usually in a daze of alcohol. The goal of Sharon's life is a scholarship to college where she will receive an education and continue her basketball career. But over and over again, the frustrations of home and personal life prove too much. She misses school and basketball practice and she has constant fights with her deadbeat boyfriend. It is this constant warring between home life and school life, amid her struggles to grow up and carry on a mature relationship, that keeps Sharon from realizing her full potential, both on and off the basketball court.

At the end of the school year, Sharon graduates—with the generosity of two teachers' grades—but there is no scholarship and no basketball. She is living with Randy. They finally marry, and she becomes pregnant. Colton tries to help her get a scholarship to at least a community college. Randy, who is alcoholic and abusive, fights it. Finally, she does get a scholarship to a two-year college. It is difficult for Sharon, what with being a mother and the constant trouble between herself and her husband. Colton despairs for what seems like another bright life stomped out by the drudgery and blank walls facing those on the reservation and from a dying culture. Then, many months later, he receives a letter from Sharon. She is graduating with an associate arts degree in Business Administration.

Even more, she has won a scholarship to Rocky Mountain College, a small, academically respected private college in Billings. This scholarship is not based on basketball ability but on academic merit.

Sharon makes the dean's list during her first year. But near graduation time, she feels as though she will have to drop out. She now has two children, and her life with Randy is a nightmare, but she can't find the strength to leave. Colton meets her, expecting the worst, but goes away with the knowledge that this young woman will find the strength to graduate, to be a mother, and to put her life together. She is a warrior who has counted many coups.

Suitability and Critical Comment

This is a sad, often depressing but fascinating look at life in the world of modern-day Native Americans. It shows the day-by-day existence of young people who have long been cut out of the American dream. Sharon is shown as a talented, charismatic, but troubled young woman in a bitter struggle to maintain her sense of self-worth and her love of the game of basketball. It is recommended for most teen readers in grades nine through twelve.

Themes and Subjects

Abuse, alcoholism, basketball, depression, family relationships, friend-ship, Indian reservations, Native Americans

Passages for Booktalking

Colton meets Sharon (pp. 4–15); the coach deals with Sharon's absen-teeism (pp. 45–51); fathers at the game (pp. 126–34); Colton discusses what is wrong with Sharon (pp. 239–42); Sharon goes to Little Big Horn (pp. 400–402).

Additional Selections

P. H. Mullen's *Gold in the Water: The True Story of Ordinary Men and Their Extraordinary Dreams of Olympic Glory* (St. Martin's, 2001) is the inspiring story of the U.S. swim team's journey to the 2000 Olympics.

A dramatic retelling of the 1999 Women's World Cup championship match between the United States and China is contained in Jere Longman's *The Girls of Summer: The U.S. Women's Soccer Team and How It Changed the World* (HarperCollins, 2000).

The lives of four hoop stars of Abraham Lincoln High School and their pursuit of athletic scholarships are featured in *Last Shot: City Streets, Basketball Dreams* (Houghton Mifflin, 1996) by Darcy Frey.

A Whole Other Ball Game: Women's Literature on Women's Sports (Farrar, 1997) edited by Joli Sandoz is a lively adult anthology of stories, poems, and novel excerpts about women in sports.

About the Book

Booklist, Aug., 2000, p. 2068.
Kirkus Reviews, July 15, 2000, p. 1007.
Library Journal, July, 2000, p. 104.
New York Times Book Review, Jan. 28, 2001, p. 19.
VOYA, Aug., 2001, p. 220.

About the Author

No information available.

Crutcher, Chris. *Whale Talk.* Greenwillow, 2001. $13.95 (0-06-029369-1) (Grades 8–12).

Introduction

This is Chris Crutcher's (1946–) sixth novel for young adults. His first, *Running Loose* (Greenwillow), was published in 1983 to great critical acclaim. All six novels explore similar themes, such as the importance of values and the struggle for justice, honesty, and tolerance. Each also uses the pursuit of a particular sport as a metaphor for the struggles and choices that teenagers face on their road to physical and emotional maturity. Although sports action is an important element in each plot, the central focus is always adolescent problems and moral development. In *Whale Talk,* the specific sport is swimming and the setting is a town in eastern Washington State, the area where the author was born and still lives. The title refers to a passage in the book during which the father of the central character, T. J. Jones, tells his son about the mysterious and beautiful method of communication used by whales.

Principal Characters

The Tao Jones, also known as T. J., the seventeen-year-old narrator who is known for his honesty, integrity, and independence

John Paul Jones, T. J.'s fifty-three-year-old adoptive dad, who shares his son's commitment to justice and fair play

Abby Jones, T. J.'s adoptive mother, who is a respected lawyer working for children's rights in the local DA's office

Mr. Simet, T. J.'s favorite English and journalism teacher

Chris Coughlin, a brain-damaged special education student at T. J.'s school

Mike Barbour, a star footballer who is also a prejudiced bully

Daniel Hole, a studious, somewhat pompous student who becomes a member of the swim team

Tay-Roy Kibble, a musician and bodybuilder who also becomes a team member

Rich Marshall, the bigoted, intimidating high-school alumnus who once was the school's most famous sports hero

Oliver Van Zandt, nicknamed Icko, a denizen of the All Night Fitness Center

Georgia Brown, a sympathetic child psychologist

Simon DeLong, an obese, affable student who joins Jackie Craig, a quiet, introverted boy, and Andy Mott, the surly, psychotic loner, as members of T. J.'s swim team

Carly Hudson, T. J.'s bright, attractive girlfriend

Heidi, the biracial child who has been adopted by Rich Marshall

Plot Summary

T. J. Jones is a multiracial (part black, Japanese, and white) seventeen-year-old senior at Cutter High School in a town about fifty miles away from Spokane, Washington. At birth, he was named The Tao by his drug-addicted mother, who was somewhat interested in Eastern religions; but since his adoption at age two by Mr. and Mrs. Jones, he has usually been known as simply T. J. His adoptive mother, Abby Jones, a lawyer, is a successful defender of children's abuse cases, and John Paul Jones, his adoptive father, works part time as a motorcycle repairman and is also a fervent defender of the rights of the innocent and underprivileged. Before his marriage, T. J.'s father suffered a traumatic experience that continues to haunt him, in which he accidentally caused the death of the baby of a young woman with whom he was having an affair. As a child, T. J. had a difficult time accepting his multiracial status and working through the anger and hurt caused by his abusive childhood. He has emerged a smart, likable youngster who is able to withstand the racial slurs and prejudice he continues to experience at his lily-white high school. Part of this remarkable adjustment is the result of working with Georgia Brown, a multiracial child psychologist, who continues to be his friend. Though he is a natural athlete and well built, T. J. has refused to join organized sports at school because he loathes the exaggerated attention and privileges given to the players. Two incidents change his mind. First, he intervenes when the school's ace linebacker and notorious bully, Mike Barbour, harasses Chris Coughlin, a brain-damaged youngster, because he is wearing the sports letter jacket once owned by the boy's late brother. Second, Mr. Simet, T. J.'s favorite English teacher, approaches him about forming the school's first swim team. T. J. realizes that this is an opportunity to challenge the misplaced authority and prestige of the school's sports establishment. He gathers around him a group of volunteers who represent the major losers and misfits of the school. As well as Chris, they are Daniel Hole, a bookish nitpicker who is nevertheless a likable kid; Simon DeLong, an extremely overweight, anxious-to-please boy; Jackie Craig, who is so shy he scarcely speaks; Andy Mott, a surly, irascible outcast who has lost a leg through childhood physical abuse; and Tay-Roy Kibble, a bodybuilding, solitary type. Because there is no pool at school, the team is forced to practice during off-hours at the town's All Night Fitness Center. There T. J. meets Oliver Van Zandt, nicknamed Icko, a middle-aged man who spends his nights hiding in the steam room because he cannot afford a proper home. T. J., Mr. Simet, and Icko become the team's coaches, and somehow, the boys gain enough polish and strength to compete in local contests without totally embarrassing themselves. What is more important, the boys learn to open up to each other and reveal their innermost problems and concerns. Often their long bus rides resemble group therapy sessions. Throughout all these events, T. J. gains support and love from his steady girlfriend, Carly Hudson. Eventually Chris and the other team members earn their letter jackets, but these activities incur the enmity of the powerful alumnus and former sports hero of the school, Rich Marshall, a bullying bigot, who resents the upstart swim team. Rich is so abusive toward his wife, Alicia, and the biracial child, Heidi, that Alicia had before her marriage, that the court issues a restraining order against him. When Georgia Brown persuades the Joneses to take in Heidi, Rich's fury turns on the girl and her protectors. At a sports gathering, he attempts to shoot the child, but Mr. Jones falls into the bullet's path and dies in T. J.'s arms. In a coda to the novel, T. J. accidentally locates the son that his father did not know he had. Mr. Jones unknowingly fathered the child during the tragic affair he had had before his marriage. T. J. now has an older brother and a new friend.

Suitability and Critical Comment

This is a gripping and compassionate story that uses the smart, witty, slangy remarks of its narrator, T. J., to tell a convincing story of the triumph of justice, humanity, and the underdog. T. J. emerges as a witty, self-assured, fearless, and wise hero who possesses a strong moral sense. His character remains with the reader long after finishing the novel. Because of the many adult situations described and strong language used, this book is best suited for readers in grades eight and up.

Themes and Subjects

Adoption, fair play, friendship, integrity, mentally handicapped, prejudice, racism, school stories, sports, swimming, team spirit

Passages for Booktalking

T. J. introduces himself and his name (pp. 5–8); Mr. Simet introduces the idea of forming a swim team (pp. 9–12); Chris Coughlin and the letter jacket incident (pp. 13–17); Dan Hole joins the team (pp. 22–24), as does Tay-Roy Kibble (pp. 24–26); T. J. incurs the wrath of Rich Marshall (pp. 35–38); and T. J. meets Oliver Van Zandt at the All Night Fitness Center (pp. 43–45).

Additional Selections

Eighteen-year-old Theo tries to sort out his feelings toward Kit, a bull rider from his rodeo camp in Jean Ferris's *Eight Seconds* (Harcourt, 2002).

Barry "Bones" Austin who lives for his friends and soccer finds that a girl is coming between him and his best friend in *Shots on Goal* (Knopf, 1997) by Rich Wallace.

The brutal world of boxing comes to life in *Redhanded* (Viking, 2000) by Michael Cadnum, the story of teenager Steven and his desire to get into the fight game.

At his new military academy, Mike discovers racism and intimidation in Adam Rapp's *Missing the Piano* (Viking, 1994), a story about values, basketball, and friendship.

About the Book

Booklist, April 1, 2001, p. 1462.
Bulletin of the Center for Children's Books, April, 2001, p. 3000.
Horn Book, May-June, 2001, p. 8.
Kirkus Reviews, March 1, 2001, p. 328.
School Library Journal, June, 2001, p. 119.

About the Author

Authors and Artists for Young Adults, vol. 9, Gale, 1992; vol. 39, Gale, 2001.
Children's Literature Review, vol. 28, Gale, 1992.
Continuum Encyclopedia of Children's Literature, Continuum, 2001.
Crutcher, Chris. "The Outsiders," *School Library Journal,* August, 2001, pp. 5–6.
Davis, Terry. *Presenting Chris Crutcher,* Twayne, 1997.
Drew, Bernard A. *The 100 Most Popular Young Adult Authors,* Libraries Unlimited, 1997.
Lives and Words: Young Adult Authors, vol. 2, Grolier, 1999, pp. 85–87.
Major Authors and Illustrators for Children and Young Adults, vol. 2, Gale, 1993.
St. James Guide to Young Adult Writers (2nd ed.), St. James, 1999.
Seventh Book of Junior Authors and Illustrators, Wilson, 1996.
Silvey, Anita. *Children's Books and Their Creators,* Houghton Mifflin, 1994.
Something about the Author, vol. 52, Gale, 1988; vol. 99, Gale, 1999.
Twentieth Century Young Adult Writers, St. James, 1994.

Deuker, Carl. *On the Devil's Court.* Little, Brown, 1988. $13.95
(0-316-18147-1) (Grades 7–10).

Introduction

Carl Deuker is considered one of the best writers of thoughtful, exciting sports novels for young adults. Two of his popular works are *Painting the Black* (Houghton Mifflin, 1997) and *Night Hoops* (Houghton Mifflin, 2000). In the first, high-school senior Ryan Ward forms a friendship with Josh Daniels, whose family has moved across the street. Josh is everything Ryan isn't: confident, handsome, charismatic, and a two-sport star in football and baseball. But Ryan discovers that his idol has participated in an assault on a girl and must decide whether or not to tell the authorities. In *Night Hoops,* Nick Abbott finds himself trying to cope with his parents' divorce and with many other personal problems such as deciding about the status of his friendship with neighbor and teammate, Trent Dawson, who is overly aggressive and in trouble with the law. *On the Devil's Court,* a third work, is a variation of the Faust legend and tells how a senior high basketball star believes he has sold his soul to have a perfect season. All three are taut physiological novels that feature believable characters and plenty of sports action.

Principal Characters

Joe Faust, seventeen years old

Joseph Faust, Sr., Joe's well-known father

Mrs. Faust, Joe's talented mother

Ross, Joe's new friend

John, whom Joe meets through his parents

Mr. Raible, the basketball coach

Plot Summary

Seventeen-year-old Joe Faust moves to Washington for his last year in high school because his famous father has accepted a position as chairman of the Department of Genetics at the University of Washington. Joe's main love in life is basketball. He feels inadequate in his own household; his father is a brilliant scientist, and his mother is a talented sculptor. In addition, his father is hot on Joe's going to Stanford and pursuing a brilliant career. Joe knows he doesn't have the grades for Stanford, and he really wants to go somewhere to college where he can keep playing the game he loves. But try telling that to his father.

During the summer before his senior year, Joe decides to rebel. He meets Ross, a kind of wild guy who loves basketball also and attends the local public high school. With promises of good grades and hard study, Joe gets his parents to consider his enrollment at the local school instead of Eastside, the private school his father wants him to attend. Things look good for Joe until he attends a party at Ross's house. The party is unchaperoned, Joe gets drunk and sick, the police are called in, and Joe's chances of going to public school are destroyed. He is enrolled for his last year at Eastside.

The only person Joe knows at Eastside is John, whom he doesn't like very much at first. What's worse, Joe doesn't even make the basketball first team. But when injuries occur and Joe's hard work is noticed, he gets some playing time. Joe is determined to make the team and stay on it. One day he finds an abandoned building. He breaks into it and discovers a perfect place to practice his basketball shots. He does this frequently and with relentless determination. In fact, considering how things are going in his family and his own loneliness and inadequacy, Joe wants so much to succeed that he makes a pact with the devil. If the devil will give him a perfect season, twenty-four games with incredible power, the devil can have his soul. After that, Joe's shooting is remarkable. The coach puts him on the first team. Things go so well for Eastside that Joe begins to wonder if all this can be real. He even breezes through his final exams.

Then Joe's father has a heart attack, and Joe begins to think that perhaps his pact with the devil was not such a good idea. Was the devil giving him what he wanted only to take his father instead? His father recovers, although he remains very ill. By the time Eastside gets to play a tough rival Bellarmine for the perfect season, Joe is in such a state that he performs badly. But in the fourth quarter, he questions what he is doing to his teammates. Is he making sure they will lose the game so he doesn't have to keep his vow to the devil? Joe decides he can't let the team down; he plays to win, and Eastside takes the game. But after the game, he is told his father has had another heart attack. Joe rushes to the hospital to find it is a false alarm—just some indigestion. His father isn't going to die, and Joe is free from his vow with the devil! Even better, Joe's relationship with his father looks like it is going to develop into something special, and Joe gets an offer from a Washington college that will include playing basketball.

Suitability and Critical Comment

This is a good bet for sports-minded teenagers, especially boys from twelve to seventeen. The writing is crisp, and the author exhibits real feelings for the fears and hopes of teenagers who feel inferior to their own parents. It is easy to identify with Joe, a bright, likable boy who wants to please, but who also wants to find his own way and determine what is right for him. For grades seven through ten.

Themes and Subjects

Basketball, competition, friendship, loneliness, parent-child relationships, rebellion, Washington State

Passages for Booktalking

Joe meets Ross (pp.14–16); the party (pp. 54–59); Joe's pact with the devil (pp. 119–20); Joe's father has a heart attack (pp. 192–97); the championship game (pp. 240–49).

Additional Selections

"Slam" Harris, a talented basketball player, has problems controlling his temper in *Slam* (Scholastic, 1996) by Walter Dean Myers.

A tiny high school produces a prize-winning basketball team in Thomas J. Dygard's *Tournament Upstart* (Farrar, 1998).

Lonnie plays basketball in spite of his coach, a has-been named Cat, in Walter Dean Myers's *Hoops* (Dell, 1981).

T. J., a basketball hopeful, goes to a basketball camp where he meets a girl from a religious cult in James Bennett's *Blue Star Rapture* (Simon, 1998).

About the Book
Booklist, Dec. 15, 1988, p. 703.
Horn Book, March, 1989, p. 216.
Kirkus Reviews, Jan. 1, 1989, p. 47.
School Library Journal, Jan., 1989, p. 92.
VOYA, April, 1989, p. 27.

About the Author
Authors and Artists for Young Adults, vol. 24, Gale, 1998.
Drew, Bernard A. *100 More Popular Young Adult Authors,* Libraries Unlimited, 2002.
St. James Guide to Young Adult Writers (2nd ed.), St. James, 1999.
Something about the Author, vol. 82, Gale, 1995.

Jenkins, A. M. *Damage.* Harper, 2001. $14.95 (0-06-029100-1)
  (Grades 10–12).

Introduction
The author A. M. (Amanda McRaney) Jenkins was born and raised in Texas, where she currently lives in the town of Benbrook. In her first novel for young adults, *Breaking Boxes* (Delacorte, 1997), she tells the story of two brothers, teenager Charlie, the narrator, and his older brother, Trent, and of an unexpected friendship that is formed between independent, self-absorbed Brandon and Trent, a rich, spoiled kid who is leader of an important school clique. Brandon ends the friendship abruptly when he learns that Trent is gay, leaving Charlie to cope with his loss and with his confused feelings about his brother and himself. *Damage* deals with another controversial theme, teenage depression. It is narrated in the second person (for example, "You shave, shower, get dressed") by Austin, the central character. This unusual literary device adds both intimacy and also a sense of distance to this powerful novel that effectively captures the dialogue, feelings, interests, and concerns of today's teens.

Principal Characters
  Austin Reid, a seventeen-year-old senior and football hero who is suffering bouts of depression
  Mrs. Reid, Austin's mother, a widow and successful businesswoman
  Becky Reid, Austin's younger sister

Curtis Hightower, Austin's best friend and teammate
Dobie, another of Austin's dear friends
Stargill and Rhinehart, two of Austin's teammates
Heather Mackenzie, a beautiful blond girl who becomes Austin's girl-friend
Coach Van Zandt, Austin's hated coach, whom Curtis calls "a Nazi asshole"

Plot Summary

Seventeen-year-old high-school senior Austin Reid appears to have everything going for him. He is tall, handsome, well liked, owns a pickup, and, as the school's star football player, has been dubbed "Pride of the Parkersville Panthers." Parkersville is the small, typical town in Texas where Austin lives with his mother, a forty-year-old office administrator, and Becky, his sister, who is three years younger. Austin's father died of cancer when he was only four, and the boy still misses him and remembers the times they would "shave" together—his father with his ornate straight razor and Austin with a tiny toy one. Austin is also blessed with a number of good friends, including teammates Dobie, Brett Stargill, and best buddy and next-door neighbor, Curtis Hightower. Recently, however, Austin has been feeling increasingly listless and empty. He often wants to stay in bed in the mornings, suffers from loss of appetite, and, increasingly, is forcing himself to be his usual congenial, outgoing self. As he says to himself, "What you really want to do is give up trying. Lay your head down on the steering wheel and quit squeezing, quit breathing, quit trying." At times he fondles his father's razor and thinks abstractly about suicide. He feels unable to discuss his problems with anyone, not even his loving mother or Curtis, who suffered a similar emotional jolt when his father left his family for another woman five years before. Austin experiences a serious diversion when Heather Mackenzie insinuates herself into his life. Heather is the most sought-after girl in the school. Also a senior, she is beautiful, blonde, composed, and mature for her years. Together, they become the school's ideal couple, inseparable to the point where Austin neglects his old friends, including Curtis, who does not approve of Heather and her controlling hold over Austin. Austin clings to Heather as a desperate affirmation of his worth and value. While Austin's love life flourishes, so does his football career. Through his brilliant plays, Curtis helps the Panthers win several important games, but Coach Van Zandt remains his brutal, dictatorial self and never bestows compliments. Instead, he continues the cruel game known as Bull-in-a-Ring, where anyone who goofs during a game is punished, at the next practice, by being tackled and thrown to the ground by his fellow teammates. Austin and Heather become both sexually and emotionally intimate, and Heather begins to reveal her complex inner self. She has been deeply scarred by the suicide of her father, eleven years ago, and feels that in shooting himself he betrayed and abandoned her, his only child. Gradually, Austin becomes aware that his periods of weariness and detachment are returning; even sex with Heather is becoming more mechanical and unexciting. After he clumsily fumbles a catch during a game, he endures the humiliation and pain of being the Bull in the Ring. Only Curtis refuses to participate and stomps off the field, quitting the team. At home, a despondent, desperate Austin, once again, caresses his father's razor. Afterward, he confesses to Heather his suicidal feelings. But Heather, obsessed with keeping an orderly life, can't bear to hear of flaws similar to her father's in the young man she thought was perfect. Instead of sympathy, she calls him sick, attacks him verbally, and tells him their relationship is over. Dazed, Austin returns home. He sees that Curtis is next door, preparing to paint the front porch. He sits next to him and blurts out his story and thoughts about suicide. Curtis listens sympathetically. In this patient and devoted friend, Austin seems to have found someone with whom he can communicate, and perhaps he has also gained an entry into understanding his own fragile mental state.

Suitability and Critical Comment

This is an unflinching, realistic portrait of teenage depression that offers no easy solutions or pat endings. It also portrays the cruel, often savage, nature of the high-school sports scene and the importance of friendship to young people. Because of this mature subject matter, and its graphic portrayal of sex (including one scene depicting oral sex), this novel is best suited to readers in grades ten through twelve.

Themes and Subjects

Broken homes, death, depression, family problems, football, friendship, love, school stories, sex, suicide, Texas

Passages for Booktalking

Austin's morning routines (pp. 1–4); Curtis comments on Austin's problems (pp. 9–11); Heather flirts with Austin (pp. 18–20); Austin takes Heather home in his pickup (pp. 36–41); Rhinehart is the victim of a Bull-in-a-Ring session (pp. 72–74).

Additional Selections

Fifteen-year-old Keegan, who feels continued guilt that he survived a premature birth and his twin brother didn't, finds an outlet when he joins a wrestling team in Neil Connelly's *St. Michael's Scales* (Scholastic, 2002).

A small-town high-school football player gets a chance to redeem himself during a championship game in *Roughnecks* (Harcourt, 1997) by Thomas Cochran.

During his senior year, Louie fights with his football coach and falls in love, but loses the girl in a fatal accident in Chris Crutcher's *Running Loose* (Greenwillow, 1983).

Rick Norman's *Cross Body Block* (Colonial Press, 1996) is the moving story of a middle-aged football coach and his personal tragedies, including the death of a son.

About the Book
Booklist, Sept. 15, 2001, p. 227.
Bulletin of the Center for Children's Books, July, 2001, p. 410.
Horn Book, Sept.-Oct., 2001, p. 587.
Kirkus Reviews, Oct. 15, 2001, p. 1485.
School Library Journal, Oct., 2001, p. 162.
VOYA, Oct., 2001, p. 279.

About the Author
No information available.

Remnick, David. *King of the World.* Random, 1998. $25.00
(0-375-50065-0) (Grades 10–12).

Introduction
David J. Remnick (1958–) is a distinguished journalist and writer who, at the age of forty, became editor of the *New Yorker* magazine in 1998. From 1982 to 1991, he worked as a reporter for the *Washington Post,* spending four years in Moscow, where he wrote extensively about Russia and his experiences there. From this stay, he also produced the book *Lenin's Tomb: The Last Days of the Soviet Empire* (Random, 1993), which won the Pulitzer Prize for general nonfiction. He joined the *New Yorker* as staff writer in 1991. He has been described as "an editor with extremely broad interests and a sense of what a piece is about." *King of the World* is a biography of Mohammed Ali and recounts the legendary boxer's exploits, mainly in the1960s when he gained and defended the heavyweight championship. The book has been praised highly for both its writing and the thoroughness of the research involved. He used only retrospective sources like first-hand accounts, tapes of fights, and interviews with surviving participants. The result is a fresh, compelling biography of a fascinating, complex man.

Principal Characters

Cassius Clay, aka Muhammad Ali
Lonnie, his fourth wife
Sonny Liston and other stars of the boxing world

Plot Summary

Born Cassius Marcellus Clay in Louisville, Kentucky, in 1942, he adopted the Muslim name of Muhammad Ali and became the first and only boxer to win the heavyweight championship three separate times. Ali, who changed the world of sports, became the most recognized face in the world. Handsome and charismatic, he boasted, "I am the greatest!" which became his personal slogan.

This story of Ali covers his growing up in the Jim Crow South at a time when boxers were generally at the mercy of the mob. But Ali refused the mob's aid and rebelled against them and everyone who would keep him down. He fought racism and stereotypes. In 1960, he won the Amateur Athletic Union light heavyweight, the Golden Gloves heavyweight, and the Olympic Games light heavyweight championships. Soon after, he turned professional and became the world heavyweight champion in 1964 by knocking out Sonny Liston in seven rounds.

As the author notes, Ali had unusually fast reflexes and excellent hand-leg coordination among his boxing talents. He successfully defended his title nine times from 1965 to 1967. He was universally recognized as world champion after defeating the World Boxing Association champion Ernie Terrell in fifteen rounds on February 6, 1967. Then Ali joined the Nation of Islam (Black Muslims), adopted his Muslim name of Muhammad Ali, and refused to answer the call to military service on religious grounds. Subsequently, he was convicted of violating the Selective Service Act, stripped of his title, and barred from the ring for life. The conviction was reversed by the Supreme Court in 1971.

The book also covers the other important events that occurred during Ali's years in boxing, such as those involving Malcolm X, Elijah Muhammad, and John F. Kennedy. It details the civil rights movement, political assassinations, and the war in Vietnam. These historical events form a backdrop to the career of Ali.

Ali resumed boxing but lost to heavyweight champion Joe Frazier in 1971. For the next three years, Ali fought numerous contenders for the number one ranking, such as Jerry Quarry, Floyd Patterson, making a brief comeback, and Ken Norton. In 1974, Ali won a unanimous decision over Frazier. That led to his meeting with the new champion, George Foreman, later that year. Ali knocked out Foreman in the eighth round and once more was crowned heavyweight champion of the world.

From then until 1978, Ali successfully defended his title, eventually losing to Leon Spinks in a split decision that February. He regained the WBA title later that year on a unanimous decision over Spinks. That made him the first boxer to win the heavyweight championship three times.

Ali retired from boxing in 1979, having lost only three decisions in fifty-nine fights. He did fight Larry Holmes in 1980 and Trevor Berbick in 1981 but lost both times. By the mid-1980s it was confirmed that Ali was suffering from Parkinson's disease. Today, he has slurred speech, poor balance, and difficulty walking. But Muhammad Ali is still a much-beloved figure and hero, not only in the sports world.

Suitability and Critical Comment

This is a book suited to good readers of all ages, especially to those interested in boxing or in Ali himself. Ali is shown as a mirror of his era, a strong figure in the racial battles of his time. His rebellion against stereotypes and his refusal to compromise what he considered his religious rights make a compelling civil rights story as well as an exciting and personal biography of a beloved sports figure. For grades seven through twelve.

Themes and Subjects

Assassination, boxing, civil rights, Muslims, Parkinson's disease, racism, stereotypes, Vietnam, war

Passages for Booktalking

The defeat of Patterson (pp. 27–36); the defeat of Liston (pp. 199–203); Ali changes his name (pp. 213–14); Ali refuses the draft (pp. 285–91); Ali retires (pp. 300–306).

Additional Selections

In Nathan McCall's *Makes Me Wanna Holler: A Young Black Man in America* (Vintage, 1994), the author remembers his youth in a working-class African American neighborhood, his time in prison, and his rise to an important position at the *Washington Post.*

Interviews and photos are used to profile various figures in the world of boxing in Arlene Schulman's *The Prizefighters: An Intimate Look at Champions and Contenders* (Lyons and Burford, 1994).

In Dave Anderson's *In the Corner: Great Boxing Trainers Talk about Their Art* (Morrow, 1991), twelve of the best-known trainers reveal their secrets.

For middle-school readers, Walter Dean Myers has fashioned a tribute to the great boxer in *The Greatest: Muhammad Ali* (Scholastic, 2001) that tells about both his public and personal life.

About the Book

Booklist, Sept. 15, 1998, p. 172.
Kirkus Reviews, Nov. 1, 1998, p. 1586.
Library Journal, Oct. 1, 1998, p. 108.
New York Times Book Review, Feb. 4, 1999, p. 40.

About the Author

Contemporary Authors New Revision Series, vol. 92, Gale, 2001.

Sweeney, Joyce. *Players.* Winslow, 2000. $16.95 (1-890-81754-6) (Grades 7–10).

Introduction

Joyce Sweeney (1955–) considers herself a country girl. Her father died when she was very young, and she lived with her mother in the country until they moved to Dayton, where she felt like an outsider. Being bookish, she relied on her interest in reading for pleasure. By the fourth grade, she was reading Steinbeck and had decided to become a writer. After college and marriage, she held many jobs until her husband convinced her to begin writing full time in 1980. Her first novel, *Center Line* (Delacorte, 1984), was intended for an adult audience but was sold as a young adult novel after winning the Delacorte First Young Adult Novel Prize. It tells about the adventures of five young brothers who are on their own after escaping from an abusive father. They learn about family responsibilities as they travel from town to town in true road-novel fashion. Ms. Sweeney is particularly interested in writing about the dynamics of friendship and family structure. These themes are explored in *Players,* the story of Corey Brennan, the captain of the school's basketball team, and his problems with a competitive new player and his disintegrating family ties.

Principal Characters

Corey Brennan, star on his high-school basketball team
Luke, the starting center
Antawn, team member
Theo, team member
Noah, newcomer to the school and team

Renee, Corey's younger sister
Beth, Corey's older sister
Franny, Corey's girlfriend

Plot Summary

Corey is really excited about St. Philip's varsity basketball team this year. It looks like they can make all-city, except that their terrific center has graduated and gone off to college. Noah, a newcomer to the school, tries out for the team and is accepted as a second-stringer. Luke will play center. It is obvious from the start that Noah expected to be given the starting center spot. Luke has suspicions about the newcomer right away, but Corey has to acknowledge that Noah is very talented, which makes him pretty much okay in Corey's book because Corey really wants to win.

Corey is elected team captain, and he encounters problems right away. There is animosity between Luke and Noah, and the rest of the team doesn't care much for Noah's pushy ways, either. In addition, Corey has problems concentrating at home since the household is in chaos with the approaching wedding of his older sister, Beth. He also is uncomfortable with the fact that his younger sister, Renee, whom he truly loves, is carrying on conversations with young men through e-mail.

On the opening night of the season, Luke, who sustained an injury colliding with Noah at practice, needs Tylenol before the game. Noah hands the Tylenol to Corey to give to Luke, who takes three and collapses at game time. Noah plays center and is the star. Corey is suspicious at first, but is caught up in the excitement of a big win and a big season for the team.

Noah has caused dissension among the team members, however, and the next two games do not go well. Then Theo startles everyone by announcing that he is quitting the team. He will not say why, and he will not be persuaded to change his mind. Corey's dream of the great season is collapsing before his eyes. The ultimate disaster occurs when a gun is found in Luke's locker. Corey knows Luke was framed, and he suspects it was Noah but cannot prove it. Luke is off the team until the case is settled.

With everything falling apart, Corey realizes that he has to do something as the team captain. He goes to Theo's home and says he knows that Noah must have something on Theo to make him desert the team. Theo finally acknowledges that Noah has found out he is gay and will make the knowledge public unless he quits the team. Theo is afraid to lose his college scholarship. Corey makes him promise to wait just two weeks before quitting. Theo agrees.

Next, Corey fools Noah into meeting him at the gym, where Corey tells him that he knows about Theo and what Noah has done. Corey says he only wants Noah to promise not to hurt Theo because all Corey cares about is winning the all-city tournament. In their talk, Corey gets Noah to confess that he also planted the gun in Luke's locker. This conversation is overheard by the police, whom Corey had alerted to the conversation, and by the rest of the team members.

Noah is taken away by police and vows revenge. It comes on Beth's wedding day, when Corey suddenly realizes that Renee's e-mail friend is Noah, who has kidnapped her. The boys speed off after Noah and catch him before Renee is harmed. When it comes time for the all-city championship game, Corey is the star. He also learns that he loves his teammates more than he loves winning.

Suitability and Critical Comment

This is an easy-to-read, fast-paced sports story with the focus more on the reactions and emotions of the players than on the game itself. It concentrates on the feelings of young men thrust into competition, when they must come to terms with friendship and trust and their own ambitions. A good read for all teenagers, sports minded or not. For grades seven through ten.

Themes and Subjects

Ambition, basketball, drugs, envy, family relationships, friendship, greed, racism, romance

Passages for Booktalking

Noah makes the team (pp. 4–8); Luke collapses on game day (pp. 60–68); Theo quits the team (pp. 92–97); the gun is found in Luke's locker (pp. 125–27); Corey confronts Noah (pp. 184–94).

Additional Selections

Two teenaged brothers get a chance to fight in the underground boxing circuit to earn money for their financially strapped family in the Australian novel *Fighting Ruben Wolfe* (Scholastic, 2001) by Markus Zusak.

For a younger audience, *Throwing Smoke* (HarperCollins, 2000) by Bruce Brooks is a sports fantasy in which Whiz, the cocaptain of the school baseball team, is able to create star players for his losing team.

Twenty-one players on a local girls' softball team tell about a feud between a Japanese girl and a girl whose father died at Pearl Harbor in Virginia Euwer Wolff's *Bat 6*, set in Oregon in 1947.

Todd, age sixteen, must cope with a soccer-team bully, homophobia, peer pressure, and girlfriend problems during an eventful school year in *Twelve Days in August* (Holiday House, 1993) by Liza Ketchum Murrow.

About the Book
Booklist, Oct. 1, 2000, p. 337.
Book Report, Nov., 2000, p. 62.
Bulletin of the Center for Children's Books, Jan., 2001, p. 199.
Kirkus Reviews, Oct. 1, 2000, p. 1433.
School Library Journal, Sept., 2000, p. 238.
VOYA, Dec., 2000, p. 355.

About the Author
Authors and Artists for Young Adults, vol. 26, Gale, 1999.
Contemporary Authors New Revision Series, vol. 86, Gale, 2000.
Something about the Author, vol. 108, Gale, 2000.

Wallace, Rich. *Playing Without the Ball.* Knopf, 2000. $15.95
(0-679-88672-9) (Grades 7–9).

Introduction
Rich Wallace (1957–) was born in Hackensack, New Jersey, where he began writing "little stories" in first grade. He gravitated to sports later in school and confesses that his aim as a teenager was to become the best runner possible. Heavily into a number of sports, he specialized in track and cross-country running. In high school, he also began to write seriously and worked conscientiously on the school newspaper. In college, as an assignment in creative writing class, he wrote his first novel. After graduation, he began working on the magazine *Highlights for Children,* where he is now senior editor. His first published novel was *Wrestling Sturbridge* (Knopf, 1996), in which Ben, a high-school senior, decides to challenge his best friend for the top spot on the school's wrestling squad. Ben is also pursuing the tough-minded Kim, an attractive girl who believes in him. Also set in the town of Sturbridge is the novel *Playing Without the Ball,* but here the focus is on basketball.

Principal Characters
Jay McLeod, who lives for basketball
Jay's father, absent in Los Angeles
Spit, a punk-rock genius
Julie, Jay's love interest
Alan, a teammate

Plot Summary
Jay McLeod is a five-foot-eight seventeen-year-old high schooler who lives for basketball. He has no illusions about making it to the NBA one day. He

knows he's a borderline player, but he keeps on the team because he hustles and has good speed and good legs. Jay lives in Sturbridge, Pennsylvania, in a room above Shorty's Bar. His father is in Los Angeles trying to find himself. He wants Jay to join him, but Jay refuses. His mother isn't around, but Jay has friends such as Spit, who is a punk-rock genius with a terrific voice—if she could stay off the drugs and alcohol. However, she and Jay have a good relationship, and he likes her. She thinks he has some potential to get up on the stage with her, but he never does. Jay also likes Julie, who comes into Shorty's once in a while, but he doesn't know how she feels about him.

Jay is crushed when the coach cuts him and teammate Alan Murray from the team to go with a younger lineup. The coach suggests that they should join a church team. Alan says he's a Methodist and that they do have a church team. Jay doesn't really go to any church, and besides, he has no desire to play in that league.

Life becomes purposeless for Jay without the opportunity to play basketball. One night, Spit almost dies of an overdose, and he has to get her to the hospital. The holidays roll around, and he is alone. His father calls from L.A. and offers again to have Jay join him there. Jay still says no. His relationship with Julie is going nowhere, and Jay thinks maybe she comes into Shorty's to meet other guys. Then Alan persuades him to join his church team. Now desperate for a chance to play, Jay agrees to join the team, which is awful. But at least it's basketball.

Jay has no experience with sex or drugs, but he begins a romance of sorts with Spit. At least, they have a physical relationship, but something is wrong. He knows this just isn't the way things should be. He is afraid that he is merely becoming Spit's latest addiction, and he doesn't want her to become his addiction, either. Finally, he summons up the courage to talk to her. He says he feels they are losing what brought them together in the first place, and it wasn't sex and drugs. Spit good-naturedly agrees and tells him he's off the hook.

With Alan and Jay on the Methodist team, the team is getting better. In fact, they play so well that they will come up against Jay's old team for the number one spot. In a tough game, Jay's team wins. It is his best game ever. He scores 31 and Alan scores 29 points. Jay is feeling pretty good about himself and his future. He figures that he will put in an application for community college. Alan is going there; so is Julie. It won't be the NBA, but at least he'll get to play some basketball.

To add to his feeling that better things are coming, he finds out that Julie keeps showing up at Shorty's Bar to see him. He likes that idea, but Jay wants this one to be right. So he asks if he can call her sometime for a real date. She agrees, and they make a date for the movies.

After he leaves the party following the winning basketball game, Jay knows he'll run into Spit, and he does. She tells him her band has finally got a chance for a real gig. He tells her that one of these days, he will get up on the stage with her and do something. He thinks that time is coming. She tells him it is, just don't rush it.

Suitability and Critical Comment

An easily read book but one that is best reserved for the older reader due to its realistic language and frank dealing with drugs and overdoses. It handles fragile adolescent egos in an intelligent, direct manner. The basketball fan should be interested, although the game is not central to the story. Jay is a likable young man who remains surprisingly level-headed in his less-than-ideal world. For grades seven through nine.

Themes and Subjects

Alcohol, basketball, drugs, family relationships, friendship, overdoses, Pennsylvania, sex

Passages for Booktalking

Jay gets cut from the team (pp. 44–49); Spit overdoses (pp. 64–68); Jay joins the church league (pp. 70–71); Jay talks to Spit about their relationship (pp. 178–79); the championship game (pp. 204–10).

Additional Selections

T. J. realizes that he has been invited to basketball camp because he protects the learning-disabled Tyrone in James W. Bennett's *Blue Star Rapture* (Simon & Schuster, 1998).

High-school soccer and the friendship of the team's two top players are featured in *Shots on Goal* (Knopf, 1997) by Rich Wallace.

When No One Was Looking (Fawcett, 1987) by Rosemary Wells is a story about tennis and a mystery that includes the death of the heroine's arch rival.

Chris, who has accidentally injured an opponent in a basketball game, is guided back to the sport by a sensitive coach in Thomas J. Dygard's *The Rebounder* (Morrow, 1994).

About the Book

Booklist, Sept. 1, 2000, p. 116.
Book Report, March, 2001, p. 65.
Horn Book, Nov., 2000, p. 763.
New York Times Book Review, March 11, 2001, p. 26.
School Library Journal, Oct., 2000, p. 173.
VOYA, Oct., 2000, p. 270.

About the Author
Authors and Artists for Young Adults, vol. 34, Gale, 2000.
Contemporary Authors, vol. 189, Gale, 2001.
Something about the Author, vol. 117, Gale, 2000.

Weaver, Will. *Farm Team.* HarperCollins, 1995. $14.95
  (0-06-023589-6) (Grades 7–9).

Introduction
  Will Weaver (1950–) was born in Park Rapids, Minnesota, to a farming
family. After college and a graduate degree, he returned to farming and
began teaching creative writing. When his own children became adolescents,
he started writing young adult novels using as subjects two of his own interests, farming and baseball. His first young adult novel was *Striking Out*
(HarperCollins, 1993). In it, the reader is introduced to Billy Baggs, a farm
boy who is strengthening his pitching arm through chores like lifting bags of
fertilizer and cleaning out cattle pens. Weighed down by his guilt at accidentally causing the death of his older brother, Billy has grown up dominated by
his grumpy father. The coach of the local baseball team, however, gives him
encouragement, and the boy begins his career in baseball. *Farm Team* is the
first sequel, and in the second, *Hard Ball* (HarperCollins, 1998), the baseball
rivalry between Billy and wealthy King Kenwood is partially solved when their
coach suggests that each boy live with the other for a few days.

Principal Characters
  Billy Baggs, teenaged farm lad
  Abner, his father
  Mavis, his mother
  King Kenwood, ace pitcher and Billy's rival
  Coach Anderson
  Aaron Goldberg, who becomes Billy's friend
  Skinner, the dog

Plot Summary
  Billy Baggs is a fourteen-year-old with lots of baseball talent and no place
to put it. He is also a farm lad on a dairy farm in the heartland of Minnesota, worked by Billy, his cantankerous father, and his mother. Coach
Anderson wants Billy on the high-school baseball team because he is a very
talented pitcher, but Billy has little time for sports—although he loves
baseball—because he has so much work to do at home. There is even more

work after Abner Baggs, Billy's cantankerous father, gets sent to jail. Abner got very riled up after Randy Meyers, a local car dealer, sold Billy's mother a car that turned out to be lemon. When Meyers refused to exchange the car, Abner drove the caterpillar tractor over to the car dealership and right down a row of used cars.

Abner's temper and loud mouth get him sentenced to ninety days in jail and a fine of $6,000. That leaves Billy and his mother with more work than ever and no time at all for baseball. But Billy is astounded when Abner tells him about the money he has been saving, enough to pay the fine and then some. Billy thinks of all the improvements they could have made on the farm with the money. Abner tells Billy to take out the fine money but to go to the bank and get it exchanged into dimes. The bank is rather surprised at the request and says it will take some time to fill it.

In the meantime, it is summer and there is lots of work for Billy and his mother. Billy uses some of his father's savings—without his father's knowledge—to buy special additives for the dairy cows. He has been reading up on farm improvements. The improvement in the milk output begins to show. When the dimes arrive at the bank, Billy takes them in the pickup—as per his father's instructions—and dumps them in front of Meyers's place. The sheriff says it's all legal. Billy also cleans up the barn, gives it a coat of whitewash, and spruces up the place in general. His mother, knowing that Billy would have liked to have been in the summer baseball league, comes up with the idea of what they call a Farm Team, calling in anyone to come over and get together for a game. They put up fliers around town for the following Friday night. Billy and his mother map out a baseball diamond in the field and wait for the results.

Surprisingly, some people do show up, such as the Gonzalez family, on their way up north to work in the fields for the summer. Two of their sons are pretty good ball players. With Mavis on first, that takes care of the infield. Billy will pitch. Two girls he knows arrive, and one of them becomes the catcher. But when all are counted, they are short an outfielder. Skinner the dog is recruited for his ball-catching ability.

The Friday night games become an attraction, and more and more people show up, including the high-school coach. Pretty soon there is a bleacher section and concession stand—of sorts. All this is fun, Billy thinks, but no matter how good the team gets, they have no one to play with. So he suggests a game against the high-school team. The coach agrees. This will pit Billy against his rival, King Kenwood.

On the night of the big game everyone is there, including Abner. He has been let out of jail for the night because no one wants to stay at the jailhouse and miss the game. Billy is afraid of his father's reaction to all the people stamping around the farm. Although Abner seems a bit dazed, but he gets into the spirit of things. Amazingly, the Farm Team plays the high-school team well, and at the end of the seventh and final inning, it is Farm Team 2, Town Team 1. All Billy has to do is get the final batter out. But the batter hits a high ball to the outfield. It looks like a certain hit and win for the Town Team. But streaking across the field is Skinner. He leaps high in the air and catches the ball in his mouth. Victory for the Farm Team and not a bad summer at all for Bill Baggs.

Suitability and Critical Comment

This book is easily read, with enough baseball action and humor to delight any young sports fan. The author has drawn likable and believable characters. Billy is a sympathetic young man who shoulders the responsibil-ities of his home life with quiet courage and determination. He accepts the challenges of the farm and still hangs on to the dream of doing the thing he loves most. For grades seven through nine.

Themes and Subjects

Animals, baseball, family life, farming, jail, responsibility

Passages for Booktalking

Abner plows into the car lot (pp. 13–17); Abner goes to jail (pp. 75–77); Billy finds the savings money (pp. 109–10); Billy and his mother clear the field (pp. 137–40); Skinner wins the game (pp. 278–81).

Additional Selections

Baseball and race relations in Boston in the early 1970s are subjects in Chris Lynch's *Gold Dust* (HarperCollins, 2000), the story of the unlikely friendship between two seventh graders, one white and one black.

A star pitcher's best friend must help his buddy when he is injured by a line drive in Scott Johnson's *Safe at Second* (Philomel, 1999), a coming-of-age sports story.

In *Danger Zone* (Scholastic, 1996) by David Klass, a young basketball star tries to prove to himself and his teammates that he deserves a place on the American High School Dream Team.

Jake's father, a preacher, forbids him to pitch with his left hand because he believes it is the instrument of Satan in John H. Ritter's *Choosing Up Sides* (Putnam, 1998).

About the Book

Booklist, Sept. 1, 1995, p. 66.
Bulletin of the Center for Children's Books, Sept., 1995, p. 32.

Kirkus Reviews, June 1, 1995, p. 32.
School Library Journal, July, 1995, p. 96.
VOYA, Oct., 1995, p. 226.

About the Author

Authors and Artists for Young Adults, vol. 30, Gale, 1999.
Hipple, Ted. *Writers for Young Adults,* supplement 1, Scribners, 2000, pp. 325–34.
Lives and Works: Young Adult Authors, vol. 8, Grolier, 1999, pp. 52–54.
St. James Guide to Young Adult Writers (2nd ed.), St. James, 1999.
Something about the Author, vol. 109, Gale, 2000.

7

Biography and
General Nonfiction

Alexander, Caroline. *The Endurance: Shackleton's Legendary
Antarctic Expedition.* Knopf, 1998. $29.95 (0-375-40403-1)
(Grades 10–12).

Introduction

In an interview for Barnes and Noble's Web site, Caroline Alexander
explains the origins of her book on Sir Ernest Shackleton and his amazing
attempt to journey to Antarctica: "I am American English and had heard
his name (Shackleton's) from my British parents. Then someone gave me a
book about him, and I fell into it and started reading obsessively every book
I could get my hands on. But I didn't think of doing a book at this point. I
wrote a whimsical book of the ship's cat called *Mrs. Chippy's Last Expedition.*
But in researching Mrs. Chippy, I discovered an extraordinary collection of
photos and realized they'd never been comprehensively exhibited. I
worked on an exhibition for the Natural History Museum (in New York),
and once that was in place, they asked for a book to accompany the exhibit
and that is how the book came to be." In commenting on the current interest in Shackleton, she said, "there is a real wistful nostalgia for the age we
are leaving behind and Shackleton's story exemplifies many of these old-
fashioned virtues that we know we have lost."

Principal Characters

Ernest Shackleton, explorer
Frank Hurley, photographer
Frank Wild, second in command
Crew of the *Endurance*

Plot Summary

This is the story of one of history's greatest epics of survival. In August 1914,
shortly before the outbreak of World War II, Ernest Shackleton and his crew

of twenty-seven set sail on the *Endurance* bound for the South Atlantic. Their aim was to be the first to cross the continent of Antarctica on foot. By December the ship had battled unusually heavy ice conditions and sailed more than 1,000 miles from the island of South Georgia. After weaving a treacherous path through the ice-packed Weddell Sea, they neared eighty-five miles of their destination. Then the *Endurance* became trapped in the ice pack. Despite attempts to free the ship, the ice held it fast. Before long, the ship was crushed like so much firewood, and the crew was left stranded on the ice floes. So began their terrible twenty-month ordeal before they would be rescued.

Shackleton was born in Ireland into comfortable middle-class circumstances. He joined the British Merchant Navy at age sixteen and had sailed on the ship *Discovery* to Antarctica's McMurdo Sound in 1901. This, too, was a terrible ordeal, and Shackleton's health suffered. In 1907, he obtained money for a new expedition and the following year went back to Antarctica as leader of the *Nimrod*. This time he got within ninety-seven miles of the pole before the ice stopped him. On his return, Shackleton was knighted. The *Endurance* voyage, part of the British Imperial Trans-Antarctic Expedition (1914–16), was his next try to reach the pole.

Shackleton and the crew of the *Endurance* settled down more or less to wait for the ice pack to melt so the ship could be freed. They waited for ten months and still the ice would not release the ship. The crew busied themselves as best they could with ship's chores, caring for the dogs they brought with them, playing chess and other games, and keeping up each other's spirits. But by October 1915, Shackleton knew it was no use. The ice had caught the ship and would not let go. At 5 P.M. on October 27, he gave the order to abandon ship. He was the last to leave.

The crew spent the first three nights on the ice after the ship went down. Then they attempted a futile march to land, which was some 364 miles away. They set up their first camp on a solid ice floe about a mile and a half from the wreck. It was called Ocean Camp, and they drifted for the next five months on the ice. Finally, they escaped in boats to Elephant Island in the South Shetland Islands. Next, Shackleton and five others sailed 800 miles to South Georgia to seek aid. It took four relief expeditions, led by Shackleton, before the crew was rescued from Elephant Island. Interestingly, although the British government was overjoyed at the news of Shackleton's and the crew's survival, it could spare no ships for the rescue because the country was still engaged in World War I. Two foreign ships were offered, but they had to turn back because of ice. Finally, the *James Caird* was able to get through.

Shackleton's health never returned after that voyage. He died in South Georgia at the beginning of the Shackleton-Rowett Antarctic Expedition in 1922.

Suitability and Critical Comment

This is a true adventure story for all readers in grades ten through twelve. The remarkable black-and-white photographs add to the stark reality of the beauty and treacherousness of the Antarctic. The straightforward account of the disaster brings out the leadership qualities of Shackleton, which in large measure accounted for the survival of the crew. This is a true story of human endurance and courage.

Themes and Subjects

Antarctica, courage, explorers, ice floes, leadership, South Atlantic, survival

Passages for Booktalking

The *Endurance* heads south (pp. 15–25); the ship gets stuck in the ice (pp. 41–44); they abandon ship (pp. 83–89); making Ocean Camp (pp. 101–5); on Elephant Island (pp. 171–85).

Additional Selections

Details on his voyages on the *Beagle* and his findings on the Galapagos are given in Dorothy Hinshaw Patent's illustrated *Charles Darwin: The Life of a Revolutionary Thinker* (Holiday House, 2001).

Shipwrecked! The True Adventures of a Japanese Boy (HarperCollins, 2001) by Rhoda Blumberg tells the true story of a young Japanese fisherman who was saved from a deserted island by an American whaler, and who later lived in Massachusetts before returning to Japan at the time of Commodore Perry's visit.

Ann Cook's *Running North: A Yukon Adventure* (Algonquin, 1998) is an adventure-packed account of training for and racing in the 1,000-mile Yukon Quest.

For younger readers, use Jennifer Armstrong's *Shipwreck at the Bottom of the World* (Crown, 1998), which is subtitled, "The Extraordinary True Story of Shackleton and the *Endurance.*"

About the Book

Booklist, Oct. 15, 1998, p. 389.
Kirkus Reviews, Oct. 1, 1998, p. 1423.
Library Journal, Oct. 15, 1998, p. 81.
New York Times Book Review, Dec. 27, 1998, p. 10.

About the Author

No information available.

Aronson, Marc. *Sir Walter Ralegh and the Quest for El Dorado.* Clarion, 2000. $15.95 (0-395-84827-X) (Grades 7–10).

Introduction

Marc Aronson has spent most of his adult life working in the field of publishing. He was an editor of books for children and young adults at Harper and Row, and later for Henry Holt. Currently, he is the editorial director and vice president for nonfiction publishing at Carus Publishing in Chicago. He also teaches courses in publishing at such institutions as New York University and Simmons College in Boston. As a writer of nonfiction for young adults, he combines a lively writing style and unique approaches to presenting his material. This is certainly true of his biography of Sir Walter Ralegh, which was the first winner of the annual Robert F. Sibert Award for the "most distinguished informational book for children published in 2000." In commenting on this book, the awards committee stated that it is "beautifully researched and written with a passion" and that "Aronson not only details Raleigh's career as soldier, sailor, explorer, writer, and schemer but constantly discusses causes, effects and the broader significance of events large and small."

Principal Characters

Walter Ralegh (usually spelled Raleigh), English adventurer and favorite of Queen Elizabeth I
Elizabeth I of England
Elizabeth Throckmorton, Ralegh's wife
Earl of Essex, Robert Devereux
James I of England
Walter, Ralegh's son
Lawrence Keymis, friend and member of the El Dorado expedition

Plot Summary

Walter Ralegh (c.1554–1618) led a most adventurous life. He was a favorite of Queen Elizabeth I, who knighted him in 1585, but was accused of treason by her successor, James I, imprisoned in the Tower of London, and eventually put to death.

This book focuses on Ralegh's quest for El Dorado, the fabled city of gold supposedly located in South America.

Ralegh was born in Devon, England, to Walter Ralegh and his third wife, Katherine Gilbert. By 1582, Ralegh had become a favorite of Queen Elizabeth I, a position that gave him wealth and influence. Elizabeth's favorites were men who helped her run the country, and she often treated them as pets or lovers. She made Ralegh a knight in 1585 and, two years later, he was named captain of the queen's guard. But in 1592, his secret marriage to Elizabeth Throckmorton became evident when she gave birth to their son. A jealous queen imprisoned Ralegh and his wife in the Tower of London, but he was able to buy their release.

Between 1584 and 1589, Ralegh established a colony near Roanoke Island in present-day North Carolina, which he named Virginia. He never visited the colony himself. Then, in 1595, Ralegh led an expedition to what is now Guyana in South America. He sailed up the Orinoco River, into the heart of the Spanish holdings in the New World. He later wrote of this expedition in *The Discoverie of the Large, Rich and Bewtiful Empyre of Guiana*. Ralegh was seeking a legendary and fabulous city of gold in the interior of South America. It was called El Dorado, and stories by natives as well as Spanish documents convinced him that the city existed. However, Ralegh did not find El Dorado, although he did locate some gold mines.

In 1596, Ralegh fought against the Spanish city of Cadiz, and was rear admiral to Robert Devereux, earl of Essex, on a 1597 expedition to the Azores. King James came to the English throne upon Elizabeth's death in 1603. Ralegh's fight against Spain did not endear him to the pacifist king, and Ralegh was accused of plotting to dethrone the monarch. He was imprisoned in the Tower of London. In 1616, his sentence was suspended, and he was released but not pardoned.

Ralegh still dreamed of El Dorado. With the king's permission, he financed and led a second expedition to Guyana. He told the king he would open a gold mine there but would not offend the Spanish in the area. But Ralegh fell ill of a fever on the ocean voyage, and he could not lead his men upriver. That left the expedition in the hands of Ralegh's son Walter (called Wat) and Lawrence Keymis, a longtime friend. No gold was found, but a Spanish settlement was attacked and burned. Ralegh's son was killed. James I revoked Ralegh's suspended sentence in 1603. Ralegh wrote a spirited defense of his actions in South America, but to no avail. He was executed in 1618.

Ralegh's last voyage proved the myth of El Dorado once and for all. It was a European dream with no reality, for which many gave their lives. It even led Sir Walter Ralegh to his death. Ralegh was a man of great courage and daring, but not a man popular with his contemporaries.

Suitability and Critical Comment

Filled with many historical facts and details, this book is well suited to the young reader who prefers a dose of history with adventure. For grades seven through ten.

Themes and Subjects

Adventure stories, biography, England, explorers, Queen Elizabeth I, Sir Walter Ralegh, South America

Passages for Booktalking

Ralegh's early life (pp. 13–14); Ralegh becomes the queen's favorite (pp. 31–37); the queen learns of Ralegh's marriage (pp. 113-14); the quest for El Dorado (pp. 125–42); the contest between Ralegh and the king (pp. 180–86).

Additional Selections

Albert Marrin's *Terror of the Spanish Main* (Dutton, 1998) is a rousing biography of Henry Morgan—buccaneer, enemy of the Spanish, and knight-governor of Jamaica.

Behind the Mask: The Life of Queen Elizabeth I (Clarion, 1998) by Jane Resh Thomas is an entertaining portrait of a charming, intelligent, and powerful woman who was one of the world's great rulers.

Elizabethan culture and theater and the life and plays of Shakespeare are the subjects of Michael Rosen's *Shakespeare: His Work and His World* (Candlewick, 2001).

A contemporary of Ralegh, Sir Francis Drake, who voyaged around the world and conquered the Spanish Armada, is featured in Albert Marrin's *The Sea King: Sir Francis Drake and His Times* (Atheneum, 1995).

About the Book

Booklist, Aug., 2000, p. 2130.
Bulletin of the Center for Children's Books, July, 2000, p. 388.
Kirkus Reviews, May 15, 2000, p. 710.
School Library Journal, July, 2000, p. 113.
VOYA, Oct., 2000, p. 282.

About the Author

Aronson, Mark. "Acceptance Speech—Boston Globe Award for *Sir Walter Raleigh*,"
    Horn Book, Jan.-Feb., 2001, pp. 49–52.
Contemporary Authors, vol. 196, Gale, 2002.
Something about the Author, vol. 126, Gale, 2002.

Bober, Natalie. *Abigail Adams: Witness to a Revolution.* Atheneum, 1995. $17.00 (0-689-31760-3) (Grades 7–9).

Introduction

Natalie Bober (1930–) wrote her first biography for young readers while being laid up with a bad knee and unable to go to work as a reading teacher. She was challenged to write by her husband and, because she was attracted to the life of Wordsworth, she chose him as a subject and began doing research and a great deal of reading. Four years later, she completed the work and, after twenty-one rejections, she finally found a publisher for *William Wordsworth* (Thomas Nelson, 1975). In an interview for *Something about the Author,* she stated that "my books describe the milieu from which my subjects sprang—the forces that shaped their lives—and show how their accomplishments were an outgrowth of the lives they lived." Her sixth biography, *Abigail Adams,* won the Boston Globe-Horn Book Award for nonfiction. It combines, in a perfect balance, selections from Abigail's letters and the material collected during the author's research. The result is a stunning portrait of a fascinating woman.

Principal Characters
Abigail Adams
John Adams
John Quincy Adams
Thomas Jefferson
George Washington
Louisa Smith, Abigail's niece

Plot Summary
This young adult novel of the life of Abigail Adams presents this extraordinary woman in the background of her times and through her detailed and remarkable letters to her family and friends. These letters give an intimate and vivid portrayal of life in the young United States. Adams is shown here as a woman in her own right, even though the main historical focus on her has always been through her role as wife of the second president of the United States, John Adams, and mother of the sixth president, John Quincy Adams.

Abigail Smith was born in Weymouth, Massachusetts, in 1744. Her father, a parson, had attended Harvard College, and he passed on his love of books to his three daughters. Abigail's formal education was meager, but she grew up to be remarkably knowledgeable and an avid reader of history. In 1764, she married a young Boston lawyer, John Adams. Their lifetime partnership of love and respect was considered by many to be an ideal union.

Abigail and John had four children and made their home in Quincy, Massachusetts. For about ten years after 1774, she was largely separated from John as he attended to business in the Continental Congress in Philadelphia. This forced separation began the flow of letters that led to her genius as a correspondent. She witnessed the growing storm of revolution and watched the Battle of Bunker Hill from a nearby hilltop. Through her letters, she gave firsthand reports to her husband and other leaders of the American Revolution as the people who played vital roles come alive in her correspondence. After the peace treaty in 1783, when Abigail joined her husband at his diplomatic posts in Paris, The Hague, and London, her letters to friends and family were filled with the strange sights and different customs of foreign lands.

John Adams served as vice president and then president between 1789 and 1801. During this period, Abigail moved back and forth between Massachusetts and Philadelphia, then the capital. Her letters once more described the scenes and the times as a new country was trying to establish itself. In mid-November 1800, she became for a brief time the first First Lady to live in the White House in the new capital city of Washington, D.C.

Abigail and John spent the next seventeen years in quiet retirement at the family home in Quincy. She died there of typhoid fever on October 28, 1818. John Adams said a part of him had died, too, because he had lost his best friend.

Abigail Adams was remarkable in her intelligence and candor, in her gift for portraying her times with truthfulness and humor. Her story is remarkable because she lived in an age in which women were largely treated as second-class citizens, without the right to vote, with no political and little legal status. Her letters document the lives of most women of the times, called on to make life-and-death decisions for their children, asked to run the farms when their husbands were away for months or years, educating their daughters when formal education was not available to them. Abigail Adams lived through a crucial period of our nation's history, and her letters have helped to preserve the true flavor of those unsettled times.

Suitability and Critical Comment

This young-adult biography can be enjoyed by most teen readers, and especially those with a love of early U.S. history. Abigail's letters in themselves make lively historical reading, filled with the details of day-to-day living in colonial America and then in the new country. Her intellect and sense of humor present this crucial period in history in a straightforward, lively account that reads more like a novel than a biography. For grades seven through nine.

Themes and Subjects

John Adams, the American Revolution, colonial life, diplomats, family life, First Ladies, friendship, marriage, presidents, Washington, D.C., the White House

Passages for Booktalking

The romance of Abigail and John (pp. 16–23); in Paris and London (pp. 129–41); the presidential years (pp. 179–80); in the White House (pp. 198–202); her death in Quincy (pp. 219–21).

Additional Selections

Such important historical characters as Jefferson, the Adamses, Benjamin Franklin, and John Hancock come to life in Natalie S. Bober's *Countdown to Independence: A Revolution of Ideas in England and the American Colonies, 1760–1776* (Atheneum, 2001).

The story of President Jefferson's family, including the links to his slave Sally Hemings, is recounted in *Jefferson's Children: The Story of One American Family* (Random, 2001) by Shannon Lanier and Jane Feldman.

Albert Marrin's *George Washington and the Founding of a Nation* (Dutton, 2001) presents a dramatic picture of our first president and the colonies' fight for freedom.

Samuel Adams: The Father of American Independence (Clarion, 1998) by Dennis Fradin is an attractive, large-format biography that introduces Samuel Adams, his wife, and his contributions and flaws.

About the Book
Booklist, Jan. 1, 1996, p. 737.
Bulletin of the Center for Children's Books, July, 1996, p. 377.
Kirkus Reviews, May 15, 1995, p. 707.
School Library Journal, Dec., 1995, p. 20.
VOYA, Aug., 1996, p. 149.

About the Author
Contemporary Authors, vol. 151, Gale, 1996.
Something about the Author, vol. 87, Gale, 1996.

Fradin, Dennis Brindell, and Judith Bloom Fradin. *Ida B. Wells: Mother of the Civil Rights Movement.* Clarion, 2000. $18.00 (0-395-89898-6) (Grades 7–9).

Introduction

Dennis Fradin (1945–) has written almost two hundred books of fiction and nonfiction, principally for middle-grade readers and chiefly for series like Best Holiday Books, Young People's Stories of Our States, Disaster, Thirteen Colonies, From Sea to Shining Sea, and Enchantment of the

World. His publishers are usually Children's Press and Enslow. He researches each of his books through travel, interviews, and a thorough perusal of both primary and secondary sources. In an interview for *Something about the Author,* he said that for each book, "I research extremely carefully and rewrite about five or six times. I also check over all my facts line-by-line to make sure everything is accurate." In the same interview he gives the following philosophy that he has adopted toward his own writing: "When I realized that I wanted to become an author, I couldn't live and die by other people's opinions but should do it out of my own desire and need to write."

Principal Characters

Ida B. Wells, African American journalist
Ferdinand Lee Barnett, her husband
Charles, Herman, Ida, and Alfreda—Ida's children
Ferdinand Jr. and Albert, her stepchildren

Plot Summary

Born in Holy Springs, Mississippi, in 1862, Ida Bell Wells was the daughter of slaves. She became a teacher in rural Mississippi and Tennessee and began a career in journalism in the late 1880s. Under the pen name of Iola, she wrote articles for black-owned newspapers on such issues as the education of children. By 1892, she was a part owner of the *Memphis Free Speech.* When she wrote an editorial denouncing the lynching of three of her friends, the newspaper office was stormed by whites and destroyed. That only made Wells more determined. She began a crusade to investigate the lynching of blacks in the South, using the argument that lynching stemmed from a white fear of black economic competition, not an excuse to protect white Southern womanhood. For this crusade, Wells traveled throughout the United States and England on lecture tours. She also founded anti-lynching societies and black women's clubs. Her crusade against the deplorable practice of lynching would become her main work in life.

Wells organized a black women's club in Chicago in 1893, and two years later she married Ferdinand Lee Barnett, editor of the *Chicago Conservator.* She founded the Chicago Negro Fellowship League to help migrants from the South and founded what is probably the first black women's suffrage group, the Chicago's Alpha Suffrage Club. She also started a newsletter for the organization. By that time she was fifty years old and running two newspapers, the other being the *Fellowship Herald,* in addition to holding a full-time job as a probation officer and writing numerous articles on segregation. In 1913, thousands of women went to Washington, D.C., for the inauguration of

Woodrow Wilson to demand the right to vote. Wells went to march with the Illinois delegation but was told she could not because her presence might annoy Southern white women. She would have to march in a segregated section. Wells said it was too bad if the Southern white ladies were annoyed, she was marching with the white Illinois suffragists and that was that.

In 1928, Wells began her autobiography, *Crusade for Justice*. It was published in 1970. Wells wrote it because she realized that most of her fight against lynchings had taken place before many of the young blacks she knew had been born. She wanted them to know the true story. In 1920, when women finally received the right to vote, a number of women began to run for office. Wells decided to run for the Illinois state senate in 1930. Although she lost to a male candidate, she made history as one of the first black American women to run for public office.

Wells died on March 21, 1931, of uremic poisoning, a condition associated with kidney disease. She was sixty-eight years old. By the time of her death, lynching had virtually disappeared in the United States, largely due to her work. In 1974, her Grand Boulevard home in Illinois became a National Historic Landmark. Many of her achievements were long forgotten because she did her pioneering work so many years ago. But as the women's civil rights movement gained momentum in the 1970s, she was rediscovered, which resulted in the publication of her autobiography. Today, she is remembered as an American whose courage and determination laid the groundwork for the modern Civil Rights movement.

Suitability and Critical Comment

This is a well-written, easily read biography of a courageous American that should be of interest to most readers. The authors' direct approach tells a chilling story of lynching and segregation practices in early America. Any young reader with an interest in the history of civil rights in America will find this book a fascinating and informative read. For grades seven through nine.

Themes and Subjects

African Americans, civil rights, family relationships, lynching, racism, segregation

Passages for Booktalking

Yellow fever outbreak (pp. 13–16); writing as Iola (pp. 27–30); the lynching of her friends (pp. 38–56); her marriage (pp.75–76); the march on Washington, D.C. (pp. 139–40).

About the Book
Booklist, Feb. 15, 2000, p. 1105.
Book Report, Nov., 2000, p. 67.
Bulletin of the Center for Children's Books, April, 2000, p. 278.
Horn Book, May, 2000, p. 331.
School Library Journal, April, 2000, p. 148.

About the Authors
Contemporary Authors New Revision Series, vol. 100, Gale, 2002.
Something about the Author, vol. 29, Gale, 1982; vol. 90, Gale, 1997.

Freedman, Russell. *Eleanor Roosevelt: A Life of Discovery.* Clarion, 1993. (0-899-19862-7) (Grades 7–10).

Russell Freedman (1929–) grew up in San Francisco in a house full of books and book talk because his father was a representative of a major publishing house. Through his father's work, he met great writers when he was young, such as John Steinbeck and William Saroyan. He attended school in California and, after serving in the army during the Korean War, gravitated to the fields of writing and publishing. From his interest in adolescents who accomplished great things while young, came his first book about young adults, *Teenagers Who Made History* (Holiday House, 1961). He is now a full-time writer, chiefly of award-winning biographies for young readers, which are noted for the meticulous research involved and the author's lively writing style. Among the innumerable awards heaped on him and his work, was the Newbery Award in 1988 for *Lincoln: A Photobiography* (Clarion, 1987). *Eleanor Roosevelt* was a Newbery Honor Book in 1994. Mr. Freedman has said that a nonfiction book, "should be just as absorbing an any imaginary story because it is, in fact, a story, too."

Principal Characters
Eleanor Roosevelt, First Lady of the United States, 1933–1945
Franklin Delano Roosevelt, president of the United States, 1933–1945
Elliott Roosevelt, Eleanor's father
Anna Hall Roosevelt, Eleanor's mother
Marie Souvestre, an inspired teacher
Sara Roosevelt, Eleanor's mother-in-law
Anna, James, Elliott, Franklin Jr., and John Roosevelt—Eleanor and Franklin's children

Plot Summary

In this photo-filled biography, the author details the extraordinary life and accomplishments of Eleanor Roosevelt, First Lady of the United States and one of the most influential women of her time. Born in 1884 into a wealthy and influential family, Eleanor was a timid, shy child whose unhappy parents made her life lonely. She adored her father, Elliott, a deeply troubled man who often went off on drinking sprees. Eventually his dependence on drugs and alcohol caused the family breakup and, although her mother tried to keep the family together, Eleanor desperately missed her father. When she was ten years old, he died from a fall while intoxicated.

When Eleanor was fifteen, the family sent her to London for schooling. She responded well to an inspired teacher, Marie Souvestre, of whom she later said, "she shocked me into thinking." She would later call her three years in London the happiest of her life. On her return to the states, Eleanor was a young woman of grace and character but not beauty. Therefore, she was somewhat surprised at the attentions of her handsome fifth cousin once removed, Franklin Delano Roosevelt. He was attending Harvard at the time, and they were married in 1905. The couple would later have six children, of whom five lived to adulthood.

Thirteen years after her marriage, Eleanor discovered that her husband was having an affair with Lucy Mercer, her social secretary and a family friend. Eleanor felt her life was over, but a divorce was unthinkable. For the sake of the children and his career, Eleanor and Franklin decided to try to hold the marriage together. But their relationship had changed forever.

Eleanor Roosevelt had no interest in politics and was truly troubled when Franklin ran for the presidency in 1932. She dreaded the thought of living in the White House. But when Franklin won the election, she became a gracious, tireless First Lady and would call the White House her home until 1945.

During World War II, Eleanor earned the world's admiration as she made several wartime trips as a goodwill ambassador. She visited U.S. troops overseas and even earned the respect of Admiral William F. Halsey, chief of naval operations in the Pacific. She was a woman who radiated warmth and genuine sympathy. The country had never seen a First Lady like her.

After her husband's death in 1945, Eleanor thought she might fade from the world stage. Instead, President Harry Truman called on her for advice. She served as an American delegate to the first meeting of the United Nations General Assembly, and was Truman's UN delegate throughout his administration. She also continued to lecture, broadcast, and write on subjects that filled her with passion, such as human rights and dignity. She remained an influential figure in the Democratic party throughout her life, speaking on nuclear disarmament and other important issues. After her UN duties, she traveled around the world, meeting with women's groups and everyday citizens.

Eleanor Roosevelt died on November 7, 1962, of a stroke. At her death she was regarded as the most respected and influential woman in the world.

Suitability and Critical Comment

This Newbery Award–winning author has written an intriguing biography of one of the nation's most respected and loved citizens. His many fine details of her life and numerous insightful quotes allow the warmth and dignity of Eleanor Roosevelt to come across to the reader. This is well recommended for all young adult readers who love a good story in nonfiction form. For grades seven through ten.

Themes and Subjects

Family relationships, marriage, politics, war, wealth, the White House

Passages for Booktalking

Family troubles (pp. 8–13); Eleanor goes to school in London (pp. 23–29); Eleanor meets Franklin (p. 37); Eleanor discovers Franklin's affair (pp. 59–61); Eleanor becomes First Lady (pp. 97–100).

Additional Selections

Nancy Mace destroyed many sexist images when she entered South Carolina's historical military college, the Citadel, and reported it in her book, *In the Company of Men: A Woman at the Citadel* (Simon & Schuster, 2001), by Nancy Mace and Mary Jane Ross.

Penny Colman's *Where the Action Was: Women War Correspondents in World War II* (Crown, 2002) profiles a number of talented female journalists like Margaret Bourke White and Martha Gellhorn.

Gena K. Gorrell's *Heart and Soul: The Story of Florence Nightingale* (Tundra, 2000) re-creates the life of this difficult, demanding humanitarian and the contradictions of life in Victorian England.

For a more advanced biography of Eleanor Roosevelt, use *Eleanor Roosevelt: A Passion to Improve* (Facts on File, 1996) by Raymond Spangenburg and Diane Moon.

About the Book

Booklist, July, 1993, p. 1962.
Bulletin of the Center for Children's Books, Oct., 1993, p. 44.

Horn Book, Jan.-Feb., 1994, p. 81.
Kirkus Reviews, July 1, 1993, p. 858.
School Library Journal, Aug., 1993, p. 196.
VOYA, Feb., 1994, p. 394.

About the Author

Authors and Artists for Young Adults, vol. 4, Gale, 1996; vol. 24, Gale, 1998.
Children's Literature Review, vol. 20, Gale, 1990; vol. 71, Gale, 2002.
Continuum Encyclopedia of Children's Literature, Continuum, 2001.
Dempsey, Frank J. "An Interview with Russell Freedman," *Horn Book,* July-Aug., 1988, pp. 452–56.
Hipple, Ted. *Writers for Young Adults,* vol. 2, Scribners, 1997, pp. 1–10.
Lives and Works: Young Adult Authors, vol. 3, Grolier, 1999, pp. 88–90.
Major Authors and Illustrators for Children and Young Adults, vol. 2, Gale, 1993.
Marcus, Leonard S. *Author Talk,* Simon & Schuster, 2000.
McElmeel, Sharron L. *The 100 Most Popular Children's Authors,* Libraries Unlimited, 1999.
"Newbery Award Acceptance," *Journal of Youth Services in Libraries,* Summer, 1988, pp. 421–27.
"Newbery Award Acceptance Material, 1988," *Horn Book,* July-Aug., 1988, pp. 444–51.
"1998 Laura Ingalls Wilder Acceptance Speech," *Journal of Youth Services in Libraries,* Summer, 1998, pp. 353–56.
St. James Guide to Young Adult Writers (2nd ed.), St. James, 1999.
Silvey, Anita. *Children's Books and Their Creators,* Houghton Mifflin, 1995.
Sixth Book of Junior Authors and Illustrators, Wilson, 1989.
Something about the Author, vol. 16, Gale, 1979; vol. 71, Gale, 1993; vol. 123, Gale, 2001.
Twentieth Century Young Adult Writers, St. James, 1994.
Zvirin, Stephanie. "The Booklist Interview—Russell Freedman," *Booklist,* Jan. 15, 1999, pp. 926–27.

Krakauer, Jon. *Into Thin Air: A Personal Account of the Mt. Everest Disaster.* Villard, 1997. $24.95 (0-679-45752-6) (Grades 10–12).

Jon Krakauer (1954–) was born in Brookline, Massachusetts, but moved with his family when he was two to Corvallis, Oregon, where he experienced his first mountain climb when only eight. His father was an ardent climber. The young boy's childhood heroes were famous mountaineers, and his dream was to conquer Everest. Several of his climbs became the material he used for his first writing attempts. For example, his first published article was commissioned by the American Alpine Club as a report on his expedition in 1974 in which he climbed the previously unexplored

Arrigetch Peaks in Alaska's Brooks Range. At this time, his life was split equally between working as a carpenter and scaling mountains. With the increased demand for articles, he gave up his carpentry job and, in 1983, became a freelance writer. When his expedition to climb Everest ended in tragedy, he was so haunted by the deaths of his comrades that he felt he could secure peace of mind by writing about them. The result was a magazine article that was later expanded into the book, *Into Thin Air.*

Principal Characters

Jon Krakauer, mountain climber
Rob Hall, guide
Scott Fischer, guide
Lou Kasischke, climber
Other climbers of Mt. Everest

Plot Summary

Journalist and author Jon Krakauer is also an accomplished mountain climber. In 1996, he went to the Himalayas on an assignment for *Outside* magazine to report on the growing commercialization of Mt. Everest, the world's tallest mountain and the one that each year draws would-be climbers with an almost hypnotic fascination. Krakauer's guide was Rob Hall, the world's most respected high-altitude guide. A New Zealander, Hall had climbed to the summit of Mt. Everest four times between 1990 and 1995, leading thirty-nine climbers to the top.

This climbing expedition, which included six other climbers, began in early May 1996. On May 10, Krakauer reached the summit in the early afternoon. Suffering from oxygen depletion and without sleep for fifty-seven hours, he was nearly delirious. He had been told that reaching the summit would trigger a unique surge of intense elation, but his exhaustion and pain were too intense. Besides, reaching the summit is only half the battle; one must survive the long and dangerous descent. As he started back down from 29,028 feet, he passed twenty other climbers still trying to make it to the top. Some hours later, when he had descended 3,000 feet, he collapsed into his tent, hallucinating from oxygen deficiency and freezing, but alive.

That could not be said for Krakauer's companions. A 70-knot storm with blinding snow hit the mountain. Five fellow climbers would not make it back to camp. When the storm passed, the sixth climber returned but with a hand so frostbitten that it later had to be amputated. In addition, disaster struck the companion climbing expedition led by Scott Fischer, a forty-year-old American who had climbed the peak without added oxygen in 1994. Fischer died in that storm, and so did Krakauer's guide, Rob Hall.

Krakauer gives a vivid account of surviving the rogue storm that struck Mt. Everest in May, 1996. He speaks of finally achieving his goal of standing on top of the world, with one foot in China and the other in Nepal, but being too tired and exhausted to care. On his way down, he remembers passing guide Scott Fischer, who would soon be trapped in the storm fast approaching the mountain. Krakauer speaks of the toll in human life and suffering that the mountain exacts from those who try to reach the summit. Fellow climber Lou Kasischke, who survived that day in May, later wrote that it was the worst experience of his life. Krakauer himself speaks of how even the most experienced climbers and guides are often left to chance, such as the terrible and unexpected storm that hit Everest as he was descending the mountain to safety and others were still climbing to what would be their deaths.

Hypnotic as Everest may be for some climbers, it also seems to have poisoned many lives. Those who return, says Krakauer, often suffer great guilt for surviving when their colleagues died. In addition, they must live through the taunts and accusations of relatives of those who were left behind. Was enough done to save their fellow climbers? The survivors may suffer doubt about their own actions. Marriages break up, friendships die. But the mountain and its fascination survives.

Suitability and Critical Comment

This book is written on a level that should be entertaining and well understood by most teen readers. The author does not dramatize the events, but his stark and simple narration paints a vivid picture of the intense suffering and physical toll that the mountain exacts of those who try to climb it. Also well described throughout is the almost mysterious fascination that Mt. Everest holds for so many climbers, even when they realize the grave dangers they face and the small chance of success without harm. For grades ten through twelve.

Themes and Subjects

Friendship, frostbite, guides, journalists, mountain climbing, Mt. Everest, Nepal, oxygen deprivation

Passages for Booktalking

Reaching the top (pp. 5–9); the trek begins (pp. 41–54); at 21,300 feet (pp. 123–31); the summit (pp. 199–214;) getting back down (pp. 260–64).

Additional Selections

Several survival narratives are used to describe what happens to the human body when pushed to its limits as reported in Peter Stark's *Last*

Breath: Cautionary Tales from the Limits of Human Endurance (Ballantine, 2001).

Linda Greenlaw tells her story of being captain of a fishing boat and her month-long, backbreaking swordfish expedition in *The Hungry Ocean: A Swordfish Captain's Journey* (Hyperion, 1999).

The Lost River: A Memoir of Life, Death and Transformation on Wild Water (Sierra Club, 1999) by Richard Bangs tells the exciting story of rafting the Takeze River and of Ethiopia's land, people, and wildlife.

In Matt Dickinson's *The Other Side of Everest* (Times Books, 1999), subtitled "Climbing the North Face through the Killer Storm," the author describes his successful ascent under terrible conditions.

About the Book
Booklist, April 1, 1997, p. 1276.
Kirkus Reviews, March 1, 1997, p. 357.
Library Journal, April 1, 1997, p. 117.
New York Times Book Review, May 18, 1997, p. 39.
School Library Journal, Nov., 1997, p. 150.
VOYA, April, 1998, p. 37.

About the Author
Authors and Artists for Young Adults, vol. 24, Gale, 1998.
Contemporary Authors, vol. 153, Gale, 1997.
Something about the Author, vol. 108, Gale, 2000.

Lobel, Anita. *No Pretty Pictures.* Greenwillow, 1998. $16.00
(0-688-15935-4) (Grades 7–10).

Introduction
Anita Lobel (1934–) was born in Krakow, Poland. In this country, she is best known as the author and illustrator of many picture books, concept books, fantasies, and retold fairy tales for young children. Sometimes she works independently, other times with such authors as John Langstaff and Charlotte Zolotow. She also collaborated on many projects with her late husband, Arnold Lobel. Her work is usually in line-and-wash or watercolor. *No Pretty Pictures,* the story of the artist's childhood during World War II, is the story she has waited years to tell. During the war, her family, who were Jewish, were separated, and she was placed in the care of a loving Polish woman. Eventually, she was caught and sent to a concentration camp. Two years after the war, the family was miraculously reunited. Ms. Lobel cur-

rently lives in New York City, where she is able to indulge her interest in acting and attending the theater.

Principal Characters
   Anita Lobel, the author
   Lobel's father
   Lobel's mother
   Lobel's brother
   Niania, Lobel's nanny
   Uncle Samuel
   Aunt Bella
   Cousin Raisa

Plot Summary
   Lobel's story begins in Krakow, Poland, in 1939, as Nazi soldiers burst into her apartment, which she shares with her parents, brother, and nanny, Niania. They take things such as candlesticks, a silver coffeepot, and an expensive rug. Not long after, Lobel's grandparents and aunt are deported. With her father's whereabouts unknown, it is decided to send Lobel and her brother into the country, where there will be less danger from the Nazis. Niania will accompany them. They leave for the small village of Lapanow, where her father's relatives live. They spend the winter there but the Nazis are getting closer. Niania decides to take them to her own village, where there are no Jews.
   The children and Niania go to her village where they hide until Lobel's mother arrives, saying the Nazis have taken everything from them in Krakow. Lobel's mother takes the children back to Krakow, where they move in with her aunt, uncle, and cousin. They are in the ghetto, growing more and more trapped and more and more fearful of the Nazis. It is decided that the children must sneak back to Niania's village. She finds them shelter at the convent of Benedictine sisters. Life is good at the convent until the Nazis arrive one Christmas Day to find the Jews. Lobel and her brother, who had been masquerading as a girl, are taken away.
   Thus begins a succession of concentration camps for Lobel and her brother. One night after a long march they arrive at the dreaded Auschwitz. What follows is a nightmare of starvation, diarrhea, and constant fear and terror. In 1945, Lobel and her brother are miraculously rescued and sent to Sweden by the Red Cross. The children are sick with tuberculosis, and Lobel must stay in a sanatorium for about a year. It is there that Lobel is introduced to books. She is brought Jewish stories, but screams because she

says she is not Jewish, but Christian. Then Lobel gets a letter from her mother, who has found out that the children are alive. Later she learns that her father has survived also.

Eventually, Lobel's mother and father go to Stockholm, where she has been sent. She hardly knows them. The family settles down in Stockholm, and Lobel is able to go to school, which she loves. That is where she begins her great interest in and discovers a talent for art. When she is sixteen years old, Lobel and her family emigrate to the United States, which Lobel does not want to do at first. Sweden has become her home. But Lobel does come to the United States, where she has lived ever since. She has become a painter, a fabric designer, and an honor-winning illustrator of books for children.

Lobel has often traveled to Europe since she emigrated. Each visit rekindles her memories of those terrible years of her youth. But now she feels that she is an American. She has never gone back to Poland and will never do so. She says she cannot stand on the preserved grounds of Auschwitz or the other concentration camps that will forever live in her memory. But she has returned to her beloved Sweden, a place that gave her life after her living nightmare.

Suitability and Critical Comment

This book is best suited to the older teenager with some knowledge of the Nazi persecution of the Jews during World War II. The writing is not graphic but realistic, and the horror is all too evident in the simple words of the children who survived this terrible ordeal. For those who like stories of survival against great odds, Lobel's story should be of particular interest. For grades seven through ten.

Themes and Subjects

Auschwitz, concentration camps, family relationships, Germany, Jews, Nazis, persecution, Poland, racism, survival, Sweden, terror, World War II

Passages for Booktalking

The Nazis come the first time (pp. 5–9); Lobel and her brother go to Niania's village (pp. 27–35); living in the convent (pp. 54–59); in Auschwitz (pp. 100–103); freedom in Sweden (pp. 122–25).

Additional Selections

Combining fact and fiction, the twelve stories in *Shattered: Stories of Children and War* (Knopf, 2002) edited by Jennifer Armstrong tell about young people and wars, ranging from the Civil War to the present.

The true story of Jack Mandelbaum, a Polish Jew, who spent three years in Nazi death camps as a teenager, is told in Andrea Warren's *Surviving Hitler: A Boy in the Nazi Death Camps* (HarperCollins, 2001).

In Gary Schmidt's *Mara's Stories: Glimmers in the Darkness* (Holt, 2001), an inmate of a Nazi death camp retells twenty-two Jewish folktales to fellow adult inmates and children.

A young Polish Jew with his mother and older sister live five years during World War II as German Catholics in Yehuda Nir's memoir, *The Lost Childhood: A World War II Memoir* (Harcourt, 1989).

About the Book
Booklist, Aug., 1998, p. 1988.
Bulletin of the Center for Children's Books, Oct., 1998, p. 65.
Horn Book, Nov., 1998, p. 755.
Kirkus Reviews, Sept. 1, 1998, p. 755.
New York Times Book Review, Nov. 15, 1998, p. 44.
School Library Journal, Sept., 1998, p. 220.

About the Author
Major Authors and Illustrators for Children and Young Adults, vol. 4, Gale, 1993.
Silvey, Anita. *Children's Books and Their Creators*, Houghton Mifflin, 1995.
Something about the Author, vol. 6, Gale, 1974; vol. 55, Gale, 1989; vol. 96, Gale, 1998.
Third Book of Junior Authors, Wilson, 1972.
Twentieth Century Children's Writers, St. James, 1995.

Marrin, Albert. *Sitting Bull and His World.* Dutton, 2000. $27.50 (0-525-45944-8) (Grades 7–9).

Introduction
Albert Marrin (1936–) is a professor of history and chairman of the history department at Yeshiva University in New York City. In addition to his teaching and administrative duties, Mr. Marrin has found time to write approximately thirty nonfiction books for young adults, beginning with *Overlord: D-Day and the Invasion of Europe* (Atheneum, 1982). His books are highly readable, well-organized, unbiased accounts that are noted for the thorough research behind each. He brings history alive by using interesting details and by creating dramatic tension in his books. Mr. Marrin has written expansively of World War II, its battles, and such leaders as Hitler and Stalin. War history is another of his interests, and he has several volumes on important American wars and historical figures like George Washington, Robert E. Lee, and Lincoln. *Sitting Bull and His World* is an

example of another area of concern—the history and fate of Native Americans and their conflicts with Europeans.

Principal Characters

Sitting Bull, warrior chief
Crazy Horse, Sioux chief
George Armstrong Custer, U.S. Army

Plot Summary

Sitting Bull, born around 1831 near Grand River, Dakota, became the great chief of the Lakotas and united the Sioux tribes in a fierce struggle for survival on the North American Great Plains. He distrusted white men all his life and fought against their domination. He was born into the Hunkpapa division of the Teton Sioux and fought his first battle at age fourteen. By the time he became a leader in the powerful Strong Heart warrior society, he was known for his fearlessness in battle. Sitting Bull helped to extend Sioux hunting grounds westward. After the Minnesota Massacre in 1863, when the U.S. Army retaliated against the Santee Sioux, Sitting Bull had his first skirmish with U.S. soldiers. As the army encroached ever more on Native American hunting grounds, Sitting Bull was in frequent hostile contact with the soldiers. In 1866, he became principal chief of the northern hunting Sioux, with Crazy Horse, who was the leader of the Oglala Sioux, as his vice chief. The following year he was made principal chief of the entire Sioux nation, cited for his courage and wisdom.

The U.S. government granted the Sioux a reservation in what is now southwestern South Dakota in 1868. But when gold was discovered a few years later, prospectors began to violate the treaty and invade Sioux lands. By 1875, the Sioux were ordered to return to the reservation, which they had been leaving to fight the intruders, but when the retreat did not meet a government deadline, General George Crook set out after them. Sitting Bull rallied the Sioux, Cheyenne, and Arapaho to his camp in Montana Territory. When Crook was forced to retreat in the Battle of the Rosebud on June 17, Sitting Bull and the Sioux moved to an encampment in the valley of the Little Bighorn River. Now Sitting Bull performed a sun dance in which he said he saw soldiers falling into their camp. On June 25, 1876, Lieutenant Colonel George Armstrong Custer rode against Sitting Bull and the Sioux, and all men under Custer's immediate command were annihilated at the Battle of the Little Bighorn.

The victorious Sioux were now subject to battle after battle from the U.S. troops, and it was a war they could not possibly win in the end. The buffalo, on which the Sioux depended for livelihood, were steadily declining as the white invaders took more and more land. Famine caused many of the Sioux to surrender, and Sitting Bull led his remaining soldiers into Canada. But famine finally forced him to surrender in 1881. In 1885, an Indian agent allowed Sitting Bull to join Buffalo Bill's Wild West Show, where he gained international fame. In 1890, there were rumors that a Ghost Dance prophesied the coming of an Indian messiah who would sweep away the white settlers. As a precaution, Sitting Bull was seized on December 15, 1890, and was killed while his followers tried to rescue him. His remains were moved to Mobridge, South Dakota, in 1953, where a granite shaft marks his resting place.

Sitting Bull was perhaps the most revered warrior of the Plains Indians. He was a visionary leader whose courage and determination influenced generations of Native Americans.

Suitability and Critical Comment

This is a well-researched, highly readable account of the life and death of a great Native American warrior. It also details the vast differences between white and Indian cultures in the nineteenth century that kept the two sides in constant battle and shows how part of the United States was created at the expense of an entire people. This is suitable for most readers in grades seven through nine and especially those interested in U.S. history.

Themes and Subjects

Battle of Little Bighorn, courage, honesty, Native American culture, Native Americans, reservations, U.S. Army, war

Passages for Booktalking

Minnesota uprising (pp. 75–76); at Rosebud Creek (pp. 127–28); Battle of Little Bighorn (pp.132–57); Wild West Show (pp. 200–203); the Ghost Dance (pp. 210–16).

Additional Selections

The electrifying, tragic story of the last major battle between the U.S. Army and the Sioux people of the Great Plains is re-created in Neil Waldman's well-illustrated *Wounded Knee* (Atheneum, 2001).

Cochise: Apache Chief (Chelsea House, 1992) by Melissa Schwarz is the story of the Apache chief who opposed the white Americans' attempts to subdue his Southwestern people in the 1860s.

Russell Freedman's *The Life and Death of Crazy Horse* (Holiday House, 1996) tells an uncompromising story of bloody wars, terrible grief, and the loss of the land so dear to the Sioux tribe.

The Indian Heritage of America (Houghton Mifflin, 1991) by Alvin M. Josephy is a fine survey of the culture and history of Native Americans from both North and South America.

About the Book

Booklist, May 1, 2000, p. 1666.
Book Report, Jan., 2001, p. 16.
Bulletin of the Center for Children's Books, July, 2000, p. 412.
Horn Book, July-Aug., 2000, p. 474.
New York Times Book Review, Aug. 13, 2000, p. 16.
School Library Journal, July, 2000, p. 119.
VOYA, Aug., 2000, p. 206.

About the Author

Authors and Artists for Young Adults, vol. 35, Gale, 2001.
Children's Literature Review, vol. 53, Gale, 1999.
Seventh Book of Junior Authors and Illustrators, Wilson, 1996.
Something about the Author, vol. 53, Gale, 1988; vol. 90, Gale, 1997; vol. 126, Gale, 2002.

Murphy, Jim. *Blizzard! The Storm That Changed America.* Scholastic, 2000. $18.95 (0-590-67309-2) (Grades 6–9).

Introduction

Jim Murphy (1947–) grew up in suburban Kearny, New Jersey. He read little as a youngster except those books that he was forbidden to read by his teachers, like Ernest Hemingway's *A Farewell to Arms.* After college, he worked as an editorial secretary at Seabury Press (now known as Clarion Books) and rose to the position of managing editor. In 1977, he decided to become a freelance editor and writer. He is best known for nonfiction works on a variety of subjects and historical periods. *The Great Fire* (Scholastic, 1995) was a Newbery Honor Book in 1996. It tells the story of one of the great disasters of the nineteenth century, the great Chicago fire of 1871. As a result of this fire, some one hundred thousand people were left homeless, and about three hundred were killed, many of whom drowned in the city's river while trying to escape the fury of the fire. Like *Blizzard!,* it re-creates an awesome event vividly and accurately in words and pictures, using exhaustive research involving original documents, eyewitness accounts, and selected secondary sources.

Principal Characters

Americans from Maine to Virginia who lived through the blizzard of 1888

Plot Summary

At the time, it was the warmest winter on record on the East Coast, from Maine to Virginia. The year was 1888, and even on March 10, it was unseasonably warm. In fact, President Grover Cleveland and his wife decided to enjoy the weather with a weekend vacation at their country home. Other families were actually picnicking. A hardware buyer for a Manhattan department store had previously ordered 3,000 wooden snow shovels, and he was worried that he might lose his job because they would never be sold. He needn't have worried.

Two days later, on March 12, 1888, the snow began. It turned into a huge, awesome, destructive blizzard, which was actually two storms. One was sweeping across Minnesota, Wisconsin, and Michigan. The other was in the South, soaking Pensacola, Florida, and sending cyclone-force winds tearing around Mississippi, Tennessee, and Alabama. But the weather forecasters said not to worry; maybe it would rain on the East Coast.

Blizzard! is the story of three days in the lives of people who survived—and some who didn't—the blizzard of 1888. New York City got twenty-one inches of snow; fifty-five inches hit Troy, New York. Trains were stalled everywhere; power lines snapped. Some two hundred ships were lost at sea, and eight hundred people lost their lives in New York City alone. By Tuesday morning, New York City was paralyzed. Fire engines could not get through the snow-drifted streets. Several thousand laborers were called in to clear out the city streets. They piled the snow into wagons and hauled it to the river to be dumped. People dug tunnels through the snow to move around. The mounds of snow grew so high that kids were sleigh riding at the level of second-story windows.

The storm that some called "the Great White fire" stretched along the north Atlantic seaboard and as far west as the Mississippi River. Food and fuel became scarce.

Included in this riveting tale are many dramatic stories from survivors of how people coped with the crisis. The great blizzard officially ended on March 14. Shortly thereafter, the temperature hit 40 degrees in both Philadelphia and Boston. The storm passed as quickly as it came, but its effects would live on. For one thing, it changed the way the weather was forecast. The federal government wanted to know why the Signal Corps, which at the time was in charge of making weather predictions, had failed to predict the storm. Three years later, the Signal Corps was removed from army control and handed over to the Department of Agriculture. Its name was changed to the present-day United States Weather Bureau. And instead of focusing on advance storm warnings, the bureau began to concentrate more on why and how weather happens, in order to give more and better warnings of upcoming blizzards or similar potential tragedies. Those changes have improved safety and given better advance warnings, but they are not 100 percent accurate. For example, in January 2000, a storm that had been predicted to die out over the Atlantic came back and closed down Washington, D.C., for two days.

Suitability and Critical Comment

Suitable for most teen readers, this riveting account of a dramatic storm is a true story that reads like fiction. The author highlights the tremendous power of the awesome storm and colors the story with anecdotes, newspaper accounts, and contemporary photographs of the terrible tragedy that took the lives of hundreds of Americans. For grades six through nine.

Themes and Subjects

Blizzards, East Coast, human interest, snow, tragedy, weather bureau

Passages for Booktalking

The day before the storm (pp. 10–24); a child goes out in the snow (pp. 37–40); John J. Meisinger sells his shovels (pp. 63–64); tragedy on the water (pp. 75–78); the aftermath (pp. 103–24).

Additional Selections

Through firsthand accounts of workers, farmers, sharecroppers, veterans, and professionals, Milton Meltzer re-creates the Great Depression in the United States in *Brother Can You Spare A Dime? The Great Depression, 1929–1933* (Facts on File, 1991).

The story of the underwater explorer's expeditions to the remains of the sunken Titanic are retold in Robert D. Ballard's *Exploring the Titanic* (Scholastic, 1988).

Victoria Sherrow's *The Triangle Factory Fire* (Millbrook, 1995) tells about the deadly fire that exposed the shameful labor exploitation in this country prior to World War I.

The causes, effects, and the methods of tracking El Nino are discussed in Caroline Arnold's *El Nino: Stormy Weather for People and Wildlife* (Clarion, 1998).

About the Book

Booklist, Feb. 15, 2001, p. 1135.
Bulletin of the Center for Children's Books, Jan., 2001, p. 190.
Horn Book, Jan., 2001, p. 113.
Kirkus Reviews, Nov. 15, 2000, p. 1617.
School Library Journal, Dec., 2000, p. 161.
VOYA, June, 2001, p. 145.

About the Author

Continuum Encyclopedia of Children's Literature, Continuum, 2001.

Seventh Book of Junior Authors and Illustrators, Wilson, 1996.

Something about the Author, vol. 32, Gale,1983; vol. 37, Gale, 1989; vol. 77, Gale, 1994; vol. 124, Gale, 2002.

8

Guidance and Health

Abner, Allison, and Linda Villarosa. *Finding Our Way: The Teen Girls'*
Survival Guide. Harper, 1995. Pb. $13.00 (0-06-095114-1)
(Grades 9–12).

Introduction

Allison Abner and Linda Villarosa, two African American women, both
work in publishing, one as executive editor of *Essence* magazine and the
other as a freelance journalist. The two also have written *The Black Parenting*
Book: Caring for Our Children in the First Five Years (Broadway Books, 1998). In
addition, Villarosa has written or edited books on obesity, heart disease,
stroke, and diabetes and how they relate to the black community. *Finding*
Our Way is a candid look at young women and their concerns. The tone is
light and often chatty, but never flip. Hailed for both the quantity and quality of its information, its covers such topics as body image, puberty, sexual
development, nutrition, relationship, birth control, and even plastic sur-
gery. As one reviewer said, it is "a unique illustrated guide that helps teens
discover who they are, what they want in life, and how they can get it in
today's complex world."

Principal Characters

Teenaged girls

Plot Summary

The authors' stated goal of the book is to help teenaged girls think for
themselves and make the right decisions. The thirteen chapters cover all
aspects of what concerns young girls and touches their lives. Chapter 1
deals with good bodies, covering body image and its effects, obesity, eating
disorders, and exercise, and how to feel good about whatever body you
have. Chapter 2 covers good outsides—tips on skin, hair, eyes, teeth, and
nails, the outside parts that everyone sees. It discusses common problems
young girls experience and how to deal with them. Chapter 3 goes to good

insides, providing suggestions on healthful eating and exercise and avoiding substance abuse. In chapter 4, the authors discuss the more general topic of what teenagers should know about health care, including school-based or school-linked clinics; physical, including pelvic, exams; ten questions that girls should ask their doctors; and considerations of a career in the health field.

Sex in all aspects is covered in chapters 5 through 7, beginning with a general examination of the female and male bodies, naming body parts. It covers menstruation and the questions girls never want to ask their mothers. It discusses sex, from what changes occur in the body to emotional feelings. Chapter 6 talks about "doing the right thing," that is, avoiding pregnancy and disease. Is abstinence and postponement the answer? It covers the use of condoms, both male and female, myths about birth control, safe sex, and AIDS. Chapter 7 concerns babies: the biology of making a baby, abortion and abortion rights, adoption, and the reality of becoming a teenaged parent.

Chapter 8 gets into the moodiness of the teenage years and how emotions affect how people feel about themselves. There are tips on raising self-esteem, on how to deal with sexism and racism, and handling stress and depression, including suicide, which is noted as the third leading cause of death of young people aged fifteen through twenty-four.

In chapter 9, the authors talk about the importance of family—even if they can be totally annoying. It provides suggestions on dealing with too many fights in the family relationship, living with one parent gone, getting along with siblings, what happens when the family becomes a stepfamily, how to live through a divorce, and how to survive when one parent goes to jail.

Perhaps nothing seems so crucial in the teenage years as friends, which is the topic of chapter 10. It provides tips on how to be a good friend, things one must never do—such as lie—to maintain friendships, and how to avoid just going along with the crowd. The ins and outs of peer pressure and the need to be popular are discussed.

Falling in love and sexual orientation are the subjects of chapter 11. Chapter 12 deals with the second leading cause of death for all young women aged fourteen through twenty-four—homicide. After a general discussion of the growing violence in society both inside and outside of the home, the authors provide ways to avoid violent situations, including date rape, and how teenagers can help to curb the growing violence in society today. The subject of abuse is covered in chapter 13, how to deal with abuse inflicted by one parent on another, substance abuse, how abuse affects the teenage years, and what to do about it, even running away. Each chapter in the book ends with recommended reading and other suggestions about where the teenager can turn for help.

Suitability and Critical Comment

Teen girls of all ages should find this matter-of-fact, easily read book to be beneficial. The authors cover most aspects of the troubling teen years and are especially helpful with practical suggestions of where to turn for advice and aid if it doesn't come from the home. The authors have presented a reassuring kind of manual that offers aid and suggestions without being overbearing or dictatorial. For grades nine through twelve.

Themes and Subjects

Abuse, body image, depression, family life, friends, friendship, health, pregnancy, sex, teen years, violence

Passages for Booktalking

Body image (pp. 1–4); naming body parts (pp. 87–93); avoiding pregnancy and disease (pp. 131–38); how to get and maintain friends (pp. 219–24); dealing with abuse (pp. 286–302).

Additional Selections

Using the subtitle, "Successful Teens Tell Us What Works," Barbara Littman's *Everyday Ways to Raise Smart, Strong, Confident Girls* (St. Martin's, 1999) supplies over one hundred tips to help girls to flourish.

The title tells all about the contents of Deborah Harris-Johnson's *The African-American Teenager's Guide to Personal Growth, Health, Safety, Sex and Survival: Living and Learning in the Twenty-first Century* (Amber, 2000).

Gutsy Girls (Free Spirit, 1999) by Tina Schwager and Michele Schuerger contains autobiographical sketches of women who engage in such activities as skydiving, drag racing, and mountain climbing.

About fifty girls, ages ten to sixteen, give advice and tips on everything from slumber parties to coping with death in *Girls Know Best 2* (Beyond Words, 1998) edited by Marianne Monson-Burton.

About the Book

Booklist, Feb. 15, 1996, p. 1016.
VOYA, Aug., 1996, p. 174.

About the Authors

No information available.

Canfield, Jack, Mark Victor Hansen, and Kimberly Kirberger.
Chicken Soup for the Teenage Soul: 101 Stories of Life, Love, and Learning. Health Communications, 1997. Pb. $12.95 (1-55874-463-0) (Grades 9–12).

Introduction

Jack Canfield was born in Fort Worth, Texas. After college, he became a teacher and gravitated to self-motivational work with people. He began conducting very successful seminars and is now the president of a California-based company known as Santa Barbara Self Esteem Seminars. He says, "I started my writing career as a high school teacher who collected and published classroom activities to build self esteem in my students." With this collection of case studies and the help of Mark Victor Hansen, his first book, *Chicken Soup for the Soul* (Health Communications, 1993), was created but rejected by about 150 publishers. When it was finally published, it took about fourteen months before it took hold. This first volume of an increasing numbers of sequels remained on the *New York Times* best-seller list for 125 weeks and has sold over 6 million copies in twenty-three languages. Like its predecessors, *Chicken Soup for the Teenage Soul,* a spin-off, is a collection of uplifting stories about kids from all around the world. As one young fan commented, "It is so inspiring, I cry every time I read this book. It is great for kids who are depressed and need a way to cheer themselves up."

Principal Characters

Teenagers who contributed to the book

Plot Summary

This book is composed of 101 stories, mainly by teenaged writers, who contributed their experiences on life, love, and learning. It covers eight main topics: Relationships, Friendship, Family, Love and Kindness, Learning, Tough Stuff, Making a Difference, and Going for It.

Mary Jane West-Delgado speaks of her first romantic interlude in "My First Kiss, and Then Some." She was a very shy teenager and was anxious to be kissed, but her first boyfriend was quite shy and nervous, too. They were sophomores in high school. One day they were sitting on her living room couch and he finally got up the nerve, but she put up a pillow just in time, so he kissed that. He moved closer, and she moved to the end of the couch. Finally, she got up and walked to the door. He followed. She closed her eyes, and he managed to kiss her teeth. She said she could have died, and he left. They never dated again. After a year at college, she saw him again in an old hangout. She tapped him on the shoulder and boldly kissed him, saying, "So there!" He nodded to someone next to him and said, "Mary Jane, I'd like you to meet my wife."

An anonymous contributor learned a lesson in friendship with "Always Return Your Phone Calls." Angela was aware that her best friend Charlotte was having a rough time, arguing with her sister and mother, feeling moody and depressed. It got so bad that no one was on speaking terms with her that summer. But Angela kept trying and spent as much time with Charlotte as she could. Then Angela's family moved, and she couldn't see Charlotte every day. One day when she came in, her mother said Charlotte had called. Angela called her back but Charlotte didn't answer, so Angela left a message. Shortly after that, Charlotte called back to say she had just been about to commit suicide when she heard Angela's voice on the machine. Charlotte said she realized that someone did care about her, and she was going to get professional help. Angela went over to Charlotte's, and they sat on the porch swing and cried.

Jennifer Love Hewitt talks about love and kindness in "Bright Heart." A television actor, she attended a carnival for Tuesday's Child, an organization that helps children with AIDS. She saw one little boy painting a heart in dark colors because he said his own heart felt sick. He said his sickness was not ever going to get better and neither was his mom's. Jennifer tried to make him feel that there were things people could do to help, even if it was only giving a bear hug, which she did. A little later, the boy came to her and said his heart was feeling better. Maybe bear hugs really work.

Chris Laddish, age thirteen, remembers his brother, Michael, in "Just One Drink." Seven years earlier, Michael and three friends went out for dinner and had a few drinks. They swerved into the opposite lane on the way home, and Michael was killed. The driver, Joe, was charged with manslaughter. There is a small cross on highway 128 that tells Michael's sad story.

Jennifer Philbin talks about not being afraid to try things anymore in "Wild Thing." She'd always been impressed with people who participated in Outward Bound; now she decided to try it herself. It was her junior year in high school. First, she rafted a hundred miles down the Deschutes River, then climbed the second highest peak in Oregon. She was dropped off alone in the woods for a few days and found her way out. She thinks it made her a new woman, and she thinks she won't be afraid to try new things anymore.

Suitability and Critical Comment

These letters, ranging from humorous to serious topics, are suited for all teen readers. They give insights into teen problems and concerns. The book is set up for jumping around from topic to topic as the reader wishes. A panel of readers graded the stories to try to include all types of stories that can bring inspiration or guidance to the young reader. For grades nine through twelve.

Themes and Subjects

Courage, death and illness, education, family, friendship, growing up, learning, love and kindness, relationships

Passages for Booktalking

Mary Jane's first kiss (pp. 14–15); the returned phone call (pp. 55–56); the AIDS patient (pp. 114–16); drunk driving (pp. 216–17); the Outward Bound success (pp. 316–18).

Additional Selections

A cross-section of American teens talk candidly about their lives, opinions, and beliefs in *Seen and Heard: Teenagers Talk about Their Lives* (Stewart, Tabori, 1999) by Mary Motley Kalergis.

Chapters on topics like anorexia, purging, steroids, and cosmetics are included in *Body Image: A Reality Check* (Enslow, 1999) by Pamela Shires Sneddon.

Sol Gordon's *The Teenage Survival Book* (Times Books, 1981) discusses the important concerns and worries of adolescents and gives practical advice.

Practical advice on the emotional changes that accompany puberty and adolescence is given in *It's My Life* (Watts, 1997) by Pete Sanders and Steve Myers.

About the Book

Booklist, Oct. 1, 1997, p. 34.
VOYA, April, 1998, p. 39.

About the Authors

No information available.

Packer, Alex. *Bringing Up Parents: The Teenager's Handbook.* Free Spirit, 1992. $15.95 (0-915793-48-2) (Grades 8–12).

Introduction

Since this guide, Mr. Packer has written *How Rude! The Teenager's Guide to Good Manners, Proper Behavior and Not Grossing People Out* (Free Spirit, 1997).

Bringing Up Parents is a candid, often humorous guide to good manners for teenagers that avoids being preachy while covering such topics as rude noises and table manners plus unusual subjects such as line skating, computer hacking, and sex etiquette. The book discusses in detail the art of coping with parents: building trust, diffusing family power struggles, waging effective verbal battles, developing listening skills, and expressing feelings nonaggressively. This sound advice is combined with enough wit and humor to produce a feeling of oneness between the author and the reader. As one reviewer said, "It promotes maturity and responsibility. The text is easy to read, insightful, and should spark the beginning of a healthy relationship between parents and young adults."

Principal Characters

Parents

Teenagers

Plot Summary

In an amusing vein, but with strictly serious information, the author discusses the problems of teenagers relating to their parents and vice versa. The idea is to give tips and techniques for turning parents into what teenagers want them to be; that is, people who listen and trust, who respect opinions, and who let their children be themselves.

The book is divided into six chapters. Chapter 1, "The Nature of the Beasts," deals with living with both parents and teenagers. It encourages teenagers to try to understand why parents sometimes have such great expectations for their children, even though those expectations may have little in common with the actual desires and needs of the child. It talks honestly and openly about the difficulties of being a teenager, the fears, needs, and innate behaviors of the adolescent species. Chapter 2, "Getting Down to Basics," is a look at basic issues at the core of every parent-child relationship. The author makes a point that in order to get along better with one's parents, the teenager has to understand them and accept them for what they are. It is necessary to connect the parents' past with the present in order to understand why they act as they do. And in order to get parents to act as the teenager wants them to, the teenager him- or herself must accept responsibility.

Chapter 3, "Tricks and Treats," takes on time-tested tactics designed to get what you want, such as an act of kindness. It discusses when to ask for help and even when to cry, and certainly when to apologize. In chapter 4, "Taking Charge of the Fight Brigade," the emphasis here is on attitude or style. "It's not what you say, it's how you say it." Style includes body language, timing, facial expressions, tone of voice, and choice of words. Techniques for getting parents to become active listeners are discussed, as are methods of communication for the teenager to follow. Chapter 5, "Close Encounters of the Worst Kind," focuses on a very serious issue—family problems and how to solve them.

Some tips include focusing on the future, not the past, because what's done is done. It encourages the teenager to look behind the argument at the true reason for the disagreement. The reason is not always on the surface. It is important to find the hidden agenda, to discover what's really behind the message. For instance, if parents harp on adhering to a curfew, it may be because they themselves like to go to bed early. Honest discussions can lead to peaceful solutions. Chapter 6, "Cures for the Common Conflict," is an appendix of helpful hints in solving the problems of living together as a family. It covers such issues as room sharing, cleaning up after oneself, bathroom habits, sibling fights, money, the boyfriend/girlfriend issue, parties, drinking, sex, drugs, child abuse, and others.

This is straight talk with specific suggestions delivered with lots of ideas and laughs. The aim is to show teenagers that, with a little effort and understanding on their part, they can have the kind of parents they think they deserve. The result will be more privileges for the teenager, more say in family decisions, and an all-around better home atmosphere for all.

Suitability and Critical Comment

Aimed at readers from twelve to seventeen, the book covers most aspects of family problems that occur with teenagers in the house. It is peppered with humor and down-to-earth suggestions that young readers can understand and live with. Most teenagers should find this how-to easy to read and follow; grades eight through twelve.

Themes and Subjects

Cleanliness, curfews, dating, family problems, fights, parents, responsibility, teenagers, trust

Passages for Booktalking

Parents' expectations (pp. 21–22); teenage freedom (pp. 76–83); how to choose your parents (pp. 110–11); troubleshooting problems (pp. 156–74); problem appendix (pp. 207–46).

Additional Selections

Facts for teens on budgeting, saving, investing, dealing with debt, and other monetary matters are given in *Teen Guide to Personal Financial Manage-*

ment (Greenwood, 2000) by Marjolin Bijlefeld and Sharon K. Zoumbaris.

Eight case studies on such subjects as adoption, problems with siblings, drug abuse, and assuming responsibilities are featured in *Staying Out of Trouble in a Troubled Family* (Millbrook, 1998) by Rose Blue and Corinne J. Naden.

Family problems such as single parenting and abuse are discussed in Ruth K. J. Cline's *Focus on Families* (ABC-CLIO, 1990).

Haim Ginott's *Between Parent and Teenager* (Avon, 1982) is an excellent guide to developing good relationships between parents and their teenage children.

About the Book
Booklist, May 1, 1993, p. 1596.
Book Report, May, 1993, p. 35.
VOYA, Aug., 1993, p. 180.

About the Author
No information available.

Pollack, William S., with Todd Shuster. *Real Boys' Voices: Rescuing Our Sons from the Myths of Boyhood.* Random House, 2000. $25.95 (0-679-46299-6) (Grades 9–12).

Introduction
William S. Pollack is a psychologist, director of the Center for Men at McLean Hospital in Boston, and a faculty member at Harvard Medical School. He believes that "the stereotypes of boys as being stoic, tough, sex-oriented, and sure of their emotions leads to confusion and is not conducive to emotional health." The result is a series of mixed, conflicting messages on what constitutes masculinity. His book, *Real Boys* (Random, 1998), is subtitled, "Rescuing Our Sons from the Myths of Boyhood." In it, he states that mothers should not try to make their sons independent too early and that it is wrong to tell them that crying, sadness, and separation anxiety are signs of being a sissy. It is also wrong to teach boys that anger is the only acceptable emotion. One result of this faulty teaching is the production of emotionally crippled youngsters who have lost their sense of creativity. He also offers suggestions and advice on raising psychologically healthy boys. *Real Boys' Voices* reinforces these ideas through a series of case histories.

Principal Characters
Boys of all ages all across America

Plot Summary

Instead of advising boys on what to do, this book first listens to what they have to say and then comments. Boys from big and small towns in the United States, including Littleton, Colorado, speak about their fears and dreams, about drugs, sports, violence, parents, body image, anger, love, sex, and more. The five main parts and twenty-four chapters cover the secret emotional lives of young men; bullying and teasing and the difference between fitting in and being left out; rage and suicide; reaching out and connecting; how to deal with loss, loneliness, and shame; and the place of boys in the world.

The author finds that young boys are really desperate to talk about themselves, their feelings, and their fears. He offers this book as a way of getting them to open up to be able to talk more openly. In this book, the boys discuss things that hurt them, such as harassment from their peers or a troubling relationship with their fathers, or their embarrassment in front of girls and their troubling confusion about sex.

The author contends that the outdated expectations in society today toward young men force them to mask many of their real emotions. This book can help to spot the danger signals of actual depression and how to grow closer to a boy in the family or a boy as a friend.

Using Part 2, "The Cycle of Rage and Suicide," as an example, boys from Columbine High School in Colorado speak about the role of fear and violence in their lives. A sixteen-year-old talks about how he used to play the saxophone but after the violence at the high school, he generally doesn't play anymore. A twelve-year-old says he doesn't want to grow into the type of kid who goes to school and just takes out a gun and starts shooting.

Throughout the book, the author, who is a clinical psychologist at Harvard Medical School, offers insights into the feelings of these young men and clear advice on how such feelings might be channeled or handled in order to deal with them effectively.

At the end of the book, after the boys have spoken, the author offers a fifteen-step program that is designed to help others help the boys in their lives to develop emotionally and physically. These steps include: create safe, "shame-free" zones where the boy can relax and be himself; identify at least one mentor the boy can lean on for love and support; develop a sensitivity to the way one boy may communicate; talk about the "gender straitjacket" about always being tough and never evidencing a softer side; discuss the fact that there are many different ways of becoming a real man; create trust; train boys themselves to be mentors; encourage creative expression; bully-proof the neighborhood and school; validate a boy for being real, not for being so-called manly.

Suitability and Critical Comment

This book on emotional help for boys is intended and suited for boys aged twelve and up. The writing is clear, direct, and crisp. Some of the writings of the boys themselves are touching in their honesty and directness. Both teenaged boys and those who love them will find this book helpful. Grades nine through twelve.

Themes and Subjects

Depression, family relationships, friendship, gender roles, love, peer pressure, school, sex, sexual orientation, teenaged boys, violence

Passages for Booktalking

Boys describe the angst they feel about coming-of-age (pp. 48–58); the pressure of success (pp. 77–85); fitting in and being left out (pp. 106–41); the problem of abuse (pp. 214–22); when addiction is a problem (pp. 325–41).

Additional Selections

Girls Speak Out: Finding Your True Self (Scholastic, 1997) by Andrea Johnston gives accounts from various girls who participated in speakout groups and suggests activities for girls trying to find their true selves.

Using interviews with four teenagers as a focus, the author discusses the causes, effects, and treatments available in *Teen Alcoholics* (Lucent, 1999) by Gail B. Stewart.

You Hear Me? Poems and Writings of Teenage Boys (Candlewick, 2000) edited by Betsy Franco is a fine anthology of poems and short prose pieces in teen voices about coming-of-age and the problems of adolescence.

From pimples to pornography, *The Teenage Guy's Survival Guide* (Little, Brown, 1999) by Jeremy Daldry is a frank discussion of adolescent problems whose subtitle is "The Real Deal on Girls, Growing Up and Other Guy Stuff."

About the Book

Booklist, May 15, 2000, p. 169.
Kirkus Reviews, June 1, 2000, p. 777.
Library Journal, June 15, 2000, p. 102.
New York Times Book Review, June 25, 2000, p. 20.
School Library Journal, Oct., 2000. p. 197.
VOYA, Dec., 2000, p. 380.

About the Author

Contemporary Authors, vol. 177, Gale, 1999.

9

Challenging Adult Novels

Buck, Pearl S. *The Good Earth.* John Day, 1931. Pb. Washington Square $6.99 (0-6715-10126) (Grades 9–12).

Introduction

Pearl S. Buck (1892–1973) was born in China, the daughter of American missionary parents, and grew up in a small house overlooking the Yangtze River. She learned to speak Chinese before English and absorbed both Eastern and Western cultures as a child. She spent most of her first forty years living in China, and it was there that she met her husband, John Buck, who was an American agricultural specialist assigned to teach modern farming methods to the Chinese. Because of the political upheavals that racked China in the 1930s, she was forced to leave and return to the United States, where she continued her career as a best-selling writer. *The Good Earth* is set primarily in rural China during the late nineteenth and early twentieth centuries and covers a period of over fifty years in the life of Wang Lung, a peasant who begins in extreme poverty and eventually becomes a wealthy landowner. It ends when his life is waning and he is about to be claimed by the good earth.

Principal Characters

Wang Lung, an ambitious, hardworking farmer who is obsessively anxious to succeed

O-lan, his stoically passive, industrious wife, who is very plain in appearance

Lotus Blossom, Wang Lung's playful, spoiled concubine

Nung En, Wang Lung's eldest son, given to spending his father's money

Nung Wen, Wang Lung's second son, a frugal, shrewd businessman like his mother

The Fool, Wang Lung's simpleminded first daughter

Pear Blossom, Wang Lung's slave, who cares for him in his old age

Ching, Wang Lung's faithful, honest friend

Plot Summary

Wang Lung, the son of a poor farmer, enters the House of Hwang—the palace of the area's richest landowning family—to claim as his bride, the slave his father has chosen and paid for. She is O-lan, a plain but hard-working and uncomplaining young girl. Together they work long back-breaking hours cultivating Wang Lung's small bit of land. O-lan also frugally and efficiently manages their humble family home and cares for Wang Lung's father. She gathers twigs and wood so they don't have to buy fuel, and mends every inch of their clothes so they can avoid buying new ones. She even works in the fields on the day their first son is born. In time, she gives birth to a second son, and also a simpleminded daughter they nickname the Fool. Wang Lung purchases more land from the Hwang family, but when a severe drought strikes, the family flees to the south to find work. In the city, Wang Lung becomes a rickshaw driver, and O-lan and the boys beg on the streets. Caught up in a peasant revolt, Wang Lung and O-lan witness the looting of the city. O-lan accidentally gains possession of a cache of jewels and silver taken during an attack on a rich man's house. With this small fortune, they return home, where Wang Lung sells the jewels, allowing O-lan to keep two small pearls that she fancies. He purchases more land, hires a number of farm laborers, and appoints his faithful friend and neighbor, Ching, to be their overseer. O-lan gives birth to twins, a boy and a girl, and no longer works in the field but only cares for the family and the newly enlarged house. The two eldest boys attend school in the village, where the schoolmaster names the older one Nung En and the younger one Nung Wen. Wang Lung is growing increasingly dissatisfied with his docile and uninteresting wife. In a tea house run by Cuckoo, a former concubine of the Hwangs, he finds and falls in love with kittenish Lotus Blossom and brings her and Cuckoo home to live in a new wing of his home. This breaks O-lan's heart, though she never speaks of her betrayal. The household is further increased with the arrival of an indigent uncle, his wife, and their licentious son. Because the uncle was a member of a gang of local bandits, Wang Lung's home is spared when the gang goes on a rampage after there is severe flooding in the area. Wang Lung encourages his aunt and uncle to form an opium habit to make them harmless. O-lan is stricken with a fatal form of cancer, and a contrite Wang Lung cares for her. Before her death, O-lan has the satisfaction of seeing her eldest son, Nung En, marry the daughter of a prosperous grain merchant. O-lan and later Wang Lung's father are buried on a hillock on the family's land. Nung En, who revels in displays of the family's wealth, persuades his father to buy the now-deserted House of

Hwang and renovate it. The family moves to their luxurious new quarters but, as his death is approaching, Wang Lung, now nearing seventy, moves back to his former home accompanied by a faithful slave named Pear Blossom and a few faithful servants. After Ching's death, Wang Lung does no more farming himself but now only rents his land. He hopes that his youngest son will work it after his death, but when Wang Lung takes Pear Blossom as his slave, the young boy, who was secretly in love with her, runs away from home to become a soldier. One day while strolling the land with his sons, Wang Lung overhears their plans to eventually sell off the property. He protests because this land has been both his livelihood and his salvation. They reassure him, but glance at each other and smile knowingly.

Suitability and Critical Comment

Pearl Buck's writing style is reminiscent of Dreiser and other naturalist writers. The tone is objective and detached, neither commenting on the action nor offering critical judgments. This point of view adds to the reader's involvement in the plot. The novel is both the saga of a family history as well as a minuscule view of China as it emerged from feudalism into the twentieth century and the events that led to the Japanese invasion and the triumph of communism. Still in print after three-quarters of a century, this modern classic is suitable for readers in grades nine and up.

Themes and Subjects

China, family stories, farming, land ownership, poverty

Passages for Booktalking

Wang Lung claims his bride (chapter 1, pp. 10–28); his early married life (chapter 2, pp. 20–23); the birth of his first child (chapter 3, pp. 23–28); his relationship to the land (chapter 6, pp. 38–41); and the great drought (chapter 8, pp. 47–53).

Additional Selections

A young Taiga Indian girl in Florida is caught between modern life and her native culture when a rare panther is killed in *Power* (Norton, 1998) by Linda Hogan.

Trapped in her home by a domineering mother, Sarina, a twelve-year-old white American girl living in Liberia befriends a gentle African boy in Amy B. Zemser's *Beyond the Mango Tree* (Greenwillow, 1989). For a slightly younger audience.

James Clavell's sweeping novel *Noble House* (Dell, 1981) is an action-filled story about a Chinese trading firm in Hong Kong.

Modern China is the setting in Betty Bao Lord's novel *The Middle Heart* (Knopf, 1986) about three youths who forge an alliance that survives for five decades.

About the Book
No reviews are available.

About the Author
Authors and Artists for Young Adults, vol. 42, Gale, 2002.
Buck, Pearl S. *My Several Worlds,* Buccaneer, 1992.
Contemporary Authors New Revision Series, vol. 34, Gale, 1991.
Doyle, Paul A. *Pearl S. Buck,* Twayne, 1980.
LaFarge, Ann. *Pearl Buck,* Chelsea House, 1988.
Something about the Author, vol. 1, Gale, 1971; vol. 23, Gale, 1981.

Chevalier, Tracy. *Girl with a Pearl Earring.* Dutton, 1999. $28.00 (1-56895850-1); pb. $12.00 (0-452-28215-2) (Grades 9–12).

Introduction
Tracy Chevalier was born and raised in Washington, D.C., and earned her bachelor's degree in English from Oberlin College in Ohio. She moved to London in1984, intending to stay for only six months. She lives there still, now with a husband and a son. She worked for several years as an editor for a reference books publisher (for example, she edited *Twentieth Century Young Adult Writers*). *Girl with a Pearl Earring* is Ms. Chevalier's second novel. It deals with the last three years in the life of Jan Vermeer (1632–1675), the Dutch painter who lived and worked in Delft, with a focus on the imagined genesis and execution of his painting *Head of a Girl,* also known as *Girl with a Pearl Earring.* Little is known about Vermeer's life except that he was an artist and art dealer who suffered perennial financial problems. At his death, the court appointed Anthon van Leeuwenhoek, the "father of microbiology," as executor of Vermeer's bankrupt estate. It would appear that they were friends, as depicted in the novel. As well, Vermeer's works are so involved in light and shadow that it seems likely he used the lens maker's camera obscura, as described in the novel. The story is told from the standpoint of the enigmatic serving girl, Griet.

Principal Characters
Griet, a resourceful girl who becomes a servant at the Vermeer household
Jan and his wife, Griet's parents

Frans and Agnus, Griet's younger brother and sister
Jan Vermeer, the Dutch artist
Catharina, his willful, sensuous wife
Maertge, Cornelia, Lisbeth, Aleydis, Johannes, and later Fransiscus, the
    Vermeer children
Maria Thins, Catharina's mother
Tanneke, the Vermeers' cook
Van Ruijven, a rich merchant who is Vermeer's patron
Van Leeuwenhoek, a scientist friend of the family
Pieter, the butcher
Pieter, his son

Plot Summary

The time is 1664 and the setting, the Dutch city, Delft. Griet's family has recently suffered a major misfortune. Her father, Jan, a talented tile maker was blinded when a kiln exploded, killing two of his coworkers. Now he is unable to work, and the family must find new ways to earn a livelihood. In addition to sixteen-year-old Griet and her parents, the family consists of Franz, age thirteen, who has left home to become an apprentice tile maker, and young Agnes, a ten-year-old daughter. After the painter Vermeer and his wife, Catharina, visit Griet at home and observe her work habits, Griet learns that she is to become their live-in servant, working a six-day week and earning a small stipend. She packs up her few belongings and moves to a strange Catholic part of the city where she becomes acquainted with the Vermeer family. The couple has five children with another on the way. They are four girls—Maertge, the oldest, Cornelia, Lisbeth, and Aleydis, the youngest—and one boy, the baby Johannes, a well-behaved infant. Also in the household are Maria Thins, Catharina's crusty, wily mother, and the moody, unpredictable cook, Tanneke.

Griet is a resourceful, enterprising young woman who makes every effort to fit into the household. Her greatest problem is the unpredictable and ungovernable Cornelia, who delights in getting Griet into trouble. Griet sees little of the master, who spends most of his free time in his studio, but in their chance encounters, they seem to form an unspoken bond of respect and understanding. Visitors to the Vermeer household include the painter's patron, van Ruijven, a wealthy, lascivious merchant who often tries to grope Griet, and the lens maker and scientist, van Leeuwenhoek, whose camera obscura is used by the painter to reveal new dimensions in light for his paintings. As well as the special privilege of cleaning the master's studio, Griet's duties include shopping at the local outdoor market. Here, she meets Pieter, the butcher, and his son and helper, also named Pieter. The young Pieter shamelessly flirts with Griet, who is flattered by the attention she receives from such an attractive young man. Catharina, who is distant and perhaps a little jealous of Griet, gives birth to another boy, Fransiscus, and within weeks she is pregnant again. Misfortune again strikes Griet's family. The plague comes to their quarter of the city, and young Agnus is one of the victims. As the months pass, Griet sees the young Pieter as often as possible, and talk of marriage is heard.

The master slowly realizes that Griet possesses an innate sense of taste, composition, and a knowledge of color values. He assigns her special duties, including grinding and mixing the colors for his paints in an attic room. The bond between them grows. An awkward situation arises when van Ruijven commissions a painting of himself with Griet. Vermeer realizes the merchant's ulterior motives and secretly begins painting Griet alone. To add color, she drapes her head in blue and yellow cloths and, at his insistence, pierces one ear so she can pose in one of her mistress's pearl earrings. Griet is excited by the project, but fearful that Catharina will find out and dismiss her. The morning of her eighteenth birthday is an eventful one. The painting is completed, and the young Pieter proposes marriage and is accepted. Though she loves Pieter, she realizes that there is a mutual unspoken attraction between her and the taciturn painter. She is saddened to think that their hidden moments together are coming to an end. Through Cornelia's scheming, Catharina sees the painting and is furious at Griet for secretly posing and for wearing her earring. In the middle of her savage verbal attack, Griet rises and leaves the painter's household, vowing never to return. In an epilogue dated ten years later, Griet, now married and the mother of two sons, is summoned to the Vermeer house by Tanneke. The painter has died and, in a last request, has bequeathed the earrings to Griet. Reluctantly she accepts, but knowing that she can never explain their presence to Pieter, she sells them to a local jeweler who is noted for keeping secrets.

Suitability and Critical Comment

Vermeer's painting has often been called the Dutch *Mona Lisa*. In this eloquently developed story, life in seventeenth-century Delft comes superbly to life. The artistic process, from the mixing of paints to the final product, is well presented, as are elements involving suppressed passion, class differences, and familial duty. This novel is suitable for readers in grades nine through twelve.

Themes and Subjects

Family life, historical novels, jewelry, marriage, Netherlands, painting, religion, servants, Jan Vermeer

Passages for Booktalking

The Vermeers visit Griet's home and hire her (pp. 3–6); Griet meets the Vermeer children and the maid, Tanneke (pp. 14–17); she also meets Maria Thins and gets a tour of the house (pp. 18–20); Griet's first encounter with Cornelia (pp. 21–23); she goes to market and meets Pieter (pp. 26–28).

Additional Selections

Fifteen-year-old Maya, a modern American teen, discovers her Indian heritage when she spends a summer with her grandmother in India in *Motherland* (Soho, 2001) by Vineeta Vijayaraghaven.

Jill Paton Walsh's *Grace* (Farrar, 1992) is a novel on the life of Grace Darling, who saved shipwrecked sailors in 1838 by her acts of heroism.

The flowering of Dutch art is traced in text and reproductions in Claudio Pescio's *Rembrandt and Seventeenth-Century Holland* (Belrick, 1996).

Information about Vermeer and the Dutch school is contained in *The Story of Painting* (DK, 1994) by Wendy Beckett and Patricia Wright.

About the Book

Booklist, April 1, 2000, p. 1444; April 1, 2001, p. 1460.
New York Times Book Review, Jan. 14, 2001, p. 28.
School Library Journal, June, 2000, p. 173.
VOYA, Aug., 2000, p. 186.

About the Author

Contemporary Authors, vol. 193, Gale, 2002.

Dickens, Charles. *Oliver Twist*. Oxford University Press, (nd). $25.00 (0-19-2544505-1) (one of many editions) (Grades 8–12).

Introduction

Charles Dickens (1812–1870) was born in Portsmouth, England, the second child of John Dickens, a clerk in the Navy Pay Office. Dickens Sr. had one trait in common with Mr. Micawber, a character in *David Copperfield:* he was unable to manage the family finances. In 1822, after the family had moved to London, Charles's parents and the younger members of the family were sent to Marshalsea, a debtor's prison. Charles was left to fend for himself. He had to leave school, where he was a prize pupil, and work under miserable conditions as a sealer of pots of shoe polish. He never forgot the shame, fear, and loneliness of this experience and later wrote often of abandoned and victimized children like Oliver Twist. Dickens's first writing success came with *Pickwick Papers*. While it was still running as a serial in a London periodical, he began to publish another serial in a magazine he edited. This was the much more somber *Oliver Twist or The Parish Boy's Progress*. It appeared in book form in 1838.

Main Characters

Oliver Twist, a workhouse waif of unknown parentage

Mr. Brownlow, a kindly gentleman who becomes Oliver's benefactor

Mrs. Maylie, a sweet lady who also befriends Oliver

Rose Maylie, her adopted daughter

Fagin, a Jewish ruffian who lives off the earnings of young pickpockets

Bill Sikes, a barbarous criminal and confederate of Fagin's

Nancy, a young girl who loves Bill Sikes in spite of his mistreatment

The Artful Dodger (Jack Dawkins), one of Fagin's prize young pickpockets

Bumble, a scheming, evil workhouse official

Monks (Edward Leeford), a mysterious gentleman who is plotting against Oliver

Plot Summary

Oliver Twist was born in a workhouse about seventy-five miles from London to an unmarried woman who died at his birth. He lives for his first nine years at an "infant farm" run by Mrs. Mann, who starves her young charges until some die. Taken by Mr. Bumble, the corrupt parish beadle, back to the workhouse, the boy gets into trouble by daring to ask for a second helping of gruel. Apprenticed to an undertaker named Mr. Sowerberry and forced to sleep in the coffins, Oliver runs away after he is locked up for trying to defend himself from another apprentice, the bullying Noah Claypole. On the way to London, Oliver meets a street-smart, sharp kid named Jack Dawkins, also known as the Artful Dodger, who takes him into the slums of London to his boss, a miserly, filthy old man named Fagin, and his group of child criminals. Oliver begins his training as a pickpocket. On his first trial expedition, Oliver is caught but rescued from the police by Mr. Brownlow, the intended victim. In frail health, Oliver gradually recovers, but while on an errand for Brownlow, he is intercepted by Nancy, girlfriend of Bill Sikes, another criminal in league with Fagin. Oliver is brought back to Fagin's lair and becomes part of a robbery plot led by Sikes that requires the help of a child of Oliver's size to creep through a small window of the targeted house and open the outside doors to the robbers. The plan is botched, and Oliver is left wounded in a ditch. He crawls feebly back to the house and is taken in by its owner Mrs. Maylie, her son Harry, and her adopted daughter Rose. They nurse him back to health in their country home. In the meantime at the workhouse, Beadle Bumble marries the widow Corney, who appears to know something about Oliver Twist's origins and is in possession of jewelry that the pauper Sally had stolen from Oliver's mother on her deathbed. The Bumbles are contacted by a mysterious Edward Leeford, nicknamed Monks, who buys the jewelry and then throws it in the river. Monks, who is obviously trying to hide the truth of Oliver's past, hires Fagin to help him. Nancy overhears their plotting and learns through them of Oliver's whereabouts. She warns Rose Maylie that danger is near. During this time, Oliver is reunited with Mr. Brownlow, who continues to show an unusual interest in the boy. Sikes learns of Nancy's defection and cruelly murders her. Monks is apprehended and explains to Mr. Brownlow why he has been plotting against Oliver. Oliver's father had married a woman older than himself. After years of quarreling and the birth of a son, Edward (Monks), the couple separated. In time, the older Leeford met a young girl and proposed marriage, but before the wedding could take place, he died, and his fiance, trying to hide her pregnancy, went to a workhouse to bear her child who became known as Oliver Twist. Afraid that his inheritance will diminish if Oliver's identity is known, Monks has tried to keep Oliver in Fagin's clutches. Later it is determined that Rose is the younger sister of Oliver's mother and Mr. Brownlow, his father's best friend. Fagin and his gang, including the Artful Dodger, are arrested. Fagin is hanged publicly at Newgate, and the rest of the gang is transported out of the country. Sikes is trapped by the police and, in an attempt to escape, slips into a loop of rope and accidentally hangs himself. His identity revealed and inheritance assured, Oliver generously restores Monks's share. The Bumbles, now thoroughly discredited, lose their positions and become inmates of the workhouse they once controlled. Oliver is adopted by Mr. Brownlow. It appears that his years of hardship and misery have ended.

Suitability and Critical Comment

Though filled with sentiment and coincidence, *Oliver Twist* presents a realistic, harrowing portrait of London's underground criminals and the exploitation of children that existed during Dickens's time. The plot is complicated and is filled with cliff-hanging scenes and frequent switches in setting, but the story moves naturally and at an exciting pace. This classic, made popular by its many screen and television adaptations, including a musical version, is enjoyed by good readers in grades eight and up.

Themes and Subjects

Crime, foster homes, London, murder, orphans, pickpockets, poverty, robberies

Passages for Booktalking

Oliver, in the workhouse, asks for more food (chapter 2, pp. 11–13); Oliver is taken to the Sowerberrys by Bumble (chapter 4, pp. 26–28); Oliver fights Noah Claypole, another worker at Sowerberrys (chapter 7, pp. 40–43); Oliver meets the Artful Dodger (chapter 8, pp. 52–54); and later meets Fagin (chapter 8, pp. 55–57); and adjusts to life with Fagin's boys (chapter 9, pp. 558–63).

Additional Selections

Four-feet-tall Wick gets a taste of sought-after adventure when he is kidnapped by pirates and sold into slavery in Mel Odom's *The Rover* (Tor, 2001).

In Reconstruction days, fifteen-year-old African American Gabriel and his friend James run away to join a group of cowboys herding cattle to Texas in David Anthony Durham's *Gabriel's Story* (Doubleday, 2001).

After his father's disappearance, eleven-year-old Sam Webber and his mother move to a smelly apartment in a racially tense Baltimore neighborhood filled with druggies and muggers in Jonathon Scot Fuqua's *The Reappearance of Sam Webber* (Bancroft, 1999).

In Victorian England, Sally Lockhart, age sixteen, is being stalked by an arch villain when she tries to claim her inheritance in Philip Pullman's *The Ruby in the Smoke* (Knopf, 1986).

About the Book

No reviews are available.

About the Author

Achroyd, Peter. *Dickens*, Harper, 1990.

Bloom, Harold. *Charles Dickens*, Chelsea House, 1992.

Hipple, Ted. *Writers for Young Adults*, vol. 1, Scribners, pp. 353–64.

Hobsbaum, Philip. *A Reader's Guide to Charles Dickens*, Farrar, 1972.

Johnson, Edgar. *Charles Dickens: His Tragedy and His Triumph*, Simon & Schuster, 1952.

Lives and Works: Young Adult Authors, vol. 2, Grolier, 1999, pp. 101–4.

Major Authors and Illustrators for Children and Young Adults, vol. 2, Gale, 1993.

Murray, Brian. *Charles Dickens*, Continuum, 1994.

Nelson, Harland S. *Charles Dickens*, Twayne, 1981.

Something about the Author, vol. 15, Gale, 1979.

Wilson, Angus. *The World of Charles Dickens*, Academy Chicago, 1985.

Haruf, Kent. *Plainsong.* Knopf, 1999. $24.00 (0-375-40618-2); Pb.
Vintage $13.00 (0-375-70585-6) (Grades 10–12).

Introduction

As in his two previous novels, Kent Haruf uses as his setting the American High Plains areas of eastern Colorado. Specifically, it is the fictional town of Holt, Colorado, and its surrounding farmland—a place where everyone knows one another by name and where there are few secrets. The author defines plainsong as "any simple and unadorned melody or air" but, as a book title, it could also refer to the rhythm of life in this remote area. Though told completely in the third person, the story is narrated in alternating chapters from the points of view of several key characters, principally Victoria, Tom Guthrie, his two sons, and the McPheron brothers. The two seemingly separate plot lines (one involving Victoria and the other Tom Guthrie) intersect throughout the novel and, in the end, converge when the two families share a Memorial Day dinner. The time span of the novel is about eight months, from the fall of one year through the following spring.

Principal Characters

Victoria Roubideaux, a seventeen-year-old high-school senior
Maggie Jones, one of Victoria's teachers
Tom Guthrie, a social studies teacher at Victoria's school
Ike and Bobby, Tom's two sons, aged ten and nine
Ella Guthrie, Tom's wife, who suffers from chronic depression
Lloyd Crowder, principal of the high school
Russell Beckman, a surly, incorrigible delinquent who is in Victoria's
    class
Harold and Raymond McPheron, two elderly bachelor brothers who
    operate a small cattle farm outside of town
Dwayne, Victoria's abusive boyfriend
Mrs. Iva Sterns, an elderly recluse who befriends Ike and Bobby

Plot Summary

Seventeen-year-old high-school senior Victoria Roubideaux is in terrible trouble. She is three months pregnant by a boy named Dwayne, who has left town, and her mother, a single parent, has discovered her secret and has thrown her out of the house. In desperation, Victoria seeks help from Maggie Jones, one of the teachers at her high school in Holt, Colorado. Maggie, who lives alone with her senile father, takes Victoria in, but when the father, in his dementia, attacks the girl, she must find the girl another home. One of Maggie's colleagues is Tom Guthrie, a handsome, well-liked social studies teacher who is also facing personal problems. His wife, Ella, has suffered a mental breakdown and is now in a state of chronic depression. To sort things out, she moves first across town to another house and then to Denver to live with her sister. She leaves behind a distraught Tom and her two young boys, Ike, aged ten, and Bobby, aged nine, both of whom are confused and unhappy without their loving mother. One night, the boys slip out of the house to investigate a light in an abandoned house, and there they see two teenaged boys having sex with a girl. One is identified as Russell Beckman, who, unknown to Ike and Bobby, is constantly a troublemaker in their father's classroom. Ike and Bobby are inseparable and protective of each other. In their loneliness, they find company and diversion through visits to an equally lonely old woman named Mrs. Iva Sterns, one of the customers on their paper route. Tom turns to other women to fill the void in his life: first, a short fling with the school secretary, Judy, and later with Maggie Jones, whom he really loves. Maggie has been able to place Victoria in the home of two reclusive bachelor brothers, Harold and Raymond McPheron, who operate a small cattle farm seventeen miles out of town. Since their parents died fifty years ago, the two men have had little contact with the outside world, and both are as apprehensive and frightened at the thought of having a pregnant teenager in their home as Victoria is about getting along with these two well-meaning but taciturn old men. Somehow, with Maggie's help, they work out their differences and form an unusual family unit. However, one day Dwayne appears at school and persuades Victoria to move to his apartment in Denver. She leaves without having the courage to tell the McPherons.

In the meantime, trouble is brewing for Tom at school. After he reprimands Russell Beckman for unruly behavior, the boy attacks him, and the school principal, Lloyd Crowder, suspends Russell. Russell's brutish redneck parents object and promise revenge. It comes one night when Russell and the other two teenagers that Ike and Bobby saw in the deserted house kidnap the boys and leave them half-naked five miles out of town. They manage to find their way back and reluctantly tell their father what happened. When Tom confronts Russell and his parents the next day, the three gang up on him, and the police are called.

In Denver, Victoria realizes she has made a terrible mistake in thinking that she could find a life with her brutish, selfish seducer. In spite of Dwayne's threatened violence, she leaves and arrives at Maggie's in Holt, hoping for a reconciliation with the McPheron men. Cautiously, they let her return, and soon their love seems to have been strengthened by the ordeal. When the baby arrives (a girl), they are as proud and happy as any parents could be. On Memorial Day, the McPherons and Victoria are joined by Tom, Maggie, Ike, and Bobby for a happy picnic dinner.

Suitability and Critical Comment

With sensitivity and spare, objective writing, the author explores dramatically the lives of a group of people who are isolated from the mainstream but represent the essence of American life. This is a haunting story, rich in detail, that also creates a vivid locale and atmosphere as it traces the cycle of life, death, and birth and the importance of family relationships. Because of its explicit sex scenes and depiction of the brutal side of farm life (such as a detailed description of an autopsy on a horse), it is best suited for mature readers in high school.

Themes and Subjects

Abuse, cattle, Colorado, families, farm life, friendship, love, mental problems, nontraditional families, old age, pregnancy, sex, small-town life

Passages for Booktalking

Victoria's mother throws her out (in paperback edition, pp. 8–11); Ike and Bobby deliver their papers (pp. 12–14); and they stop to visit their mother (pp. 12–14); Victoria tells her story to Maggie (pp. 33–38); Ike and Bobby collect for the paper from Mrs. Sterns (pp. 43–47); and together they make oatmeal cookies (pp. 144–51).

Additional Selections

Told from the standpoint of a teenaged army brat, *Yokota Officers Club* (Knopf, 2001) by Sarah Bird is a humorous and heartbreaking story of family secrets and a young girl's search for identity.

Jim, the Boy (Little, Brown, 2000) by Tony Earley is a touching novel of a ten-year-old boy, Jim Glass, growing up in the 1930s without a father in rural North Carolina.

Homer Hickham's nonfiction *Rocket Boys* (Delacorte, 1998) tells of the author's adolescence in a 1950s West Virginia coal mining town and of his interest in rockets.

Set in a quiet 1960s Minnesota community, Leif Enger's *Peace Like a River* (Atlantic Monthly, 2001) tells how the Land family, including eleven-year-old Reuben, leave their land to find the son who killed two men who threatened the family.

About the Book

Booklist, Aug., 1999, p. 1986.
Kirkus Reviews, Aug. 15, 1999, p. 1245.

Library Journal, Sept. 1, 1999, p. 232.
New York Times Book Review, Oct. 3, 1999, p. 7.

About the Author
Contemporary Authors New Revision Series, vol. 91, Gale, 2001.

Hurston, Zora Neale. *Their Eyes Were Watching God.* Harper, 1931.
Pb. Perennial Classics $3.50 (0-06-093141-8) (Grades 10–12).

Introduction

Zora Neale Hurston (1891–1960) was born in Eatonville, Florida. She was an outspoken, adventurous girl who was absorbed in local stories and gossip. Her hometown was isolated, and therefore, she grew up without the racial hatred and segregation that was common in the rest of the South. She attended Howard University and, after graduation, moved to New York City, where she became a respected member of the Harlem Renaissance, a movement that saw African American arts flourish between 1919 and 1930. After studying anthropology at Barnard College, she traveled extensively in the South, collecting African American folklore. Four novels were published during her lifetime, the most popular being *Their Eyes Were Watching God,* first published in 1931. It portrays the life of Janie Crawford, an independent black woman and folk heroine. Ms. Hurston died penniless in Florida, her work all but forgotten. However, she was rediscovered during the 1990s, and is now considered one of the great African American writers.

Principal Characters

Janie Crawford, a self-reliant black woman
Phoeby Watson, a friend of Janie's
Nanny, who raised Janie
Logan Killicks, Janie's first husband
Joe Starks, Janie's second husband
Tea Cake, the man with whom Janie finds fulfillment

Plot Summary

Janie Crawford is much talked about in her Florida town. Self-reliant and aloof, no one knows much about her since her return. As the story opens, she tells her tale to Phoeby Watson. Janie begins with her upbringing by Nanny in west Florida. One day when Janie is sixteen years old, Nanny catches her kissing a neighbor boy. Knowing that she will not be around to care for her, and fearful of Janie's future, Nanny talks her into marrying Logan Killicks, many years her senior but the owner of sixty acres of land. He will protect her. Naïve Janie thinks that with marriage must come love, so she waits for love to bloom. It never does.

About a year later, Janie meets Joe Starks, citified and stylishly dressed. She calls him Jody. He talks of a different world. Janie leaves Logan and goes to Green Cove Springs with Jody, where they are married. They take the train to a forsaken spot called Maitland, where Jody decides to organize a town. He talks the few townspeople into an organizing committee, gets a road built, and also gets himself elected mayor. Jody is a whirlwind of activity, and Janie is not always sure she likes the big talker and important person he has become. But people just naturally respond to Jody. He is not a fighter, although he takes to hitting her sometimes just to show how important he is. Something else dies in her when that happens. Some twenty years pass and, after a while, Janie withdraws inside herself. When Jody dies, the town stages the biggest funeral Orange County has ever seen.

Then one day, along comes Vergible Woods, a younger man whose friends call him Tea Cake. He makes Janie laugh. Pretty soon the town notices that something is going on between Tea Cake and Mrs. Mayor Starks. Tea Cake leaves town and tells her to meet him in Jacksonville. Her friends warn her not to go, but Janie feels she has found happiness this time. She meets Tea Cake in Jacksonville, and they marry.

So begin Janie's years of blossoming. Tea Cake is a roustabout who frolics around the Florida swamps as the mood strikes him. Life is not ideal and rarely secure, but Janie loves him and she knows he loves her. Their house is always full of people, at least the doorstep is always crowded. People just naturally take to Tea Cake. Sometimes he shoots a little pool with them, and sometimes he wins. Janie learns about jealousy, too, although Tea Cake swears she has no reason to worry. But Tea Cake also takes to hitting her on occasion. She knows that what she calls "slapping around" is to justify the awful fear inside of him.

One season a destructive hurricane hits Florida, and Janie and Tea Cake are caught in it. The town is almost destroyed, but they manage to survive. However, Tea Cake is bitten by a dog during the storm, and sometime later he becomes ill. Janie calls the doctor and learns that the dog must have been rabid. Tea Cake is going to die. Out of his mind with pain and afraid, Tea Cake tries to shoot Janie, but she kills him with a rifle to save her own life. Her trial clears her of any wrongdoing.

Janie returns home to take up her life again. She ends her story to Phoeby by talking about love: "Love is lak de sea. It's uh movin' thing, but still and all, it takes it shape from de shore it meets, and it's different with every shore."

Suitability and Critical Comment

This is a beautiful story of a woman's development, written with sensitivity and compassion. However, the black dialect of much of the narrative may make this a difficult read except for the better students in grades ten through twelve.

Themes and Subjects

Abuse, the black experience, feminism, friendship, love, marriage, maturity

Passages for Booktalking

Janie marries Logan Killicks (pp. 21–25); she marries Joe Starks (pp. 32–33); they go to Maitland where Jody becomes mayor (pp. 46–50); Janie reflects on her marriage (pp. 71–72, 76–80); Jody's death (pp. 85–87); Janie meets Tea Cake (pp. 95–99); life with Tea Cake (131–35); the hurricane (pp. 158–67); Tea Cake dies and the trial (pp. 183–89).

Additional Selections

Sarah, age seventeen, weighs the pain of peer pressure against the excitement of first love during one summer in Cape Cod in Rosa Guy's *The Music of Summer* (Delacorte, 1992).

Allic Bynam and her African American family encounter unexpected racial prejudice when they move to Georgetown in the 1920s in Breena Clarke's *River, Cross My Heart* (Morrow, 1999).

When their father's business fails and their mother suffers a mental collapse, three African American sisters are placed in foster care in *Tempest Rising* (Morrow, 1998) by Diane McKinney-Whetstone.

Eleven-year-old Tempest and her family move from an inner-city neighborhood to an upscale gated community with unforeseen results in *Only Twice I've Wished for Heaven* (Crown, 1997) by Dawn Turner Trice.

About the Book

No reviews are available.

About the Author

Authors and Artists for Young Adults, vol. 16, Gale, 1996.
Bloom, Harold, ed. *Zora Neale Hurston,* Chelsea House, 1986.
Contemporary Authors New Revision Series, vol. 61, Gale, 1998.

Contemporary Literary Criticism, vol. 7, Gale, 1977; vol. 30, Gale, 1984; vol. 61, Gale, 1990.

Hemenway, Robert E. *Zora Neale Hurston: A Literary Biography,* University of Illinois Press, 1977.

Lives and Works: Young Adult Authors, vol. 4, Grolier, 1999, pp. 61–62.

Nathiri, M. Y., ed. *Zora! Zora Neale Hurston: A Woman and Her Community,* Sentinel Communication, 1951.

St. James Guide to Young Adult Writers (2nd ed.), St. James, 1999.

Witcover, Paul. *Zora Neale Hurston,* Melrose Square, 1994.

Yannuzzi, Della. *Zora Neale Hurston: Southern Storyteller,* Enslow, 1996.

Lamb, Wally. *She's Come Undone.* Washington Square, 1992. Pb. $14.00 (0-671-00375-5) (Grades 10–12).

Introduction

Wally Lamb (1950–) was born in Norwich, Connecticut. After graduating from college, he became a high-school English teacher at the Norwich Free Academy and eventually the head of their writing center. The morning after his first child was born in 1981, he began his own creative writing career. His first novel, *She's Come Undone,* was published in 1992. It is the story of the narrator, Dolores Price, a woman who is struggling to overcome a lifetime of misfortune. She is a lovable, self-deprecating survivor, whose massive problems are lightened partly by her sense of humor. Mr. Lamb claims that a series of conflicting emotions are present both in his writing and his life. As an example, in *Contemporary Authors,* he lists his religion as "questioning Catholic." In an interview, he stated, "I'm most responsive to artists who juggle three balls in the air: hope, pain, and humor. I aim for just such a juggling act in my own fiction."

Principal Characters

Dolores Price, thirteen-year-old obese heroine
Bernice, her emotionally unstable mother
Tony, her abusive father
Grandma Holland
Jack Speight, the upstairs neighbor who is a rapist
Mr. Pucci, high-school counselor
Dante, Dolores's lover

Plot Summary

This novel follows Dolores Price, four years old in 1956 when her story begins, on the day a free television set is delivered to her house. She survives almost unbelievable turmoil, which leaves her an emotional basket case and follows her into young womanhood, where she billows to 257 pounds, and then into her own marriage and divorce. Sassy and not always likable, Dolores experiences one painful event after another. Almost every known abuse and travesty that exists in a family happens to Dolores. She is an only child. Her mother, Bernice, is vulnerable and weak and later slips into mental illness. Her father, Tony, is an abuser and a womanizer and liar. He walks out on the family, and a divorce follows.

Dolores tries to deal with that by hiding from the world behind a smart mouth and an I-don't-care demeanor. Once again, the men in her life betray her. She is raped by Jack Speight, the handsome upstairs neighbor whom she has a crush on. That betrayal throws Dolores's life severely off course. At age thirteen, she settles into a life like a beached whale in front of the television set, nourishing herself with potato chips, Pepsi, and Mallomars, which her mother supplies. Through 1,001 nights of television in which she feeds on sitcoms and melodramas, she tries to eat her way into forgetting. When she finally reaches young womanhood, she is 257 pounds. At first, she simply tries to retreat from life, her overwhelming anger and defiance blinding her to the needs of others. Even her surrogate family is dysfunctional, except for Mr. Pucci, her former high-school guidance counselor, who helps to give her a few small moments of happiness. Other oddball characters also drop into and out of her life, such as an ancient Polka Queen disc jockey who has Parkinson's disease and the six-foot-ten owner of Existential Drywall.

By the time Dolores is into her late teens, she is obese, unhappy, and sarcastic. A freak accident causes her mother's death, and it sets Dolores into thinking about her adamant decision not to attend college. Finally, Dolores herself goes to a mental hospital, where she pulls herself together for one more attempt at some kind of normal life.

Dolores meets Dante, and they begin a romance. In time, Dolores becomes pregnant and she has an abortion, but she is very ambivalent about doing so. After that, they are married, and her Grandma comes to the wedding. Dante talks Dolores into using Grandma's wedding present money to buy a van so they can take a cross-country vacation. When they return, he tells her he has lost his job. One day she comes home from work to find him in bed with another woman. He leaves, but she calls him back a few days later because Grandma has died. Dante returns, and the two move into Grandma's house, which she has left to Dolores. But the marriage does not work, and she finally tells Dante to leave.

In 1982, Dolores gets the deed to Grandma's house and also gets a divorce. Her life continues on its normal path of disaster. Her dear friend

Mr. Pucci has terminal AIDS. But Dolores is in college, and she will keep on trying even if she is an old woman before she gets a diploma, she says. Now maybe she is strong enough to consider marriage again, this time with someone she can truly love.

Suitability and Critical Comment

This novel is suited for the more mature teenager, both for the language and the social content. The heroine is not a particularly likable character, yet the author manages to show her vulnerable side as well as her sarcasm. The book is well written and there is just enough humor to keep the novel from descending into depression, but there are descriptions of physical, sexual, and/or mental abuse. For grades ten through twelve.

Themes and Subjects

Abortion, AIDS, divorce, humor, lesbians, marriage, mental illness, obesity, physical abuse, rape, television

Passages for Booktalking

Ma returns from the mental hospital (pp. 53–56); Dolores is raped (pp. 107–10); Dolores has an abortion (pp. 338–39); Grandma's death (pp. 374); Dolores decides to live again (pp. 457–58).

Additional Selections

A hardworking high-school student is driven to a nervous breakdown because of the pressure and expectations of others in Josiah Bunting's *All Loves Excelling* (Bridge Works, 2001).

Though she outwardly appears to be a bright, precocious young woman intent on a writing career, Esther Greenwood is slowly descending into madness in Sylvia Plath's *The Bell Jar* (HarperCollins, 1966).

Set in Newfoundland, *Kit's Law* (Houghton Mifflin, 2001) by Donna Morissey features Kit; her deranged mother, Josie; and her loving, protective grandmother in this story of poverty, conflict, and triumph.

Alice Hoffman's *Local Girls* (Putnam, 1999) contains a series of vignettes about Gretel Samuelson and her teenage years.

About the Book

Booklist, Aug., 1992, pp. 1995, 2001.
Kirkus Reviews, April 15, 1992, p. 487.
Library Journal, May 1, 1992, p. 118.

About the Author

Contemporary Authors, vol. 140, Gale, 1993.

Updike, John. *Gertrude and Claudius.* Modern Library, 2000. $12.95
(0-375-40908-4) (Grades 10–12).

Introduction

John Updike (1932–) is a successful author, essayist, poet, and dramatist.
He grew up in a small town in Pennsylvania, where his father was a junior-
high-school teacher, At thirteen, he moved with his family to an isolated
farm. To assuage his loneliness, he haunted the local library and read vora-
ciously. After high school, Mr. Updike attended Harvard and graduated
summa cum laude. He intended to become a cartoonist and won a scholarship to England to study art, but after marriage and the birth of his first
child, he turned to writing fiction. He usually writes about ordinary people,
husbands, wives, homes, children. This is true of his most famous creation,
the four Rabbit books. Each of the books traces a decade in the life of
Harry "Rabbit" Angstrum, beginning with *Rabbit Run* (Knopf, 1960), which
covers the optimism and eventual disillusionment of the 1950s. *Gertrude
and Claudius*, a departure from this pattern, traces the events that occurred
before the play *Hamlet* begins. A reviewer in *Publisher's Weekly* said that the
novel was "precisely honed . . . with masterful character analysis, and subtly
observed historical detail."

Principal Characters

Gertrude, queen of Denmark
Horwendil, who becomes King Hamlet of Denmark
King Rorik, Gertrude's father
Feng, younger brother of Horwendil, who becomes King Claudius
Corambis, lord chamberlain, who becomes Polonius
Amleth, son of Gertrude and Horwendil, who will become Prince Hamlet
Ophelia, whom the prince loves

Plot Summary

Most readers know of the melancholy Dane, Prince Hamlet, who falls
into despair after the death of his father. His father's brother, Claudius, has
taken the throne and married Hamlet's mother, Gertrude. The ghost of
Hamlet's father appears, accuses Claudius of murdering him, and demands
revenge. Hamlet dies in the attempt to avenge the murder of his father.
The tragedy is the most famous of Shakespeare's plays. In *Gertrude and
Claudius*, modern-day novelist John Updike takes the reader back to the
very beginnings of the Hamlet tragedy and to the youth of Hamlet's
mother. He fills in the events that might have happened before Hamlet was
born and might have led to the death of his father.

At the age of sixteen, Gertrude, beloved daughter and only child of King Rorik, is betrothed to Horwendil. She does not love him and questions her father about why she must marry. He tells her that Horwendil is the most suitable heir to the throne of Denmark. Because she loves her father and because she is aware of the importance of the Denmark throne, she obeys his wishes and consents to marry Horwendil. This pleases her father, who is satisfied that the future of his country has been ensured. Gertrude marries Horwendil. When King Rorik dies, Horwendil becomes king of Denmark and Gertrude becomes the queen. They have one son, Amleth, who will become Prince Hamlet. The marriage between Gertrude and Horwendil is harmonious, but the king is a detached and unemotional man. Young Hamlet grows up in his father's image. He is not close to his mother and spends most of his time away from the castle.

When Gertrude reaches middle age, she becomes restless and bored with an unemotional husband and son. She finds herself attracted to Feng, the king's younger brother, who is about her age. The two begin to meet in a secret retreat, with the help of Corambis. Their affair becomes torrid and emotional, but both Gertrude and Feng feel that they have been clever enough to keep their meetings secret from the court at large.

One day, however, the king openly accuses Feng of the affair and threatens him with banishment. Not willing to live without the love of Gertrude, Feng plots his brother's death. With the help of Corambis, the king is poisoned. It is done so cleverly that a venomous serpent is found to be the cause. Not even Gertrude suspects what has really happened.

Within two months, Feng, who takes the name of Claudius, and Gertrude are married. The new king insists that young Hamlet return to the castle to live with them. Feeling content that he has gotten away with the murder of his brother, Claudius settles down to what he envisions as a long and peaceful reign with the woman he loves. But, as we know from Shakespeare, that is not to be.

Suitability and Critical Comment

Written in the style of the ancient Scandinavian legends, this novel is best suited for good readers with an interest in history and old superstitions in grades ten through twelve.

Themes and Subjects

Adultery, Denmark, loyalty, marriage, murder, passion, Scandinavia

Passages for Booktalking

Gertrude argues with her father about marrying Horwendil (pp. 4–9); Gertrude and the king discuss their son (pp. 52–54); Feng longs for

Gertrude (pp. 72–78); Gertrude discusses a retreat with Corambis (pp. 95–102); Gertrude and Feng meet at the retreat (pp. 102–13); the king confronts Feng about the affair (pp. 143–50); the murder (pp. 154–62); Gertrude and Claudius are married (pp. 169–79).

Additional Selections

After reading *Hamlet*, students might wish to dip into *Readings on Hamlet* (Greenhaven, 1998) edited by Don Nardo, with essays on the play's structure, themes, plot, and characters.

Set in sixteenth-century Venice, the novel *Shylock's Daughter* (Putnam, 2001) by Miriam Pressler reexamines the characters and situations of Shakespeare's *Merchant of Venice*.

The rebuilding of the Globe theater in London from its inception in the 1890s to the present is chronicled in *Rebuilding Shakespeare's Globe* (Routledge, 1989) by Andrew Gurr and John Orrell.

West Side Story: A Musical (Random, 1958) by Arthur Laurents is a contemporary variation on Shakespeare's *Romeo and Juliet* that uses gang warfare in New York City as its backdrop.

About the Book

Booklist, Jan. 1, 2000, p. 835.
Kirkus Reviews, Dec. 15, 1999, p. 1909.
Library Journal, Feb. 15, 2000, p. 200.
New York Times Book Review, Feb. 27, 2000, p. 9.
School Library Journal, Aug., 2000, p. 213.

About the Author

Authors and Artists for Young Adults, vol. 36, Gale, 2001.
Current Biography, Wilson, Oct., 1984.
Hunt, George. *John Updike and the Three Great Secret Things,* Eerdmans, 1980.
Luscher, Rober M. *John Updike: A Study in Short Fiction,* Twayne, 1993.
Newman, Judie. *John Updike,* St. Martin's, 1992.
Thorburn, David, and Howard Eiland, eds. *John Updike: A Collection of Critical Essays,*
    G. K. Hall, 1982.
Updike, John. *Self-Consciousness: Memoirs,* Knopf, 1989.
Uphaus, Suzanne Henning. *John Updike,* Ungar, 1980.

Wright, Bill. *Sunday You Learn to Box.* Scribner Paperback Fiction, 2000. $17.95 (0-684-85795-2) (Grades 9–12).

Introduction

This poignant story of a black youth, Louis Bowman, and his coming-of-age problems in a hostile urban environment, is the first novel by Bill

Wright. The author, a native New Yorker, has taught English, acting, and writing in various colleges in New York and has had many short stories published in prestigious publications. He has also worked extensively teaching communication skills to adolescents and adults living with HIV and AIDS. Many of these students commented on the lack of characters they could relate to in the books they read. Concerning this novel, the author has said, "I can't say that I wrote the book specifically for this group, but I definitely wrote it knowing that there are Louises in the world who might have found 'the ring' of their environment a little easier had they seen themselves in print and understood that there were other kids in comparable situations struggling to get through."

Principal Characters

Louis Bowman, a sensitive fourteen-year-old black boy who narrates the novel

Jeanette Stamps, Louis's hardworking mother

Ben Stamps, Louis's harsh stepfather

Lorelle Stamps, Louis's five-year-old half-sister

Ray Anthony Robinson, a chipped-toothed seventeen-year-old hoodlum from the projects whom Louis adores

Ed Macmillan, a pedophile who befriends Louis

Grandaddy, Louis's grandfather, who is retired and lives in Harlem

Dr. Davie, a kindly counselor who takes an interest in Louis

Plot Summary

The time is 1968, and the setting is the housing projects in the Connecticut city of Stratfield, within commuting distance of New York City. Here, just before Christmas, fourteen-year-old Louis Bowman, a black kid, witnesses his stepfather, Ben Stamps, die of a heart attack during a particularly violent fight with his wife, Louis's mother, Jeanette. Through a series of remembrances, Louis's story unfolds. The boy never knew his real father, but remembers leaving the brutal public housing projects of New York City at the age of three for what, his mother hopes, will be a temporary home in the less-violent projects of Stratfield. She plans and works for the day when she can move to a regular suburban home. Jeanette is a vibrant, hardworking, intelligent woman who is a department manager at the local branch of Saks. Partly to further her plan to move and partly because Ben Stamps, a coworker, gives her the attention she needs, Jeanette marries him when Louis is eight. Within a year they have a daughter, Lorelle. Jeanette is aware of her son's passive, sensitive, bookish nature and, to provide him with the ability to protect himself from the project's bullies, she asks Ben to teach

Louis how to box on Sundays after they return from church. This plan, however, proves to be a dismal failure because Ben increasingly uses these sessions to act out the hostility he feels toward his noncommunicative, passive stepson. To supply a role model for Louis, Jeanette arranges for her son to spend his weekends in Harlem with his Grandaddy. Again the scheme backfires, because the taciturn old man spends the time tinkering with old radios while Louis remains alone in his assigned bedroom. On one of these trips, Louis is approached on the train by an older, married man, Ed Macmillan, who begins touching him affectionately. Louis encourages the man's advances, but narrowly escapes being sodomized when Macmillan takes him to a motel room. Filled with confusion and guilt about this experience and upset about his home life, Louis sinks into a depression. This affects his schoolwork so drastically that the school authorities recommend that he receive guidance at a local mental health clinic. Here, he comes under the influence of the understanding Dr. Davies, a West Indian counselor who befriends Louis. When Louis receives a bicycle for his thirteenth birthday, he again becomes the object of physical abuse by the project bullies, who try to take it from him. On one occasion, he is protected by seventeen-year-old Ray Anthony Robinson, a tough, enigmatic hood who dresses flamboyantly in purple polyester pants and patent leather shoes. Ray Anthony is considered the coolest cat in the projects. Louis develops an obsessive crush on the older boy and seeks him out whenever he can. Usually aloof and seemingly unaware of Louis's attention, Ray Anthony, nevertheless, at times, appears to encourage Louis. A few days after Ben's death, events reach a climax when Ray Anthony's jealous girlfriend, along with some of her tough male cronies, tease Ray Anthony by calling him a faggot. He becomes enraged and attacks one of his tormentors. Only Louis's physical intervention prevents Ray Anthony from committing murder. Ben's seemingly abortive boxing lessons have proven useful. When Ray Anthony returns to the projects after being temporarily in police custody, he singles out Louis for a show of tenderness by placing his hand on his shoulder. Louis glows and basks in this sign of affection.

Suitability and Critical Comment

This novel candidly explores the emotional and sexual confusion of a sensitive black youngster who is coming of age in a hostile environment. The author has also created a gallery of other memorable characters, including Jeanette, a caring mother who remains unfulfilled because of her poverty. Although often grim in its depiction of life in the projects, the novel also shines with moments of humor and gentleness. Though written for adults, it is also appropriate for readers in grades nine and up.

Themes and Subjects

Blacks, coming-of-age, Connecticut, death, family problems, grandfathers, Harlem, homosexuality, housing projects, New York City, obsessions, poverty, sexuality, stepfathers

Passages for Booktalking

Ben's death (pp. 11–16); Jeanette brings Ben home from work (pp. 26–29); Jeanette describes meeting Billie Holiday (pp. 339–41); Louis encounters racism at school (pp. 42–46); Louis meets Ray Anthony (pp. 52–56); and Ben gives Louis his first boxing lesson (pp. 61–65).

Additional Selections

In Nikki Grimes's *Bronx Masquerade* (Dial, 2000), eighteen Bronx teenagers get to each other through Friday afternoon readings of their poetry.

The nonfiction *Honky* (University of California, 2000) by Dalton Conley tells about a white boy growing up in the mainly black and Hispanic housing projects of Manhattan.

Nancy Garden's groundbreaking novel *Annie on My Mind* (Farrar, 1982) tells the story of Annie and Lisa, who fall in love after meeting at the Metropolitan Museum of Art in New York.

Landon appears to be an average high-school senior, but his experiences falling in love, running for class president, and starring in the Christmas play make him special in *A Walk to Remember* (Warner, 1999) by Nicolas Sparks.

About the Book

Booklist, Feb. 15, 2000, p. 1086.
Kirkus Reviews, Jan. 1, 2000, p. 16.
New York Times Book Review, Feb. 20, 2000, p. 21.
School Library Journal, Sept., 2000, p. 260.

About the Author

No information available.

AUTHOR INDEX

Titles fully discussed and summarized in *Teenplots* as well as those cited in the text and in "Additional Selections" are included in this index. An asterisk (*) precedes those titles for which both summaries and discussions appear.

TITLE INDEX

Titles fully discussed and summarized in *Teenplots* as well as those cited in the text and in "Additional Selections" are included in this index. An asterisk (*) precedes those titles for which full summaries and discussions appear.

SUBJECT INDEX

This listing includes only those titles fully summarized in the book. Unless otherwise noted with the label nonfiction, the subject headings refer to fictional treatments of the subject.

333

About the Authors

JOHN T. GILLESPIE is former Dean and Instructor of Library Science at Long Island University, New York. He has authored numerous books in the areas of library management, school libraries, and children's and young adult literature.

CORINNE J. NADEN is a freelance writer and editor and has published more than thirty books.